Risë Stevens:

a life in music

by
John Pennino

Great Voices
10

BASKERVILLE
PUBLISHERS

Baskerville Publishers, Inc.
2711 Park Hill Drive
Fort Worth, Texas 76109

www.baskervillepublishers.com

Pennino, John.
  Risë Stevens : a life in music / by John Pennino.
    p. cm. — (Great voices ; 10)
  Includes discography (p.   ) and bibliographical references.
  ISBN 1-880909-75-8 (alk. paper)
  1. Stevens, Risë, 1913- 2. Mezzo sopranos—United States—
Biography. I.
Title. II. Series.
  ML420.S84P46 2005
  782.1'092—dc22

                                        2005024048

Manufactured in Canada

First printing, 2006

Table of Contents

CD Track Listing

ACKNOWLEDGEMENTS

Elizabeth Aarons, Mannes College of Music; Allan Altman, VAI; Lucine Amara; Julia Aries, Glyndebourne Festival Opera; Donald Arthur; Rose Bampton; JoAnne E. Barry, Philadelphia Orchestra; Mary Baskerville; Bibliotek der Friederich-Ebert-Stiftung; Jaroslav Blecha, Oddeleni Dejin Moravskeho Zemského Muzea, Brno; Natalie Bodanya; Ruthanna Boris; Lucielle Browning; Matthew Buff, San Francisco Performing Arts Library and Museum; Bruce Burroughs; Semyon Bychkov; James Camner; the late Walter Cassel; Andrea Cawelti, Chicago Symphony Orchestra Archives; Center for Motion Picture Studies; Columbia Artists Management; Anthony Coggi; Clare Colvin, English National Opera; the late Nadine Conner; George Dansker, New Orleans Opera Archives; George Darden; Joy Davidson; Elizabeth Davis; Deborah Davis, Mannes College of MusicLibrary; Claudia Depkin, BMG Entertainment Archives; Detroit Public Library; the late Annamarie Dickey; F. Paul Driscoll, Metropolitan Opera Guild; Dr. Paul Eckstein; the late Otto Edelmann; Carl Edwards, Metropolitan Opera Guild; Rosalind Elias; Family History Center; the late Marita Farell; Andrew Farkas; Jane Fenwick, Glyndebourne Festival Opera Archives; Johanna Fiedler; Regina Fiorito-Sokol; Gino Francesconi, Carnegie Hall Archives; Warren Fremling; Herta Glaz Redlich; Ellen Godfrey; Metropolitan Opera; Margaret Goostray, Boston University, Special Collections; Dr. Howard Gottlieb, Boston University, Special Collections; Jane Gottlieb, Juilliard School of Music Library; John Grande; Michael Griebel, Metropolitan Opera; Roger Gross; Paul Gruber, Metropolitan Opera Guild; Frank Guarrera; Nimet Habachy; Eva Harmannová, National Theater, Prague; the late Margaret Harshaw; Philip Hart; Barbara Haws, New York Philharmonic Archives; Loren Hightower; Richard Horowitz, Metropolitan Opera; Joan Ingpen; Juilliard School of Music, Alumni Office; Sena Jurinac; Miriam Kartch; Prof. Charles Kaufman, Mannes College of Music; Alan Kayes; the late Carlos Kleiber; Prof. James Kleinsasser, University of California, Bakersfield; Dr. Vlasta Koubská, Norodni Muzeum; Robert La Marchina; Herman Krawitz; Dr. Barbara Lesák, Österreichisches Theater Museum; Library of Congress, Interlibrary Loan Division, Music Division, Periodicals Division; the late Michael Manuel; Mary Jane Phillips Matz; Temple University; the late Dennis McGovern; the late Angelo Mercuriali; Nathanial Merrill; the late Robert Merrill; Mildred Miller; the late Richard Mohr; Patrice Munsel; John A. Murphy, Pennsylvania Research Associates; New York Public Library, Music Research Division, Reference Division, Rodgers and Hammerstein Archives of Recorded Sound, Slavonic Division, Special Collections, Theater Collection; Patricia Neway; the late Elena Nikolaidi; Charles Niles, Boston University, Special Collections; Sean D. Noel, Boston University, Special Collections; Norwegian Emigration Center; Toni Palladino; Mary Beth Peil; Roberta Peters; Paul Plishka; Jane Poole, Metropolitan Opera Guild; Dr. Svetlana Pribanova, Moravské Muzeum, Brno; Don Roberts, Northwestern University; Jack Rokahs; Dennis Rooney; Jonathan Rosenthal, Museum of Broadcasting; John Russell, Metropolitan Opera; Safka andBareis Autographs; the late Bidú Sayão; the late James Shomate; the late Brooks Smith; the late Zachary Solov; Sophia Smith Collection, Smith College; Julius Spivák, Slovak National Theater, Bratislava; Statsarkivet I Bergen; Naomi Stewart, Community Concerts; Hana Stranska; Joanne Sylvester; Rosemary Summers, Metropolitan Opera; Robert Sutherland, Metropolitan Opera; George Swope, Community Concerts; Teatro alla Scala Archives; the late Walter Taussig, Metropolitan Opera; Ron Tavitz; Dean David Tcimpidis, Mannes College of Music; Elizabeth Thorne, Community Concerts; Giorgio Tozzi; Robert Tuggle, Metropolitan Opera Archives; Pierre Vidal, Opéra National de Paris; Edgar Vincent; Murad Wahba; Marlene

Wehrle, National Library of Canada; Jeannie Williams; the late Dino Yannopoulos; Walter Zvonchenko, Library of Congress, Theater Division.

Many others were contacted but through unfortunate circumstances or reasons of their own they did not respond.

Special thanks to:

Astrid Varnay, a legend in her own time, who graciously consented to write the Introduction to this book. Mme. Varnay holds a significant place in my early opera going experiences by introducing me to some of the most memorable interpretations of Wagner's heroines. Her own biography, *55 Years in Five Acts,* written with Donald Arthur, is a must for opera lovers.

Dr. Carmen Mayer whose recollections of Risë Stevens in Prague are invaluable additions to the biography. Her dedication to the project has been unfaltering and highly treasured. She is a remarkable woman whose admiration for Risë Stevens equals my own.

Vilma Georgiou for her comments on and rare photographs of the Athens Festival.

The late Jo Mottola and Rita Mottola, for a complete run of *Metro-Lark* , candid photographs and other memorabilia relating to Risë Stevens' career.

The entire *Metro-Lark* staff whose contributions to the biography are numerous and meaningful. Their first-hand accounts add another dimension to the book.

Peter Clark, Roger Rose and Sergio Stefani for their skillful translations of French, German and Italian reviews.

Ron Moore, F. Ann Whitaker, Mark Moore, and Dick Kriegbam of Baskerville Publishers deserve my thanks in more ways than I can put down on paper.

Most significantly, my deepest thanks to Risë Stevens, the late Walter Surovy and Nicolas Surovy who graciously consented to be interviewed for this book even though it is not authorized by them.

Risë Stevens: a life in music

PREFACE

One of the highest forms of national recognition was bestowed on Risë Stevens in 1990 when she was named a recipient of a Kennedy Center Award along with Dizzy Gillespie, Katharine Hepburn, Jule Styne and Billy Wilder. All of them were cited for the contributions they made to the advancement of culture in America; Stevens, Gillespie and Styne for music, Hepburn and Wilder for film. Although she was primarily an opera singer, Risë Stevens' career touched on both classical and popular forms of entertainment. As such, she is harder to classify.

With Risë Stevens, Carmen comes immediately to mind for a large number of those who saw her in that role or heard her recording. For others, *Going My Way*, the Academy Award winning film in which she appeared is why she is remembered. If for no other reason, the by now classic recording of *Carmen* and the regularly revived, *Going My Way*, keep Risë Stevens firmly before the public in spite of her having retired more than forty years ago. Unlike Maria Callas, Judy Garland and Elvis Presley, she has not attained legendary status. Very few do, and more often than not, performers who achieve that status attain it for the wrong reasons. Troubled lives, early deaths both natural or self inflicted, sensationalism, often obscure the artistry behind the artist; they are reduced to fodder for gossip mills, exploitation of the most sordid. Callas is a case in point. Subject of dozens of biographies that range from accurate to nonsense, her turbulent life is in danger of outstripping the supremacy of her art. She is a cultural icon but at a very high price.

The question arises as to why Risë Stevens is worthy of a biography. Actually two in her case since there is an earlier one. The answer is not difficult. As an American woman who attained the highest rank in her chosen field, she is an example of what can be accomplished through a combination of natural talent and the will to succeed. Risë's career is unique in that it encompassed opera, recordings, radio, films, television, academic and arts administration. She was a mainstay at the Metropolitan Opera for twenty-three seasons. In the 1940s she had her own radio show, she appeared in a classic film, in the 1950s she was a popular guest on television, her recordings sold in the thousands, the complete *Carmen* has been in print for over fifty years, the Mannes School of Music survived a bleak period in the 1960s because of her, the Metropolitan Opera National Company was launched under her aegis, she is now a managing director of the Metropolitan Opera. This biography will attempt to show a career that extended from Brooklyn to Prague, from Canada to South America, from parts of America where a *lied* or aria had never been heard to the centers of culture, Paris and Milan.

Written in her tenth decade, it can objectively reflect on a life well managed. Compared to Callas, Stevens has lived a long life and has escaped notoriety. Her accomplishments are no less significant as a result.

All biographers choose their subject for a variety of reasons: admiration, topicality, remuneration or even detestation. With Risë Stevens, admiration for her as a performer is my reason for writing, and it makes writing about her, without bias, difficult. A smiling woman dressed as a gypsy holding a cigarette in a Chesterfield "ad" captured the imagination of a very young boy. She accomplished that without singing a note, without reciting a line but merely looking out from a page in a magazine. Subsequently, seeing Risë Stevens on stage and in films, the singing, acting, and then the living presence provided the third dimension which led to total capitulation.

Biographies, however, at least those that are valid, must be unbiased. The central character must be observed and evaluated from both sides, the positive and the negative. Throughout the "big career", Stevens was given her fair share of space in print. While what was written about her portrayed her as she and her staunchest supporter, her husband, Walter Surovy, wanted her portrayed; it presented, at times, a one-dimensional picture. Walter, an expert public relations man, was the source of many of the news items and he controlled this aspect of the career. With the passage of time, we can now gain new and more complete perspectives on the various aspects of her life and her career.

Introduction

An Operatic Chameleon

Recollections of Risë Stevens
by
Astrid Varnay

The tyranny of repertoire often keeps kindred spirits apart, which explains why I never got a chance to collaborate with Risë Stevens anywhere near as much as I would have liked to. From the time of my début at the end of 1941, I was fairly locked into the Wagnerian canon, and although Risë had done one or two Wagner roles in her early New York career, we never made it onto that terrain in tandem. As to my infrequent excursions into Italian opera, the works I sang offered no roles for a mezzo soprano of her stature. Nevertheless, there was one opera in which I was solemnly convinced we could make beautiful music together, and that was Richard Strauss's *Rosenkavalier*.

I had always thought the Marschallin would be a natural choice for me, which was why I had made it my business to learn the role. Then one day Frank St. Leger, General Manager Edward Johnson's deputy at the Metropolitan asked me if I knew the opera, and I replied in the affirmative, hoping to be scheduled for a couple of performances in coming seasons, but Mr. Johnson told me he felt that a soprano in her late twenties-early thirties (my age at the time) was simply too young for the part. I was tempted to reply: "were I to have to step in as the Marschallin, would anybody ask my age?" but I decided discretion was the better part of valor, and so I went back to Wagner, and the possibility of a stage get-together with Risë was tabled for possible – but not guaranteed – future reference.

Of course, even then, I was more than aware of Risë

Stevens's artistic quality and her professional experience. Of all the promising young American élite who had joined the Metropolitan roster in the years when World War II made the Atlantic impassable for many European singers, Risë was one of the few locals who had actually received European training and also sung leading roles on that continent. Risë had launched her career in the remarkable Prague German Theatre during the years when the influential Dr. Paul Eger, that theatre's General Manager and General Music Director George Szell, were nurturing artists like Zinka Milanov and Hans Hotter, preparing them to launch their international careers. Risë was the only native-born American to emerge from that eminent Central European crucible. When she made her début in her home town of New York in 1939, she was one of the few home grown singers who could handle herself adroitly in the rarefied polyglot surroundings of that house, fluent in every language she sang and very much at home in all the diverse roles she delineated, especially her definitive characterizations of those two ultimate operatic seductresses – Bizet's Carmen and Saint Saëns's Dalila, both of which set the woods on fire.

In an innocent day and age like the 1940's and '50's when characters like Carmen and Dalila were at best hinted at by other artists, who might have come to terms with the vocal demands of those roles but were either unable to exude much sensuality or else reluctant to portray a convincing seductress on the stage of a theatre where suburban ladies brought impressionable grandchildren to the opera. Risë told it like it was, managing the sensational feat of exuding captivating, totally credible voluptuousness without corrupting her interpretation with so much as a microgram of vulgarity. On top of all that, Risë's Carmen did her own dancing and played her own castanets, two accomplishments that were anything but standard operating procedure in those years.

It was this incredible ability to associate so symbiotically with the quintessential femaleness of these two characters that frankly had me wondering if she could put it all aside to make a believable male teen-ager come to life as Octavian, but I was more than willing to find out, if only somebody would give me a crack at it.

Oddly enough, my first opportunity to essay the role; on October 5, 1952, came about not in New York but in the composer's own home town of Munich during a two week stint the Bavarian State Opera had kindly devoted to introducing me to one of the best educated and discerning audiences in the world. When the management of the theatre asked if they could include *Rosenkavalier* in that "Varnay Week", in a spasm of enlightened chutzpah I agreed to step out on the stage of that city's prestigious *Prinzregententheater* as Strauss's passionate princess, discovering only after the performance that among the patrons was no less an expert than Franz Strauss, the composer's son, who kindly came backstage to congratulate me on a portrayal I had launched with only a minimum of rehearsal.

I never told Mr. Strauss that this was the first time I had ever sung his father's magnum opus.

Having nevertheless acquired that Good Housekeeping Seal of Approval on the composer's home turf, I was pleased to discover that Mr. Johnson's successor, Rudolf Bing, had scheduled me for almost a dozen *Rosenkavalier* performances in the following year, including the broadcast matinée and four dates on the road during the company's annual tour, most of them featuring Risë Stevens as my youthful swain, Octavian, with the exacting Fritz Reiner presiding over the musical interpretation.

What I experienced at the first performance on January 23, 1953, was nothing short of a revelation. The same lady who had been so paradigmatically female in the French operas had undergone more than just a gender change on the Strauss-Hofmannsthal piece, transmuting into a totally adolescent scamp, who, for all his mischievousness, also communicated that his experience with the princess before the curtain rises had been a rite of passage, thus confirming a theory I had always held about the first act of the opera – namely that this was not only Octavian's one and only night of intimacy with the Marschallin but also his own sexual awakening.

There is no way I could define how Risë did it, it was all far too subtle for detailed analysis, but the fact remains that both the masculinity and the innocence had become utterly interwoven with her stage deportment and her musical interpretation to the point that even I fully accepted her as a member of the opposite sex.

This kind of total identification, which she brought to every role she touched, made each Stevens performance an event, whatever she undertook. Those two other very different young men that became her own, Mozart's ungainly, adorable Cherubino and Johann Strauss's ultra-sophisticated, definitively Slavic and terminally bored Prince Orlofsky, along with her vast array of utterly diverse female characters, the waif-like Mignon, the intensely spiritual Marfa, the ambitious Marina, and all the other grand figures of operatic literature were accorded the ultimate accolade of being given breath and redefined histrionically and musically by the consummate artistry of Risë Stevens.

It is a source of great joy to me that her story is now being told, and it is a special satisfaction that the teller of that story is John Pennino, whose operatic expertise and grasp of fact, detail and nuance were an invaluable support to me when setting down my own memoirs. Readers of Risë's biography can be assured that the account they are about to enjoy will be accurate, well-documented, perceptive and entertaining.

Now, if you'll please excuse me, I'd like to read Risë's story for myself.

THE LIFE THE CAREER

Part I
Early Years: 1913-1938

I had success beyond my Mother's fantastic dreams. She was a determined woman and she was wildly ambitious for me. [1]

John Pennino

Chapter 1

For the 1920 census, Christian Steenberg recorded that he was thirty-five years old, his wife, Sadie, thirty-one, his daughter, Risë, six and his son, Lewis, three. The family resided on Bergen Avenue in the Bronx and that he was born in New York.

Christian Steenberg, in fact, was born in Christiana, Norway, today's Oslo. It was not an uncommon practice in the early part of the last century for non-native born citizens to say they were American by birth if they arrived in this country at an early age. Steenberg was only five years old when his father, Olaf, decided to relocate from Christiana to Bergen, Norway, and from there to America. Olaf had married into a ship-building family whose business faltered. The move was no doubt prompted by financial exigencies, the motivating factor behind seeking the gold-paved streets of America for thousands of immigrants.

The elder Steenberg (his wife who would die quite young leaving her husband Olaf to take care of the two girls, Elsie and Christina (Tina) and their son, (Christian), arrived in New York in 1890. Olaf Steenberg was a strong willed man and a hard drinking one as well. His drinking proved to be fatal later in life when in a drunken stupor he was trampled by a horse and wagon crossing a street. Christian Steenberg, hard working but as much taken to drink as his father, always had an independent streak that contributed to a very serious falling out in later years with Olaf, when Risë was about seventeen years old. The disagreement was kept between themselves and no one learned its cause. Most likely it was a contest of wills between two strong minded men.

Risë was her father's favorite and she was as fond of him as he was of her but she could not forgive his drinking. Fortunately, for both, Christian was away from home a good deal of the time which shielded Risë from having to deal with it on a daily basis. Once when he was in a New York for a brief visit, returning home from Juilliard one afternoon, she found him dead-drunk and stopped speaking to him until he stopped drinking. He did for a while but being on the road was no doubt lonely and eventually, he went back to his old ways. It was only after Risë made her debut with the Metropolitan Opera, he vowed never to drink again to protect her from any embarrassment.

The family was Lutheran and Christian Steenberg's choosing to marry the Jewish, Sarah Mechanic, was in conformity with his independent nature. They met when Sadie fell out of a boat in the Central Park lake and he jumped in to save her. It was a romantic beginning to a sometimes troubled marriage.

Sarah Mechanic or Sadie as she was commonly called was Russian on her father's side, Polish on her mother's and Jewish on both. What cities the families came from is not known nor is the true family name. Since her father gave his trade as a carpenter, "Mechanic", was assigned to them by a clerk on Ellis Island who either could not understand or spell their real name. Sarah Mechanic's father died soon after his seventh child was born and like the Steenberg children, she was raised in a one-parent family. There were four boys, Abraham, Edward, George, and Benjamin and three girls, Dorothy, Sarah and Augusta. As was the custom in poorer families, the boys went to work early to earn some money but the girls stayed home to help their mother.

Risë never knew her paternal grandmother or maternal grandfather but she did get to know her maternal grandmother who was a cold, stern woman left with a large family and very little means of support. Lewis and she dreaded visiting her.

Christian's two sisters eventually married; Elsie started the Hanberry branch of the family, converted to Catholicism in deference to her husband and had three daughters and six sons. Tina married a Grunbech and adopted several children among whom was a boy who died at age twenty-one. The only child she bore was a daughter also called Risë (who married and became Knudson) a name handed down for generations in the Steenberg family. When Risë decided to change her name from Steenberg to Stevens (borrowed from a married relative), her father was disapproving but accepted the change. However, even though she was regularly called Rose, Rosa or Rise, Risë never had the nerve to change her given name (which means "laughter" in Norwegian) since her father would never have forgiven her. Her middle name, Gus, came by way of her Aunt Gussie (Agusta), her mother's sister, who died at age twenty. Gussie was the favorite as was Ed and like Gussie died young at forty years of age, leaving a wife and a daughter, Lucille. On the Mechanic side, domestic arts were not neglected and Risë's Aunt Dorothy, who lived nearby, taught her how to embroider while Sadie saw to it that she learned how to knit and use a sewing machine.

Risë was born on June 11, 1913. If she was indeed six years old in 1920 as reported on the census (and there is no reason to question Christian on this point even though he did misstate the place of his birth), then the date as given is correct. A second child, Lewis, or Bud, was born three years later. Christian sold advertisements, he was very successful but his drinking ate up most of the money he earned leaving his wife to manage as best she could on the little that was left over. A railroad apartment at 1286 Stebbins Avenue, a strictly blue-collar neighborhood of the Bronx, was all the family could afford.

When Risë was six and Bud three, the family moved to a somewhat better apartment on Bergen Avenue. Another railroad flat with a living room in front, a kitchen with a huge coal stove in back and one bathroom off the kitchen. In between her mother's and father's room, a small windowed dressing area was fashioned into a bedroom for Risë, only big enough for a bed and a chiffonier. Bud's room abutted the kitchen and, at first, Risë shared it with him, but his terrified awakenings to nightmares of goblins and horrid faces prevented her from sleeping. Lacking central heating, the apartment was made bearable in winter by coal heaters that Sadie would light to take the chill off the bedrooms before the family retired for the night. Both children would be bathed in a large wash basin in the kitchen since there was no heat in the bathroom. Afterward, they would huddle around the coal burner to warm themselves before getting into bed.

Risë was, by then, of school age and was enrolled in PS 10 which was a fair distance from where the family lived. Walking to and from school was not safe for a young girl since gangs of thirteen and fourteen year old boys who would stand around street corners making comments, heckling, menacing passers-by, frightened her and made going to school something she dreaded. They were not much older than Risë but she had to pass them to get to the school always fearing what they might do.

Whereas some other girls might have caved in and let the boys prevail, Risë vowed to get even by taking steps to show that they had more to be afraid of than she. Across the street from her apartment was an Armour meat packing plant and visible from the street were the butchers moving large sides of beef on conveyers equipped with lethal looking hooks. After school, she would wait for the butchers to leave and sneak into the plant and hang by her arms from the hooks to build up her strength. She had seen the boys from the gang horsing around nearby and in a show of bravery, mainly to impress one another, did calisthenics on a steel bar which was above a flight of cement cellar stairs. One trick they did impressed her sufficiently to want to try it herself, knowing that if she slipped, she would crash head first on the cement steps below. The stunt consisted of sitting on the bar and positioning herself so that it was behind her knees, slowly bending all the way back hanging upside down over the stairs, pulling herself up to a sitting position and sliding forward and off. She repeated it over and over until she did it with such ease that she was ready to show the gang that she was as tough as they were. A bunch of smirking boys were not won over that easily. The harassment continued.

A confrontation was triggered by a pogo stick her father gave her, a gift meant to soften his absence from home so much of the time. They are difficult to manipulate but Risë was determined to master it and in no time, she could go up and down stairs, travel the entire length of the street without a mishap much to her father's delight and the neighbors' amusement. The boys from the Bergen Avenue gang, never missing an opportunity to cause trouble, were intent on stealing it. One afternoon, she was playing with it in front of her house and no one was around. They boldly marched up and made a grab for it but she held her ground and swung the stick menacingly, frightening them away - so she thought. Without knowing it, behind her, two brawny Irish brothers somewhat older than she, who lived on the top floor of the building, happened to come out and saw what was going on. All her stick waving could not compete with the sudden appearance of those two.

Whatever the situation, Risë was developing a greater self-assurance that masked the insecurities she had around people. When Sadie became quite friendly with a German Methodist minister, she decided that Risë would receive religious instruction in his church located a good distance from where they lived. Getting there meant traversing a tough neighborhood early on Sunday mornings without anyone around to help her should an incident arise. Her qualms were quieted by the confidence in herself she had developed as a result of her standing up to the members of the gang. The effort she had made to strengthen herself physically resulted in the sharpening of her motor skills and had a long-term effect. When she was appearing regularly as Carmen at the Metropolitan Opera, the conductor, Fritz Reiner, marveled at the consistency with which she caught a tambourine tossed to her from a distance in Act 2. She never missed.

In the parlor of the Steenberg apartment there was a player piano and Christian enjoyed entertaining the family whenever he was home,

> He'd pump out When Irish Eyes are smiling, Sympathy and Mother Machree, singing at the top of his pleasant untrained tenor voice. Risë - six, seven, eight years old - brother Bud naturally got into the habit of singing with him. 'Goodness', neighbors and relatives and friends used to exclaim, 'that Bud certainly has a lovely voice! And little Risë sings pretty too Bud's voice being what it was, Mrs. Steenberg thought of a brother and sister act. The sister part was so that Risë's feelings wouldn't get hurt. [2]

When Bud showed more interest in the violin than in singing, Sadie turned her thoughts to Risë since it was obvious that she had a voice. There was a program on WJZ on Sunday mornings called the *Children's Hour* that was described in *Radiogram and Guide* as a program of "vocal and instrumental solos by boys and girls under eighteen." [3] It was hosted by Milton Cross, Uncle Milt, as he was referred to then, a vigorous twenty-six year old who was to become the voice of the Metropolitan Opera broadcasts in 1931. In the past, Sadie listened to this program without much thought but now she realized that if other children could be on the radio so could her daughter. The show originated from a studio on Forty-second Street in Manhattan, a long ride on the "El", but her efforts were rewarded when Risë was accepted as one of Uncle Milt's juvenile artists. She was entrusted to the care of Orry Parado who served as music teacher, coach and accompanist for the children. His lessons, consisting mainly of scales to help them get through the selections they were to sing, were the first training in music Risë had. The love of music was already there and it was not uncommon to see her sitting by the radio at home with her head leaning against it, listening to music with tears in her eyes. Music always had the ability to move her and when she was on the stage, there were places in the operas she sang where she had to be very careful to control her emotions. The ending of Act 1 in *Der Rosenkavalier*, especially when Lotte Lehmann was the Marschallin, Orfeo's "*Che farò*", carried with them intense feelings which did not escape her.

On the *Children's Hour*, the children sang opera and operetta arias, duets and ensembles. Risë's determination to be an opera singer was not born with this program, however. It was through later studies that it became the focus of her professional life. For now, appearing on the show was an unknowing step toward that goal and a start in developing a show business savvy. It made no difference to Sadie that Risë was paid one dollar a week. She hoped that appearing on the *Children's Hour* would encourage Risë to study music and become a professional singer. In school, Sadie knew she was only average. Lewis was the studious one who went to extreme lengths to improve his mind.

Risë made no pretense at being an intellectual; she got by in school, no more than that and while she enjoyed a normal childhood in spite of her radio work, studying music came before everything else. Moreover, it was something she was good at and, similar to her tests of strength, helped raise her self-esteem. She could not compete with her brother or many of her peers in scholastic matters but she had the capacity to rise far above them as a singer. However, unlike her brother who mastered an instrument, one thing frustrated her with respect to her music studies– no matter how hard she tried, she never learned how to play the piano or any musical instrument, as Lewis had. She blamed that failing on a martinet piano teacher found by her mother who with his Prussian ways instilled in his young students a fear that made some physically ill. Risë vowed never to return to his studio when one day she found the piano bench soaking wet courtesy of the previous student whom he had succeeded in terrifying. Later in life, she discussed this inability to play the piano with an acquaintance, an analyst, who explained that a mental block had developed because of this experience. The lack of mastering the piano did not go unnoticed when she was at Juilliard.

For now, however, her closest friend, Florie Hynes, who was also on the *Children's Hour,* and she, enjoyed one another's company on the long ride home after a show, talking and eating the pickles they bought with their dollar from a stand near the entrance to the "El". It didn't bother Risë that her friend was considered the child most likely to succeed by those connected with the program, since she had begun to realize, much to her mother's relief, that music would be her chosen profession. Florie, in spite of her potential, turned away from show business and became a nurse instead. She remained very close to the Steenbergs, Sadie in particular, who looked on her as one of her own after her mother died. When Risë went to Europe to further her career, Florie moved into the Steenberg apartment and became quite close to Lewis who was invited into her circle of friends, eventually marrying one of them.

Fame came early to Risë even if it was only at a local level, for she began to be written about in the newspapers as a result of her radio appearances,

> Demure and dainty and only 13 years old, little Miss Risa (sic) Steenberg, contralto, 1184 Sherman Avenue, has already achieved a reputation as a radio and concert singer of which a seasoned veteran may well be envious. Risa broadcasts every Sunday from Station WJZ during Children's Hour and hordes of letters from children all over the country attest to her popularity. What makes her achievements all the more unusual is that Risa

has been taking vocal lessons since last September. In February, just five months after she started her training, Risa was featured in a concert in the Waldorf-Astoria Hotel. So famous were the comments on her singing by critics that the following months found her singing at numerous benefits. Risa attends P. S. 53, 638 East 168th Street, where she is considered a good student. Despite her artistic ability, Risa is considered just an average girl when it comes to the enjoyment of the pleasures of her companions. She likes to read. She enjoys games and is even said to be a good athlete for her size and age. [4]

The move to Sherman Avenue was thought necessary after Sadie's mother became ill and in order to help her, the family relocated to a building around the corner from where she lived. The apartment was a step backward from the one they left. There was only one bedroom which Sadie reserved for herself and Christian, a kitchen, bath and a living room that doubled as a bedroom for both Risë and Lewis. When Christian returned home and saw how they would have to live, he was none too happy with the cramped quarters. As if out of sympathy for his concern, his mother-in-law died soon after and Sadie made up her mind to leave the Bronx for good. What led her to Jackson Heights, Queens, is not clear but she found an apartment and the children transferred (again) to the neighborhood school,

> Though only fourteen years old, Risë Steenberg of 31-26 Eighty-eighth Street, Jackson Heights, a talented girl attending PS 127 East Elmhurst is already a radio artist of wide reputation. Jacob Greenberg [principal of PS 127] and a connoisseur of music says that Risë has a wonderful future in opera before her and in February Risë will leave the East Elmhurst school...to attend Newtown High School, Elmhurst. After Newtown, Risë will study in Italy. [5]

PS 127 was newly founded when Risë entered in 1927 but she was not there for very long. As a member of the first graduating class on January 26, 1928:

> "the enthusiastic audience of parents was charmed by her beautiful voice, at the first commencement exercises ...yesterday...District Superintendent, Stephen F. Bayne... declared that the memory of Risë's singing would always be connected with the first class...The vocal solos given by Risë were 'I Dreamt I Dwelt in Marble Halls', 'Still Wie Die Nacht' and 'The Song is Ended'." [6]

Jacob Greenberg had recommended that Risë be enrolled in Newtown High School because of its superior music department that was endorsed by the American Academy of Teachers of Singing. The principal, a Mr. Dillinger, was told by Greenberg that his new student should be treated with special care on account of her potential. Accordingly, she was placed in the music program that was picturesquely housed in the school's tower. Her two music teachers were Irving C. Valentine, organist for a church in Flushing, who occasionally invited her to sing during Sunday services and Miss Anderson (her given name lost to the appellation, "Miss", since she was referred to in no other way) who taught her sight reading, church music, counterpoint and tried to interest her in a career in music education.

Sadie clashed head on with Miss Anderson over a career in music education for Risë and with what can only be termed *chutzpah* made an appointment for her to be auditioned by no one less than Samuel L. (Roxy) Rothafel. Roxy's claim to fame centered around his introduction of stage presentations in movie theaters thereby making him a very powerful presence on Broadway. Mistakenly thinking it was Sadie who was to audition, he was dismayed when he learned it would be Risë. He asked her how old she was but before Risë could answer, Sadie snapped, "forget her age and hear her sing." If Roxy was affronted by Sadie's manner, he did not take it out on Risë. He asked her to sing and after she ended her last number, he went over and put his arm around her shoulder but addressed his remarks to Sadie. "Madam, let the child finish her schooling and then come back again." The highly indignant Sadie told Roxy, "someday you will regret not hiring her because she is a future Metropolitan Opera star." With that, the bemused Roxy said that he hoped her prediction proved correct and the audition was over. Risë, in spite of the statements in the newspapers about her training for opera and her mother's retort to Roxy, had no fixed notion about where her musical talent would lead her. She thought her voice better suited for musicals at that time and the prospect of appearing on Broadway very exciting.

Not long after arriving at Newtown in 1928, Risë's teachers recommended her to Reverend Willard, the pastor of St. James Episcopal Church. He offered her a place in the choir and a weekly salary with the chance to earn extra money singing for weddings and funerals. Risë learned a great deal about church music which stood by her when she performed oratorios later on as did the additional experience singing before a live audience. Equally important, Reverend Willard succeeded in imparting to her a love for the Episcopal Church. A product of a Lutheran, Jewish home and a Methodist Sunday school, Risë had no religion that she truly embraced. At sixteen years of age, the Episcopal Church became the answer to her religious needs and Reverend Willard baptized her into the faith. When she married Walter Surovy, a Catholic, she consented to raise any children they might have in his faith, in deference to him. Although never renouncing her adopted religion, Risë had many connections with the Catholic Church after she appeared in *Going My Way* with Bing Crosby. Through Crosby she was introduced to New York's Francis Cardinal Spellman who took a personal interest in the spiritual development of her son, Nicolas.

Risë was chosen to star in *Newtown Band Wagon*, a Christmas musical, that called for her to sing as well as dance and Sadie, as ever, determined to insure her success, made an attention-getting dress that left one arm bare. She could not have pleased her daughter more since Risë reveled in the aura of sophistication it gave her. An awareness of the importance of making a visual impact on an audience began to grow. On the countless recital tours she made when her career was in full swing, whether the newspaper reviewer was male or female, her gowns never failed to draw notices of their own. A letter written in 1984, provides an insight to the effect Risë had on one of her classmates while still in school: "Many, many times tears ran down my cheeks as she sang in the auditorium of Newtown High...her beautiful voice touched me and made chills run through me - each time - as not only that sound, but her most charming smile pervaded the room. My high school days were as a part of Heaven - only because of [her]." [7]

In her last year at Newtown, the February 18, 1930 issue of the school newspaper, the *Newtown X-Ray*, reported on a concert presented by the vocal training class at the Aeolian Hall the previous week. The program was designed for the American Academy of Teachers of Singing to illustrate that instruction in singing could be taught to high school students to train them to appreciate singing as amateurs or even prepare them for a professional career. Risë was among the twelve students chosen to prove this theory and obliged by offering "Oley Speaks", "Sylvia" and d'Hardelot's, "Because" as the closing numbers of the Newtown portion of the program. The *New York Times* reported on the event and felt that the student performers had acquitted themselves exceptionally well both in voice and diction.

The school newspaper can be forgiven a bit of chauvinistic crowing,

> We are rightly proud of the performance of our accomplished young singers. They were the youngest on the programme and had the least training...the selections

14

rendered by our representatives were the most difficult and their position as first on the programme was most trying. [8]

With this appearance, Risë had a more mature outlet for her abilities. Three years earlier, on the *Children's Hour*, and specials like "The Reindeer Express" where she was introduced as "a little German Miss" [9], she was still in the talented child performer category, one that she was quickly outgrowing.

Another step towards her goal as professional singer came with her engagement by the Queens Symphony to appear with them at their inaugural concert at Newtown High School's Dillingham Hall in 1930,

> Risë Steenberg, who is professionally known as Risë Stevens... has sung at several concerts and is continuing with the Queens Symphony Orchestra. Madame De Koven, wife of Reginald De Koven, composer, praised her voice when she made her debut at the first concert of the season 1930, with the Queens Symphony Orchestra, where she sang all Reginald De Koven's compositions. She also sang at a concert given by her instructor Professor Parado, at the Chemists Club. Her next concert with the Queens Symphony Orchestra will be sometime in May. Unless she goes abroad to study music, she will attend the Juilliard School of Music, after she graduates from Newtown. [10]

Significantly, Risë changed her name to "Stevens" about the time she was about to graduate from Newton. She billed herself that way for public appearances but only after she graduated from high school did she drop "Steenberg" all together. Of the inaugural concert, Herman Epstein reported that, "In the second part of the program a group of 3 songs by De Koven sung with finished style by Miss Risë Stevens, of most pleasing appearance, were beautifully rendered; she has a rich contralto voice." [11] He went on to say, "Her singing of 'O Promise Me' was rich and sweet and received such a warm reception that she was obliged to repeat it. She also sang two other numbers of the late Reginald De Koven, 'Persian Love Song' and 'The Angelus'." [12]

* * * *

On December 6, 1927, the *New York Times* reported that "A new attempt to establish a permanent 'Little Theatre' opera company with American singers was begun in Brooklyn last night with a sprightly performance of Nicolai's...'Merry Wives of Windsor' at the Brooklyn Little Theatre...If its standards are kept high this enterprise may succeed in bridging the gap between the school and the professional stage." [13]

Kendall K. Mussey, former Director of the Brooklyn Music School Settlement, was engaged by the Board of Directors to manage the company that was heartily embraced by a number of well-known professional artists. The *New York Times* article recorded that Amelita Galli-Curci sent a telegram that was read between acts of *Merry Wives* commending the venture. The renowned coloratura had been instrumental in raising the necessary funds by giving a benefit recital several years earlier that helped build the St. Felix Street Playhouse in Brooklyn where the opera school had its headquarters.

The 1928 offerings identified it from the start as an adventurous company. Reginald de Koven's, *Robin Hood*, Georges Bizet's, *Djamileh*, *Phoebus and Pan*, set to music by J. S. Bach and Oscar Strauss', *The Chocolate Soldier*, attracted a group of subscribers who were influential backers as well.

In order to increase their pool of talent, the Little Theatre announced the formation of an opera school that would enroll thirty students on a scholarship basis the following season. Each student would receive $100.00 a month for expenses during the seven-month season. Auditions were scheduled for April 28th to May 3rd at Brooklyn's Little Theatre in St. Felix Street. Classes in *mise en scène*, acting, gesture, fencing, sight-reading and diction as well as stage experience would be available to the lucky winners.

Sadie saw the article in the *New York Times* and promptly entered Risë as a contestant with full confidence that she would be offered a place in the program. On September 30, 1930, a news release stated that,

> 26 singers chosen from 312 began yesterday their studies in the first all-scholarship opera school to be organized in New York. E. Roland Harriman, President of the Board of the Little Opera Company announced classes are being held at the Brooklyn Little Theatre...Among the winners of the scholarships [was]...Risë Stevens. This week, Risë abandoned her course at Newtown High School...to place one foot upon the ladder that leads to the Metropolitan. Until now she has studied with Professor Orry Parado of Manhattan. [14]

The company was in its fourth year in Brooklyn and its third in Manhattan when Risë entered on September 29, 1930. The season began in Brooklyn on November 12th and on November 17th in Manhattan with Karl Millöchers, *Beggar Student*. The opening in Manhattan was for a "people's theater," a high society event with debutante program girls and many social sponsors guaranteeing its six month season. The company had already started rehearsing its second presentation, *Orpheus in Hades* at the Brooklyn workshop for a December hearing. Subsequently, on a monthly basis, *The Marriage of Figaro*, *Don Pasquale*, *Phoebus and Pan*, *Bartered Bride* and *Waltz Dream* were scheduled.

William Reddick, the conductor, was thirty-nine at the time of Risë's entering the Little Theatre's training program. He already had a varied career behind him. As a pianist and organist, he was accompanist to some of the world's leading singers, among whom were Edward Johnson, David Bispham,

17

Alice Nilsen and the violinist, Maude Powell. During World War II, he produced the National Broadcasting Company's symphonic series and was director and founder of the Ford Sunday Evening Hour reuniting him with Risë when she appeared as a guest on the show in the 1940s.

The *New York Times'* review mentioned Risë in the cast listing of *Orpheus in Hades* but erroneously referred to her as "Rose Stevens". A colleague in that performance was Eleanor Steele, a three year veteran of the company, who was to play an important part in the furthering of Risë's career by helping finance her studies for one year. Steele, herself, had a respectable career as a concert and opera singer abandoning it at the start of World War II for marriage to an Idaho rancher, Emmet P. Reese. As the daughter of Charles Steele, lawyer and partner of J. P. Morgan and shareholder in the Metropolitan Opera Real Estate Company, she was born into wealth, married into it and became a philanthropist backing charities in Idaho and Appalachia. Her great niece, mezzo-soprano, Frederica von Stade, in a letter (undated) to the author, confessed of little knowledge of Steele's helping Risë, "I have heard that my Great Aunt Lela may have helped at one point but I have no direct knowledge and sadly she died long ago." [15] Eleanor Steele was also one of the principal backers of the company and an ally Risë was lucky in having.

Life with the Little Theatre was a grueling round of hard work, classes in the morning, rehearsals in the afternoon and, if chosen to appear in a production, performances at night. For Risë it was even more exhausting since she still lived with her family in Jackson Heights. A long subway ride to Brooklyn early in the morning and another late at night left little free time. Risë's apprenticeship in the Little Theatre encompassed every phase of activities both behind the scenes and on stage. For one run of performances she would be in the chorus, for another she would have a role and then back to the chorus. It was hectic but she was learning her craft.

After the *Marriage of Figaro* and *Don Pasquale,* the *Bar-*

tered Bride offered her an opportunity to have a solo role. It wasn't her debut in opera as is often stated, since the company was in actuality semi-professional and, moreover, Risë was still a student in the opera school. Entrusted with the smallish part of Ludmilla, the mother of the heroine, Marenka, in the premiere on March 23, 1931, Francis D. Perkins of the *New York Herald Tribune* commended her on her vocal performance but felt she looked much too young for a character twice her age.

On May 14th, the board of the Little Theatre which included Cornelius N. Bliss, Clarence MacKay, J. P. Morgan, John D. Rockefeller, Charles Steele, among others, voted to officially change its name to New York Opéra-Comique, Inc. believing the new name would impart a greater sense of purpose to the company's endeavors. The search for a centrally located theater in Manhattan was also announced, one which would enable more ambitious programming.

The 1931-1932 season of the New York Opéra-Comique, the last to be given in the Hecksher Theater, began its Manhattan series on November 16, 1931 with Albert Lortzing's seldom-heard work, *The Poacher*. The next program, devoted to the less than successful world premiere of Ernest Carter's, *The Blonde Donna*, which took place on December 14, 1931, elicited a harsh review from *Musical America* damning not only the new opera but the entire enterprise "The Opera Comique...is hardly professional in its technical attainments. Its singers lack operatic style and their acting is often amateurish. There is needed an efficient stage director to tell these young singers what to do." [16]

Risë was in the ensemble and escaped the wrath of the critics unlike Eleanor Steele and Hall Clovis who were the stars. One member of the cast, Sonia Essin, a contralto soloist formerly of the *Staatsoper* in Düsseldorf, sufficiently aroused the curiosity of voice teacher, Anna Schoen-René, to make her purchase a ticket for a performance in spite of the reviews. On the night of her visit, the announcement came that at the last minute Essin was too ill to go on and a talented newcomer, Risë Stevens, would take her place. Schoen-René sank lower in her seat and debated whether to leave but something told her not to. Pandemonium reigned back stage. Risë, with no forewarning or rehearsal, was fitted into Essen's costume and wig, makeup was hastily applied and she was practically pushed on stage with no time to panic. It did not augur well but instinct, natural talent and luck overcome the obstacles and she acquitted herself quite respectably. At least, capably enough to impress one member in the audience, Madam Schoen-René.

Chapter 2

Anna Eugenia Schoen-René was born in Coblenz, Germany, on January 12, 1864, the last of eight children of the Baron von Schoen who was the Royal Master of Forestry and Agriculture in the Rhine provinces. She was only ten years old when the Baron died and the family moved to Treves. In her autobiography, *America's Musical Inheritance: Memories and Reminiscences*, she recalls that, "As a child, I was brought up more or less as a boy because my brother Otto needed a companion." [1] In her adult years, there was always something mannish about her appearance that no doubt stemmed from her identification with her brother. Drawn to music as a career, she applied for a place in the Royal Academy of Music in Berlin and when speaking about her audition for the conservatory, she recalled, "In the entrance hall, I had quickly swallowed two raw eggs, to make sure that my voice was clear for singing." [2] She impressed the judges (among whom was Johannes Brahms) and was admitted as a student of the German *lied*.

Upon the advice of Joachim, who was the director of the Royal Academy, she sought out the illustrious Pauline Viardot-Garcia. Daughter of Manuel Garcia, the tenor for whom Rossini wrote Almaviva in *Il Barbiere di Siviglia*, *Tancredi* and *Otello*, sister of Manuel Garcia Jr., a celebrated teacher of singing and Maria Malibran, the mercurial creator of Donizetti's *Maria Stuarda* who died at age twenty-eight from injuries sustained when falling off a horse; Viardot, herself, was the creator of the role of Fidés in Meyerbeer's, *Le*

Prophète in 1849 and Gounod's, *Sappho* in 1851. It was for her that Hector Berlioz in 1859 restored Gluck's, *Orfeo ed Euridice* to the Paris Opera and in retirement, she was, along with Mathilde Marchesi, *the* singing teacher of the last half of the nineteenth century. About sixty-five in 1886 when Schoen-René visited her in her studio in Paris and sang an aria from *La Sonnambula*, "Connais-tu le pays" from *Mignon* and a German *lied*, she pronounced her a soprano with mezzo coloring and took her on as a student. Their working relationship was to endure on and off for eighteen years during which Schoen-René learned much about the training of voices.

After two years of study, Viardot-Garcia thought her pupil ready to return to Germany and sing for Kaiser Wilhelm I. An engagement with the Ducal Opera of Saxe-Altenburg was offered whereupon she adopted the stage name, René, to conceal her identity and spare her noble family any embarrassment, later adding it to her own. America beckoned in 1893 and one of her sisters, who taught at the University of Minnesota, suggested she settle in Minneapolis. There she started to come into her own as a conductor, her singing career cut short because of ill health.

In 1893, Schoen-René formed her own orchestra, the Northwestern Symphony, which was the predecessor of today's Minneapolis Symphony. Returning to Paris in 1909 to accept a position as Viardot-Garcia's assistant, she was caught up in the onset of the first World War but as an American citizen since 1906, she felt obliged to return to her adopted country when it too became involved in hostilities. Taking up residence in New York, she opened a studio and in 1925 joined the faculty of Juilliard School of Music. Ever the evaluator of the true singing voice, Schoen-René mentioned in her autobiography an early encounter with Anton Seidl, Wagner's proselytizer and conductor at the Metropolitan Opera from 1885 to 1897, "I used to be often with Anton Seidl when I attended the Metropolitan Opera season in Chicago. One day, when I invited him to have lunch with me, he came in carrying a picture of [Emma] Calve which she had just autographed for him. On it she had written, 'Your future Brünnhilde'. He seemed very sanguine about it, but I felt I knew her musical abilities better than he, as she had once been a pupil of Viardot. I told him 'if Calve sings the Brunnhilde, than I will sing Wotan!' For all her great gifts...she was entirely a French singer...it would have harmed her voice." [3]

Similarly with Risë, Schoen-René could evaluate her abilities in spite of the lack of preparation for her performance, "I first heard her at the Opera Comique in New York at age 17...I had the immediate impression of an extraordinary talent and fine personality, and for that reason I gave her a scholarship." [4] In actuality, the scholarship commenced in October, 1932, since Risë felt obliged to honor her commitment to the Opéra-Comique. Prior to her introduction to Schoen-René, Risë had applied for a scholarship to Juilliard in the spring of 1931. She was highly recommended by Mr. Valentine of Newtown High who in his letter of May 1, 1931 to the Admissions Office stated, "She has a quick ear, a retentive musical memory, good musical intelligence, and a voice of rare quality, range and power. In addition she is graceful, good to look at, and has a very pleasing personality. In fact, I believe she has just the requisites to succeed as a singer." [5] Orry Parado confirmed these sentiments in his letter of May 18th, and told the admissions committee, "you may be proud of a student who sincerely loves music and is willing to sacrifice much for it." [6]

On September 3, 1931, Ernest Hutchinson, Assistant Dean of Juilliard, wrote Risë, "Before the Committee on Applications gives us its decision as to your eligibility or ineligibility for entrance to our Fellowship examinations, I should like to inquire whether you are to sing this season with the Little Theatre Opera Company. It is not possible for singers to carry our first year required studies and do justice to the Opera Company. Their rehearsals and our classes come at the same hours so often that it is impossible for a first-year Fellowship holder to combine the two. The Opera Company is quite right in having sufficient rehearsals and in demanding attendance at them. The point is, that the course demanded of a Fellowship holder in Voice is so heavy that almost the only thing that can be combined with it during the first year is a church or synagogue position, or radio." [7]

Juilliard was dismissed as a possibility for the time being until the accidental meeting with Schoen-René made it a possibility for the future. In the meantime, Risë was given her biggest role to date at the Opéra-Comique which helped ease Juilliard's rejection. Jacques Offenbach's, *La Vie Parisienne* was scheduled for a January 11th opening and she was cast as Michelle. The performance took place before an audience which boasted Offenbach's niece, Mrs. Mason Redlich, and garnered a good review from the *New York Times* the following morning, "...Miss Stevens as the deeper voiced beauty in the 'Eugénie hat' and curls ... had much to do...the operetta moved with smoothness and speed of a previous half-week in the Brooklyn Little Theatre." [8]

The Opéra-Comique, in serious financial trouble by January of 1932, hastily structured a plan to ensure the completion of its season of six productions. The Womens' Committee and the subscribers were called on to guarantee the payroll of the company for the remaining three productions. Volunteering to raise the amount needed for one of the operas, the ninety-seven members of the company accepted a ten-percent salary cut and launched a ticket selling drive to increase box office sales. By the beginning of February, half of the necessary funds had been secured with Mrs. Cravath contributing $1,000 of it. Both Mrs. Patrick Campbell, the actress, and Mrs. Lawrence Tibbett lent their support to the fund raising drive as well. Tibbett, himself, gave a recital of Handel, Brahms and "Di Provenza il Mar" from *La Traviata* before an audience of three hundred at the Colony Club on the 14th of February for the benefit of the scholarship school.

The various efforts were successful and the remainder of the season was guaranteed.

February 8th, saw Risë in the small role of Aurelia in *The Chocolate Soldier* and the Sunday edition of the *New York Times* prior to the opening had published a photograph of her and colleagues, Eleanor Steele and Alice Atkins. After the opening, the *Times* mentioned that Risë, Eleanor Steele, Hall Clovis, et al., were part of a lively ensemble. Francis D. Perkins in the *Herald Tribune* found the production "enjoyable and spirited and the average standard of singing was unusually high." [9] At that time the thought would never have occurred to Risë that a dozen years later, Hollywood was to again unite her with the operetta in a totally different format but with her as the star.

A month later, *Orpheus in Hades* returned as promised with Risë as Public Opinion. It was an updated version as described in the *New York Times* on May 8th, "The gates of Olympus are ...slyly suggestive of a speakeasy. Pluto arrives by plane. The Seabury investigation.*..pop[s] out of the topical songs...the changing scenery... delicately burlesques *Das Rheingold*." [10]

During the intermission, Kendall Mussey pointed out to the audience that the company had progressed from one that had an ensemble without experience to one that paid its principals and chorus enough to insure their service full-time. The profile of the company was changing from one which originally was to serve the community on a not for profit basis to one which was a strictly professional group. A Broadway house proved unrealistic and equally unrealistic was the belief that the company could endure. However, before the lights went out for the once "Little Theatre", Johann Strauss', *Die Fledermaus* opened on April 4th. Risë was given the part of the forever bored Prince Orlofsky and her concept "followed

---

* The Seabury investigation examined alleged corruption in the police and lower courts.

excellent traditions of opera comique." [11] The role is not large but skillfully handled it can be made to seem more important than it is, which is what happened when she essayed Orlofsky in the 1950 Metropolitan Opera production.

The Opéra-Comique was nearing its end. An announcement for Town Hall auditions for only experienced singers who have sung leading roles and speak English without an accent appeared on April 17th in the New York Times, and a benefit by Beniamino Gigli, Claudio Frigerio and Katherine Newman at Carnegie Hall on May 9th which proved highly successful, were among last ditch efforts to save the company. On June 22nd, the Times reported that Mrs. Paul D. Cravath was elected President of the Board. Long a patron of the company, the former Agnes Huntington was once a singer herself, having appeared with the Leipzig Gewandhaus concerts under Carl Reinecke, the New York Philharmonic and the Boston Symphony, among other venues. In spite of her excellent credentials, she could not save the Opéra-Comique, and the *New York Times* announced on October 29th that the forthcoming season was suspended. When it was determined that sufficient funding could not be raised, the Company closed its doors permanently.

* * * *

Kyle Crichton's* biography of Risë, *Subway to the Met,* fills in the events which followed, "It was summer, and there were no openings for a singer. She landed with a dress house on West 37th Street, modeling coats. The pay was $28 a week,

---

* Kyle Crichton (1896-1960) the author of *Subway to the Met* was as colorful as the biography he wrote. Early in his literary career, using the alias, "Robert Forsythe", he wrote leftist articles, at the same time he was an associate editor of *Collier's Weekly* where he specialized in interviewing celebrities. A product of the Maxwell Perkins school of editing at Scribners, prior to his coming to New York in 1929, he worked as a coal miner and machine shop operator, among other occupations in Pennsylvania.

she specialized in fur coats, and it was one of the hottest summers in the records of the New York weather bureau. Along
about July she thought she was going to die at the modeling
job (this was before air conditioning) but she stuck it out." [12]
The Schoen-René scholarship (financed by Eleanor Steele)
was to start the following year and while it was a boon for
her career goals it was not going to provide the necessary
money she needed to help out at home. Schoen-René wanted
her as a pupil as much as Risë wanted to study with her so
she found her a job as a member of the chorus on the radio
show, "Palmolive Beauty Box Theater", which featured Metropolitan Opera singer and Hollywood hopeful, Gladys
Swarthout. She was paid eighty dollars per week and "stayed
two years with the Palmolive show, raising her salary to $100
per week and eventually working into small roles. Risë enjoyed every minute on the Palmolive show and was sorry when
it was all over for her. The money made all the difference in
the world at home." [13]

Risë never had any problems with Swarthout even though
they were in the same vocal category, because she accepted
the fact that it was Swarthout's show. If anything, it gave her
added incentive to try harder with the stylish Swarthout as a
model. When the Palmolive show ran out, Risë went back to
singing in churches for twenty-five and thirty-five dollars a
Sunday.

The time came for zeroing in on the next phase of developing a career. Risë had said that she would pursue studies
in Europe right after high school but The New York Opéra-
Comique and Schoen-René intervened. The former provided
invaluable stage experience and the latter the guidance in
career choices and, more basically, instilling in her a sound
technique. The method that Schoen-René followed was based
on the classic approach to vocal training that made no concessions to outside distractions. One's whole physical and
mental being was to be subservient to the two vocal cords
housed in your body. The length of study averaged from

one to two years depending on your progress in mastering the Garcia method that stressed *bel canto* line, scales and exercises in legato. Risë recalled,

> Schoen-Rene always thought of me as a mezzo rather than a contralto. She started lightening the voice; she gave it the quality that was not always that heavy sound...she was after something that was not so...'forced' in sound...always a big tone. So now she was after the piano...the crescendos....decrescendos...the finesse singing...It was a struggle because it was unknown to me. And then the voice got more and more even...easy on the top. It began to flow more. I had no difficulty in hitting a high G, or A. [14]

The eminent soprano, Margaret Harshaw, also studied with Schoen-René and remembered her saying "every note you sing should come from the bridge of your nose." [15] "[She] would start with very slow scales...In other words try to find the focus of the voice...then she would give me grace notes to do...to give it flexibility." [16] There were no songs or arias until the second year of study. Schoen-René emphasized *lieder* for breath control since it is the basis for even vocal production. Risë cites passages from *St. Matthew Passion* where Schoen-René would not let her take a breath. "The actual proof of breath control is: sing as many phrases in one breath as you possibly can, and you time yourself." [17] Bach was also extolled for a legato line. You can do anything if breathing is in control. "Ombra mai fu" and other Italian Art Songs were assigned for their long drawn out phrases. This, Risë maintains, is how she successfully spun out the legato phrases of both Orfeo and Dalila. The voice had to be focused for support, that is what Harshaw meant by its coming from the bridge of the nose. In her autobiography, Schoen-René speaks of breath control, "[it] should not be noticeable to the audience...use the diaphragm in order to avoid having to raise the shoulders...the throat must be relaxed and the diction perfect. The voice should never be used as a declamatory organ." [18] With Harshaw, "Du bist die ruh" by Schubert and Brahms songs were the first pieces she was allowed to sing.

> Mannerism in singing 'Lieder' show very bad taste. The singer who develops them, emphasizing, for instance, single words instead of keeping them in the correct phrasing, as the composer had done in co-operation with the poet, has no understanding of the 'Lied'. In singing 'Lieder', especially those of Schubert, Schumann, Franz, Hugo Wolf and Brahms, the singer must first visualize them. He should get the feeling of the songs by meditating on them, to put himself in tune with the composer's thoughts...The execution of the 'Lied' is the happy combination of two people, singer and accompanist, who have found each other. [19]

What Schoen-René is expressing here is the basis for all interpretation whether it is a *lied* or an aria. The word and the music suggest the interpretation. Maria Callas was fond of saying that she did not have to study the background of a character, it was all in the music.

With Stevens, Schoen-René worked at lightening the voice, moving it from contralto to mezzo, with Harshaw she heard a future soprano in the sound. Harshaw emphasized that Schoen-René did not try to push the voice up, it was allowed to happen naturally. "How far apart is Ortrud from Brünnhilde or Amneris from Isolde?" [20] Harshaw asked the author in a telephone conversation. "She predicted I would be a soprano by age thirty-eight." [21] Harshaw was quick to express her gratitude, "She taught me everything I know." [22] She gave credit to the Viardot-Garcia method with having stood by her for her entire career and served as the basis for her own methods of teaching.

On September 23[rd,] 1933 Risë received notification from Dean Hutcheson of the Julliard School of Music that she was awarded a Fellowship to the Graduate School for one year. Schoen-René's recommendation was sufficient to secure a place for her, which was fortunate since the basic requirements that included proficiency in at least one musical instrument would have doomed her application from the start. She was told to report to the School on Friday, October 6th for lesson assignments, knowing full well that besides not playing the piano or any instrument, she had no knowledge of theory and composition. Courses in these were to prove her bête-noir since her overriding interest was training to be a performer not a composer. Happily, studies with Schoen-René would continue albeit in a different setting.

When she first entered Juilliard, Risë was still living with her family in Jackson Heights. She drove to school in the Essex automobile that belonged to her father. She followed this routine for the first two years but her mother was petrified at the thought of her driving across the Queensborough Bridge (the bridge which connects Queens and Manhattan) in winter. It could become very icy and slippery, sufficient reason for Sadie to give into her fears, pack everything and move once more when she could stand the anxiety no longer. This time, Queens was left behind for Manhattan and the new apartment was located at 415 West 115th Street and Morningside Heights near the Cathedral of Saint John the Divine. For her mother's peace of mind, Risë would be able to walk to school.

At that time, Albert Stoessel was the motivating force behind Juilliard's Opera program. Born in St. Louis, Missouri in 1894, at age fifteen he was enrolled as a scholarship student in Berlin's, *Königliche Hochschule für Musik*. He mastered the violin with proficiency and was considered a virtuoso after his Berlin debut in 1913. The threat of war forced his return to America in 1915 and his highly successful American debut with The St. Louis Orchestra occurred that same year. In 1925, he became Director of the Worchester Festival and in 1927, he began his association with Juilliard when he was appointed Director of the Opera and Orchestra Department of the Graduate School of Music.

In May of 1934, Risë sang Bach's solo cantata "Schlege doch gewünschte Stunde" in the Oratorio Society's Bach Festival at the Juilliard School. Her next engagement came through Dr. Stoessel, who, in his capacity as Director, was able to introduce many of his Juilliard students at the Worchester Festival. Given its prominence, the *Worchester Telegram and Gazette* covered the pre-opening festivities in detail and Risë, dressed in the height of fashion, posed with her colleagues for a photograph. From a brief item in the paper it is learned that she had one of her earliest supporters with her, "Miss Risë Stevens...was accompanied by her mother, Mrs. Christian Stevens [sic], at the rehearsal in the auditorium this morning. Miss Stevens wore a gown of black crepe with metallic embroidery. A frill of lace finished the neckline and a smart close fitting hat harmonizing with the black and silver of her gown completed her costume. Mrs. Stevens was attired in midnight blue crepe." [23]

In an article headed, "Says Contraltos Envy Sopranos", Risë confessed that contraltos would like to sing coloratura soprano roles but she stressed that she loved her vocal range nonetheless. On a more serious note, she also expressed her belief in young people's support of the opera and the need for American opera for Americans. Professing a love for singing to audiences of children, she also revealed that she had a Spitz terrier, Toots, and that "some day...she is going to buy a cabin in Maine in the lake country, and live there with 'Toots' and other assorted canines. Before she picks out her cabin, she has first another desire...It is to play Amneris...'I think I would call that my greatest operatic ambition. After that, I'd be content to pick out that cabin in Maine'." [24]

On the evening of October 1st, an audience of three thousand crammed the Municipal Memorial Auditorium to witness the opening of the seventy-fifth Worchester Music Festival among whom were Risë's mother and father. The program was the traditional mixture of the old and the new for which the Festival was known and it was an extension of the philosophy which Stoessel professed in the opera department of Juilliard. Through the years, he championed works which were modern and gave them early hearings in both venues. The Cesar Franck's, "Psalm", one of the programs works is a short piece but a review noted that the "festival chorus of 450 voices swung into [it] with an assurance and authority that has come to be associated with a chorus trained and directed by Mr. Stoessel." [25]

The final work, *Le Roi David*, had Risë among the soloists in a performance that was notable for its "dashing sweep of enthusiastic treatment." [26]

Brangäne, in a concert reading of Act 3 of *Tristan und Isolde*, was the first of her final three performances, and she "added materially to the excellent impression she created on opening night and although the part allotted her was a small one, nevertheless she surprised her listeners with the breadth of her range through which she maintained a quality of musical merit." [27]

In a childrens' concert, Risë, having earlier professed her love for singing for boys and girls, was "the ideal choice for the afternoon's program, for in the two arias 'Che Farò Senza Eurydice'...and 'Oh Mio Fernando'...she demonstrated to her young listeners the heights which youth may achieve; and following an explanation of the numbers by Mr. Stoessel she proceeded in a portrayal of the roles with that unassuming charm and musical grace that will lead her far in her chosen field." [28]

The concert on Saturday evening, October 6th, saw Risë's fourth assignment, Kate Pinkerton, in a staged presentation of *Madama Butterfly* with Suzanne Fisher in the title role. This was to be the only complete Puccini role Risë would ever sing apart from an occasional "Vissi d'Arte" from *Tosca* in recital and the "Flower Duet" from *Madama Butterfly* with Gladys Swarthout on the *Palmolive Beauty Box Theater*. Puccini was not interested in mezzos as leading ladies and, although Risë was temperamentally suited for Tosca, vocally it was beyond her mezzo range.

Risë's first year at Juilliard was a time for the continued laying in of technique coupled with classes in theory, sight reading and performance practice but she had already caused comment among other students, among whom was Annamary Dickey, herself, a future member of the Metropolitan Opera, "Risë came to Juilliard with her usual charisma and we who had been there for several years marveled at her." [29]

It was in the second year when the hard work of her year of studying privately with Schoen-René and her first year of formal studies at Juilliard began to pay off. She was singled out not only for her voice but also for her poise and outgoing disposition and Albert Stoessel could not help but take note.

On May 16, 1934, Risë was told, formally, by Dean Hutcheson that, "We take great pleasure in informing you that your Fellowship at the Juilliard Graduate School will be continued for the school year 1934-35, subject to good work in all your studies." [30]

While Risë had appeared in the chorus of the opera productions the first year, the second brought with it her first solo role, Dryad, in Richard Strauss's, *Ariadne auf Naxos*. Schoen-René approved of this assignment since it contained a great deal of legato singing in harmony with a soprano and another mezzo. Even though Risë was stage-wise from her apprenticeship with the Opéra-Comique, Schoen-René knew it was better to start in a part that would show her to advantage but not be too big a burden. Gluck's, *Orfeo ed Euridice* was the second offering of the season and Schoen-René was determined that Risë would be chosen as one of the two students who would play the lead. Orfeo needs an interpreter with a seamless vocal line and her long hours coaching Risë in legato singing would make her ideal for the part. Also, Schoen-René's teacher, Viardot-Garcia, was a famous Orfeo and she was convinced that Risë was her natural heir to the role.

Prior to the opening of *Ariadne*, Risë gave a song recital at the Monday Afternoon Club on November 18th. The *Palmolive Beauty Box Theater* that she joined in the spring of 1934 eased the anxieties of how to make ends meet for a good two years and subsequently, the Sigmund Romberg radio show performed the same function. The summer between her first and second years at Juilliard was the hellish one modeling fur coats, but it did pay and that was all that mattered. The financial situation of her parents was still touch and go, what with her father's being away from home so much and his unabated drinking problem. Then, too, there was Lewis who was trying to find a means of support at a time when the nation was heading towards a major recession. Risë's studies served as a giant escape where she could insulate herself from the harsh reality of day to day exigencies. Lewis was not as fortunate and, needing to support himself and carry his weight at home, followed in his father's footsteps and became a traveling salesman.

Wednesday evening, December 5th, saw the first New York performance of Strauss' sixth opera, *Ariadne on Naxos*, as it was called in Arthur Kalisch's English translation. The opera is arranged in two parts, a prologue and the opera proper. Originally composed in 1912, it was intended by Strauss as a companion piece to Moliere's, *Le Bourgeois Gentilhomme*. It was not a success and the 1916 revision was the one used by Juilliard. The libretto centers around the whim of an wealthy old man who in order to get more quickly to a fireworks display which is to conclude a gala evening, commands that an *opera seria* be done simultaneously with the *Commedia del Arte* divertisement. The *New York Sun*'s critic, W. J. Henderson's opinion that "in the end it must be confessed...most of [it] is tedious, heavy, dull stuff." [31] was pretty much the general consensus of the press. For them, it suffered greatly against the merits of *Der Rosenkavalier* and was considered to be a pastiche of the composer's earlier works. Henderson thought, however, that "The performance of such an opera by students was a courageous undertaking." [32] As for the production by Frederick Kiesler, Winthrop Sargeant (12/6/34) in the *Brooklyn Eagle* thought that "detail after detail was in atrocious taste. The Greek nymphs wore cellophane aprons over their pleated gowns, Zerbinetta sported the hat of an American "gob", Arlecchino...wore goggles and a pair of ordinary gymnasium sneakers." [33]

The cast came off quite well with Josephine Antoine as Zerbinetta garnering the highest praise. A highly thought of student of Marcella Sembrich, she would go directly from the stage of Juilliard to that of the Metropolitan. "Zerbinetta was the heroine of this performance...her high D was true and she managed cleanly the intricate florid passages." [34] She won the ovation of the evening from the invited audience among which were Geraldine Farrar, Lawrence Tibbett and Eleanor Robson Belmont. In a far less showy part, Risë was nonetheless singled out by Pitts Sanborn in the *New York World Telegram*, "an uncommonly good voice was heard in the minor part of the Dryad." [35]

With the combination of a handful of good reviews and the influence of Schoen-René, Risë was given the role of Orfeo. Francis D. Perkins thought Risë's, "impersonation was expressive in action and vocal inflection; her voice, in the first scene, was handicapped by some unfocused tones, but she gave some noteworthy singing later on with remarkable volume, resonance and emotional potency, although a more rounded quality could, at times, have been a further asset. In the main, however, her performance merited warm praise." [36] Other reviewers felt, "Risë Stevens more than fulfilled expectations." Harold Strickland, critic for the *Brooklyn Times Union* without disguising chauvinistic pride in their St. Felix Theater alumna, singled her out as "about the best of Mr. Stoessel's singers at the moment." [37] For the most part, the simplicity in design for the production was commended (it had a modern touch with Risë's wig made of wool) but apart from certain shortcomings the general consensus was that it was the, "most successful venture into the operatic realm undertaken thus far by the Juilliard forces, there can be only praise for the artistic sensitivity and smooth professionalism with which the classic tale and its ethereal musical counterpart were unfolded." [38]

The third and final presentation for the season was a premiere of a new opera, *Maria Malibran*, with music by the well-known orchestrater, Robert Russell Bennett, and a libretto by the chief music critic of the *New Yorker*, Robert A. Simon. The opera would be the third American opera staged by the school, the others being *Jack and the Beanstalk* by Louis Gruenberg presented in December, 1931, and *Helen Retires* by George Antheil in February, 1934, both with librettos by Juilliard's President, John Erskine. The Bennett-Simon work was composed between 1932 and 1934 and was submitted to the Metropolitan Opera which, wisely, demurred from taking an option on it citing financial exigencies. Erskine and Stoessel saw in it possibilities for the opera program and shortly after the announcement was made to present it at Juilliard, WJZ scheduled a half-hour pick up of Los Angeles Philharmonic Orchestra concert under the baton of Alfred Wallenstein playing music from the opera.

The cast called for fifteen singers and Risë was again in the first cast, her assignment, Cornelia Bayard, described as an early nineteenth century "deb". The action set in New York in the mid 1820's is a fictionalized account of a period in Malibran's life prior to her becoming a big star. Robert A. Simon was most forthright in his evaluation of this product by two neophytes, "Mr. Bennett and I shall be amply satisfied if an audience attends 'Maria Malibran' without regretting it hadn't gone to the movies instead." [39] Mr. Bennett expressed a definite resigned feeling about his efforts, "I write music like 'Malibran' for fun. I make my living orchestrating - by the yard. More or less serious music I write as it comes to me, without too much fuss, and if the public likes it, well and good. But if not I needn't worry, I have my living anyway." [40]

The first performance was witnessed by the customary invited audiences among whom were Lawrence Tibbett and Walter Damrosch. The reaction on the part of the critics was decidedly mixed with Howard Taubman declaring the score "a curious melange." [41] He did declare it a good show but one which "might be recommended to the Hollywood moguls, who are reported to be in search of material for the operatic stars they have been engaging in hordes lately." [42] At various places in the score, Malibran sang "Home Sweet Home", "Una Voce Poco Fa" and an aria from *Giulietta è Romeo* by Nicolò Zingarelli, all of which made the lack of a melodic line in the Bennett score more pronounced. W. J. Henderson agreed with the composer's own self-evaluation, "melodic inspiration…is not his greatest gift." [43]

Chapter 3

Outside of Juilliard, Risë was being closely watched on another front as well, one that would play an important part in the future. Eric Simon, artist representative with Organization Artistique Internationale and talent scout for the Metropolitan Opera in Europe, wrote Edward Ziegler, Assistant General Manager of the Metropolitan Opera, on July 30, 1935,

> During my last visit to New York I heard Miss Stevens taking a lesson with Mme. Schoen-Rene and also in a performance of the opera 'Malibran'...I mentioned the 21 year old artist to Bodanzky and Mr. Witherspoon several times and introduced Mr. Witherspoon to her at a party at Hutcheson's. I had strongly advised Miss Stevens to go to Europe in order to study the part of Octavian in Der Rosenkavalier with Mme. Gutheil-Schoder in Salzburg, while of course continuing under the guidance of...Mme. Schoen-Rene. Miss Stevens, who is in very modest circumstances, was able to follow my advice and is now in Salzburg. To judge from her letters things are going very well. We have a great talent and I ask you to speak with Mr. Johnson about her - he already knows her name. Miss Stevens has faith in me and has entrusted me with building her career, which of course I undertake with the greatest care and sense of responsibility. I ask that, after her return to New York, you hear Miss Stevens at the earliest opportunity. In addition to everything else, Miss Stevens makes a very at-

tractive appearance both in person and on stage. [1]

On August 8th, Ziegler answered, "we all know about her, and the suggestion that she sing an audition for us is an echo of our own desires. We asked this of her before she left for Europe but Mme. Schoen-Rene refused to let her sing an audition." [2]

The school year was over and Risë received her scholarship renewal letter on May 21st stating that she was to be admitted to the 1935-36 term with the bothersome proviso that she was to repeat Harmony II and piano. The opinion of Eric Simon concerning her abilities and his suggestion to study with Marie Gutheil-Schoder in Salzburg meant more to her than Juilliard's approval or disapproval. Moreover she had Schoen-René's support in spending the summer abroad. For some time, Risë had been saving money out of the little left over to finance a trip to Europe in order to gain valuable experience performing in smaller houses. She had confided this to Schoen-René and acting on Simon's advice, Schoen-René told her the time for Europe was now and not the future. Risë looked on the suggestion with utter amazement. As much as she wanted to go, there were not enough funds for the passage let alone living expenses. Schoen-René countered every argument with- if Eric Simon felt that Risë must study with Gutheil-Schoder that was were she was going. Cutting off all discussion, she took Risë to Chemical Bank and drew a check for the sum wanting payable to her "as a loan". Risë protested that she might never be able to repay the amount but her teacher squelched the protests with an irrefutable statement. As a pupil of hers, Risë was bound to have a good career and payment could be made at some unspecified time in the future. In truth, she probably did not hope to see the money again since Risë was not the first student who was similarly helped. The difference was that unlike many others Risë, or more accurately her husband, Walter, made sure that every cent was repaid with interest. As a final gesture, before she left for Europe, Schoen-René rejected the offer by the Metropolitan Opera to audition Risë believing that the time was not right.

Risë's first European trip in the spring of 1935 was at a time of increasing global tensions. Declaring Europe unsafe for foreign travel was premature, nor was an ocean voyage considered hazardous. In spite of that, Risë was relieved that Schoen-René was to make the crossing with her. She insisted, however, that the money she saved be used for the price of a ticket in Tourist Class, and Schoen-René objections could not win Risë over to the idea of the First Class accommodations that she was willing to pay for. A dedicated believer in living life in as much comfort as possible, Schoen-René always traveled First Class on her annual summer sojourns to Europe. As part of her program to broaden Risë's awareness of life's niceties, she knew that the people she would socialize with in Tourist would not have the advantages of those in First. In this respect Schoen-René could be arrogant. She was brought up in comfortable surroundings while Risë knew what doing without meant.

As it turned out Risë loved everything about Tourist Class. Her fellow passengers were her age and, no doubt, from working class homes, students with little money, hopeful artists as she was, schoolteachers and others she could relate to. Her cabin mates were, in fact, three schoolteachers from the Midwest, young like herself and good company.

The Crichton book fictionalizes much of the trip and relates that Schoen-René insisted on Risë joining her for dinner in First Class every evening and that Risë acquiesced to this request. After the last mouthful, the author says, she would immediately head for the Tourist section and join in the festivities. Implying that she was almost a wreck from partying by the time the ship docked at *Le Havre*, Crichton omits the fact that she was seasick most of the time. It is certain Schoen-René noticed that Risë was ill and knew the hard work ahead of her would test all her reserves of strength since Gutheil-

Schoder was as demanding a perfectionist as she was. According to their arrangement, as soon as Risë disembarked, her living expenses were underwritten by Schoen-René. Careful account of each cent had to be maintained so that Risë would know how much of the stipend was left. When all their baggage was collected and Risë deemed well enough to travel, they set out together for Salzburg where Schoen-René would accompany Risë to the *Mozarteum* and introduce her to Gutheil-Schoder. There they would separate with Schoen-René off to her annual visit to the baths of Bad Gastein.

* * *

Founded in 1841, the *Dommusikverein und Mozarteum* was an artistic institution designed to serve all branches of music. Originally, the emphasis was on church music and the director, at the time Risë entered, Bernhard Paumgartner, paid homage to that tradition each year when he conducted Mozart's, *Mass in C,* in St. Peter's Church. Almost one hundred years later, secularism had won, and the *Mozarteum* took on the form of the traditional conservatory.

One of its foremost instructors, Marie Gutheil-Schoder, was born in Weimer on February 10, 1874, and had made her debut as the First Lady in Mozart's *Die Zauberflöte* in her native city in 1891. Gustav Mahler looked on her as a musical genius when she appeared under his aegis with the Vienna Opera, where she created the part of Octavian in the Vienna premiere of Strauss', *Der Rosenkavalier.* In spite of Mahler's benediction, she had detractors who claimed she had no voice but great interpretive abilities. Cherubino, Isolde, Carmen, Elektra and the Woman in the premiere of Arnold Schoenberg's, *Erwartung,* were among the diverse roles that highlighted a career that continued until the late 1920's. Upon retiring from the stage, she was appointed to the faculty of the *Mozarteum* in Salzburg where she taught interpretation rather than voice.

Schoen-René and Gutheil-Schoder were friends for many years and she knew that the doors of her prestigious studio in the *Mozarteum* would open to accept a student upon her recommendation. Risë soon learned that Gutheil-Schoder was a formidable presence. In Crichton's book, she is described as having "a heart condition and hid her paleness with excessive rougeing, but she was a tall, handsome, fascinating woman. She was thin and held herself stiff as a ramrod, but she had great elegance and charm." [3] Her photographs bear out the fact that she had the perfect build for male roles. She looked well in the fitted jacket and breeches of Octavian and the length of her face gave it a more masculine cast. The same could be said of Risë and it is certain that Gutheil-Schoder saw that immediately. Schoen-René had left instructions that Gutheil-Schoders's accompanist, Hans Pichler, was to go over the musical values of one score in particular for the entire summer. *Der Rosenkavalier* would be learned note by note, semi-quaver for semi-quaver, until the notes were firmly in place and wedded to the text. Risë already knew Acts 1 and 2 but not Act 3. Since she was not conversant in German at that time it was exceedingly difficult for her to absorb the text, especially the amount of Viennese dialect used by Hugo von Hopfmannsthal in the libretto. While she could not play the piano, she was a good sight-reader so the musical values came easier.

The vocal line for Octavian is written for the soprano voice but is quite often played by mezzos. Even though Schoen-René knew Risë was a true mezzo she also felt she could handle the musical line because of the solid training in "bel canto" singing she had imbued her with. "I was one of the first mezzo Octavians - Kirsten Thorborg and Maria Olszewska had done it before - and the first to really set the style. As you know, it was written as a soprano role. Octavian's music is actually higher than the Marschallin's, except for the high B flat." [4] Later in her career, at an informal gathering in Paris, Risë asked the French soprano,

Germaine Lubin, to sing passages from the opera with her. When she declined, Risë sang bits of both parts prompting Lubin to predict that someday she would be a fine Marschallin. Although flattered by Lubin's comment, Risë was never tempted to essay the role on stage. The Marschallin's line is difficult to sustain since it remains high with very little relief as there is with Octavian.

Another reason for her dismissing it for the future was that she was always in awe of Lotte Lehmann's interpretation and that alone would have placed a definite obstacle in not being merely an imitation of her. She had that problem when she started singing *Der Rosenkavalier* with Lehmann. A conscious effort was made to blend their voices seamlessly, with Lehmann finishing one phrase and Risë beginning another, coloring her voice to match Lehmann's. While it was quite effective when she and Lehmann sang together, it became noticeable in her vocal production that she was beginning to mimic Lehmann even when she was not singing with her. It took great effort to rid herself of these mannerisms, however, some of Lehmann's vocal coloring remained in Risë's voice throughout her career.

In addition to note for note correctness, Schoen-René wanted the words to be definite, clear in their enunciation and it was left to the accompanist to teach the role word for word with his pupil learning it painstakingly by rote. It was Gutheil-Schoder who would ignore the music as such and concentrate on the creation of the character, Octavian, in all his aspects. She worked from the standpoint of *mise en scène* never mentioning the voice for when the character is set, the voice follows.

Octavian Maria Ehrenreich Bonaventura Ferdinand Hyacinth, Count Rofrano is a young man of eighteen years, a Count by birth, with the Field Marshal's thirtyish wife as his mistress. It is not the first dalliance for either but, perhaps, the first "affair" of any duration and seriousness for the young man. It is implicit in the action that the Marschallin, Marie

Therese, has turned Octavian into a lap dog, a pet for her boudoir, an amusement to take the place of an unloved and quite often absent husband. She has already grown tired of him before the opera starts but she is not quite ready to turn him loose. Octavian has for her on the other hand an adolescent ardor which turns him into a lover so possessive of this Circe he will even change his sex temporarily to save her honor (and protect his own) by donning woman's clothes and impersonating a chamber maid. As such in Act 1, he will subject himself to being pawed by her oafish royal cousin, Baron Ochs, propositioned by him and all but sexually attacked in her presence, to protect her when he barges unannounced into her home (and affair) seeking advice on a fitting candidate for presenting the engagement rose to his intended fiancée, the nouveau riche, Sophie von Faninal. The male Octavian is chosen to present the rose to Sophie upon which a mutual love is born in Act 2 and the female Octavian in the guise of the chamber maid, Mariandl, goes off in Act 3 on a pre-arranged assignation to rid everyone of the decidedly unwelcome Baron. Sophie as an unknowing catalyst frees Octavian from his bondage and the Marschallin's final words, "Ja, Ja" (yes, yes) resign her to the thought of growing old gracefully or more likely giving up this particular youth.

The difficulty inherent in the role of Octavian is the fact that it is written for a woman who plays a man who for a while plays a woman. Masculinity must be encased in "satins and laces and smell of cologne" but must not be effeminate and the contours of the female figure can spell defeat that even expert costuming cannot hide. Arguably, it is this very femaleness that gives an added dimension of sensuality to the text since an Octavian who is clearly feminine making love to another woman gives true meaning to a role, *en travestie* (literally, cross-dressing). Perhaps, Octavians are meant to look like a woman in disguise to add piquancy to the story but what to do with Mariandl if Octavian is clearly female to begin with. Mariandl must be played in the gauche tradition of men playing women much in the same manner as a Harvard Hasty Pudding Show. The femininity must be exaggerated with the maleness emerging at various times, the legs too far apart when sitting, the stride, even the tilt of the chin, make Och's attraction to her laughable. It is the most difficult role in *Der Rosenkavalier* and one of the most difficult to bring off correctly in operatic literature. Risë has been known to offer a rare negative criticism of another singer when she recalls the Octavian of Maria Olszewska who did the role at the Metropolitan just prior to herself. She found her too matronly in appearance, too rigid in her acting, not sympathetic as a man.

Gutheil-Schoder from all accounts had mastered every nuance of the part and unlike Olszewska conjured up the character by skillful illusion. It was this knowledge that she was mandated to give to Risë not only by Schoen-René but also by the natural order of succession. The notes could be learned from any good *répétiteur* but not the gesture. In spite of her sixty-one years and failing heart, she demonstrated the visual side of every facet of the role. Hiking up her skirt to demonstrate what she was after, she would stride across the studio like a youth of noble lineage, she would walk the walk, strike the stance, hold her head, move her wrist, turn her hand, her body language speaking as loudly and clearly as the notes which once issued from her throat. Octavian is all about court behavior, a true son of the Rococo period and once this is mastered the role falls into place. She showed how her legs could be turned in such a way as to become a man's legs and how that would provide the amusing side to Mariandl. Risë would not only learn this but take it one step farther in transforming herself into a young man, she would wear an elastic band across her chest to erase all traces of breasts (a device she adopted for all her male roles). Her jackets were cut in such a way that the shoulders were wider than the skirt and the skirt, itself, devoid of pleating or flaring which would call attention to her hips. Edward Ziegler bestowed on her the nick-name, "Legs Stevens" not only because she played pants roles but because she had the legs which went well with them. Her powdered wigs at first sporting side curls as in the 1938 painting of her as Octavian by Nikol Schattenstein which hangs in the Metropolitan Opera's Founders Hall, were discarded for sleeker ones which again drew one's eye away from the feminine. The sword, too, was given careful attention for it was made to sit by her side by cutting a slit in the jacket so that it would lie flat.

* * * *

Risë's lodgings were in a family owned *pensione* where the daughter of the proprietor spoke English and was able to help her by translating the dialect that is sprinkled through the text of *Der Rosenkavalier*. Another plus was that William Schuman, who was enrolled in the *Mozarteum* as a conducting-composition major, was also staying at the *pensione*. The future President of Juilliard, Metropolitan Opera Board member, President of Lincoln Center and recipient of the first Pulitzer Prize in Music, had just completed his Bachelor of Science degree in Music Education from Columbia University's Teachers College. The two soon became fast friends and accompanied one another to the free *Domkonzertes* where they could hear Arturo Toscanini and Bruno Walter conduct. The Salzburg Festival that year was enjoying a resurgence that was unlike anything in the past with attendance at a new high. The presence of Toscanini, who was conducting opera in Salzburg for the first time and who had disappeared from the opera scene after renouncing Bayreuth and the Nazis in 1931, added to the air of expectancy. His performances of *Falstaff* and *Fidelio* were eagerly awaited and garnered notices that added to his legend, "He gives you nothing but the score and that perhaps is the marvel." [5] As a student of the *Mozarteum*, Risë was eligible for passes for the Gallery of the *Festspielhous* where she spent afternoons in the glorious company of Toscanini rehearsing *Fidelio* with Lotte Lehmann, Josef Krips conducting *Der Rosenkavalier* with Lehmann, Jarmila Novotna and Emmanuel List, Bruno Walter pacing *Don Giovanni* for the incomparable Ezio Pinza and *Die Entführung aus dem Serail* for Margherita Perras, who would be her Sophie in Vienna in 1938, and Charles Kullman with whom she would appear at the Metropolitan and other venues.

On evenings when Risë opted to attend a performance at the *Festspielhous*, especially if Lotte Lehnmann was singing, and Schuman went to a piano recital or symphony concert, they would arrange to meet afterward at the opera house and eat at the restaurant which was located on the top floor, accessible only by a creaky old elevator. There they would feast on a frankfurter and a beer, before boarding the trolley to the end of the line followed by a fifteen minute walk to the *pensione* arriving there well after midnight. At the *Mozarteum*, classes began at nine A.M. which meant getting up a good two hours before. On top of that, each day, she and Schuman would return to the *pensione* for their lunch since it was included in their board and hungrily consume a thin soup, cold cuts, bread and butter. This was not a regimen that allowed much in the way of sleep or nourishment. There was very little time left over for casual fun but Kurt, a young man who was a friend of the daughter of the *pensione*'s owner, was attracted to her. They would date casually, nothing serious, a swim, a walk, that was all. He called her "Reizl", he spoke little English and she as much German but he was her age and fun to be with. He was also being arrested periodically for certain transgressions. Risë presumed they were political given the nature of the times. A Nazi sympathizer, she suspected, as she feared were the owners of the *pensione*.

While Risë fell in love with Salzburg, she was not overly happy with her stay at the *Mozarteum*. It was a conservatory after all as was Juilliard, she did not speak the language and working with Gutheil-Schoder day after day added to her sense of exhaustion, which she never really shook off from the trip over. She was not entirely free from professional appearances either since on June 27th, she traveled to Berlin to sing at the American consulate. The summer came to an end none too soon and home and family looked very inviting. When it was time to leave, Kurt unexpectedly showed up at the railway station and begged her to take him with her to America. She told him that that it was entirely out of the question and after much back and forth of pleas and refusals he reluctantly left minutes before her train was to leave. Before Risë could board, two female security guards approached her and took her to the station office where she was searched and interrogated. They asked if she knew the young man, how he knew she was leaving, what he had said to her and on and on and when she answered all their questions to their satisfaction they told her she was free to go. Fortunately, the train was held until the procedure was over and she got on much to her relief amid a chorus of grumbling from the delayed passengers. When she returned to Salzburg the following summer, she learned Kurt was dead, shot and killed by whom or for what, no one would say. Out of curiosity, she went to his lodgings and the owner would not let her in. At her old *pensione*, they knew or said nothing. Risë's suspicions that he was involved with the Nazis seemed all too true.

The ocean voyage back was less of a strain than the one over and it gave her time to think about all that she had learned from Gutheil-Schoder. She had no need to worry about her ability to draw upon this knowledge since an unaccredited reference to a letter cited by Crichton written by Gutheil-Schoder to Schoen-Rene said, "...Risë is one of the most interesting pupils I have ever had. She already shows signs of being a great Octavian." [6]

* * * *

The Metropolitan Opera was experiencing transition

pains in 1935 what with the retirement of Giulio Gatti-Casazza as General Manager since 1908 and the unexpected death of his successor, former baritone, Herbert Witherspoon. Irving Kolodin describes the situation in detail: "What no one could anticipate when Herbert Witherspoon, of long and varied experience in opera, was nominated for the post by the heavily committed Juilliard Foundation, was that a successor would have to be found when he died a few weeks later. Almost automatically, the choice fell on Edward Johnson, who had been assigned to organize the following season's experimental spring season..." [7]

Edward Johnson, a Canadian, was a tenor of renown who besides pursuing a successful career on the Continent as Eduardo di Giovanni, built a solid reputation as a leading singer with the Metropolitan Opera from 1922 to 1935, where he created the tenor roles in Deems Tayor's, the *King's Henchman* and *Peter Ibbetson* as well as being the Metropolitan Opera's first Pelléas. Born in 1878, he was fifty-seven when he retired from opera and accepted appointment as the Met's General Manager, thereby becoming the "boss" of colleagues he had sung with. He was still active professionally when his appointment was announced and was in fact appearing in Detroit. His acceptance telegram thanked both the board of the Metropolitan and that of Juilliard for the confidence they had in him. Supporting Witherspoon's dedication to keeping the Company the way it was, he also embraced his and Erskin's concept of a spring season which would be given by a predominantly different group of singers than was heard in the main season, that it was to commence in May, 1936, and that it was to charge popular prices. It was also to change Risë's life.

In February of 1936, Risë appeared in three performances of Honegger's, *Le Roi David,* with the Philadelphia Orchestra under the direction of Fritz Reiner. The concerts received good notices with Reiner being commended for "a most sympathetic and artistic reading of the score" [and the vocal soloists] "in fine form, singing with good tone quality." [8] This marked the first encounter Risë had with Reiner but definitely not the last. Delighted to learn that she had gone to Europe to further her studies, he cautioned her against devoting too much time to Octavian since he felt she would have no place to perform it.

In March, along with several of her Juilliard colleagues, she entered the first rounds of The Metropolitan Opera Auditions of the Air which were held during December through March of 1935-1936. Quite possibly Schoen-René or Dean Hutcheson encouraged her to do so but it would have been better had she avoided it entirely. This was the first year for the program called The Metropolitan Opera Auditions of the Air sponsored by the Sherwin-Williams Company and broadcast over NBC in the United States and in Canada over the CBC network on Sunday afternoons. More than seven hundred singers competed but only forty-eight were heard on the air. It was a first for the Metropolitan Opera to have public auditions that could be transmitted to listeners at home. The auditions also offered the promise of a one-year contract commencing with the newly formed spring season to two of the contestants who made it to the finals. Wilfred Pelletier, the Metropolitan Opera conductor, was Director of the Auditions with John Erskine, Edward Ziegler, Earle Lewis (Assistant General Manager of the Metropolitan), Edward Johnson and himself as judges.

In the first of two auditions, Risë sang, "O mio Fernando", from La Favorita on December 29th. The second set of auditions were in March and the participants included Nicholas Massue, Lucielle Browning, Emily Hardy, and Dale Jones on the 15th. Arthur Carron, Annamary Dickey, Anna Kaskas, Lionel Daunais and Risë in perhaps the earliest rendition of the "Habañera" from Carmen were heard on March 22nd.

On March 29th it was announced that Arthur Carron and Anna Kaskas were the first place winners with the understanding that they would be given one year contracts with the

Metropolitan. Risë was passed over and while this no doubt upset her and raised doubts in her mind as to her abilities, it opened up prospects for her that a beginner's contract with the Metropolitan Opera could not have done. Since both Carron (who was recommended to the Metropolitan by soprano Florence Easton) and Kaskas, prior to their winning, failed private auditions for the Metropolitan in 1935, they improved considerably or other factors were involved when choosing the winners. In subsequent interviews, Risë maintained that there was nothing unfair about the results. She did not sing well and lost.

Mezzo-soprano, Rose Bampton, who was married to Pelletier, is quite frank in her appraisal of Risë's voice *vis-à-vis* Kaskas', "Risë had a far richer voice, more even in scale with a wonderful top." [9] Soprano, Natalie Bodanya, expressed a similar feeling, "Kaskas' and Risë's voices were not comparable, she was not in the same league as Risë." [10] The outcome of the Auditions remains a mystery further obscured by Pelletier's assertion that Risë was offered the choice of a cash stipend to study abroad or a contract with the Metropolitan – an offer Risë adamantly denies.

Schoen-René engineered her next move, however, by enlisting Dean Hutcheson's support in persuading Risë to seek out concert management so that her career would not be based on opera alone. She had no less a personage than Arthur Judson backing her in this request. Judson, a former music critic and one of the most powerful concert managers of the period, was chief operating officer of Columbia Concerts and quite interested in Risë. His management would place her alongside some of the world's leading artists, Lotte Lehmann, Lily Pons, Vladimir Horowitz, Serge Prokofiev, Jascha Heifetz, to name only a handful. A canny businessman, he also had under contract artists who were not in the upper echelon as yet. Josephine Antoine, Helen Marshall and Nelson Eddy, for example, were represented by him. Judson controlled the Community Concert Service that booked artists for recitals throughout the country. If a community could not afford one of his top line clients, he could offer another who did not command as high a fee. The Community Concert Service would play a significant part in Risë's extensive concertizing in the forties and fifties. On March 26th, Schoen-René again wrote to Hutcheson apprising him of the fact that she and Judson agreed on a three-year contract for Risë and that Hutcheson should review it and offer advice on its contents. The contract was signed but Schoen-René insisted that no concerts be arranged for Risë for at least a year. She wanted her to be sufficiently prepared for her debut as a concert artist.

A letter on file in the Archives of the Juilliard School of Music dated March 15, 1936, from Schoen-René to Dean Hutcheson may help explain the events leading up to Risë's loss of the auditions, her rejection of a Metropolitan Opera contract and her decision to return to Europe,

> ...when you referred to Risë in your criticism about her manerisms [sic] in acting and facial expression...I could have given you the reason for her extrem [sic] nervousness during the performances. That week Risë went through the most humiliating experience with the Metropolitan and it did crush the girl completely, she felt as if she could sing no more in the School or anywhere, she was under an awful nervous strain and still is suffering from it, and I, as her teacher was also very much offended, nevertheless I had to give her courage and confidence. I tell you this before the examination so that you may be lenient in your criticisme [sic] because she feels very nervous and depressed to go throu [sic], she will sail May 20th and is the only salvation now for her, as she is more than ever determinate [sic] to make a success ...in Europe. I told her that she has you as a friend on her side and that we still have perfect confidence in her ability to make a great career. Mr. Judson...does not want her to sing next year in America and even of-

fered financial assistance - that speaks for itself. [11]

Risë was scheduled to appear as Mistress Page in the final opera which Juilliard presented that season, Otto Nicolai's rarely performed *Die Lustigen Weiber von Windsor* in an English translation by critic, H. E. Krehbiel. Annamary Dickey was in Risë's cast, and Danton Walker of the *Daily News* commented, "It is taking little risk to predict bright professional futures for such competent singers (none of whom is a beginner) as Annamary Dicky...[and] Risë Stevens." [12]

On April 24th, Risë wrote the following letter to the Metropolitan Opera Board of Directors,

> I regret to say that this great opportunity You have offered me, unfortunately, I am unable to accept. Several months ago, in fact, directly after the Metropolitan Opera Auditions of the Air, I made plans to sail for Europe where I intend to study and sing, I had little idea that you would be considering me for "Orfeo". However, several days ago, Mr. Johnson spoke to me in regards to the same. I immediately tried my utmost to alter my plans, but everything was so definitely arranged, it was impossible. I have spoken with Mr. Johnson in regard to all this, but I felt it my duty to also explain the situation to you Gentlemen. I am indeed flattered to think you had even considered me for such a responsible role. Let me convey my sincere gratitude to you, and tell you how deeply sorry I am about this most unfortunate situation. [13]

It is a plausible assumption that Risë was told of the Metropolitan's wanting her for the Spring Season's *Orfeo* and she auditioned but quickly lost interest or was advised against doing it when the nature of the production was revealed. Although the letter was sent on April 24th, the *New York Times* on May 3rd had an article that claimed the Metropolitan had tentatively offered her the role. The article also said that George Balanchine's American Ballet would be a prominent component of the production. Balanchine had been engaged by the Metropolitan as Ballet Master that season and it was his idea to have the singers in *Orfeo* confined to the orchestra pit and their on stage personages represented by dancers. While hailing the idea behind the concept as praiseworthy, its actual realization was damned by most critics with Olin Downes at his most vitriolic when his review appeared on May 23rd, "it is regrettable to be obliged to say that it ranks as the most inept and unhappy spectacle this writer has ever seen...It is an absurd interpretation of the opera. It is ugly and futile, impudent and meddlesome...there is no genuine relation between the style of the pantomime and the style of the opera." [14] Danton Walker in the *Daily News* called it "Balanchine's greatest opportunity and his greatest defeat." [15]

Lincoln Kirsten claimed that Balanchine did not want a female voice as Orfeo but rather a tenor. The Metropolitan insisted it be female but allowed the dancer on stage to be male, the very masculine Lew Christianson. Anna Kaskas was offered the part when Risë withdrew and she received warm praise for her vocal interpretation. Her career at the Metropolitan lasted eleven seasons and secondary roles dominated her assignments. Risë knew that a debut in the orchestra pit was not the way she wanted to be introduced to the Metropolitan Opera, nor, as she explained later, "the Met isn't a training ground for young singers. They end up playing smaller roles and go nowhere." [16] The Spring Season lasted a mere two years giving way to the concentrated effort that was needed to plan the 1939 World's Fair activities. Balanchine was not invited back for the 1938-39 season since his choreography was not to the liking of influential patrons. His goodbye consisted, in part, of the following statement, "I try to adapt myself to the Metropolitan but no use. The tradition of ballet at the Metropolitan is bad ballet." [17]

On the 21st of May, Risë's status as a Juilliard student

came officially to an end. A letter from Dean Hutcheson stated that the Faculty agreed to her graduation and, in view of her excellent record, extended the privilege of doing post-graduate work with Schoen-René. The thought of spending another year at Juilliard ran counter to her plans of getting on with a performing career so the news of the Faculty's decision to free her from any obligation to stay a fourth year was particularly welcome. (Her diploma was not issued until June 3, 1942, however, and she had to apply for it formally). If Schoen-René was correct when she gave May 20th as the date of Risë's departure for Europe, the letter did not reach her in time nor did she have the pleasure of savoring the reviews of a fiasco she almost was a part of. During an interview on the January 1st 1939 segment of the "Auditions of the Air", Risë mentioned that a Hollywood contract was proffered around the time the offer to sing Orfeo was made. In a most cultivated speaking voice with a touch of the mid-Atlantic accent some singers affect, Risë gave an overview of her accomplishments to date to Edward Johnson, the host of the program, and to the listening audience. She had to make a choice of either entering the Metropolitan, tying her future to the West Coast or going abroad. She chose the latter and in so doing opened the way for the start of her professional career. Both the Metropolitan Opera and Hollywood would have to wait for a future meeting and when that occurred she would do that on her own terms.

Chapter 4

Risë had no intention of returning to America, at least not until she had proven to herself that she could be an opera singer of the first rank. She would enter the Metropolitan as a lead singer or not at all, but first she needed an *entrée* into a European opera company where she could gain the requisite experience. Had she auditioned immediately upon arrival, she no doubt would have found a place but she delayed because of a promise to Schoen-René that she would spend one more summer at the *Mozarteum*. Gutheil-Schoder was dead at age sixty-two, her weak heart finally giving out in October of the preceding year. Herbert Graf, stage director at the Metropolitan, would now be her mentor and coach her in the *mise en scène* for Amneris, among other roles. Risë reported dutifully to the conservatory but it did not take her long to realize that the thirty-three year old Graf was not for her. She could not relate to his theory that outworn traditions in opera must be eliminated in the same way she did to Gutheil-Schoder's fanaticism in preserving them. Coupled with that was the difference of learning a role from someone who actually performed it as opposed to someone who theorized about it. Never questioning Graf's abilities, she questioned his being right for her at this early stage of her development. After all, she had to learn the rules before she could bend them to her needs. Conservatory life was over when Juilliard gave her its blessing and freedom and the *Mozarteum* became oppressive. Leaving before the term was over, she returned to Paris hoping to find employment. Her stay in

Salzburg was not a total loss, however, since she did witness the now legendary revival of *Die Meistersinger* led by Toscanini with Lehmann as Eva. She attended the rehearsals where as Paul Stefan, correspondent to *Musical America* reported, "occasionally the Maestro has one of his famous fits of temper, but they are very rare and are confined to a fanatic emphasis on a knowledge which he regards as irrefutable and which has not yet dawned on others." [1] The opera was scheduled for no fewer than forty rehearsals and the result was termed "not only perfect in itself but it opens new paths for every further interpretation." [2] Toscanini also opened and closed the Festival with *Fidelio,* conducting a second act that left the audience limp and a Brahm's program featuring his *Requiem*. Bruno Walter offered *Orfeo ed Euridice, Don Giovanni* and *Tristan und Isolde*, Kirsten Thorborg was heard in Mahler's Third Symphony, Elisabeth Schumann (Susanna) and Jarmila Novotna (the Countess) appeared in a Felix Wingartner led *Le Nozze di Figaro* and Novotna sang Frasquita in Hugo Wolf's, *Die Corregidor,* a role which was to figure in Risë's future. The Festival was at its pre-war peak with more than two hundred thousand dollars in ticket sales.

When Risë arrived in Paris, Schoen-René was about to return to New York and resume teaching at Juilliard. She entrusted Risë to the care of Eric Simon who, knowing of her impatience to get started on her career and a need for money, tried to find her a place with the opera house in Zurich. Unfortunately, it was too late. All the vacancies were filled earlier in the summer and this proved to be true with other companies as well. However, he did succeed in getting her an audition with Artur Bodanzky, principal conductor of the German wing at the Metropolitan Opera. He heard her on June 16th in Vienna in selections from *Aida* and *Der Rosenkavalier*. His comment on her audition card reiterates an earlier impression of her outstanding talent recorded on April 14th by Simon (quite probably since Bodanzky was still in New York on April 6th) after hearing her in selections from *Orfeo*.

If it were not for the Simons' faith in her abilities and their kindness in treating her as one of the family, she would have admitted defeat and gone back to the States. Luck again played a part in determining the next phase of her life. A *deus ex machina* came in the form of George Szell, the quixotic but brilliant conductor who was music director for the *Neues Deutsches Theater* in Prague. Szell could be difficult and many years later when someone commented that he was his own worst enemy, the Metropolitan Opera's, Rudolf Bing retorted, "Not while I'm alive." Szell was an acquaintance of Simon and one of his business partner's, F. Horwitz. Mr. and Mrs. Horwitz, learning of Risë's inability to find a place to practice in her very cramped quarters, graciously opened their home to her. She was free to retreat to their music room where she could vocalize on a daily basis in order to keep in shape. Szell called on Mrs. Horwitz one day and through the closed door of the study heard Risë singing Frika's music from *Die Walküre*. Impressed with what he heard, he asked if he could be introduced. Showering compliments on her, he mentioned that Dr. Paul Eger, General Director for the *Neues Deutsches Theater*, needed a resident mezzo for leading roles. While the Theater engaged many internationally known artists as guests, it depended on local singers to perform on a regular basis. It sounded perfect but there were several very serious considerations on Risë's part. She did not speak German and certainly not Czech, moreover, her repertory was small and as an American she might be resented for taking the place of a native born singer. Szell who found a willing ally in Simon squelched these reservations and an audition was arranged for her with Dr. Eger.

* * * * * * * *

Germany obtained a stronghold in medieval Bohemia through marriage of their royal families and the desirability of Prague, a hub of commerce, with its foot in both east and west. A strong German element took hold and by the mid nineteenth century, German was the official language of the secondary schools. Resentment grew especially in Prague between the German interloper and the native Czech. However, the German love for drama and music were shared by the Czechs as well and in Prague alone the Germans had two theaters, The *Neues Deutsches Theater* and the *Ständetheater,* and the Czechs one, the National Theater. Both the German and National Theaters dated from the end of the eighteen-eighties but the *Ständetheater* traced its origins to the seventeenth century. When the Germans renounced their claims to it in 1920, bending to public pressure, they were given in compensation a subsidy for the *Neues Deutsches Theater* and financing for a new theater, the 400 seat *Die Kleine Bühne*, which would be run by the older organization and used exclusively for drama.

Carmen Mayer, a native of Prague, recalled, "Tickets were not expensive...the thirties were the time of the Depression and high unemployment. Money was tight. There was no competition between the National Theater and the German, at that time. The German definitely had better singers. [3] The Czechs ignored the German scene, mostly because of nationalism. Wagner was almost never performed in the Czech opera." [4]

Prague had some 900,000 inhabitants and was a Western-oriented city but nonetheless, as Risë feared, she was at a language disadvantage. She knew some German from Salzburg, but it was barely rudimentary. This was a serious handicap, she realized, but getting through the audition was a more pressing concern. Her anxiety was not made any less acute when she arrived at the opera house and found the stage door blocked by a gaggle of women. Not wanting to be late, she pushed her way through with the athletic skills she mastered in the Bronx. At the center of the commotion was the blond, matinee idol of the *Kleine Bühne Theater* and several films, who was known as much for his acting abilities as he was for his attraction to and for women. His name was Walter Géza Ladislau Szurovy, and with a combination of good looks, personality, charm and theatrical abilities, he had become the heartthrob of Prague's female sector. As Carmen is intrigued by Don José when he ignores her, so, too, was Walter taken with Risë when she jostled him along with the rest, not stopping for even a minute out of curiosity to find out who he was. Later, he would confess to a physical attraction from the first although she did not have the elegance that was a must in the women he courted. Following her into the theater, he sat next to Dr. Eger in the darkened auditorium. Not wasting any time, he suggested to Eger that the woman who was to audition would be a great addition to the *Kleine Bühne Theater*. Eger looked at him in disbelief and informed him that the lady spoke no German. Walter got up and left.

In later interviews, the initial meeting was changed somewhat with each retelling. In one, Walter is quoted as saying that, "Risë bumped him. He whistled wolfishly, followed her." [5]; in another, "He asked her in a bored way where the program was that she wanted him to sign...she stepped on his foot hard as he passed. Surovy followed her into the theater and sat in the auditorium while she auditioned." [6] Risë, on a Metropolitan Opera questionnaire, said she saw him first in a play, went back to compliment him and they went to dinner. That happened - but later.

The audition was recalled in a 1955 article in *Musical America*, "her first offering was 'O mio Fernando'...It went well enough...and now, did she know Fricka? She obliged with a few pages before the director stopped her. The same strange procedure followed with a half-dozen other roles-just a short sample, and she was shut off. The unseen voice from the first row kept saying 'thank you, thank you, that will do...'." [7]

The voice from the darkened theater was Dr. Eger and he

watched in amazement as Risë, hearing all of the curt "thank-you's" and then "*Genug, Danke*" (that's enough), convinced she had failed the audition, was packing up and heading for the door. "Kommen Sie zurück!," cried Dr. Eger sharply, and at her elbow was the little pianist, showing her by smiles and motions that she was to come back. From the halting translation of the pianist she found that Dr. Eger had thought she had done extremely well." [8] A contract was offered for one thousand two hundred *kronen*, the equivalent of twenty-five dollars a month and it was agreed that she would make her debut in December as Mignon. She hastily wired New York about her engagement to tell her parents and Schoen-René the good news. When her mother heard how little she would earn, she began sending a steady flow of care packages to make sure Risë was eating properly and dressing well.

Erich Simon did not waste time, either, in notifying Edward Ziegler about Risë's success in a letter dated September 25th. Ziegler, answered on October 2nd, that he noted the news of Risë's engagement and requested periodic reports on her activities. He was not to wait long, since another message came from Simon dated October 13th informing him that word had got out that Risë was to be a guest artist for a German season in Cairo that was to take place in January and February of the following year. This revelation refutes the notion that the Crichton biography advances that Eger packed her off to Cairo when, after her debut, she faltered badly as Amneris. It also underscores Eger's conviction that she would be a success and that singing for other companies as a guest did not violate her contractual arrangement with the German Theater.

With her debut more than two months away, Risë could enjoy the luxury of settling in before the fateful night when she would make her first professional appearance in opera. She had to find an apartment which would have been a daunting experience had she not been introduced to Harriet Henders (née Henderson), an American soprano from

Marengo, Iowa, who had first appeared with the *Neues Deutsches Theater* in 1935. They took to one another immediately since their backgrounds were quite similar.

Like Risë, Henders did radio shows in order to make enough money to go abroad to study and she, too, went to Salzburg for the expressed purpose of working with Gutheil-Schoder. After two years in her studio, she entered the Graz Opera as an apprentice but progressed very quickly to lead roles. Seven years later, Prague lured her away and she consolidated her reputation there as one of its most popular performers. Harriet's command of German, her knowledge of the ins and outs of bargaining in another language helped Risë immeasurably when it was most needed. She found her an apartment in a newly constructed building at *Fochova* 182, about three blocks from her own that was located at *Fochova* 156.

The next project for Harriet as far as Risë's settling in was concerned was to get her to learn German. She took her to the gathering place of all the artists of the *Neues Deutsches Theater*, the Cafe Bazaar, and introduced her to the regulars who would occupy the same table every day. There, the conversation was only in German and if Risë wanted to communicate, she was obliged to speak it. She learned slowly with the help of her colleagues and soon could converse with them. *Mignon* had to be sung in a German translation of the original French and she needed to know the language to give proper emphasis to the words. This was always an important aspect of her approach to a role. Primarily a vocal colorist, she painted a picture of the music she was singing through the words. Whether it was an aria or a popular song, the text had to illuminate the music. In the studio of Schoen-René, she learned to be a singer but with Gutheil-Schoder she learned to be an actress. The perfect wedding of the two became natural to her and made possible the singular interpretations of Octavian, Carmen and Orfeo that were to follow. Later she was to reminisce about her first experience with the German language *Mignon*, "I was very young and rushed into the part impulsively. I knew the role perfectly, but often I didn't understand the meaning of the words I was singing." [9]

"You were so beautiful and dignified," Carmen Mayer recalled in a letter written to Risë long after, "always going and coming to the theater alone, with a bunch of music under your arm. It was on the Wenzelsplatz where I saw you most frequently, usually dressed in a two piece 'kostüm' [suit] and a hat." [10]

Risë was obliged to rehearse even on the days she sang and she sang three or four times a week. The trying out, eliminating, experimenting, putting together the pieces of the work were for her always the most enjoyable part of performing. She loved to rehearse. Word quickly got around that she loved to direct also. Instinctively, she would stage a movement differently, much to the director's surprise and some colleagues' resentment. Walter heard stories that she was taking over. This trait remained with her long after Prague. Once at the Metropolitan, when rehearsing some stage business in Act 2 of *Der Rosenkavalier* with soprano, Hilde Güden, Risë showed a flash of temper in reaction to Güden's insistence that the scene should be staged as it was in Vienna. Reminding Güden, in no uncertain terms, that this was America, Risë was determined to have the scene the way she felt it should be done. She won.

Plays were tried out in the *Kleine Bühne Theater* but if proven successful, transferred to the larger theater. Opera, therefore, was alternated with drama and neither performed every night. Each component had its own roster of players but in true repertory fashion, actors from the *Kleine Bühne* were asked to appear in operettas in mainly speaking parts.

When rehearsals for *Mignon* began, Risë learned much to her embarrassment that the cause of all the commotion at the stage door was not only one of the most popular actors of the company, but was performing the part of Frédéric in - *Mignon*. Assigning the role to an actor meant that the original version of the opera was used and a strong presence was needed to add dimension to this character without an aria.

Thomas wrote the part of Mignon for a mezzo and the role of Frédéric for a tenor/actor. The "Gavotte" lovesick Frédéric sings in his adored Philine's boudoir was added later when Zélia Trebelli, a mezzo, took over the role and Mignon was assigned to a soprano. Walter was one of the most admired young stage and film actors in Prague and no matter what the vehicle, his name on a program assured a full house. How could Risë, a complete unknown, apologize to him for her rudeness? She didn't have to since Walter was too taken with her to bear a grudge. His interest in Risë, at first, was purely physical even though, as a colleague, he wanted her to be a success. She was attractive and that would be reason enough to try to ingratiate himself with her. Soon he began joining the clique at the Cafe Bazaar where it became obvious that the American was the object of his attentions. The rest laughed, Walter's affairs did not last long but why should Risë miss out on some fun. Not quite all of the rest, however. Harriet was incensed over the obviousness of Walter's intent. He even went so far as to send box seat tickets to both Harriet and Risë for *Jean,* a play he was starring in. Before the curtain rose, a note from Walter was delivered to the box inviting Risë to a post performance supper. The invitation did not include Harriet who made a point of acquainting Risë with his reputation and told her in so many words to avoid him. Walter, nonetheless intrigued her and no matter how much the wiser Risë was about him, she still found him attractive. As far as she was concerned, his company relieved the tension that was beginning to build as the 13th approached. Having her photograph appear in the *Prager Tagblatt* on November 25th was flattering but only added anxiety to make good the hopes pinned on her. At the appointed hour, Risë was waiting at the stage door as was another woman who happened to be the female lead in *Jean.* It seems, she too, had a date with Walter for a post performance supper. When he finally appeared, Walter walked past his colleague took Risë by the arm and hastily entered a waiting taxi. After that he began to focus his attention solely on her, encouraging her to attend rehearsals in the *Kleine Bühne* to learn German better, and, of course, to watch him perform.

The much anticipated hour of seven-thirty on the evening of December 13th arrived. While Risë was waiting to go on, taking a seat in the donkey cart in which she made her first appearance, she felt something hard. Her initial surprise was not allayed when she discovered she had brushed against a toy rabbit, a type made by Czech peasants. Walter, who two hours earlier completed a matinee of Johannes Reich's, *Das Herz*, at the *Kleine Bühne*, had placed it there while the scene for the evening's opera was being set. The music for her entrance sounded so she tucked the toy away in the cart not knowing what to make of it. The mystery was cleared up later when Walter explained that he could not find a rabbit's foot for good luck so he gave her the next best thing, the entire rabbit.

The next day's review in the *Prager Tagblatt* could not have been better,

> An otherwise satisfactory evening was made special by a new singer, a genuine discovery. Risë Stevens, twenty-three years old and from America...was appearing on the operatic stage for the first time and was singing for the first time in German. She conquered all hearts with the full, dark tones of her warm mezzo-soprano voice as well as the ease of her high notes. Along with the outstanding voice there was natural acting and a feel for the stage. What's more, there was true humanity in her performance, nothing mechanical in her playing, only youthful spirit that shaded almost imperceptibly from innocent good cheer into the tragic...The singer's month-long preparation of the role in Prague was obviously highly productive...Thunderous applause...It was one of those rare performances that gives pure pleasure to eyes

and ears...An opera that one might have greeted with a certain irony became, because of the artist in the title role, a major event. [11]

The career was launched and she could not have received a warmer welcome to it than the one that was given to her that evening in Prague. In addition, the reviewer's mention of Risë leaving for Egypt further confirms the fact that she was contracted to the tour before her debut. Her reputation, as a result of this one performance, was made and her name started making the rounds in music circles on both continents.

In the March 6, 1937 issue of *Musical America*, Gerth-Wolfgang Baruch wrote, "Risë Stevens...made a brilliant debut...here. Hitherto unknown to us, the twenty-three year old singer pleased uncommonly with her singing and acting in Mignon and Rosenkavalier." [12]

On January 10[th,] with a highly successful debut behind her, Risë had her first opportunity to interpret the role she had studied in minute detail and one which is considered by far her greatest achievement, Octavian, in *Der Rosenkavalier.*

> She was literally 'the young man from the great house', altogether persuasive in her easy elegance and remarkable beauty...in the second act, one could only admire the subtlety of her movement and the way her changing feelings were reflected in her face. There is much more than musicality and a natural vocal gift, impressive as they are. The closing duet with Sophie was magical; it had the beautiful simplicity of a folk song. [13]

Her long hours with Gutheil-Schoder paid off with critical notices that were, if anything, better than the one's for Mignon. Her immediate predecessor in the role was Harriet who relinquished it during Risë's tenure.

New Year's eve found both artists participating in a review entitled, *Die Vertauschte Oper*, which was presented at the *Klein Bühne Theater*, while the Neues Theater featured the operetta by Jara Benes, *Auf der grünen Wiese*. Risë and Harriet harmonized spirituals in a number billed as, "The Two American Girls" and were scheduled along with practically everyone else, including Walter, for the finale. Unfortunately, the *Prager Tagblatt* did not see fit to record just what spirituals the two American girls sang but an eyewitness to the evening's program told of an unscheduled event. While Risë and Harriet were taking their bows, Walter and another Walter, Walter Taub, walked out on stage. Walter Szurovy asked Risë if she liked "*vögeln*" (crude term for having sex). Risë's German was still sketchy and she thought he said "*vogel*" (birds) and answered that she loved "*vögeln*". The audience howled and she couldn't understand why. Harriet hastily left the stage but Risë couldn't think of a way to get off so she stood there. She was wearing a black form-fitting gown, quite low in back and Walter started on her figure. Harriet from the wings kept telling her in a very loud stage whisper to get off the stage. Finally, Walter's comments were too embarrassing so she turned to the audience and said, "Gooood-bye", waved and made a hasty exit. The two Walters were still making comments about her after she left.

It may have been a crude beginning but it was a catalyst of sorts. Harmless flirtation began to turn serious and marked the start of what would become a life together.

The New Year brought with it Risë's first professional appearance as Orfeo on January 16th. Having learned the role originally in English for Juilliard, she had to relearn it in German. Her efforts were rewarded with another success. *Musical America* reported, "Risë Stevens gained new laurels in the title role, Harriet Henders (Euridice) and Herta Rayan (Eros) also gave outstanding contributions." [14] In the pit was Hans Georg Schick (the "Hans" was dropped eventually) who was to be brought to America by Risë and Walter where he became a conductor at the Metropolitan Opera in 1959, serving as her accompanist for two years and in 1941 coaching her for *The Chocolate Soldier.*

Dr. Eger's faith in Risë's abilities had been justified to the extent that he assigned Mignon, Octavian, Orfeo, Cherubino, Frasquita in *Der Corregidor*, La Gazette in Jacques Ibert's, *opéra comique*, *Le Roi d'Yvetot* and the Countess von Eberbach in Albert Lortzing's, *Der Wildschütz* exclusively to her. Her remaining operas were shared with other Mezzos but she had a nucleus of roles that showed her to the best advantage. The pre-debut commitment to appear in Cairo was to begin in a matter of weeks and while the fee was not good it would expose her to a different audience.

The tour was to take place between January 29th and February 26th, but since her signing of the contract she had made another commitment as well. What would Walter do in her absence? She knew what she was up against on that score. The competition for his attention was rough and she was not popular, to say the least, with the women he neglected since she arrived. If she went away, they would all come running and she was not secure enough in her abilities to hold him without physically being there. An incident that occurred at a party at the home of the wife of the producer of his last film, attested to the effect she had on him. The hostess did everything to make Risë feel uncomfortable, implying a tryst with Walter later that evening. Risë, who still had a faulty command of German, was told by Walter to be sure to thank her for inviting them when they left. Risë protested that her German did not extend that far but Walter insisted that she repeat exactly what he told her to say. She did. It was only when they were well on their way home that Walter translated the sentiment, "Thank you, I had a ghastly time."

Risë was scheduled to leave for Cairo from Genoa on the 24th and when Walter accompanied her to the train station, she was full of misgivings. Walter had doubts also, after all Risë was very attractive and she was free to look elsewhere. However, she had a contract to fulfill and he was more concerned about her refusing to leave at the last minute than any personal considerations. Ever resourceful and mindful of her reactions even in that early stage of their life together, he decided to send her off with a bit of a shove. Expecting a sentimental farewell, she was instead taken aback when he asked her to write so that he could have the stamps. It had the desired effect. Risë boarded the train with few misgivings.

Chapter 5

Joining the troupe aboard the S. S. Esperia, bound for Cairo, Risë's feelings over Walter's remark changed from anger to resignation. Some of her colleagues from the German Theater were also going on the tour, Zdenka Zika, her first Marschallin, Deszo Ernster and Pavel Ludikar, were like old friends now. The majority, however, were from Vienna where the tour was arranged by the impresario, Hugo Gruder-Gunstram, who snared Richard Tauber as star of the enterprise.

Fully staged performances were to take place in Cairo's Royal Opera House and after a three week stay, the troupe would move to Alexandria for five days. Tauber was scheduled to open the tour in both cities as Tamino in *Die Zauberflöte*. A young musician on this tour, Walter Taussig, recalled in an interview his initial horror at the thought of an American being assigned one of the most Viennese of all opera roles, Octavian, that is, until he witnessed Risë's performance. Taussig was to work with Risë for many years at the Metropolitan after his arrival in 1949. He remembered how perfect she was for every aspect of the young nobleman and, also, how well she interpreted her other assignment, Orfeo, on that long-ago tour.

An editorial appeared in the *Egyptian Gazette* on February 18, 1937 headed, "Dirty Cairo". Its theme was a condemnation of the noise and filth which pervaded this proud and ancient city. It was a place of contrasts, that is, a disregard for public amenities brought out in sharp relief against a background of art and culture.

The flamboyant King Farouk, was a ruler who rivaled the Pharaohs. On the last leg of a month long tour of upper Egypt, he and his royal entourage were to return to Cairo on February 2nd triumphant after a string of personal appearances. The poverty, hunger, dirt and disease rampant both in the cities and outlying areas seemed to disappear from the minds of the masses when faced with such pomp and ceremony. For those who could afford the pleasures of entertainment, they could indulge themselves ten fold in a city which offered it in abundance. To the visiting Viennese troupe the sights, sounds, smells of the city hit them with equal force as did the dull, cold, squally and showery weather.

The bill of fare was a mixture of some opera interlaced with operetta: *Die Zauberflöte, Der Rosenkavalier, Giuditta, Oberon, Tiefland, Das Land des Lächelns, Aida, Die Fledermaus, Orfeo ed Euridice* and *Eine Nacht in Venedig*. The pride of place was Tauber's, as if by divine right and ticket sales. Everyone had heard of Tauber but only the dedicated could recognize the names of the others. The review of *Die Zauberflöte* confirmed what everyone knew, "Richard Tauber, as Tamino, fully lived up to his world reputation as a great singer." [1] A glimpse into the nature of the enterprise concludes the review, "When one adds beautiful costumes and scenery, and an orchestra which played well...the company can certainly be congratulated on an excellent performance". [2] According to the *Egyptian Gazette*, it was a brilliant opening, the first in many years. The Royal Opera House was sold out weeks in advance for opening night and there was no dearth of royalty, politicians and money in the audience.

Der Rosenkavalier followed on the next evening, January 31, and Risë had as her Marschallin, Zdenka Zika and Sophie, Pia Boila. The critic found the performance somewhat lifeless but as for Risë, "[she] took the part of the Chevalier Octavian very well indeed and sang charmingly. Her duet with Sophie...in the second act was one of the bright spots of the evening...these two beautiful voices were so beautifully blended with the orchestra that one shut one's eyes, sat back and listened with pure enjoyment." [3]

Giuditta with Tauber on the 31st and 1st was termed a great success with "[his] haunting love songs sung with extraordinary pathos and charm." [4] He scored again in *Die Fledermaus* as a guest at Prince Orlofsky's ball in Act 2. Coupling three Schubert *lied* with his show stopping aria from *Giuditta* and conducting the orchestra in his own composition, "Le rêve chantant", he stole the performance from the rest. *Oberon* fared well with the visual elements of the shipwreck and Zdenka Zika's singing in the second act taking the honors. February 9th brought with it *Orfeo ed Euridice*. "The whole performance was magnificent: it was perhaps the best the...Company has given and the unstinting applause from the rather scanty audience was sufficient evidence of this." [5] The version that was heard was written by Hector Berlioz in 1859 for a female Orfeo and, of course, performed in a German translation by the Viennese company. "[Risë] Stevens was superb...by a gesture she was able to convey the depth of Orpheus' grief...she sang well too and her beautiful song over Eurydice's dead body was roundly applauded." [6] She impressed the reviewer with her non-acknowledgment of applause at this point in order to preserve the mood. Bachryle Nuri-Hadzic, the Euridice, it was noted "rose nobly to Frln. Stevens' Orpheus." [7] Furthermore their two voices "blended exquisitely." [8] Risë was again in *Der Rosenkavalier* on the Friday 12th evening performance, the five o'clock matinee at reduced prices was given over to *Das Land des Lächelns* with Tauber. *Tiefland* was pronounced a good presentation of a dull work and *Eine Nacht in Venedig* was praised for the dancing. The stay in Cairo drew to a close on the 18th with a farewell performance of *Das Land des Lächelns* with, of course, Richard Tauber.

* * * *

Risë returned to a troubled Prague secure in the knowledge she had made a good showing on the Cairo tour and that Dr. Eger had made note of her success. If there was any jealousy in the company because of his and Mrs. Eger's interest in her, it was not in the open. That she was resented as an American at a time when nationalism ran high was also not obvious - to her at any rate. What was scorned by some was the policy of importing guest singers, notably, Zinka Milanov, Jussi Björling and Kirsten Flagstad, to star in operas that they felt they could sing as well.

In spite of Risë's success on the tour as Octavian and Orfeo, in keeping with the repertory policy of the German theater, March found her again cast as a Flower Maiden in a George Szell led *Parsifal*. Although American, she had become very popular with operagoers who were taken by her fresh young look and voice. April saw Risë back in a starring role, Octavian, this time with Hilde Konetzni as Marschallin and Harriet as Sophie. Kurt Baum, who would be Risë's not overly welcome co-star at the Metropolitan in the years to come, was the Italian Singer and Erich Kleiber, who in 1938 would engage her for the *Teatro Colón's* German repertory, conducted.

Rehearsals for a new production of Hugo Wolf's, *Der Corregidor* began at the end of April in preparation for the premiere on May 6th. It was scheduled to receive only three performances and the *Prager Tagblatt* recalled,

> Bruno Walter, who was a strong advocate of the opera, conducted outstanding performances at the Salzburg Festival and in Vienna. In Prague, unlike Vienna, the opera is cast according to the wishes of the composer, that is, Frasquita will be sung by a mezzo (Stevens) and Mercedes by a soprano (Henders), while in Vienna, Fraquita was sung by Novatna and Mercedes by Thorborg. [9]

The Prague recreation of the opera was enthusiastically embraced by the critic from the *Prager Tagblatt* who wrote, "That Hans Georg Shick, the young conductor, succeeded so well speaks volumes for his talents...Frasquita was charmingly sung by Risë Stevens...The other singers must be content with a general recommendation." [10]

A rare staging of the Wolf opera attracted international interest and a report on the production appeared in the *New York Times* as well, "Risë Stevens...sang with pronounced acclaim as Frasquita...Harriet Henders [gave] a carefully conceived and highly finished performance." [11]

Rudolf Bing, the future General Manager of the Metropolitan Opera, who was in Prague as a representative of the Glyndebourne Festival, observed Risë at a rehearsal. He made no effort to meet her but must have been impressed with what he heard and saw in view of later developments. His presence at the rear of the Orchestra, raincoat and bowler in hand, neatly furled umbrella over his arm, provided Risë with the first glimpse of the Austrian self-styled Englishman. She did not know who he was then but this earlier sighting was brought back to her when she was offered a contract to sing at Glyndebourne in 1939.

On May 18, 1937, Eric Simon informed Ziegler, "I just got a line from Risë Stevens who had lunch with Mr. and Mrs. Bodanzky in Prague, saying that the "Rosenkavalier" performance will take place on June 5th. Will you please keep this in mind for your traveling purposes." [12] Edward Johnson, who was already in Italy, was anxious to re-evaluate Risë and observe first hand the progress she had made as a prelude to offering her a contract. Originally, he planned to be in Prague two weeks later but other commitments intervened causing him to miss Risë's final Octavian, the role that most interested him. However, in company with Bodanzky and, Hungarian baritone, Friedrich Schorr, he went to the *Neues Deutsches Theater* on May 19th in order to see the only performance Risë would give that he could attend. Frasquita in *Der Corregidor* was not the ideal vehicle for Johnson to evaluate her and, his opinion was not divulged. He departed without giving Risë the courtesy of knowing if he was interested in her or not. Subsequently Simon wrote to Ziegler that Johnson had auditioned several artists but Risë was not mentioned.

Upon his return from Europe Johnson revealed that three Americans would make their debuts in the coming season. While, he did not reveal their names, it was later learned that they were John Carter, Leonard Warren and Risë. Bodanzky was quite taken with her in Prague and at his urging, Johnson was persuaded to offer her a contract. It took two months and much negotiating back and forth for him to actually do so.

A quick trip back to the States when she concluded her season in the summer of 1937, reunited Risë with her family. Though low on funds, it was a joyous reunion at 114th Street and, of course, Schoen-René, who would never see her perform in Prague, listened to every detail Risë told her about her experiences in the German Theater. According to Crichton, although Risë was broke when she arrived in New York, she would not accept any more loans from Schoen-René. Her contract was signed for another Prague season commencing in the fall but she did not know how she could afford to return if her living expenses were not subsidized from a private reserve. A meeting was arranged for Risë by Schoen-René with John Erskine and Ernest Hutcheson at Juilliard. Through their intercession, she was awarded a five hundred-dollar loan for her re-establishment in Prague. She was also given the impression that her progress there had not gone unnoticed by the administration of the Metropolitan. Since both gentlemen were on the board of the opera, Risë's disappointment over Johnson's not making an immediate offer was somewhat relieved. Upon her return to Prague, Walter, who had just completed a highly successful engagement in Carlsberg in the

Czech play, *Perepherie*, moved in with her.

The 1937-1938 season of the *Neues Deutsches The-ater* marked the fiftieth anniversary of its founding in 1888 and Risë was given the honor of opening night.

***

Carmen Mayer: "Her Carmen was very elegant, not gypsy like, yet very attractive." [13]

Paul Eger was married to a singer and it was she who convinced him that Risë would be a perfect choice for the lead in *Carmen* that was to inaugurate the season on September 7th. In spite of being apprehensive, Risë agreed to do it out of a sense of loyalty. In truth, she was still too inexperienced to come to grips with a part that had a myriad of details and vocal demands that called for a more mature singer. In a 1948 interview for *Opera News*, Risë described Carmen as, "a blinding light which attracts the world around her." [14] A dozen years earlier, she was too much the neophyte to have begun to plumb the depths of so complex a role. Her success as Octavian and Orfeo, to name two seemingly born full-grown, were due to characters who must behave a certain way, at least in traditional stagings.

Carmen is the exact opposite, she must be unpredictable and the interpreter must find the key to this unpredictability. Carmen does not grow or change as a person during the course of the opera; she is the same free spirit when she dies in Act 4 as when she entered in Act 1. In actuality, she dies because she cannot change, "libre elle est née et libre elle mourra!" (She was born free and she will die free), she says in the face of Don José's irrational pleas. The various moods, the hardness, the playfulness, the amorality all expressed in vocal colors which reflect them, are the emotions which are in constant flux and which Risë felt she could not then command. After the opening the public disagreed, the critics concurred,

The greatest surprise of yesterday's performance, however, was the Carmen of Risë Stevens, whose singing
and acting were thrilling, who seized the attention of
the full house from her first entrance and whose generous, easily produced sound evoked storms of applause
of an intensity rarely heard. How rich in colors is this
instrument, how full and blooming at top and bottom,
how delicate in its transitions! Her conception of the
role was realized through suggestion and nuance, eschewing all exaggeration. The young American is astonishing in her temperament and theatrical flair. [15]

After the unexpected success she had with Carmen, another equally unexpected, followed. Although she was not
the possessor of the powerful organ-like tones necessary to
penetrate the thickness of Wagnerian orchestration, her first
attempt at Fricka in *Die Walküre* on September 12th was
highly praised,

First and most interesting was the Fricka of Rose [sic]
Stevens who with her fresh sound and admirable musicality convincingly embodied this most exacting of roles
for mezzo-soprano...her dignified bearing was a pleasing change from the exaggerations employed by some
of her colleagues in this role. [16]

Over sixty years later, Gebhardt records released a 1940
live performance of *Die Walküre* from Buenos Aires with Risë
as Fricka. Even through significant sonic interference, it is an
invaluable document of her portrayal. When she enters, the
dark coloring in the voice casts doubt on whether it is actually she singing. As the scene with Wotan unfolds, however,
a more recognizable quality in her voice emerges. Her mastery of vocal nuance is in full display as is the authority in
creating a characterization that was evident earlier in Prague.
When she arrived at the Metropolitan, Edward Johnson encouraged her not only to keep Fricka in her repertory but to
add Erda in *Siegfried* as well. She followed his advice but

evaded his suggestion that Venus in *Tannhäuser* join them since she knew Wagner was not for her. The New York critics agreed.

On September 14th, Prague was plunged into mourning with the death of the eighty-seven year old Tomás Masaryk. Having helped found the Czech Republic in 1918, he was the first President until 1935 when he resigned to make way for the younger Edouard Benés. Risë was so absorbed in her work in the Theater that she wasn't aware of the political upheaval taking place around her. She was aware of occasional disturbances but it was only later, after her engagement in Vienna, that she sensed danger.

Further distracting her from these events, was another new assignment for Risë, Fatima, the Arabian maid to the heroine, Rezia, in the September 19th revival of Carl Maria von Weber's, *Oberon,* in the Gustav Mahler adaptation. Fatima was well suited to her but she never had the opportunity to sing it again, "superb in the warmth of her voice and her natural acting. She transformed a supporting part into the starring role. She is a special artist: even her brief dance in the insubstantial ballet shone with the character's happiness." [17]

On October 7th, Ziegler wrote to Simon *vis-a-vis* the ongoing dance the Metropolitan and he were doing about hiring her. Johnson had taken an option on her services based on what he saw and heard on his trip to Prague but was vague as to whether it would lead to a contract, "[she] has written to Mr. Johnson and has sent him the option letter, which I am returning to you. I think her attitude is quite just that she does not wish to wait until June to know whether she is to be engaged the same winter. I would suggest that you begin negotiations with her and make a definite contract...for the season 1938-1939 with the option for the season 1939-40 and 1940-41..." [18]

On October 11th, Simon responded by sending Ziegler a copy of a letter Risë wrote to him explaining her position, "it is quite impossible for me to wait later than the end of Febru-

ary to know just what I am to do for the following year. As
you know, all European contracts are signed in every opera
house throughout Europe in January and February and I do
not want to be without an engagement of some kind...it seems
rather unnecessary to have to sign an option...if the Metropolitan has in mind of engaging me for 38/39..." [19] Simon
supported her argument by mentioning that Zurich and Basel
would engage her and that Dr. Eger had no intention of losing her to either. At the conclusion of her letter to Simon,
Risë reiterated her commitment to retaining him alone as her
Metropolitan representative.

At long last, on November 15, 1937, Risë signed her first
contract with the Metropolitan Opera. Commencing with
the 1938-39 season, she was to be engaged "for a minimum
period of eight weeks, up to a maximum period of up to sixteen weeks between about the beginning of November, 1938,
and about the end of April 1939." [20] Her fee would be two-
hundred dollars per week with ten-dollars as hotel expenses
per day in addition should she be required to travel. The roles
she might be asked to sing were spelled out by name and
included some which fell within her vocal category but which
she would never do: In German: Ortrud, Blumenmädchen,
Octavian, Venus, Brangäne, Fricka and Schwertleite (*Die
Walküre*) and Third Lady (*Die Zauberflöte*); In English:
Fatima; In Italian: Amneris, Adalgisa (*Norma*), Orfeo and
Azucena (*Il Trovatore*); In French: Carmen, Mignon and
Dalila (*Samson et Dalila*). Options for the 1939-40 and 1940-
41 seasons were included with an escalating fee schedule of
$250 and $300 for each and that she would be notified by
no later than May 31st of the year if her option was picked
up.

On March 17, 1938, Risë received the notice *via* Simon
that she was to report to the Metropolitan for preliminary
rehearsals on November 7th and that her engagement was for
eight weeks from November 21, 1938 to January 15, 1939.
Although her future plans were firmed up at the Metropoli-

tan for the first half of the 1938-39 season, she could still return to Prague in February of 1939. The contract was constructed with that in mind and with the possibility that she might be asked to return to Vienna. In a telegram, dated February 9, 1938, to Risë from Simon, who was in New York, he informed her that both Johnson and Schoen-René approved of her accepting an engagement in Buenos Aires until October 25th. Her plans for the immediate future were falling into place, however, the Prague season was by no means over, especially with the Jubilee year commencing in January.

On December 31, 1937, the *Prager Tagblatt* announced that "following the jubilee performance of 'Die Meistersinger' to celebrate the 50th anniversary of the German Theater, the second in the series of special performance will be 'Carmen' [on January 8th] under the direction of General Music Director Leo Blech. The title role will be sung by Risë Stevens, Kurt Eric Praeger will sing Don José, the Escamillo, Nicola Tvejc, is a guest from the Brno Landestheater." [21]

The production might not have come off at all since without warning, the originally scheduled conductor, Leo Blech, who was particularly famous for his Carmen, was barred by the Nazi Government from going to Prague. Relieved of his duties as conductor of the Berlin State Opera and put on pension ostensibly because of age but actually because he was Jewish and embarrassingly popular with the Berlin public, the government effectively "retired" him. The conductor, composer, Alexander von Zemlinsky, was hastily engaged as Blech's replacement and enjoyed a personal success with these performances.

H. H. Stuckenschmidt reporting on the production in *Musical America* had nothing but praise for all concerned, ...Zemlinsky, frenetically acclaimed, presided

at the desk. The evening proved one of the most impressive achievements of the Prague Oper. Not alone because Zemlinsky conducted with exemplary distinctiveness and [Friedrich] Schramm directed in a lively manner without false romanticism; but mainly because everything was concentrated on the young singer who sang, acted, lived the title part...Miss Stevens' voice is a far-carrying, not dark, mezzo-soprano with amazing facility of tone and unique brilliance of color. She handles it with sovereign technique and natural musicality. Since she does not confine herself to contralto parts, the middle register and discant are particularly well cultivated. The so-called Italian chest register is comparatively neglected (a fact which was felt as a very slight lack in the second act and in the card scene). An almost demonic temperament and a magnificent instinct for gesture and miming animate her beautiful face and tall, slender body. From the point of view of acting, neither on the Italian or the German stage have ever I seen a Carmen of more convincing impressiveness. It was a triumph of drama...stormily applauded by a brilliant audience. [22]

Robert Lawrence reporting to *Opera News* on the first repeat performance of *Carmen* in January was not favorably impressed with the production, "the German theatre presented a heavily Teutonic *Carmen*... Slow moving tempi predominated, and the stage direction was conscientious to the point of fussiness. In spite of these shortcomings, much good singing was accomplished and the playing of the orchestra was at all times creditable." [23]

In spite of the *Prager Tagblatt* calling her "a vocal and dramatic phenomenon" [adding] "with this role she has become a star," [24] Risë felt that her original trepidations about undertaking Carmen were correct. Apparently hers was a strong interpretation even then but it would be a half dozen years before she attempted the role again.

Risë's next assignment introduced her portrayal of La Gazette in Jacques Ibert's *Le Roi d'Yvetot*, conducted by Karl Rankl, on December 5th, "In the third act, a servant girl sings the brilliant chanson of the miller, a delightfully inverted piece in the manner of ancient French couplets...Risë Stevens received enthusiastic and merited special applause after the marvelously sung couplet..." [25]

* * * *

Carmen Mayer: "What I remember of Miss Stevens' Hansel is the impression that she very well impersonated a boy...somewhat tall...I remember her wearing brown pants - short and an almost white shirt and brown suspenders." [26]

In a new production under Fritz Rieger's direction, *Hänsel und Gretel* opened on December 14th with Risë and Herta Rayn in the title roles,

> Two captivating singers brought the title characters to vocal and dramatic life. Risë Stevens is the nicest, liveliest Hänsel that one can imagine. Slender, wide-eyed, with the sturdy legs of a boy, and with that combination of awkwardness and grace that only children have, she commanded the stage. Her lustrous voice caressed every subtlety of the folk songs that are incorporated into the sore, as well as holding its own in the ravishing ensembles that are so characteristic of Humperdinck's style. [27]

On March 6th, the only known Amneris she ever sang found Risë, "impressive in the nobility of her youthful bearing...precisely because of her youthful bearing-able to offer only an attractive sketch of this demanding part. The beautiful voice was lacking in weight, particularly in the low register. Her conception of the role was apt, however, and her ability to convey her ideas in music led to some moving moments." [28]

Amneris proved to be a role that she might have conquered in time but circumstances never allowed this to happen. The review of Amneris was not bad, it was merely less good than the ones she had become used to receiving from the Prague critics.

Her Cherubino in *Le Nozze di Figaro* for which she became justifiably well-known was introduced on March 24th with Karl Rankl conducting and she was "the most charming, boylike ...rogueish Cherubino conceivable." [29]

* * * *

Early in 1938, Walter signed a contract with the *Josephstadt Theater* in Vienna that was under the direction of Max Reinhardt, who would leave that post before the end of the year. He was obliged to finish his contract with the *Neues Deutsches Theater* and then relocate to Vienna for the summer. The contract was signed after Risë's for the Metropolitan which meant he realized her eventual return to America would part them, probably forever. Vienna was his second home. His Trieste born mother, Sofie Bergman, and his younger sister by ten years, Hilde (Duzie), lived there having been separated from his Hungarian born father, Imré, for many years. A cold, socially conscious woman (her father, Ladislaw Bergman, was a Knight of the Austrian-Hungarian Empire), she gave birth to Walter in Vienna on March 28, 1910 while visiting her mother. When her husband was disabled by a stroke, she left him for good, settling in Vienna with Duzie. Imré Szurovy, born in Komarom, Hungary, was one of eight boys and four girls of his father who was administrator for the railroad of the Hungarian monarchy. Imré held the rank of Major General and it was believed that he was in love with his wife's sister, a situation that weakened the marriage and caused the eventual separation after he became ill.

Walter remained with his father until the rigors of the military school in which he was enrolled caused him to flee on foot to Vienna. Shortly after his arrival, his mother entered him into a Jesuit seminary with the understanding that he would become a priest. Fate intervened when a prominent producer quite accidentally saw a photograph of Walter in the handbag of his mistress who also happened to be dating Walter. Impressed with his looks, he asked her to introduce him to Walter since he felt he might have a future on the stage. His first impression was confirmed when he met Walter and encouraged him to enter an acting competition. Without any prior training or experience, Walter won with a stirring rendition of a monologue from Schiller's *Die Räuber* along with another piece that was equally demanding. Rejecting the prize, a scholarship to study acting and, in spite of a dire need of funds, he accepted a non-paying part in a play in a small town in Czechoslovakia. He needed the experience and again, scored a success that was rewarded by his being put on salary. Engagements in Carlsberg and Marienbad followed as well as a stint with Reinhardt in Berlin in *Der Prinz von Homberg*. When Hitler marched into Berlin in 1933, Walter returned to Vienna. Hearing about him through an actor friend of Walter's, Dr. Eger engaged him for the *Kleine Bühne Theater* beginning in September, 1936. He made his debut in a German version of Dumas' *La Dame aux Camélias* and was commended for his "handsome and youthfully lighthearted Armand." [30]

At his urging, Dr. Eger presented George Bernard Shaw's, The *Doctor's Dilemma* but both the play and Walter were not a success. While *Die Katze läbt das Mausen nicht* by F. Lonsdale made him popular with the critics, ("Szurovy, a welcome new addition to the ensemble, can be praised for his youth, his sly intelligence, his piquant charm and his light touch." [31]), his appearance as the much older butler in Ladislaus Bus-Pekete's, *Jean*, made his reputation with audiences. In a career that was cut short by the war, he played everything from the classics to light-hearted comedies opposite some of the theater's and films' most accomplished actors, many of whom were to die in concentration camps because they were Jewish.

When a fellow actor tried to enroll him in the Communist Party, he went to one of the meetings in a show of comaraderie but quickly discovered that it wasn't for him. He could accept neither their ideology nor their lack of elegance.

Two years later, his reputation as a leading actor firmly in place, Vienna and the *Josephstadt* was a way to forget Risë. Even though his mother had met and approved of her, geography would win out; they would be a continent apart before the year's end. What he did not know when he signed on for the Vienna engagement was that the city would be Nazi occupied in a matter of weeks. Starting in mid-February, Germany made clear its intentions to extend its borders into Austria and by mid-March had accomplished that end. The *Anschluss* was a bloodless invasion accomplished by threats rather than bullets. Despite this, the music scene in the city was not shut down and continued almost close to normal. A month after the take-over, Joseph Goebbels, Propaganda Minister, announced that Vienna would be the center of music for the New Reich. On March 14th, however, Bruno Walter resigned as director of the Vienna Opera, in spite of having recently signed a three-year contract. Prior to that, Risë, who was in Vienna, expressed her concern for him but the Maestro brushed aside her fears, "I am Bruno Walter", an untouchable. As a Jew, he could not keep his position. He was not singled out since questionnaires were sent to other opera directors concerning their heritage. From America, Lily Pons informed the Press that she had canceled her appearances in Vienna at the end of April stating that, "There will be no more fine music in Vienna in a short time. The symphony orchestra and the opera company are being put under Nazi control, in my mind, will very soon completely ruin them. I am not in sympathy with such things." [32]

Risë was scheduled for two performances of *Der Rosenkavalier* as a guest with the Vienna Opera on March 8th and 18th. She arrived in a city that was pre-Hitler and left after the take over. For purely sentimental reasons, she asked to be assigned to Gutheil-Schoeder's dressing room. There was a plaque on the door which had her name engraved on it and the management was only too willing to honor her request. Between her two performances, Vienna was taken over and when she arrived at the opera house for her second appearance, she could not find her dressing room. The plaque with Gutheil-Schoeder's name had been removed since she was Jewish, a non-person.

Her performances went well and she and Hilde Konetzni scored personal successes along with her Sophie of the 8th, Margherita Perras. Herbert F. Peyser, reporting from Vienna to the *New York Times*, extolled Risë's debut unconditionally,

> ...I had heard [her] in Prague, but only as one of the three ladies in 'The Magic Flute'. Yet I was quite unprepared, flattering reports notwithstanding, for the big, vital artistic impression I received at the Staatsoper from her Octavian...I heard, to begin with, a lovely, blooming voice (not over-voluminous, to be sure, though with this the unfamiliar house may have had something to do)-a voice beautifully cultivated throughout its scale. Further, a skill and fastidiousness of taste in phrasing and nuance that betrayed artistry of a wholly exceptional order. And never have I seen in this opera the figure of Octavian played with such an exuberance paired with distinction or with such complete credibility of boyish verisimilitude. Miss Stevens comes about as near as humanly possible to solving the insoluble theatrical of the woman in male disguise. The Vienna Press hailed her Octavian in some respects above the late Gutheil-Schoder's. When [she] comes to America it will be a ripe and considerable artist who steps upon the scene. [33]

With this engagement a career in Vienna was opened to her but she was anxious to return to Prague and fulfill the remaining months of her contract. The forced departure of Maestro Walter from Vienna did nothing to quell her unease about her future in Europe, after all, she was half Jewish. She was witness to brutality first hand, when from the room of her hotel she heard screams from a man who was being beaten senseless by a mob shouting, "Jew", "Jew". He had been stripped naked. It was a common practice for men's pants to be pulled down in public to see if they were circumcised.

In Prague, a mixture of Cherubinos and Dryad's in *Ariadne auf Naxos* kept her busy well into May. Because of the celebratory nature of the year, the season was extended into the summer. June brought with it the final production she would appear in, *La Finta Gardiniera* by Mozart or *Die Gartnerin aus Liebe*, as it was called in its German translation, which premiered on June 26th and was staged in the gardens of the Waldstein Palace. "A well combined ensemble participated. Harriet Henders sang her farewell song to Prague as Sandrina. The German Opera loses in her one of its most admired members. Risë Stevens, her partner in the slightly American accentuation of the dialogue, will, too, not be heard before Spring, since she has been engaged to sing in New York and Buenos Aires. She gave an excellent impersonation of the young Count Ramiro." [34]

Harriet had made known her decision that she would not return for another season. Absent from America for nine years, it was time to go home and establish herself there. Risë, however, had every intention of maintaining her ties with Prague, the political situation willing. She and Dr. Eger had even discussed reviving *Samson et Dalila* for her. Then there was Walter. He would be in Prague and even if they did not resume their old life together they could at least see one another from time to time. She did not know that someone else would occupy her attention shortly. Nor could she have foreseen that Walter would make himself a *persona non grata* in Prague by openly criticizing the Nazi regime. While she could separate herself from the growing turmoil surrounding Prague, by immersing herself in her work, Walter could not. As a film and stage actor, he was too "public" to let these slights go unnoticed. Dreams on her part of his emigrating to America to join her there were also dispelled by the reality of his being an actor who did not speak English. He could pursue his career in Europe but in America, she realized, he would have to first learn the language and then start again.

On September 28th, the *Prager Tagblatt* carried the following notice, "Performances have been suspended at the *Neues Deutsches Theater*, as at most other Prague theaters. Operations will be resumed as soon as possible." [35] The political situation had climaxed in the occupation of the city but both Risë and Harriet were gone by then.

Part II: 1938-1963

Unless you are willing to go all out for
an operatic career, you might as well give
up at the start. [1]

Chapter 1

The general rehearsal for *Mignon* set for December 15th two days before the premiere on the 17th, did not pose a problem as had *Der Rosenkavalier* rehearsals. Both Lehmann and List had prior commitments that interfered with the Met's schedule. After much negotiating back and forth with the two veteran singers, the conflict was resolved to the Met's satisfaction. The *Orfeo ed Euridice* general rehearsal on November 21st with a piano run through on the 14th, 15th and 16th were also free of conflict. While not expected to appear as Orfeo, Risë was engaged to protect the performances should Kerstin Thorborg not be able to sing. This explains why almost a month elapsed between Risë's Philadelphia debut on November 22nd and her house debut on December 17th. Karin Branzell would have been only too willing to cover these performances had she been asked. In a letter to Johnson and Ziegler she begged them to give her some performances of *Orfeo* when Thorborg finished but her request was ignored. As it turned out, Thorborg sang all the performances and Risë and *Orfeo* eluded one another at the Metropolitan for a second time.

At the close of her season in Prague, Risë inquired about the cuts that were sanctioned for *Mignon* and also if the recitatives were to be sung or spoken. At first the score was to be sent to the *Teatro Colón* but since Risë had not planned to leave from Trieste until August 6th, it was decided to send it to her prior to her departure so that she could study aboard ship. Schoen-René wrote to Oscar Wagner, Dean of the

Juilliard Graduate School, on July 10th, informing him that Risë had left that day for Trieste after having spent two weeks with her in Paris. What Schoen-René did not know was that before embarking for South America, Risë joined Walter in Trieste prior to their going to Umayo (near Istria) in Yugoslavia.

The time she and Walter had spent together drew to a close and when the day came for her to board the ship, she was disconsolate. Fortunately among her traveling companions were Hilde Konetzni's sister, Anny, Karin Branzell and Editha Fleischer, who with the exception of Fleischer, by then retired, were to appear at the *Colón*. Sophisticates all in the ways of the world, Risë learned a great deal from them and, in a sense, grew up on that voyage. The three ladies possessed a European veneer which was enviable and which Risë grafted on to her American gaucheries redesigning her own persona to match theirs. Rudolf Bing was to remark on this. He did not think of her as American, which was the highest praise from someone who thought all American culture stopped west of New York. Her companions told her to forget Walter. South America was full of rich, handsome men who would take her mind off him. They plied her with good food and plenty to drink in an effort to improve her spirits. As the ship went farther out to sea, she found herself succumbing to their ministrations and began looking forward to what would await her in South America.

Risë, Konetzni, Branzell, Fleischer and their husbands were booked into a very comfortable *pensione* and it was immediately apparent that Buenos Aires was light years away from Prague in mood and ambiance. The threat of Nazi Germany was not a reality there. It was happening on the other side of the world which you read about in the newspapers. The atmosphere was light, festive, with modishly dressed people, at least within their immediate surroundings. The opera house was huge and magnificent, the audiences elegantly turned out, the ladies seemingly all beautiful and the gentlemen very appreciative. It was a city to fall in love as her colleagues hinted, however, that was not for her, she was there to work. Octavian would serve to introduce her on September 2nd, and Kleiber made known immediately that he wanted to review the role with her note for note. Their sessions lasted from ten o'clock in the morning to late at night and what Gutheil-Schoder was to the text, Kleiber was to the music. Their initial collaboration was met with praise from the critics calling Risë, "...an Octavian of importance; an expressive and fluid actress she sang with a beauty and warmth of voice coupled with perfect diction...she did everything that could be done with a difficult role." [2]

Just exactly when Norbert Bogdan entered her life is not certain but he became fascinated with Risë after seeing her at the Teatro Colón. The thirty-four year old investment banker and devotee of opera, was born in Italy, studied at the London School of Economics and emigrated to the United States in 1923. At the time of his first seeing Risë, he was Vice President of the J. Henry Schroder Banking Corporation in charge of business in Continental Europe, South America and Asia. He traveled regularly to Buenos Aires and, accomplished musician that he was, made the *Teatro Colón* high priority on his list of things to do when there.

Bogdan asked to be introduced to Risë at a reception at the U. S. Embassy, telling her how much he admired her Octavian. Subsequently, they seemed always to run into one another and slowly a feeling of mutual attraction set in. He was handsome, wealthy, cultured and very attentive to her slightest wish. She was alone with no one to share her success and welcomed his company. The time was short, her season would end in a matter of weeks. When she had to leave, they parted on the pier minutes before the Eastern Prince was to set sail for America.

The first stop was *São Paulo* and as the ship inched its way into port, Risë and Emanuel List were watching the operation from the main deck. Suddenly, List grabbed Risë's arm and pointed to a man waving at them from the dock.

She could not believe her eyes but it was Bogdan. He had timed her arrival and flew from Buenos Aires to meet the ship as it arrived, leaving them just enough time to talk briefly with promises made to meet in New York.

When Risë again took up residence in New York, she thought it best to have her own place. The quiet and the solitude away from family activities would allow her to focus solely on her impending Metropolitan Opera debut. A suite in the Beacon Hotel on Broadway and Seventy-fourth Street, not too far from her parents and the Metropolitan Opera House, became her home. Coaching sessions with Wilfred Pelletier and Victor Trucco began almost immediately since she would introduce two of her roles and quite possibly a third within a month of each other. She also needed time to learn both Orfeo and Mignon in their original languages since she knew the former in English and German and the latter only in German. Unlearning the text and relearning it in either Italian or French was not a simple matter and sometimes she would lapse into the German, correcting herself immediately.

Studies with Schoen-René also resumed, as did all the necessary preparations for creating the visual side of the characters she would portray. Costuming Octavian was not a concern, for the Egers had given her the outfits she had worn in *Der Rosenkavalier* when they learned she was to make her debut in that role. Risë wore them for almost twenty years and put them aside only when she had to have new ones made for a revised production in 1956. Mignon and Orfeo were another matter and not having costumes of her own, the house ones were fitted on her.

Amid all this activity, she and Bogdan managed to find some time to enjoy one another's company. He was as excited about her debut as she was and planned to travel to Philadelphia for *Der Rosenkavalier*. Perhaps it was there that she could introduce him to her family since in all probability they would be married in a matter of months. He had not met them as yet and no matter how many times Risë brought the subject up, he did not seem overly anxious to do so. Her family did not seem anxious to meet him either since he was of a social stratum far above theirs. This did not sit well with her. Family ties were strong and the success she was striving for was as much for them as for herself. It was a vindication for all the railroad apartments they lived in, the wanting to make good, her mother's retort to Roxy, the countless hours spent commuting to the *Children's Hour* and the *Little Theatre*, the personal sacrifices her mother made to send her welcome care packages in Prague and the ability to help her brother make a way for himself. Did any feeling for Walter remain? She was convinced it was over between them.

It was a heady experience for the Steenbergs, Schoen-René and Risë, herself, to see her picture in the *New York Times* and the other daily newspapers as one of the newcomers of the Metropolitan Opera season. The *Times* photograph was placed between Maria Caniglia and Mafalda Favero, two leading singers from Italy. The 1938-1939 season's line-up of new singers was enviable. Besides Caniglia, Favero and Leonard Warren there were Jussi Björling, Alessio de Paolis, Galliano Masini, Herbert Janssen, Hans Hermann Nissen, among others, and Beniamino Gigli who was returning after an absence of six years. Olin Downes praised Risë in print for rejecting the Metropolitan Opera until she had more experience and termed her decision an "object-lesson which could...be applied by...other young American singers..." [3] Lawrence Gilman included her in his predictions on which of the fourteen debuting artists were the most outstanding. Besides Risë his handful included Caniglia, Björling, Nissen, Favero and Marisa Morel, a soprano, who unfortunately did not succeed. Highlights of the season were *Boris Godunov* with Ezio Pinza, Grace Moore in a revival of *Louise*, Marjorie Lawrence and John Charles Thomas in *Thais* and Lawrence Tibbett as Falstaff. The incomparable pairing of Kirsten Flagstad and Lauritz Melchior explained why ten Wagner operas were scheduled as opposed to only eight by Verdi. Flagstad would also star in a major revival of *Fidelio* conducted by Bodanzky. *Orfeo*, after its disastrous outing three years earlier, would have a traditional staging by Herbert Graf, designs by Harry Horner and choreography by Boris Romanoff. Three of Risë's Juilliard colleagues were already at the Metropolitan, Julius Huehn, Josephine Antoine and Lucielle Browning. The opening of the season was scheduled for November 21st with *Otello* starring Martinelli, Tibbett and Caniglia. Johnson could rest content with the fact that the season was shaping up to be one of the financially strongest the Company had since the Depression.

Risë's debut was to take place on the second night of the season, not in the thirty-ninth street house, but, rather, in Philadelphia. This was a smart move on Johnson's part. The openings in the Quaker City were, if anything, as opulent and important as the ones in New York. Johnson needed a new face to make the Philadelphia opening that much more exciting and Risë, in what was to be arguably her greatest role, would provide that for certain. It also benefited Risë by allowing her to pass the hurdle of a debut before she actually set foot on the main stage.*

In an interview in *Opera News*, it was pointed out that, "[Risë] is happy that her debut was assigned to Philadelphia, having enjoyed the approval of the public of that city in a performance of 'Roi David'..." [4]

The article went on to say,
At nine o'clock in the morning, [she] has already breakfasted, dressed, and opened her hotel door to <u>Opera News</u>. Last evening she rehearsed Octavian until seven o'clock, today she must be at the Opera House at ten for *Orfeo*. In spite of this strenuous routine, Miss Stevens, still tanned from Buenos Aires, dark eyes shining, brown

---

* Rose Bampton told the author that her own debut in Philadelphia made her debut in New York less daunting.

curls bobbing, sits relaxed and smiling, in her olive green tweed always glad to talk of opera...This summer [she] was 'the outstanding feature of the Colon Opera season...'according to one *Opera News* correspondent, who adds, I am trying to express myself as sedately and conservatively as possible when I consider Risë Stevens one of the greatest singers of the day'...'The South American audiences were wonderful', Miss Stevens relates. 'Not as demonstrative as those in Prague, they were still most understanding and appreciative...[Discussing *Mignon*] she learned [it] in French with a coach from the Opéra-Comique in Paris, and worked so hard that she collapsed from over-work and left to recuperate in Trieste... [5]

Accompanying the article is an attractive photograph of Risë taken in Trieste no doubt by Walter but attributed to her mother in deference to propriety.

* * *

Traditions were rapidly eroding and the old Metropolitan way of functioning was in its final stages. The 'democratization' of the organization had begun. Significant in this was the enlarging of the audience to include not only those in New York but also anyone within listening range of the Saturday matinee broadcasts. Commencing in 1931 with a Christmas afternoon airing of *Hänsel und Gretel*, they were becoming a tradition in their own right. The annual tour still remained an important part of making the Metropolitan national in scope.

The mid-thirties Depression and the excesses of the Gatti regime, however, made the feasibility of touring a questionable activity. Available resources had to be reserved for the Broadway house and without adequate guarantees from host cities, the tour was deemed a risk. The box office began to rebound under Johnson and by the 1938-1939 season (although he confined himself to only one new production, *Orfeo ed Euridice*), the tour commencing on March 13th in Baltimore and ending on April 15th in New Orleans would be the longest since the early part of the century. In addition, throughout the season the Metropolitan paid visits to Brooklyn and Philadelphia at least until the Brooklyn outings were deemed too expensive and terminated in 1937. Weekly trips to Philadelphia ceased with the 1934-1935 season, cutting back to once a month visits to offset a money-losing arrangement. This season a return to more frequent appearances was to be reinstated and judging by the enthusiasm the announcement engendered, the move seemed to be a propitious one.

It was reported that over thirty-three hundred ticket buyers welcomed the company's return resulting in thirteen thousand two hundred eighty dollars in box office sales. The starting time was set for 8:30 P.M. but both the socially prominent and the gallery patrons began arriving unfashionably early, only to be kept waiting in front of still locked doors. The *Philadelphia Evening Bulletin* described the scene, "Limousine after limousine glided to the lighted marquee and discharged its fashionable cargo. Curious crowds gathered on either side. Traffic grew heavier...white caped policemen shouted orders...velvet and fur wrapped women and silk hatted men seemed to come from all directions at once...'libretto-libretto' echoed from within...The crowded lobby ablaze with crystal light and red velvet, the gaiety of the holiday season added to the general excitement." [6]

The *New York Times* sent a reporter to cover the Philadelphia opening and an article with a headline which read, "Ovation at Opera for Risë Stevens" summed up the proceedings as "the most brilliant opera inaugural this city has seen in years, the Metropolitan Opera Association opened...[its] season of ten performances tonight with a sumptuous presentation of...'Der Rosenkavalier' before a capacity audience in the Academy of Music. The house had been completely sold out well in advance, many persons were turned

away at the box office and special police reserves were required to handle the traffic along Broad and Locust Streets." [7]

A picturesque account of the musical side of the evening
was found in the *Philadelphia Record*,

> [the audience] warmed up after the first act and ap-
> plauded some. But as [the opera] went on, they shed
> their dignity...and really went to town. [They]stood up
> and cheered; and the orchestra men, too, stood on chairs
> and waved their fiddles, as cheer leaders, shouting bravo.
> And a star was born-Risë Stevens...Your reporter sat
> where he could see backstage. They danced in glee back
> there-Lotte Lehmann, Emanuel List and the others. But
> there was one cool one there; a brusque assistant stage
> manager...he told them when to take a bow...he told
> Risë Stevens to bow so often at the second curtain she
> rebelled...he grabbed her arm and shoved her out on the
> stage and she gripped the tunic of List to drag him out,
> too. But he brushed her hand away-and she was liter-
> ally hurled out for more acclaim. She cried then..." [8]

The *Evening Bulletin*'s influential critic, Henry Pleasants,
gave a balanced report of what the commotion was all about,
"...her Octavian was a delight to the eye and the ear. Her
performance dominated the proceedings...Octavian is not an
easy part for a veteran, and much less so for a debutante.
But Miss Stevens was poise itself...her voice is probably not
yet mature, but it is already even in scale and well rounded.
Certain notes at the upper extreme of her range tend to be
thin; but otherwise the voice is exceptionally well-placed." [9]

Samuel L. Lacier in the *Evening Public Ledger* hailed
Risë's contribution as "perhaps the most remarkable feature
of the performance...rarely, if ever, in Philadelphia has a young
singer made so impressive a debut. She has everything required in an operatic artist, youth, a beautiful voice, which
was exceedingly well used; a fine dramatic talent which was
skillfully employed; a most attractive stage presence and a

keen feeling for the histrionics of the role...[her] success was all the more remarkable because she was playing in the same cast with Lotte Lehmann..." [10]

An insider's report on the debut came from Natalia Bodanya, who played one of the Orphans, "Risë looked wonderful physically, the answer to all Octavians in voice and looks. She had a natural feeling for the stage. I became interested in Risë because I was interested in theater. When [Leopold] Sachse [the director] offered her suggestions there was no question that she could do them. She could take any situation and move with it. From the first rehearsals you could tell she had natural ability." [11] Lucielle Browning who played another Orphan (Anna Kaskas was the third Orphan and always spoke highly of Risë according to her son) felt that, "Risë's best role was Octavian. She was so right for that role." [12]

That Risë's house debut was to be broadcast did not cause her undue concern since only eighty stations in the United States and Canada could hear it and she was a radio veteran. Four years on the *Children's Hour*, plus several years combined on the *Palmolive Beauty Box Theater* and the *Sigmund Romberg Show*, taught her not to be afraid of a microphone. Also, the role of Mignon had taken on the feel of a "good luck" piece. It proved lucky for her debut in Prague and ushered in a tenure there that was a total success. She had been able to sing it a number of times since and the only thing that might cause trouble was the change from German to French. On the Saturday afternoon of December 17th, the Steenberg Family was assembled out front as was Schoen-René, Bogdan and a myriad group of well-wishers who came to hear one of their own. As excited, as though he were a member of the immediate family, was Milton Cross, the announcer for the Metropolitan Opera broadcasts*, who presented Risë on the *Children's Hour*. His own daughter, Lillian,

---

* Having presided over the broadcasts since the first one, he had by this time become the voice of the Metropolitan Opera and continued as host until his death in 1975.

also a member of that show died in 1933 and it was with fatherly pride that he spoke of Risë who was in a sense his child also. He remembered her as "full of life, of an athletic build and possessing poise and confidence." [13] In those days, he found it difficult to predict if her voice would be better suited for opera or popular music. Her debut that afternoon with the Metropolitan Opera settled the question.

On the eighteenth, the reviews started to appear and they, in the main, supported the positive impression she had made in Philadelphia. Olin Downes, who through the years would prove to be not one of Risë's chief supporters, had nothing but praise for this initial outing, "Yesterday afternoon a new debutante of unquestionable gifts, both vocal and dramatic, made her first appearance in the Broadway lyric theatre...She gave the part of Mignon dramatic substance...she brought the music into her service in conveying the emotional currents of the drama...the voice is obviously...fresh and its registers... smoothly joined together...it is a voice that should carry its possessor far..." [14] Francis D. Perkins, who had reviewed Risë as a Juilliard student, commented that, "her Mignon had unusual individuality and vitality and persuasive emotions." [15] He also pointed out that her "effect upon the audience was unmistakable." [16]

Risë had built-in audience appeal and throughout her career she had a divided camp of critics but a very loyal following. Two members of the radio audience wrote letters to Edward Johnson which expressed their thoughts on what they heard that Saturday afternoon: from Washington, "I feel I must tell you how shaken we were today at the close of...Mignon, with Risë Stevens. We have never missed a broadcast but it has been long since we've been touched as we have today with this girl's gorgeous performance. The entire cast was fine, but, words cannot describe the thrill she has given us here. May God bless her." [17], and from California, "Miss Stevens is tops and a worthy successor to Mme Homer." [18]

Her faith in her abilities was to be sorely tested two days after *Mignon*. Octavian met with unstinting praise in Philadelphia but on December 20th, she was to unveil her Count Rofrano in the 39th Street house. The date fell on a Monday, Society's night to attend the opera and as with Philadelphia, the audience was resplendent in dress. Jewels sparkled everywhere and there was a great sense of anticipation to see the new singer in the role that made her an overnight star in Philadelphia. The pressure on Risë was intense. Lehmann was a particular favorite on 39th Street and the fact that she was in the process of becoming an American citizen endeared her even more to the public. Risë had nothing to be concerned about with either Lehmann or List, who was again the Baron, trying to upstage her since they both were genuinely fond of her. It was the critics who might come down hard on the new girl with two successes to her credit.

Her fears were not unfounded since the reviews were mixed and did not approach the ones she had received in Philadelphia. Most felt that her Mignon was the better of the two performances.

The *Staats Zeitung* offered the most balanced account of the evening and touched on some of the advantages Risë enjoyed by studying and working abroad,

Both vocally and dramatically the young American revealed the careful schooling that she has received in European houses. The Octavian of Miss Stevens betrayed none of the understandable nervousness not to mention awkwardness, that is usually to be expected from young Americans. She gave us a fresh, lively Rosenkavalier, imbued with youthful verve and she understood how to use natural, understated gestures to convince a convincing portrayal. Her performance confirmed the earlier impression that her voice is most attractive in the middle range. Thanks to good vocal placement, however, she was able to take high passages in the second act with ease and security. The voice is warm in timbre, the soft tones carry well, and the intonation and rhythmic sense are well schooled.[19]

Chapter 2

Czechoslovakia was on the brink of a Nazi takeover in August of 1938. The Czechs had mobilized against an imminent siege. Neville Chamberlain, Britain's Prime Minister, met with Hitler in Munich on September 29, 1938, and Czechoslovakia's fate was decided. The German leader stated that Czechoslovakia would be his last act of territorial aggression. Chamberlain countered that the free world would look the other way and offer Czechoslovakia as the sacrificial lamb to avoid a greater catastrophe. The Munich pact was signed and Czechoslovakia ceased to exist as a unified nation.

At that point, Walter, who had returned to Prague after he left Risë in Trieste, tried to adjust to life without her. Their affair was no more over for him than if she were still there. When the news broke that Czechoslovakia's sovereignty was bartered for "peace', Walter quite literally packed a bag, leaving everything else behind, took a train to Bratislava where he got off with the intention of going to Vienna. His engagement with the *Josefstadt* was for December but he knew he could stay with his mother until he again had an income. He had an Hungarian passport courtesy of his father's origins, never having renounced it in favor of either a Czech or Austrian one and since Hungary was neutral, he was in less danger of being turned back. Still, to avoid calling attention to himself, he hitchhiked to Vienna thereby avoiding guard checks at train stations.

Once in Vienna, he arranged to see Dr. Heinz Hilpert,

newly appointed director of the Josefstadt, who approved his request to start his engagement earlier. The Nazis were slowly placing restrictions on what could be presented in the theaters and Walter again felt threatened. Separated for eight months, he tried unsuccessfully to contact Risë and he began to suspect that she had met someone else. He knew he must leave but this time America was his goal. Obtaining a passport was not difficult because of his Hungarian citizenship and he even managed to secure an American visa. After passage was booked on the *Deutschland*, good-byes made to his mother and sister and a leave of absence granted by Dr. Hilpert (who told him he knew he would not be back), he made one last attempt to wire Risë to tell her of his plans. She, in turn, wired back not to come, that she was engaged to be married. He calmed his anxieties during the crossing at the bar where he was never once asked to pay for a drink. The mystery of that generosity remained unsolved, but Walter felt word might have gotten around that he was a Nazi spy.

In spite of the fact she told Walter that they were through, Risë, for old time's sake, asked her mother and brother to meet him at the pier when he arrived on December 15th and escort him to the hotel where she had arranged accommodations for him. She would not be there. It would be best if she saw him later at her parents if only to reinforce the impression that she wasn't overly anxious to see him.

Surviving his first encounter with the New York subway system, he duly reported to the Steenberg household on 105th Street and Broadway. Christmas was only a week away so he came with gifts for everyone including a ring for Risë. Sadie and Bud had already taken a liking to him even though there was no means of communicating with the non-English speaking visitor. Her father was slower coming around since he and Risë were very close, closer than she was to her mother. Schoen-René, who was also there, did not like him at first since she looked on any male friend of Risë's as a

potential threat to her career. As for Risë, the whole happening made her very uneasy. It was obvious to everyone
that she and Walter had been more than just friends but in
the meantime she had made a commitment to Bogdan.
Marriage to him would give her financial independence
whereas Walter had to establish himself in America and,
most probably, she would have to support him at first. Sadie
was not in favor of Risë's marrying Bogdan. Apart from
the fact that he kept his distance, she felt that life would
become too comfortable for her to want to continue with
the rigors of a career. Sadie remained a stage mother and
she had Schoen-René's support in this desire to see Risë
make it to the top. The positive reception of her debut only
made their resolve stronger and it was Walter who might
just be the key to their plans for Risë. If she married him,
she would have to support both of them until he was settled.
It was resolved then and there that if Risë were to marry it
would be to Walter.

He, in turn, was determined to stay in America and find a
means of supporting himself even if it meant waiting on tables
at Luchows, the more than half-century old 14th Street restaurant, where speaking German rather than English was not
a handicap. However, winning Risë back was paramount.
Emboldened by Sadie's support, Walter decided to bring
matters to a head and telephoned Bogdan at his office. Fluent in German, he had no trouble understanding Walter's request to join him for a drink as a courtesy to an old friend of
his wife to be. After the usual introductory pleasantries,
Walter asked Bogdan if he would permit Risë to be his guest
at a farewell dinner so that he could say good-bye to her before returning to Europe. When permission was granted and
the meeting with Bogdan over, Walter immediately called Risë
to tell her that he was sailing the next day and that he had
Bogdan's permission to invite her out. Reluctantly, Risë acquiesced and arranged to meet him in the lobby of the Beacon. Stepping out of the elevator, she saw Walter and asked

him where they were having dinner. Walter, actor that he was, looked at her with great seriousness and informed her that room service would take care of it. Since there were no dining accommodations in the hotel, as they both knew, Walter's message was clear and the engagement to Bogdan was over.

They would have been married immediately but New York law mandated a two-week waiting period after blood tests. There was no time, let alone money, to plan a formal wedding, City Hall would have to be their chapel and the immediate family the only guests. The earliest date was the sixth of January, a Friday, and at the appointed hour, the bride (dressed in a suit and holding a bouquet someone had thoughtfully provided) and groom and guests assembled before the Justice of the Peace. Lewis was instructed to nudge Walter when the time came for him to say "I do" and upon completion of the ten minute ceremony, Walter tore the marriage certificate in half (to show that the union would endure without it) later to be stored in a safe deposit box. He presented Risë with the only wedding gift she received, a zircon ring in a silver and onyx setting. The bride took leave of the wedding party on the steps of City Hall and rushed to the Opera House where she was scheduled for a rehearsal. Afterwards, she was free to celebrate at her parents which left Walter to treat the "guests" to lunch at the automat.

Late afternoon found them all together again at 105th Street. Schoen-René had given strict instructions concerning what Risë could and could not do on her wedding night since she was to appear on the Saturday matinee broadcast of *Der Rosenkavalier* the very next day. Originally, Walter and she had planned to spend the night at her apartment but Schoen-René forbade sex before singing so demanding a role as Octavian. Risë needed to be in top form for the performance, therefore, she was ordered to spend the night at her parents and Walter was sent back to his hotel. This arrangement made sense as far as the bride was concerned but as for Walter a wedding night without Risë was an affront. However, seeing her perform Mignon on December 28th, the opera in which they first met in Prague, he knew that she had arrived where she belonged. He was genuinely happy for her and so when he returned to his hotel he asked the German speaking concierge who had taken a liking to him, where he could find something festive to do. The concierge told him of a big society wedding reception at the Waldorf Astoria Hotel and, if he mentioned his name to the doorman, he would be allowed in as a guest. Walter followed his advice and even had a dance with the bride.

The next day, before the matinee of *Der Rosenkavalier* was to start, Lehmann looked at her Octavian in a very quizzical way. She told Risë that she noticed something different about her. Risë could not lie to Lehnmann and told her in strict confidence about her marriage. No mention was to be made of it since Schoen-René felt that the management might lose interest in her thinking that she would give up her career. Her present contract was being renegotiated and there were only options on her next two. As it turned out, the marriage was not revealed in the press until March 23rd and the option renewed March 7th. Lehmann understood quite well the vagaries of management, being no novice and discreetly expressed her happiness for her. She wanted to meet Walter as soon as possible. Ironically, it was the same Lehmann who when informed several years later that Risë was pregnant told her in no uncertain terms that she and Walter would always be welcome in her home but not the child. The older singers dislike of children was well known and those in the opera chorus knew to stay away from her.

Risë appeared as a guest on the Metropolitan Opera Auditions of the Air, hosted by Edward Johnson, on New Year's day. It must have been in a way vindicating to her to be invited in light of the fact that she was not chosen as a finalist only three years earlier. For the benefit of the radio audience and the young artists participating in the contest, Risë declared December her lucky month because she made her

Prague debut and her second Metropolitan Opera debut, both great successes, in December. Briefly mentioning the other opera houses that heard her, she expressed the hope that she would be a credit to the Metropolitan Opera. Edward Johnson assured her that she already was. "Che farò senza Euridice" and "When Irish Eyes are Smiling" in remembrance of the first song she sang on the *Children's Hour*, concluded her contribution to the program. Three days later, the *New York Times* announced that the Metropolitan would present Wagner's *Das Ring des Nibelungen* uncut with prices ranging from seven dollars and fifty cents for the rear of the Family Circle to one hundred eighty dollars for a Grand Tier box seating eight for the entire cycle. The best Wagnerian singers were scheduled to appear, Flagstad, Melchior, Lawrence, Lehmann, Elisabeth Rethberg, Thorborg and Branzell among others. Originally, Risë's contract was for eight weeks only ending on January 15th. On January 12th, management extended her contact to January 29th and subsequently to March 5, 1939. Also, when it became obvious that she could not return to Prague as was originally planned due to the worsening world situation, managment saw the advantage of keeping her at the Metropolitan. Johnson, who thought of her in terms of Wagner, included her in the casting for the *Ring* cycles. Interlaced with these performances was a remaining *Mignon* and two Sunday night concerts with excerpts from *Mignon*. One reporter at the final *Mignon* on February 3rd commented on the intensity of applause for Risë by an audience that sounded as though it may have been entirely made up of Bronxites cheering one of their own.

Not only audiences but also two of America's most popular magazines were quick to jump on her bandwagon. On January 16th, *Life* ran a photograph of her as Octavian and earlier, on December 26th, *Time* reported that her debut as Mignon had created a sensation. She became material for interviews and John Selby's syndicated column informed his readers after her debut in *Mignon* that she doesn't 'just adore' anything but singing and her family...[that] she can't cook a thing, because she never tried. She doesn't care a lot for food anyway...mostly she eats what's put before her as long as it's good. She can't keep house either. That's not her job. Sewing the same. She's a well set up healthy looking girl...she looks like the winter sports type but isn't. She likes to swim a lot and likes tennis. But she hasn't the time right now for either. Most of her exercise she gets in taxicabs bouncing from her West side apartment to the Met for rehearsals and bouncing back. Her clothes are obviously good but extremely simple...she appeared in a brown tailored street dress, her short brown hair combed back comfortably. No 'upsweeps' for her. The first thing one notices about [her] is her unusually rich speaking voice. It has a warmth that singer's speaking voices usually lack...She never uses the ordinary conversational dodges and she never looks at your Adam's apple or your left ear. She always looks straight at you, and says what she means. This is all pretty refreshing, the world being what it is. [1]

It wasn't long after Lehmann learned of Risë's marriage, her own ended abruptly when her husband, Dr. Otto Krause, died on January 22nd, while she was on tour. Arriving too late to be at his bedside, the bereaved soprano lost the person who it was said helped make her the artist she became. It was a serious blow to Lehmann but trouper that she was, she canceled only one performance, *Der Rosenkavalier*, on January 25th. Grete Stückgold agreed to substitute and met with modest success but according to the *World Telegram*'s Louis Biancoli, "Risë Stevens and Emanuel List towered over the others in dramatic resourcefulness." [2] This performance even elicited a kind word for Risë from the *Sun*'s critic, Irving Kolodin (who would prove to be naggingly unsympathetic to her later on) when he termed her Octavian "charming." [3]

One of the greatest influences on Risë at this early stage

of her career was Mrs. August Belmont who instilled in her the self-confidence needed to succeed. Mrs. Belmont, née Eleanor Robson, was the widow of one of the richest men in the world. Already sixty years of age when she first met the rapidly rising young star of the Metropolitan, British born Robson, at one time an internationally acclaimed actress, had been the toast of New York and London. In spite of her stature in the theater, she chose to retire when she married financier and entrepreneur, August Belmont, Jr. in 1910. Twenty-six years her senior, widowed with grown children, he was one of the most pursued bachelors in the New York social set. As the second Mrs. Belmont, she became mistress of his vast estates and a loving stepmother to his children. Through him, Eleanor Robson was to learn to appreciate opera and horses - two passions of his which remained with her for life. What was a perfect marriage ended with his death in 1924, leaving his widow in the enviable position of being an heir to a sizable fortune. Not content with a life of ease, she championed causes, unemployment relief and the Red Cross, among others. In 1933, she became the first woman to be appointed to the Board of Directors of the Metropolitan Opera and in 1935, she founded the Metropolitan Opera Guild. Her love for children prompted her to inaugurate student matinees of opera and a concern for young performers prompted her in 1952 to establish the Metropolitan Opera National Council.

Mrs. Belmont, as she was always addressed, saw in Risë the potential for a very glamorous career. She had the voice and looks that would carry her far but she noticed as well that she lacked ease in social situations. Her observation was correct since Risë was afflicted with a great self-consciousness, not on stage, but rather in a room of people. Through the years, Walter helped bolster her confidence by deliberately getting her to circulate among other guests at a gathering. He saw it as playing a role, a method that helped him disguise his own innate shyness. In turn, Mrs. Belmont invited Risë to functions that introduced her to many of society's most prominent people. At the closing luncheon of the Metropolitan Opera Guild's membership campaign held in the Plaza, for example, the January 18th issue of the *New York Times* pictured Risë seated at a table between Mrs. Cornelius Vanderbilt and Mrs. Belmont. The Colony Club served as another excellent training ground for developing Risë's feeling of ease in social settings. The membership was limited to woman of money and social standing but Mrs. Belmont insisted that she be allowed in as a guest.

Die Walküre on January 26th unveiled Risë's Fricka to the Metropolitan Opera. Amid an assembly of seasoned Wagnerians, she found herself in the thick of a forest of voices. As for the conductor, Erich Leinsdorf, she knew him from Salzburg. During the summers of 1935 and 1936, the two years Risë was there, Leinsdorf was in residence also. He was an eligible bachelor and Risë was unattached, so it was natural that well-meaning friends tried to match them up - unsuccessfully as it turned out. Risë was not interested and refused when he asked for a date. Always the perfectionist, Leinsdorf could couple his excellent musicianship with a petty disregard for someone's feelings. In general, he was admired, but not loved, by those with whom he came in contact.

The reception for Risë's two Wagnerian heroines was decidedly mixed and played a crucial part in her coming to terms with keeping Wagner in her repertory. Lawrence Gilman thought that "this role [Erda] is not yet for Miss Stevens, who sang very creditably indeed but who did not quite suggest the immensities and eternities and who left one with the uneasy suspicion that she was about to deliver gracefully to Wotan a shining silver rose." [4] Oscar Thompson felt that "[she] sang warmly and by no means inexpressively. But the music demands a heavier and more completely settled voice. In its present estate, hers is a lyric organ." [5] He brought out an important point, "The personal charms which have played no trivial part in the young American contralto's current successes as Mignon and Octavian, were of no avail to her in the semi-darkness that surrounds the prophetess."[6]

That Fricka in *Die Walküre* on February 17th did not fare much better was exemplified by Gilman's feeling that she was "unprofitably employed." [7] Oscar Thompson again offered the most accurate evaluation when he declared "[she] sang some of her music quite well...but the voice was hard driven to achieve the sonorities required of it and, though she acted the part intelligently, there was missing that sense of authority and conviction which may be expected of her Fricka five or ten years hence." [8] He reiterated that hers was essentially a lyric voice, an observation that Pitts Sanborn reinforced, "[she] grappled intelligently and painstakingly with a task that overweighted her." [9]

Risë's first season with the Metropolitan Opera ended on March 4th with a *Siegfried* Erda. On the 18th, the *New Yorker* summed up her accomplishments, "I don't know how to catalogue Miss Risé [sic]Stevens...because she sang in both French and German operas. In "Mignon" and "Der Rosenkavalier" she proved to be a superb young singing actress, so perhaps she doesn't need cataloguing." [10] The critic, Robert A. Simon, omitted all mention of Wagner and soon Risë would do the same.

Ever mindful of the uphill struggle Bud was having in making his way, Risë offered him the opportunity to be her personal assistant and secretary soon after her debut. By this time, Bud also had changed his name to Stevens to conform with his sister's. He was performing his duties capably until the February 16th matinee of *Die Walküre* when he neglected to check the starting time of the opera. *Die Walküre* on January 26th, Risë's first, was also a matinee but the starting time was 1:45. The second matinee on February 16th was to begin at 1 o'clock. Risë's entrance as Fricka did not come until the second act and thinking that the opera started the same time as the previous one, he did not get her to the theater until the second act was to start. When they arrived at the stage door, Johnson and his assistants were nervously waiting on the street for her. One minute more and an announcement would have to be made that her cover would sing leaving Risë's future with the Metropolitan seriously compromised. As soon as she arrived, the downbeat for act two was given and Jenny Cervini, the wardrobe mistress, sped her to her dressing room where she got Risë into her costume in record time. Some makeup was applied, a wig hastily fastened and she was escorted from her dressing room to the stage for her confrontation with Wotan with no time to spare. As much as it pained her, Bud could not continue as her assistant. He returned to being a salesman until he entered the army after America went to war.

Chapter 3

On March 2ⁿᵈ, Schoen-René wrote Dean Hutcheson, "I express my great admiration and thanks for the wonderful diplomatic way you settled the dispute with Risë: Perhaps the enclosed kind letter from Mr. Carl Ebert (Agent for Glyndebourne) will interest you." [1]

The letter, dated February 15ᵗʰ, and addressed to Eric "Semon"* at his Riverside Drive apartment, was in connection with Risë appearing at Glyndebourne that summer,

> ...I would not have you think that I want Miss Stevens at Glyndebourne, no matter what. Glyndebourne has managed very well without her until now, and no doubt will suffer no great harm without her in the future. But I cannot believe that a young artist would actually pass this opportunity by...She belongs at Glyndebourne. She cannot be blamed if she does not know this. But _you_ must know it...and now you must do all that is possible to provide her with a new and perhaps decisive artistic experience. Let us be honest: the excuse of lack of time for study does not make sense. If what I say is rightly understood, then Miss Stevens will reduce her other obligations, and be prepared to discuss with us whether perhaps Fiordiligi would be more suitable to her than Dorabella. On the basis of the impression that [she] made on me in New York, and which I relayed to Dr. Busch,

---

*Simon changed his name to Semon when he settled in America in 1939. In this publication, he will continue to be called Simon.

we are definitely prepared to concentrate on this young woman. If, however, she insists on declining our offer, than I must underline Mr. Bing's words, that a later engagement is unlikely to be sought from our side..." [2]

Risë was aware that Rudolf Bing had observed one of her rehearsals in Prague. She did not know, however, that he was in the audience for one of her Metropolitan performances before recommending her for Glyndebourne. Bing and Ebert quite probably saw Risë in *Der Rosenkavalier* on the 25th, the one without Lehmann, and Bing cabled to Christie that they had found an excellent prospect for *Così* and *Nozze*. Christie was delighted to learn that not only was Risë talented but that she was attractive besides. Looks were a prime requisite as far as Christie was concerned. That Risë was cool at first to the offer is understandable since while she knew Cherubino in German she would have to relearn it in English with the knowledge that she would never use that version anywhere else. As for her consenting to sing Fiordeligi, it was out of the question. Both Ebert and Bing may have heard soprano overtones in Risë's voice but more to the point, she did not. Dorabella would be a totally new role and for the past two years, she had built an entire repertory from scratch. Adding another role so soon was a daunting factor in considering the offer.

Rudolf Bing was not about to lose her without a fight. On February 13th, in a three page letter to Eric Simon, he expressed virtually the same sentiments as Ebert but stressed that Risë's reluctance to sign a contract was more a question of fees than overwork. In January when she was first apprised of their interest, she asked for a fee of £525 with all other obligations borne by her. On February 7th, Bing cabled and made a definite offer of £515. Risë accepted on the 8th of February with a new condition that they should pay the tax. Bing made a counter offer that they would pay L30 towards traveling expenses that would be £20 more than originally offered. It is then that Risë refused blaming too tight a schedule for learning a new part. Bing intimated that should she go back on her agreeing to sing in Glyndebourne, Christie would see to it that future permits to appear anywhere else in England would be denied. The entire game of negotiating a proper fee indicated that she now knew what she was worth. That Bing did not appreciate it was not surprising.

On the 20th, Risë took matters into her own hands and wrote to Christie, himself, telling him of the amount of pressure that had been on her and the preparations she had to make for her return to the Metropolitan the next season. She hoped that her refusal to sing at Glyndebourne at this time would not lead to recriminations on their part.

It is at this point that Dean Hutcheson was asked by Schoen-René to persuade Risë to reconsider since Christie was too powerful a presence in the music world to cross. On February 20th, a much-relieved Simon wired Bing that Risë would accept the offer of L550 thereby insuring her participation in the Festival. Either Simon or Hutchinson must have convinced Risë that Ebert's statement about Bing's not being in the habit of taking kindly to rejected offers was entirely true. Ever the martinet, he would take it as a personal slight that someone who was just starting out would question his judgment. In spite of Ebert's dominance in Glyndebourne, it was Bing who actually controlled the business end of the Festival. It was Ebert who wrote the letter but it was Bing's feelings that were conveyed. Risë consented to the engagement to sing both Cherubino and Dorabella thereby, not only taking an important step in her career, but also making a positive impression on her future Metropolitan Opera boss. When Bing took over for Edward Johnson and was faced with decisions on who would remain on or be dropped from the roster, there was never a question that Risë would not be re-engaged. Risë accompanied by Walter left for Glyndebourne for what would be a vacation for him and work as usual for her. However, Walter, who had no intention of being a burden to Risë's financial situation, succeeded in obtaining a fall engagement with a fledgling German Theater in Buenos Aires.

1939 was the sixth season for the Glyndebourne festival, the last for seven years. The festival took place in the manor house on John Christie's estate in Sussex and was the brain-child of both him and his wife, soprano, Audrey Mildmay. Critics of the venture thought it to be an expensive showcase for Mildmay and while she was a featured artist, she never placed herself over the ensemble. Her artistry and astute business sense proved to be a significant factor in the success of the venture. Christie, a non-musician, originally envisioned dedicating the festival to the operas of Richard Wagner, structuring it along the lines of Bayreuth. With an increasing unpopularity of things German coupled with the realization that the theater would seat no more than three hundred eleven and the orchestra pit under forty players comfortably, all thoughts of Wagner were set aside.

Reinforcing the move away from Wagner and the adoption of Mozart as the patron saint was the engagement of Fritz Busch as Music Director, chief conductor, and Mozart proselytizer. Carl Ebert, like Busch another refugee from Hitler and former General Manager of the Berlin State Opera, was engaged as Producer. This left an opening for someone who was skilled in contracting singers and in Rudolf Bing, Christie found the right man. An Austrian of Jewish background, Bing was a known quantity to Ebert whose assistant he was in Berlin. Appointed in 1933, by 1935 he was made General Manager of the festival and he soon became a formidable presence in the international music scene.

Le Nozze di Figaro was the first opera presented at Glyndebourne in 1934 and with a nostalgic nod to the past, the 1939 season was to open with it as well. The theater by then had been expanded to accommodate a larger audience. On June 1, "Sussex was showing the greenery of it's spring dress,"[3] according to one observer and "In the brilliant sunshine some five-hundred people most of whom must have changed into evening dress within an hour of lunch met for the opening of the Glyndebourne Opera." [4]

Risë and the Icelandic soprano, Maria Markan were the Cherubino and Countess of *Le Nozze di Figaro*. Of the two, it was Risë who took top honors and was accepted immediately as an equal to the veterans Mariano Stabile, John Brownlee and Audrey Mildmay. With Dowager Queen Mary in attendance, the opening was a unique experience for Risë and the reviews the next day made her initial reluctance to accept the engagement totally irrelevant. "Real 'find' at Glyndebourne" [5] trumpeted a headline in the *Daily Mail* which termed her "quite a discovery." [6] The *Evening News* felt she had, "one of the best voices in the company." [7]

The negative comments were few and, at their worst, nit-picking: the *Glasgow Herald*, "Her special gifts are mischief, a face brimful of laughing intelligence and a generous singing capacity that almost broke the bonds of 'Non so piu' and 'Voi che sapete'. Perhaps it did and lost a mark." [8] The *Southern Weekday News* summed up the opening night proceedings, "With Mr. Fritz Busch as conductor and Mr. Carl Ebert as producer, 'The Marriage of Figaro' ran very smoothly and sweetly. The cast was quite a League of Nations since it comprised English, Scottish, Welsh, Australian, American, Austrian-Italian and Icelandic artists. If such perfect accord as they maintained could be seen on the political stage, how happy we should be!" [9]

Christie and Mildmay were both politically naive and kept up relations with the German musical hierarchy almost until bombs were exploding around them. Glyndebourne, itself, was in danger of being commandeered as a safe haven for children should the Germans attack and eventually the theater was used for that purpose when war broke out in earnest.

Così Fan Tutte entered the repertory on June 20th and introduced Risë's Dorabella. The *Sketch* described the opening, "Autocrat Mr. Christie has certainly got all musical London in good order about attending Glyndebourne...Opera 'fans' who went to the first night of 'Così Fan Tutte' this season left London in a downpour of tropical intensity, but were all gotten up in evening frocks, velvet cloaks, and silver or gold shoes. Tiaras, however, were not worn. Courage was rewarded by a splendid performance, and sunshine in the interval." [10]

Although she was not to sing the role ever again after her seventh and final performance of *Così* on July 15th, Risë's reviews were even better than for Cherubino. Richard Capell was the epitome of Anglo-tact when he stated, "To praise the 1939 Dorabella as she merits would involve something like ingratitude to her charming predecessor [Luise Helletsgruber]. Yet it must be said that the new American is the superior singer, while a no less sympathetic Dorabella. The impression made by her Cherubino was confirmed: she is an artist to meet the searching requirements of the Glyndebourne stage." [11]

Risë's stay at Glyndebourne came to an end on July 15th with the final Dorabella. The management could not have been more pleased with the outcome of her engagement and when she said good-bye she did so with a contract for the 1940 season. *Carmen* was to receive its Glyndebourne premiere in a production directed by Ebert, conducted by Busch with Risë in the part she had put aside after her Prague performances. No other details of the production were announced but as it turned out the outbreak of war shut Glyndebourne for the duration. The long-term effect on Risë, however, was that while at the Metropolitan, although Bing no longer thought of her in terms of Mozart, he made good on his Glyndebourne offer by casting her as Carmen in a production which was to be one of the highlights of his tenure and a personal triumph for her.

Risë's second season at the *Teatro Colón* was not until September when she would again appear as Octavian and in addition, Orfeo. Rose Pauly would replace Anni Konetzni as the Marschallin and it was said of Pauly by her detractors

that she was convinced that Octavian and the Marschallin
were not lovers. She would prove to be the worst Marschallin
Risë ever appeared with since she hadn't a clue as to what the
opera was about. Erich Kleiber would again conduct both
Der Rosenkavalier and *Orfeo ed Euridice* and as he did with
the Strauss he reviewed every note of the Gluck score with
her. Orfeo was a constant in her career from Juilliard to Prague
to Buenos Aires and, therefore, did not pose any difficulties
for her. The most obvious pitfall (as with Mignon) since she
had learned it in three languages (fortunately, French not being
one of them since French soprano Janine Micheau, the Sophie,
was singing in her native language) was inadvertently slip-
ping into the wrong one. The inevitable did happen once when
to Kleibar's astonishment instead of hearing "Che farò senza
Euridice", he heard "Ach ich habe sie verloren," but her immediate switching to the Italian didn't make him look any
less aghast.

Both roles were received with rapturous praise from the
critics with Octavian singled out for, "the shining beauty of
her voice, the polish of her musicality, her expressiveness and
command so much so that she made of her elegant Octavian
a creation of rare importance." [12] As for the Gluck, "[she]
brought to life the grief stricken Orfeo. It is difficult to imagine a greater psychological and musical command of the role;
a voice more expressive, a purer style and emotion more sincere." [13]

Risë's *Colón* contract called for five performances of
Octavian and three of Orfeo. Her last appearance was for
the 15th of October, and she was scheduled to report to the
Metropolitan on November 13th. With the Met approval,
however, that date was given over to her first professional
recital. On Walter's advice, she did not follow the traditional
route for many artists of making a recital debut in New York's
Town Hall. He felt she did not need the added strain of the
New York critics waiting to pounce on any false steps or mis-
calculations. Even after her career was at its height, he dis-

couraged her from Town Hall recitals fearing over exposure. More to the point, a recital debut out of town would enable her to shape a program, make mistakes, become used to the ritual of recital-giving away from home (similar to what she had done by launching her opera career in Prague).

The chosen city, Youngstown, Ohio, a regular stop on the Community Concert circuit, was not mainstream and perfect as a starting point. Risë arrived in New York from South America on the 10th and left for Youngstown on the 12th. With a very modest pre-performance admission to being a bit worried that everything would turn out all right, she embarked on the first of hundreds of recitals and concerts which covered the four corners of America and Canada in a span of twenty-five years. She had nothing to be concerned about since she beguiled both audience and critics alike. "[Her] voice is not large, but rather soft and of lovely quality with rich low tones and well-controlled high ones ...the combination of an attractive personality, a lovely voice, and attractive style, makes her a very successful recitalist." [14]

A special treat was in store for Risë on December 29th when *Der Rosenkavalier* reunited her Octavian with Harriet Henders' Sophie. This was Harriet's one and only performance with the Metropolitan Opera, her contract having been signed just three weeks earlier for an unspecified role. In spite of what were generally good reviews, she did not return. Vocal size compared with the repertory she developed abroad did not make for an ideal match in the Metropolitan. Also, she was in competition with younger singers, Eleanor Steber, Nadine Connor, Marita Farell, who were coming into their own. It was a bit too late to start over. Her career never took off in America as Risë's was beginning to do and the war put an end to returning to Europe. That the reunion of the "two American girls" was a joyful one was to be expected. What Harriet thought of Risë marrying Walter remained unsaid but she saw that Risë was exceedingly content in her new life. Harriet recognized that she was not to have the same good fortune and when the opportunity presented itself, she married and gave up her career. Harriet died in 1972 from injuries sustained in an automobile accident. With her death, a memorable part of Risë's past died also.

On the whole, the season did not offer much in the way of new assignments. Fricka, in *Die Walküre* was greeted with not much better critical reaction than the year before. Oscar Thompson still thought the role too heavy for her and with the availability of Thorborg and Branzell, he wondered why they did not give Risë roles better suited to her basically lyric instrument. Some thought she acted well but noticed spreading of tone in the upper register. While others, for example, Samuel Chotzinoff, thought, "...she was an impressive Fricka, moderate in gesture and reasonable rather than shrewish."[15] Problematically, her second season was basically a repeat of the first, three Mignons, four Octavians in the house and two on tour, two Frickas and two concerts. The one novelty was Cherubino in a major revival of *Le Nozze di Figaro,* not heard at the Metropolitan since the 1917-1918 season when Geraldine Farrar was the lovesick Page.

At this point Walter began to take more of an interest in the workings of Risë's career. He was of the "wait and see" school, that is, he told Risë they would not reject any offer out of hand but rather bargain a secondary role against a starring part. The phrase, "Speak to Walter about it", became a mantra whenever business was discussed. Whereas she would dismiss a list of suggested roles making known her displeasure then and there, Walter would take the list home and study it with her. They would discuss those which would be rejected outright, others which might be considered if a better role would balance it and still others which she wanted to do but were not offered. Wagner was definitely out and her January 19th *Die Walküre* was her last appearance in Wagner with the Metropolitan Opera. Other roles, Laura in *La Gioconda* and Marina in *Boris Godunov*, were agreed upon but balanced against Dalila and Carmen.

Risë always thought of her career in terms of opera. Walter, who was not particularly taken with it, began his program of what he called "stretching". The impression remains that he would rather have had Risë devote her time to other forms of entertainment. That very term was a sticking point between them since she did not consider herself an "entertainer". Her training was for opera and even if, early on, she had leanings toward the Broadway stage, opera was now the focal point of her life. She could have said "no" to Walter's plan for making her known outside the confines of that milicu but two people whose opinions she valued as much as his, Schoen-René and Mrs. Belmont, were also in favor of the idea.

Stretching was not a novel concept since some of the biggest names in opera both at that time and earlier did not confine themselves to opera alone. Enrico Caruso recorded semi-classical and popular music ("Over there" was an all time hit), made films (*My American Cousin*, a resounding flop so bad that his next film, *The Splendid Romance*, was never released) and lent his name and face to advertisements as well. Rosa Ponselle who got her start in Vaudeville tried to get into films after she secured a career in opera but all interest in her evaporated when she demanded too high a price. Geraldine Farrar, Mary Garden and Lawrence Tibbett went before the cameras with varying success but no staying power.

Tibbett became better known on radio, as did Gladys Swarthout who was termed the "former" opera singer in the newspapers because of her extended stays in Hollywood but her films did not cause a ripple. Lily Pons was able to transfer her Gallic charm to the screen but none of her films, though pleasant, were memorable. Grace Moore started out as an acclaimed entertainer on the Broadway and London's West End stages but yearned to sing opera. *One Night of Love* was a huge success and could have been the basis for a film career but opera was her siren's call for better or worse. What Walter had in mind was to make Risë's name equally as known outside the confines of the opera house. On her own, she would never have attempted it nor wanted it, at least the Hollywood part of it.

The 1939-40 season was well under way when on February 20th, Mozart's *Le Nozze di Figaro* was revived after twenty-two years. For Risë it meant once again learning a role in Italian which she already knew in German and English but her efforts did not go unnoticed. According to Francis D. Perkins, she interpreted Cherubino with "emotion and vitality." [16] and Grena Bennett described her as "luscious-voiced...with sly humor." [17]

This was the only Cherubino Risë had on her schedule and with it her New York season came to an end. She was to participate in the spring tour but for only two performances of *Der Rosenkavalier*. The first, a premiere for Baltimore, on March 26th, with Lehmann and List and the second in Boston, on the 28th, with Lehmann and Kipnis. Baltimore's Lyric Theater was sold out well in advance. "Yet for all its wizardry of melody, one remembers more deeply than perhaps anything else in the opera the pathos of the aging princess. More than good singing is required to bring this role alive, and Lotte Lehmann gave the kind of performance last night that has made her interpretation of the part legendary...The audience could hardly have anticipated the glorious vocalism revealed by Risë Stevens...In addition to her vocal powers, [she] has great beauty and a personality that carries with brilliance and warmth across the footlights." [18]

Boston was no less responsive to *Der Rosenkavalier* where it opened a ten-day visit. Seen two years previously, the 1937-1938 cast included Lehmann and List with Grete Stückgold as Octavian. Lehmann was again the Marschallin but Alexander Kipnis replaced List and was "thoroughly amusing." [19] Risë "looked the role of Octavian almost to perfection. Her acting was fresh and unaffected and vocally she was equal to the demands of her role." [20]

Chapter 4

More exciting prospects awaited Risë outside of the Metropolitan since during the next five years, she was offered only one new role, Dalila. Otherwise, there were repetitions of Cherubino, Octavian and Mignon, a situation that would come to a head at the close of the 1942-1943 season. For the moment, solo appearances began to play an important part and kept her commuting back and forth between the opera house and recital dates. Beginning in February after the *Le Nozze di Figaro* performance and before rejoining the company in Baltimore, Risë traveled to York, Pennsylvania, Denton and Corsicana, Texas, Topeka, Kansas and Omaha, Nebraska, among other cities. She appeared on the radio program, "So You Think You Know Music" on March 31st after her Boston Octavian and was off again to give another series of recitals. The pattern she and Walter set for the remainder of her performing career consisted of two lengthy recital tours in a designated part of the country which was compatible with her opera, radio, film and television commitments. The number of recitals were usually kept to forty and, generally, did not keep her away from home for more than two weeks at a time.

The entire undertaking had to be carefully orchestrated since she insisted on never singing in a city on the same day of her arrival. Usually she would arrive by train or plane and be met by local sponsors of the recital and the press. After having once made an unfortunate slip by stating she was thrilled to be in City X when she was actually in City Y (much to the chagrin of the sponsors and her own embarrassment), Risë avoided geographical salutations altogether. An article in Little Rock, Arkansas' The *Democrat* gives a good picture of a typical Stevens' arrival in a town,

> [she] paid a brief visit to shower-drenched Little Rock this morning en route to Beaumont, Texas, where she will present a concert tomorrow night. A native of New York City, Miss Stevens apparently never has found it necessary to surround herself with the artificial glitter which is characteristic of many of her fellow actors and actresses. Attired in a coat with matching brown accessories...[and] a tan muffler drawn high about her throat to protect it from a sharp damp wind, the star...answered most questions with a 'yes' or 'no' nod of the head and referred others with a smile to her sec-retary. [1]

Walter rarely went on these tours which left her in the care of both a secretary and accompanist on the early ones and an accompanist who served in both capacities later on. The Community Concert Organization always provided first class accommodations but that was not always the case with independent sponsors. The halls in which she would appear could range from a theater to a gymnasium. The demands on her time presented added pressure and, from experience, she insisted that she be excused from certain obligations such as post-performance parties unless she had a chance to eat between them and the end of the recital. If this were not stressed, she would go hungry for the rest of the evening since eating at the reception was impossible. The hostess might not appreciate Risë's first visiting the kitchen where a meal of scrambled eggs and a glass of milk had to be waiting but it was that or no Risë. Greeting the audience after a concert was never a problem since the adrenaline was flowing and she enjoyed talking to the people who took the time to visit with her backstage. Before the performance, she insisted on remaining by herself in her hotel. Perhaps, she might take a walk but mainly she would sleep late, the music having been reviewed on the train, the hall having been checked out by her accompanist, her dress waiting to be pressed by herself, dinner around four, some vocalizing and time to leave for the auditorium.

Walter was very impressed with the manner in which Lily Pons was presented in recital. It was her custom to wear very full evening gowns, usually light in color, to be lit by a spot light which would compliment her coloring and to have a white carpet extending the length of the stage so as not to dirty the hem of her dress. This was how he felt a star should be presented and he wanted Risë to follow a similar pattern. With the exception of the carpet which she felt could be easily tripped on, she adopted the Pons' method with equal success.

A personality that carried across the footlights was the key to her prominence as a recitalist. She had audience appeal that she carried with her in all the venues of her career. The warmth, naturally built into both her singing and speaking voice, was complimented by a manner that came across as genuine whether it be in an opera house, an outdoor arena or a television screen. Her recital in Corsicana, Texas, on March 1, stressed this very point, "Before the singer had made a sound, her beauty and personality had reached across the footlights and paved the way for the enthusiastic response each number richly received." [2]

With the cancellation of the Glyndebourne season, Risë and Walter were able to leave for South America much earlier than planned setting sail on June 14th on the Uruguay. Opera News reported that "Miss Stevens spent the entire summer in Buenos Aires, sailing with Arturo Toscanini and many other distinguished musicians, who drank her birthday health at a surprise party given for her at sea by her husband..." [3] A report in Musical America, stated that she was to sing Dalila and the Ice Queen in Weinberger's, Schwanda, another Kleiber assignment, and in the *Missa Solemnis*. The Ice Queen did not materialize since the performances scheduled for October 18th and 23rd were in conflict with her San Francisco appearances. However, Fricka, Schwertleite and the Page in *Salome* were added.

The 1940 engagement in Buenos Aires began on July 23rd with the first *Samson et Dalila* of her career. She had Albert Wolff, the venerable authority of French music, to guide her through it and preside in the pit for her four performances. He was no more than a respectable conductor but his sensitivity to the long line in singing Dalila's music was in accordance with her training in *bel canto* singing. Originally engaged only for the German repertory, the worsening world conditions and the corresponding difficulty of travel for European artists, enabled Risë to try out Dalila before unveiling it at the Metropolitan later that year. Her Samson, René Maison, would repeat his role opposite her in New York and their collaboration prior to that provided them with the opportunity to experience working together.

The critics favorably received Dalila. *La Prensa* pronounced her "a Dalila of clear and dramatic profile, seductive, with temperament and abandon." [4] The *Argentinisches Tagblatt* seconded the report, "Charming in her appearance, clever and intelligent in her gestures and actions, she knew how to make the seductive heroine convincing in each movement." [5] Even though Wagner was to be excised from her repertory, she received an affirmative critique from *La Prensa* which commented that the combination of her warm and rich voice and excellent acting made for a most impressive Fricka. The August 25th performance had Risë singing both Fricka and Schwerleite. An even stranger assignment was that of the Page in *Salome* with Kleiber conducting and Marjorie Lawrence in the title role. Later on, Risë thought of herself in the role of Salome and contacted Richard Strauss to orchestrate a mezzo version for her. Strauss, who admired her and was always amenable to change (especially if it meant more residuals) agreed readily but illness intervened. At the time of his death, no work had been done and the project was relegated to "what might have been". In all probability, not doing it worked to Risë's advantage since the critics could have been unaccepting of her having tampered with *Salome*'s musical line.

On September 13, Risë wrote in a letter to Edward Ziegler,

> You must think me a fine person not writing until it's time for me to leave this place, but truthfully, we had quite a season even though I didn't sing too often, I certainly had enough rehearsals to keep me out of mischief. I am flying from Buenos Aires, Tuesday the 17th to Rio de Janeiro, and will take the S. S. Brazil there to New York. We arrive on the 30th of September. I will by all means, come in to see you before going to San Francisco. I just received a letter from...Columbia Concerts Corp. telling me that the Ford Hour and Chicago Opera were booked for me, and the only difficulty were the dates, and getting permission from both you and Mr. Johnson to get free for this time. <u>Chicago - November 30th and December 11th Ford Hour - November 3rd</u> I will see you around the first of October and we will talk it over, but would you please let Judson's know if I can get free for those dates. Everyone here wants to be remembered to you, Marjorie Lawrence, Irene Jessner, and several others, all your New York children. [6]

On the 30th, Rudolph Polk of Artists Incorporated, Risë's West Coast representative, sent the following letter to Johnson,

> I contactedRisë Stevens and discussed the entire opera situation with her. She fully realizes the many difficulties and is perfectly willing to cooperate in any way possible. She will be very happy to do Samson performances and I would appreciate your sending me the exact dates. Before leaving New York I spoke to Mr.

Saint-Leger who informed me that only eight performances had been scheduled. I hope that you will do everything possible so that Risë will be able to do the ten performances which have been contracted for. She is particularly anxious to do a broadcast of 'Rosenkavalier'. (A postscript is added), "Risë offered the suggestion that perhaps you might be interested in doing the new production of Hansel and Gretel, in English with Leinsdorf. Should you think favorably about this suggestion, please let me know immediately so Stevens may have time to study the part in English. [7]

An English language *Hänsel und Gretel* was not to be in Risë's immediate future at the Metropolitan nor was a broadcast of *Der Rosenkavalier*. Risë's essaying Dalila at the Metropolitan Opera was not settled until October, less than two months before the premier on December 6th. Last heard in the 1936-1937 season with Gertrud Wettergren and René Maison in the title roles, it was out of the repertory for a dozen years prior to that. When news of the approaching season was carried in the daily papers on October 10th, there was no mention of reviving the Saint-Saëns opera.

Four days before her debut on October 12th, the *San Francisco Chronicle* commented that "[She] is a tall young lady who boasts two small dots over the concluding 'e' in her first name; a hearty dark velvet laugh; a Hungarian husband and a figure with 'oomph'…Unbelievably modest, [she] hopes that she'll do well in San Francisco. 'I've never been here before and I hope I make a good impression.'" [8]

Cherubino, the role chosen to introduce her to the West Coast, assured an auspicious beginning. *Le Nozze di Figaro* opened the eighteenth season and due to an oversight on someone's part, the warning bells signaling the start of the opera failed to ring leaving many in the lobby when the overture started. The conductor, Erich Leinsdorf, had to start promptly since Act 2 was to be broadcast at 9:15. It was a rocky start but quickly forgotten as Mozart and Risë worked their charms.

The dean of critics, Alfred Frankenstein, praised her ability to create the illusion of an adolescent boy without losing her femininity and commented, "She is a splendid musician and her 'Voi Che Sapete' was a memorable highlight in an evening when the lights of the performance were never low." [9]

The debut was praised unanimously but her Octavian which was unveiled on the 16th gave San Francisco a clearer idea of what the Steven's appeal was all about. "'Rosenkavalier' was probably written before Miss Stevens was born, yet one suspects that Richard Strauss and Hugo von Hofmannsthal ideally envisioned an Octavian precisely like hers." [10]

On the 16th, Edward Johnson also sent a wire to Risë, who was in San Francisco, "Following our conversation and your urgent request have succeeded placing Samson into repertoire provided you can sing Dalila and Octavian on successive nights in opening week of season." [11]

Risë responded, "Dalila thrilling. Can certainly sing successive nights. But would be obliged if you could possibly arrange to have a day come between but if impossible arrange Dalila before Rosenkavalier." [12]

A longer letter from Johnson followed on the 21st, Thank you a thousand times...for your enthusiastic cooperation. If possible, we will arrange that Dalila will come before Rosenkavalier; but, unfortunately...it may be impossible to arrange a day between the two performances. However, I feel certain that you have sung them both so often with such outstanding success, the close proximity of the two performances will not jeopardize the great favor you now hold with the great Metropolitan Opera public...We are all happy at the success you are having in San Francisco. [13]

As it turned out, Risë did have to perform Dalila and Octavian back to back which was asking a great deal of her and contrary to what Johnson said, she did not have that much experience with Dalila.

Chapter 5

Hollywood was still the "dream factory" and opera singers were tirelessly wending their way to the fabled city with very little success. Walter, who had appeared in several films in Europe, the 1939 *Hotel Sacher,* for one, was fascinated with the medium and looked upon Hollywood as a mecca. Under different circumstances, he would have wanted to be contracted to an American film studio, but ever mindful of promoting Risë's career, he dreamed that dream for her instead. He recognized the importance of film stars in the imagination of the general public. Opera was rarefied and no matter if Risë made the best dressed list for opera singers (which she did in 1941 under his careful tutelage) or gave advice on cold prevention, cookie baking or choosing the right hair style, her reputation was not as universal as he would have liked. Her name had to be a household word, her face recognizable in an instant, her voice singing popular melodies that the man on the street knew. With this in mind and very aware of happenings in Hollywood, he took action when it was rumored that Nelson Eddy was splitting up with his accustomed movie partner, Jeanette MacDonald. MacDonald had aspirations of being an opera singer with a voice that, while ideally suited for films, would prove to be no great addition to the opera scene. Eddy needed and was actively searching for her replacement and that is all Walter had to hear. Choosing photographs of Risë (one taken of her dressed in a stylish "at home" outfit and another of her with her mascots, good luck tokens, to highlight her "girl next door" side), he sent them to *Musical America*, a magazine read by nearly all of those in the classical music field. When Eddy saw the photographs he asked his agent at Columbia Artists, Calvin M. Franklin, to find out more about her. As if luck again played a hand, he was Risë's representative as well.

Franklin entered Risë's life after she had a very serious falling out with Arthur Judson over a condition in her contract that he was renegotiating. Her dissatisfaction did not sit well with him and her future with Columbia Artists could have been jeopardized had not Franklin stepped in. He agreed to manage her and it was he who negotiated her contract with M. G. M. in 1940 for *The Chocolate Soldier*, one year before he died at age fifty-four. Under Walter's skillful management, the "Hollywood era" would see changes in her professional life. The long-standing practice of paying a percentage of fees received for bookings other than concerts to Columbia Management was ended. With Risë's burgeoning career in radio, this amounted to a substantial sum. Also, Eric Simon was dropped after the first year of Risë's Metropolitan Opera debut and Walter began to assume his responsibilities in guiding her career. They were not particularly proud of the latter since Simon had been one of her first supporters but financially it was a sound move.

Before a Hollywood contract was signed, the strong reviews for her Octavian and first hand accounts by M.G.M. executives who had seen her added fuel to Eddy's entreaties that she be invited to make a screen test. The question was whether Risë was interested and in all probability while the idea was exciting, the actuality of the notion, Risë Stevens, Movie Star, did not overly impress her. In an interview for the *New York Post*, Irene Thirer learned from Risë her true feelings about taking a screen test, "I had nothing to lose...so I gladly did [it], really never dreaming anything would come of it. I'm certainly not the glamour girl type. I devoted my life to singing...I've never had any desire to go into pictures-although they are my greatest source of entertainment and relaxation. That Hollywood wants me still amazes me." [1]

Her contract in San Francisco finished with the matinee of *Der Rosenkavalier* on the 27th. She had the singular distinction of creating the role of Octavian there and it was fitting that she left content with the realization that she had made a unique contribution to its performance history. In addition, in Arthur Fried's summation of the season, he named Risë, Jussi Björling and Robert Weede as having made the most memorable debuts.

Another important debut was to take place for her on the 30th of November. *Der Rosenkavalier* was again to be her calling card, this time, in Chicago but as a result of a cold caught on route to her engagement which left her temporarily voiceless, it was postponed. Seeing that there was no chance of her keeping the engagement, she left for New York to rest before reporting for rehearsals at the Metropolitan. Her 1940-41 contract, that was the final year of her three-year contract, was renewed in May. Her salary was three hundred dollars per week for a period beginning December 2nd and ending January 26th with the option to renew it at the same rate. In August, a contract was signed for the same amount per week but commencing on December 2nd which enabled her to accept a Chicago engagement as well as prolong her recital tour. A more significant item was agreed upon in February of 1941 when her contract was renewed through April 14th but not on a per week pay schedule as was originally stated. She would now be paid two hundred dollars per performance which was a vote of confidence in her by the management.

A vote of no confidence in American culture was voiced by Zinka Milanov, Risë's colleague from Prague and South America, who was scheduled to sing Amelia in *Un Ballo in Maschera* on opening night of the season. When interviewed prior to the opening, the Croatian soprano pinpointed a major difference between the audiences of North and South America to the reporter of the *World Telegram*, "In South America an opera star is everything. Here it is a movie star." [2] It was this attitude which was soon to play an important part in Risë's life. Before Hollywood, however, there was the matter of introducing a new role in New York, one that carried with it a number of pitfalls.

Samson et Dalila is more oratorio than opera, basically, a static work which depends on arias and set scenes to advance the plot rather than dramatic situation. The singer who portrays Dalila must possess a voice that can convey the sensuous and fanatical side of her nature as well as physical allure. The criticism leveled against Bruna Castagna, Risë's immediate predecessor in the part, was that her Dalila was a thinly veiled Carmen. No two characters could be farther apart since the operatic Dalila is a fundamentalist priestess politically motivated and Carmen, as portrayed by Bizet, an amoral hedonist who takes pleasure where she will.

With the resounding success of San Francisco still fresh in her mind, Risë was not prepared for the mostly negative reviews her Dalila received by the New York press. Faced with the difficulties of bringing this part to life only a few times before, she had not found as yet the core of the role. Unlike Octavian, it was not a characterization that had been developed from the inside out but much thought had gone into it.

Judging from an interview in the *New York Post* two days before she debuted in the part, there was more interest in the look of the character she would portray than on musical values, "In the first act she wears a green brassiere and that is all except a short, short chiffon skirt. In the second act, she wears red silk and net. In the third act she wears gold lame, metal cloth." [3] The person speaking was Walter and he was dealing in some good old-fashioned showmanship of whetting the public's appetite. Her Dalila would be pure Hollywood as far as appearance was concerned. The morning after the performance, the critics, some intrigued by the visual effect, some disturbed by the vocal state, had as much to comment on the former as the latter, "she is said to be just out from a long illness, which would account for vocal weakness, but not for the eccentricities of dress, undress and deportment." [4]; "Miss Steven's Dalila gave ample reason from a visual point of view for the relative brevity of Samson's resistance to temptation...the higher notes fared best, but sometimes lacked focus while the lower register seemed occasionally muffled...the impersonation as a whole lacked the conviction which marks her Octavian or her Mignon." [5]

Olin Downes, however, was one critic who was willing to overlook vocal shortcomings as Dalila in view of her acting abilities in bringing the role to life. Lotte Lehmann's brother, Fritz, who was an actor and stage director, remarked on this aspect of Risë's artistry as well, "Look at the Metropolitan. There is my sister, there is Melchior, there is Lily Pons, there is Tibbett, there is Pinza, there is Risë Stevens. How many did I mention? Six! Six singers who are singing actors and that is all. The others are just opera singers." [6]

In an article in the *Morning Telegraph* which appeared after her debut as Dalila, Risë said, "there is a strong trend to good looks and acting ability in the opera, that opera is beginning to understand showmanship." [7] The article went on to extol her visual appeal, "[she is] the first American in 22 years to sing the role of the temptress, Delilah, at the Metropolitan Opera House [and] is the first American singer in that time to be equipped for the role of the temptress...[her] figure and face rank her with Mary Garden, Geraldine Farrar and Jeritza among the beauties of opera history." [8] The article called Risë "an accomplished actress, coached severely by her actor-husband." [9]

Walter had taken charge of this aspect of Risë's career as well as the managerial side. As her husband he knew that on the day of a performance she was moody and lost her temper easily. Everyone at home knew it was best to keep out of her way. On stage, she had little patience with non-professional behavior and cast members knew not to get in her way. Tension was at its highest when she first made an entrance and, always wanting to be her best, she was very nervous up to the point the voice came. Satisfied that it was working, her performance would come into focus. She entered the life of the character she was portraying and another mood took hold of her. During intermissions, she preferred to keep to herself, yet, she appreciated Walter's visits to her dressing room. He was her harshest critic and would sit out front evaluating every gesture. As an actor, he was able to tell her if she was in the role or merely standing beside it, never mentioning her singing since he was not a musician. After the final curtain, the role would stay with her through the night. The next day, she would ask Walter, "How was it?" He would ask her how she felt about it. They would talk it over.

With Dalila, they had a great deal to discuss. Only her acting had been termed successful. She had been ill with a heavy cold, as some of the critics took into account, and coupled with the stress of essaying a new role, she could not give it her all. In addition, she was scheduled to appear the next evening in the demanding *Der Rosenkavalier* singing opposite a new Marschallin, Maria Hussa, for the first time, and a new Sophie, Eleanor Steber. Under those circumstances, it is she who might have had to carry the performance. Hussa was called in at the last minute to replace an ailing Lehmann and would sing her one and only Metropolitan Opera performance. Steber, whose debut this would be, was the recipient of a contract with the Metropolitan Opera as a result of winning the auditions in 1940. In all probability, Risë was saving her voice for the more difficult of the two assignments. The next day's reviews could not have been better and gave no hint of even passing vocal problems, "Risë Stevens' Octavian was as it always is, beautifully sung." [10]

* * * *

Franklin Delano Roosevelt's third term in office that began in January of 1941, coincided with America's total involvement in the war that was being waged in Europe. Events came to a head with the attack on Pearl Harbor on December 7, 1941 and for the next four years, the entire nation was galvanized through a determination to defeat the Axis powers. In spite of the darkness enveloping the world, a gala evening in honor of the newly reelected President was announced with Risë included among the celebrities scheduled to appear. Her recently signed M. G. M. contract (reputed to be fifty thousand dollars per film) gave her the credentials to be invited to participate in an event of this importance.

A capacity crowd of close to four thousand people braved the wind swept chill of a January night to assemble in Constitution Hall for the occasion and,

> sang 'The Star Spangled Banner' with whatever excuse they had in their hearts. Nelson Eddy sang it and so did wonder boy Mickey Rooney and pretty Risë Stevens of the Metropolitan Opera: so did three generations of the Roosevelt family and the four colored singers and guitarist of the Golden Gate Quartet and little white haired Charlie Chaplin and Ethel Barrymore and Vice President Wallace and so did a lot of ermined celebrities in the boxes and a lot of just people who managed to scrape up the expensive tariff for seats in the gallery. [11]

Hans Kindler conducted the National Symphony and after the Orchestra played Frescobaldi's "Toccata", Risë walked out on the stage and captivated the audience immediately. Introduced by Douglas Fairbanks, she, "set the pace of the evening by winning an ovation in 'La Habañera'and 'My Hero', with full orchestral accompaniment. The thunder of applause never gained appreciably in volume after that, nor did it ever recede." [12]

Later in the year, Dalila returned on December 3rd and so did a venomous review from the *Herald Tribune*'s, Jerome D. Bohm, who was not about to be swayed by Risë's much touted acting abilities, "her voice remains inadequate to express the

various facets of the music. It has not, to begin with, sufficient volume to be heard above the orchestra for a good part
of the opera. This is especially the case in the lower and middle
registers." [13]

* * * *

A tape of the broadcast of December 13th attests to Bohm's
contention that the basic quality of Risë's voice is antithetical
to the demands of the role. Her apparent unwillingness to
darken it by using a "chest voice" makes descents into the
lower regions of the vocal line barely audible. What saves her
vocal performance is the basic quality of the voice, itself, which
has a caressing sensuousness that overrides any shortcomings. Both Leonard Warren, the High Priest, and René
Maison, Samson, have large clarion voices as opposed to
Risë's softer grained one. Whereas Maison and Warren impress through sheer vocal power, Risë uses finely shaded tones
to give meaning to the text. A dozen years later, the March
14, 1953 broadcast of the same opera, finds Risë at the height
of her powers. There is no trouble with the lower register;
the entire vocal line from top to bottom is even. The color
has darkened slightly and judicious use of chest voice gives
added weight when needed. She is more evenly matched with
the baritonal sounding Samson of Ramon Vinay and the less
overpowering High Priest of Sigurd Björling.

* * *

February found her in the Columbia recording studios
where she made her first discs. Her contract with Columbia
was signed October 11, 1940, and ran from October 20, 1940
to October 19, 1942 with an option renewable after the first
year. The session of February 21st was devoted to songs but
these selections were released after the April "Habañera",
which is often thought to be her first recording. The 1941

sessions ended on October 6th with excerpts from *The Choco-late Soldier*, which the *Record*'s John A. O'Connor, hailed as "one of the greatest albums of light classics ever recorded." [14]

With the March 20th matinee of *Nozze* her New York season with the Metropolitan Opera ended. Scheduled for the spring tour, she repeated Cherubino in Baltimore, Boston and Cleveland. "Throng Hails Mozart Opera", wrote the *Baltimore News-Post*'s, Helen A. F. Penniman, "Miss Stevens' projection of the 'Voi che Sapete' stopped the show." [15] At the second stop, Boston, the audience in the Metropolitan Theatre, gave her a reception which was no less enthusiastic. Rudolf F. Elie, Jr., correspondent for the *Boston Traveler*, commented, "She was at once convincing as the boy page and was in radiant voice." [16]

While in Boston, Risë was interviewed in the Copley Plaza by Marjory Adams of the *Boston Daily Globe*,

> to the thousands of people who have never bought or owned an opera ticket in their lives and whose nearest approach to opera is over the radio, Risë is best known because she will be Nelson Eddy's new prima donna in his picture, 'Chocolate Soldier'. She is succeeding Jeanette McDonald as his singing heroine and already the film fans are up in arms. 'Who is this Risë Stevens?' they have written in the motion picture column. And why does she think she's good enough to succeed Miss MacDonald?'. [17]

During the interview, Risë stressed that "opera is still the most important part of my life then comes the concert world and movies come only third." [18] However, when a Metro-Goldwyn-Mayer press release was issued on April 8th outlining the itinerary of its newly acquired star, it left no doubt as to who was in charge of her immediate future. Risë was to leave New York on April 12th for the West Coast with stops on route for concerts and opera. On April 14th she would join the Metropolitan Opera in Cleveland and then travel to

Davenport, Iowa, for a recital on the 21st where she substituted for the American born coloratura, Lina Pagliughi, who was detained in Italy by the war. She and Walter would arrive in Los Angeles on the 24th where filming was to start at once on *The Chocolate Soldier*. The press release pointed out that Risë's contract enabled her to sing with the Metropolitan and San Francisco Operas each year.

Chapter 6

Nelson Eddy was fond of saying that he had no special contracts with M.G.M., that he did what he was told. When MacDonald wanted out of the partnership and M.G.M. was anxiously seeking a replacement for her, Eddy recommended Risë. Roy Del Ruth, who was scheduled to direct the film, respected Eddy (although he had seen for himself that Risë on stage with San Francisco Opera had a lot to offer) and a contract was drawn up. Del Ruth, the guiding hand for the two popular *Broadway Melodies* of 1936 and 1938, was one of the top directors at M.G.M and the fact that Risë had no film experience did not faze him. From the start, luck was with her since not only was she embraced by Eddy and Del Ruth but also by two of the most powerful and dangerous women in Hollywood, the columnists, Hedda Hopper and Louella O. Parsons.

In her syndicated column, Parsons gave her benediction to Risë after their very first meeting, "I had seen an earlier test of her and I was very surprised to find when I saw her face to face that she is much more attractive than I had a right to expect after seeing her in the movies." [1] She predicted that Risë would win over the many MacDonald fans that resented her.

Rather than being offended by Parsons tactless remark about her disappointing appearance on film, Risë probably agreed with her. She had been told to slim down to 125 pounds, which entailed strict dieting to take off the ten extra pounds she needed for the opera stage. When she saw the first rushes of the film, she was so upset by the way she looked that she ran out of the viewing room and was persuaded to return only after Eddy gave her his personal assurance that she photographed perfectly fine.

Not to be outdone by her rival, Hedda Hopper proved she could be equally as tactless and created a bit of a flap over an alleged comment made on a broadcast about Jeanette MacDonald trying to have Risë removed from the film and reinstating her partnership with Eddy. The report, published in *Metro-Lark* *, incited Risë's fans and prompted a letter by MacDonald to the Club in which she expressed no knowledge of Hopper's statement. She assured them of her admiration for Risë and wished both her and Eddy a great success.

Totally immersing themselves in the making and selling of *The Chocolate Soldier*, Eddy and Risë managed to ignore any adverse comments. Soon there were photographs in the newspapers of the film couple, indulging in all sorts of activities, riding a motor scooter, sharing a soda, trying on roller skates and, in general, working hard at showing what fun they were having.

Realizing that their immediate future was tied to the West Coast, Risë and Walter decided to settle in California. They rented an apartment in the Garden of Allah**, the same complex on Sunset Boulevard where F. Scott Fitzgerald had once stayed.

After *The Chocolate Soldier* was completed, they rented a house on Palm Drive next door to the director, Rouben

---

* Early in 1941, Walter gave his approval to Risë's West and East Coast fans to publish two separate journals. In California, Fran Davis presided over *First Lady of Song* which was issued biannually and ceased publication in 1945. In New York, the Risë Stevens Music Club with Mildred Popkin as acting director issued *Metro-Lark* which survived into the sixties. Risë was honorary president of both organizations and wrote a column for each.
** The Garden of Allah located at 8080 Sunset Boulevard had a colorful history. The grounds on which it stood once housed a palatial estate belonging to the actress, Alla Nazimova. Over time, the estate was turned into a hotel and the hotel into twenty-four bungalows.

Mamoulian. It was only after Risë was expecting Nicky early in 1944, that they purchased a fifteen- thousand dollar hill-top house on Woodrow Wilson Drive near Orson Wells and Rita Hayworth.

During the shooting of *The Chocolate Soldier,* Risë was assigned a bungalow on location and each day followed a strict schedule: at exactly 5 A.M. the MGM cook arrived and made a breakfast of steak, toast and coffee; next, came a makeup call and wig fitting at 6; at 7, filming began. As for the wig, a Larry of Metro-Goldwin-Mayer creation, it was worn at the insistence of Victor Saville, the producer, who was a stickler for perfection and wanted Risë's hair to look the same in every scene. Any protest on her part did not sway Saville from his decision. Meticulous to the extreme, he re-shot an entire day's work when he noticed a hair in the wig was out of place in a close up.

Louis B. Mayer had much to do with this obsession for perfection. In Neal Gabler's insightful history of the film industry's Jewish founders, *An Empire of Their Own*, he sheds light on this aspect of Mayer's persona,

> What most distinguished MGM's films was their general air of unreality. Mayer loved beauty as an aesthete did. He particularly believed, in accordance with his somewhat antiquated nineteenth-century view of women, in idealizing his female stars, and that became one of the benchmarks of the MGM look. Camera men 'had to photograph the movie queens and make them look damn good', said George Cukor. 'Louis B. Mayer was a great believer in his movie queens 'looking right'. [2]

Gabler further points out that Mayer had a deep respect for classical music and classical musicians, "it was he who brought opera stars Grace Moore, Lauritz Melchior, and, later Mario Lanza to the screen." [3] His desire to develop Risë into a movie queen was sincere but he did not count on her in-ability to warm to the medium. She missed audience participation that made her days before the camera comparable to performing in an empty theater.

Unlike opera's orderly succession of acts, the film was not shot in sequence making it difficult to develop a role. The amount of down-time while lighting angles and camera set-ups were worked out was frustrating at best but at least the music she was going to sing gave her some satisfaction. "Mon coeur s'ouvre à ta voix", "My Hero", "Sympathy" and "Chocolate Soldier", the last three from the original score by Oscar Strauss, were a plus, however, the music department opted for originality in selecting one other number for her which was needed in a scene when she is gazing out a window into the night. The *Abendstern* or "Evening star" from *Tannhäuser*, sung in the opera by a baritone (also sung by Nelson Eddy in the film), was an unusual choice but the music rescored for mezzo suited her voice and fit the mood perfectly.

* * * *

Mr. Szurovy and I are in a lovely villa in the Garden of Allah, here in Hollywood with a swimming pool almost at our doorstep. The studio is most exciting. I have had all kinds of tests made. They like the way my voice records and I enjoy hearing it in comparison to some of the recordings I have made for records. Other tests have been makeup, costume, (by the way, Adrian is going to do my wardrobe and it is more than charming) and even tests for different hair arrangements. [4]

Risë's upbeat tone for the benefit of her fans hid the fact that she wasn't overly happy. Once the thrill of starring in a film settled into the routine of making it, she was bored. Even the California lifestyle bored her, although the climate did not. Walter still did not speak English very well, a handicap socially, but they made some friends which helped to keep the hours away from the studio a little less vacuous.

Fortunately, there was not much free time since shooting a scene was an all day affair and could be stretched over two or three days if it did not go right. Quite often scenes had to be reshot since there were no rehearsals on the actual set. Run throughs for the dialogue and for the musical numbers both solos and ensembles took place in studios. The musical portions were then prerecorded and played over loud speakers so that the actors could lip-sync them during filming. Days were also filled with countless camera angles taken to make sure the actors looked perfect in close-ups; lit from all sides, the director decided which shots were used for all but the very big stars. Everyone's appearance was scrutinized carefully on the set since publicity stills by the dozens had to be taken to promote the film.

Risë learned that the art of movie making is the art of camera angles. She was told not to look directly in the camera; she was told to laugh without squinting. Costumes had to be treated very carefully to prevent wrinkling which ruled out sitting in them. The fifteen-pound bouffant dress with a hoop designed for the finale required her to lean against a board between shots to relieve the pressure on her feet.

In spite of all the exhausting work, Risë found time to dash off a letter to Edward Ziegler that put on a good front, "Talking of the picture! You must see it and let me know your reaction. I had such fun making it. Everyone worked so conscientiously, that it <u>must</u> be a successful film." [5]

The chances that it would be rested with Roy Del Ruth who was a very skilled director but in this case he was defeated before he started. M.G.M did not own the rights to the George Bernard Shaw play, *Arms and the Man*, on which Oscar Strauss' operetta, *The Chocolate Soldier*, is based but they did have Strauss' permission to use his music. Another libretto had to be found since United Artists, as a result of Gabriel Pascal's purchasing the rights to the play from Shaw, could not be persuaded to transfer them to Metro. Ferenc Molnar's *The Guardsman*, a 1924 stage vehicle for Alfred

Lunt and Lynne Fontanne, and in 1931 a film starring the fabled duo, was grafted onto the score and proved to be a poor fit. When the film was released, one reviewer thought the title should have been *The Chocolate Guardsman*. The story centers around the age-old notion that all husbands want to test their wives faithfulness and no amount of tinkering with the plot by screen writers Leonard Lee and Keith Winter could make it any less predictable.

The action takes place in Budapest and the protagonists, a show business couple, co-starring in the operetta that gives the film its title. They are famous, rich (judging by the opulent stage setting of a house they occupy) but are at one another's throats off stage mainly due to the husband's jealousy of his wife's admirers. When the husband decides to see if his wife can be lured into an affair and disguises himself as another man intent on seducing her, the film ran into a bit of trouble. In the original play, it is left ambiguous as to whether she succumbs or not. The Hollywood code forbade any hint of implied or overt adultery and it had to be made clear that the wife sees through the disguise almost immediately. She decides to teach her husband a lesson by pretending that she is giving in to the "stranger's" advances but she knows it is her husband all along.

Nelson Eddy as the husband, Karl Lang and Risë as the wife, Maria Lanyi, try their best to keep the story line afloat. They are both quite skilled in creating characters that could have been just plain foolish. Eddy turns in a performance that is less wooden than his other films and as the husband masquerading as the very unrestrained Russian basso, Vasili Vasilovich, he is totally convincing and quite funny. His rendition of, Modest Moussorgsky's, "The Flea", is one of the highlights of the film. Risë is a good match for him and brings to her role a lightness of touch that brightens the film as a whole. She reads her lines well, sings beautifully and looks lovely *a la* Hollywood, and while there may be some awkward moments before the camera, her film debut was termed a success.

When the film was released, in spite of all the uncertainties, the reviews were flattering, to Risë in particular. Kate Cameron of the *Daily News*, one of the most influential film critics of the forties and fifties, described Risë as an, "attractive addition to the screen, not only for her golden toned voice but for her very good looks as well. She is lovely, sings divinely and needs only a little more experience before the camera to be entirely at ease on the screen."[6] The Cameron review is also noteworthy in that she never mentioned Nelson Eddy's contribution (at least in some editions).

Archer Winsten of the *New York Post*, equally as influential a critic as Cameron, found the two stars appealing but the audience in the movie theater less so,

> The little gasps of joy from feminine members of the predominately female audience at the Astor Theatre prove that Nelson Eddy still has it. His clear voice rings out strong and clear and virile. Opposite him, Risë Stevens, the pride of Queens and a genuine member of the Metropolitan Opera, is equally clear and strong. Not only has she taken the place ordinarily reserved for Jeanette MacDonald, but also looks like Jeanette from several angles. A man sitting directly behind [me] actually thought she was. But she is bigger, younger, less dental, sings as well or better and is not so cute. It hardly need be noted that Nelson Eddy is not a Lunt in acting, nor is young Miss Stevens a budding Fontanne. On the other hand, Eddy can sing in a manner Lunt could never hope to equal and Miss Fontanne simply doesn't warble in the same tree with Miss Stevens.[7]

The *National Enquirer*, the "enfant terrible" of newspapers, sized up Risë's contribution in its usual irreverent manner, "Risë Stevens' critical click in the Chocolate Soldier has other Hollywood dolls biting their nails down to here."[8]

The "Hollywood dolls" need not have worried. The entire episode did not alter Risë's resolve to continue in opera.

It was thrilling to see a giant cut-out of herself over the marquee of the Astor Theater in New York and, no doubt, gave great satisfaction to Walter. That type of glamorous publicity was not indigenous to the world of opera but no matter how much Louis B. Mayer tried to lure her away from that medium, she refused to budge. The studio saw in her another Greta Garbo type, so much so, that serious consideration was given to adapting old Garbo screenplays as musicals for her. Warmed over Garbo was not palatable to Risë nor was singing before the cold eye of a camera as seductive as singing before a live audience. Mayer realized this but she had, after all, signed a contract. Even though he did not appreciate his recalcitrant star turning down one film idea after another, he was not insensitive to her feelings. However, if she kept refusing to do any of the suggested films, her option would be dropped and her contract voided. That is what eventually happened when she turned down the starring role in *The Cat and the Fiddle*. The leading lady in the musical has a number called, "She didn't say yes, 'she' didn't say 'no'", but unlike the character she was asked to impersonate, Risë could and did say "no".

Even though her M. G. M. contract prevailed, for the immediate future, Risë's operatic activities were not curtailed. When asked by Gaetano Merola, General Manager of San Francisco Opera, to release her from her film obligations to appear in an unscheduled *Der Rosenkavalier* on October 14th, Mayer graciously consented. Kirsten Flagstad was to have sung an Isolde on that date but her returning to Norway to be with her husband removed her from the American music scene for the duration of the War. Edward Johnson in a letter dated August 8th, to Herbert Graf, commented on his visit to San Francisco, "I enjoyed meeting many old friends and seeing the new opera house. Spadoni is hard at work with his chorus and assured me that all was in order. 'Rosenkavalier' was to take the place of 'Tristan' I was informed, otherwise the program remains." [9]

Lehmann and Kipnis were available and all Marola needed to substitute *Der Rosenkavalier* for *Tristan und Isolde* was Risë. He got his Octavian and with Mayer's approval was able to squeeze in another performance in Los Angeles on November 6th in the Shrine Auditorium. Risë's performance was greeted with high praise from Bruno David Usher, the critic of the *Los Angeles Daily News*, "[she] remains one of the most spirited and finely sentimental Rosenkavaliers I have observed since that exciting night (March 11, 1911) when the Strauss grand opera comedy was presented at the Royal Opera in Dresden." [10] Gutheil-Schoder had seen to it that Risë's interpretation of Octavian possessed the attributes that Strauss, himself, envisioned. Forty years later, a reviewer who had been present at the premiere would recognize Risë's link to the past. Strauss, in a letter to her a year earlier, commented on knowing of her success with Octavian and asked her to apprise him of future encounters with the role.

On October 15th, Edward Johnson wrote and filled her in on happenings at the Metropolitan,

> You will have seen from our recent announcement to the Press that you are scheduled to open the season as Cherubino on Monday evening, November 24th. For your information, let me advise you that there will be 'Rosenkavalier' in the first week and 'Dalilah' in the second week, but Mr. St. Leger has arranged the rehearsals so that you will not find the going too conflicting with your performance dates. If our present schedule holds the first three or four weeks of the season will find you quite busy. So don't let them overwork you and bring us that vitality and energy so characteristic of you and that beautiful voice in its freshest condition. [11]

With her West Coast obligations satisfied, Risë left for New York, arriving on November 18th at Grand Central Station, with Walter and Lamby. Lamby (christened L'Ami Noir by Nelson Eddy and rechristened Lamby by Risë) was a seven-month old poodle, a parting gift from Eddy who gave him to Risë when he could no longer tolerate his black hairs on his white rugs. The party from the Coast, away from the city for six months, was met at the station by the usual complement of reporters and by four ushers from the Astor Theater. Risë, the movie star gave a "movie star" interview, "I love the climate of Hollywood. Nelson Eddy is marvelous. I've never seen anybody so conscientious. I am most grateful to the New York critics for accepting the picture so enthusiastically." [12] When the interview was completed, the four ushers who had been waiting patiently on the sidelines stepped forward and, "presented their starched bosoms and Miss Stevens autographed each." [13] Walter, when asked how he felt about Risë's successful debut in films answered, "I'm very glad. I'm her manager." [14] The usher's tossed a coin to see which of them would present her with a bouquet of chrysanthemums. With that Risë, Walter and Lamby made their way out of the station to an awaiting car.

It did not take long for the "Hollywoodization" to wear off when Risë found herself in a *milieu* more appealing to her. Though her permanent address was on the West Coast and she and Walter lived in rented space in the East, New York would always be home, the Metropolitan Opera where she wanted to perform. After *The Chocolate Soldier*, a film version of *Svengali* with John Carradine, a musical version of *Du Barry* and a remake of the 1931 film *Romance* were suggested but never made with no regrets on Risë's part. Of the latter, Louella O. Parsons reported, "I never like [sic] Garbo in 'Romance' and was bitterly disappointed in the movie but I think Risë Stevens would be swell with that God given voice of hers." [15] None of these appealed to her but Mayer still had hopes that the right vehicle would be found. One did come along but it was another studio which found it.

From the 1941-1942 season to the 1944-1945 season, Risë's Metropolitan Opera assignments saw the introduction of no new roles. Walter limited her appearances as well since he saw to it that her active repertory was not large. As her manager, he wanted her to be thought of as much a star singer as her soprano and tenor colleagues, therefore, he made it known that she was interested primarily in operas in which her character's name was in the title. This significantly reduced the roles that she would sing and the number of times she could appear. Also, dates had to be left open for film commitments should they arise (Walter still hoped that Risë would take more interest in films) and, of course, there were by now the customary recital and radio engagements to consider. She was scheduled to open the Metropolitan Opera's 1941 season as Cherubino on November 24th and end her season on January 12th as Octavian. The only other role was Dalila, although, Johnson did try, unsuccessfully, to interest Bruno Walter in conducting a revival of *Hänsel und Gretel* with Risë and Eleanor Steber. With no tour dates other than Philadelphia on December 9th, the Metropolitan Opera audience saw little of her.

Activities for the war effort began to take more of Risë's time after The Hollywood Victory Caravan was established to benefit families of fighting men. Many of the biggest names in entertainment were tapped to provide a rotating roster of talent that would travel cross-country in a variety show. Risë was honored to take part in it and had a song written especially for her, *The Moon is Down*, music by Arthur Schwartz and lyrics by Frank Loesser.

About the biggest vaudeville show there ever was opens a series of one night stands in Washington, D. C. and while it lasts Hollywood will have to mark time, account of no actors. They'll all be doing their stuff in 13 cities across the land, in hope of grossing at least one $1,000,000 for tickets, plus as many millions more as they can get in contributions for Army and Navy relief. Seats in bald-headed row, from Boston to San Francisco, will cost $100 each, boxes will sell for one. All hands are functioning for free. By utilizing upper berths, double bed rooms, and blue plate specials at lunch time, the vaudevillians expect to keep their expenses under $40,000. [16]

The company had twenty-two stars, among whom were the master of ceremonies, Bob Hope, Charles Boyer, Cary Grant, Lucille Ball, Desi Arnaz, Groucho Marx, Spencer Tracy and seventy featured players, all of whom were drafted to appear. Beginning in April, 1942 and continuing through May, they traveled in three special trains and maintained an arduous schedule, arriving in a city in the morning, appearing at night and immediately leaving for the next stop. The tour originated in Hollywood and went straight to Washington where the first show was scheduled to take place on April 30th. There they were greeted at the White House by Eleanor Roosevelt who served them tea and were photographed with her on the lawn. It was reported that a crowd estimated at one hundred fifty thousand was on hand to view the parade of stars when they arrived in the Nation's capital.

Risë enjoyed a personal success as exemplified by a Dallas review, "Nothing short of a triumph is the appearance of Miss Risë Stevens whose two songs, 'My heart at thy sweet voice' and 'My Hero' prove her not only a singer of the first rank, but a startling beauty as well. She thus makes her Dallas debut on the very stage for which her services with the Metropolitan Opera Company have been requested for some time." [17]

For the benefit of her *Metro-Lark* readers, the significance of the Victory Caravan tour was concisely stated, "the three week tour, which took us from coast to coast and brought us before countless millions of Americans, was the greatest thrill I have ever had, and the response of our audiences, as you know, was overwhelmingly gratifying." [18] The rest of the column comments on M.G.M.'s continuing search for the correct vehicle for her, "We all feel we would rather wait for the right one than take the chance of making a picture which would not be successful because of insufficient story value." [19] In the meantime, she had a series of recordings for Columbia records with Leinsdorf to keep her busy in a much more agreeable way.

A letter from Edward Johnson, dated May 2nd, was delivered to Risë's new address, 706 North Palm Drive, in Beverly Hills, which mentioned for the first time his interest in doing Carmen,

> it was good to hear from you. I am interested also in what you tell me about your studies and hope you will have the opportunity to try out your Carmen before reaching the Metropolitan. I only wish I had some suggestions in the way of new roles but, frankly, our plans for revivals are still very much in embryo and I would hesitate to indicate anything that might not materialize. However, we are counting on having you with us, as per our conversation, during the first part of the season and hope nothing will interfere to change your plans. [20]

When Risë's parents visited California for the first time, they stayed with Risë and Walter in their new home which had been accurately described in *Metro-Lark* as, "a rambling English-style home." [21] Actually, it was Walter who would be host to his in-laws, since coinciding with her parents' arrival, Risë was scheduled to, "sing for soldiers in more than fifteen camps during a period of four weeks." [22]

Army camps would have a more personal meaning by the end of the year when Walter was inducted into the Army in September amid a flurry of divorce rumors. The rumors proved to be unfounded but if the reports were true, it would not be surprising since Risë and Walter were apart a good deal of the time. Risë's career kept her constantly on the go which left Walter to not only manage her career but look after domestic matters as well. With Walter entering the Army, home life was totally disrupted. The financial rewards and professional satisfaction in touring made spending weeks on the road desirable but lonely. Home was a refuge when she had time to be there but without Walter home was lonely also. Fortunately, Irene Jessner did not live far from her, making frequent visits possible. For a few hours, she could speak German and reminisce about happier days in Prague, opting to sleep on Jessner's couch rather than going home.

As for Walter's being drafted, it apparently came about as a result of his turning down an offer from the Coordinator of Information (COI), William J. Donovan. Risë and he were invited to Washington to meet the head of the COI for a reason that they learned only after they arrived. Donovan asked Walter if he would be willing to return to Vienna for the duration of the war and serve as a spy. Walter was very well known in Vienna as a result of the films he made and if he indulged in some covert activity, it would be the equivalent of committing suicide. Expressing his regrets, the matter rested until September when he received a notice telling him to report for active duty in the Army. Considering he was not yet a citizen (that came in June of the following year while he was still in service) and still had a faulty command of English, his being inducted had a retaliatory aspect to it.

Risë's Metropolitan Opera engagements for the 1942-1943 season were to begin in Philadelphia on January 5th in *Der Rosenkavalier*. Again, she was assigned no new roles. *Werther* had been talked about as a vehicle for her and Jussi Björling and she mentioned in *Metro-Lark* that she was interested in doing *L'Italiana in Algeri* but nothing came of these. Nothing also came of the planned revivals of *Oberon* or *Boccaccio*. She could look forward to a season of only three Octavians, two Cherubinos, albeit with Bruno Walter as conductor, and two Sunday night concerts. Her contract, signed on July 23rd, called for a minimum of six performances at two hundred eighty-eight dollars each between December 28th and February 6th (the time period was later adjusted to January 5th through February 28th). There was no tour option other than the one Philadelphia appearance. The next two seasons were no better, seven performances in 1943-1944 and eight in 1944-1945. Her fee remained low, the performances fewer than even Walter sanctioned. The situation prompted him while he was still in the service to write a letter dated, May 18, 1943, to Edward Johnson,

> Risë is fortunate enough to have you as a guiding friend for many years, and this is the main reason for my writing you. I was not happy with Risë's activities at the Metropolitan last year. As you know, through experience, as long as I was around opera my main concern was in Risë's career. I felt that way because I think Risë's great talent lies in this particular field. I know what you will think when you read these lines. You will think that the reason for Risë's few appearances is mainly due to the fact of her not wanting to do Carmen, due to her limited repertoire. This is correct and will be corrected by next year. I would greatly appreciate for Risë's sake if you would talk to her, give her your valuable advise [sic] again once more, so that she can become a real valuable member of your organization. Risë changed her management from Mr. Judson to Mr. Evans, who is, in my opinion one of the few remaining managers that Columbia has who are interested in an artistic career of their clients. I advised him strongly not to book concerts near opera appearances, so that Risë will not have to cancel due to train delays. All in all I would like to see Risë as a regular member of your company, a member on whom you can count so that Risë can again sing Opera which always was and is and will be her first love. [23]

With Walter stationed in Camp Kohler on the West Coast, Risë had very little choice but to stay in California- a situation that had its rewards. At a time when a number of the foremost musicians were forced to emigrate to escape the war, settling in either New York or California, Risë had some illustrious neighbors. Jascha Heifetz was one of them in whose home she was often a guest and impromptu recitalist, joining her host, Artur Rubinstein, Gregor Piatigorsky and Emanuel Feuerman singing Brahms to their accompaniment sometimes through the night.

According to Louella O. Parsons, Mike Todd wanted Risë for a Broadway production of, *The Merry Widow*, and Max Reinhardt for a revival of *La Belle Helene*. However, relocating to the East Coast for an extended run of a show was the main drawback. Appearances at Army camps still took priority over many other engagements and her commitment to the war effort was at times potentially injurious to her well being. On one such occasion, she participated in a benefit for the Red Cross and Camp Kohler's recreation fund. The audience broke out into cheers when she entered holding a nosegay made up of defense stamps and red, white and blue flowers. The program was long, lasting close to midnight and she would have given encores until the applause stopped. No one suspected that before the show she had visited a hospital to be treated as a precaution against pneumonia.

Chapter 7

Leo McCarey, one of Hollywood's most respected directors from the silent movie era, was scouting for a film for Bing Crosby, without much success. Crosby, forty years of age and at the peak of his popularity, not only had a rich baritone voice but a nonchalance which made him highly attractive to women and a man other men could feel comfortable with. Although a strict Catholic, he was not known to be a saint and stories of his bouts of hard drinking circulated as well as rumors of a turbulent marriage to his first wife, Dixie Lee. McCarey, no saint either, was a hard drinking man himself, and understood Crosby. When he finally found what he thought would be the perfect part for him, a priest in a film called the *Padre*, no one believed he was serious in considering Crosby. Both James Cagney and Spencer Tracy had turned the role down but Crosby was immediately taken with the story. He had reservations, however, since he knew that not only would the chiefs at Paramount not see him as a priest but his audience might not accept him as one either. He was not mistaken. The studio was deeply concerned that Crosby's sex appeal would seriously suffer if he did it. Only Buddy De Silva, the Head of Production at Paramount, liked the idea and his influence made all the difference.

With the problem of who would play the central character settled, the filling of supporting roles was accomplished with comparative ease. Barry Fitzgerald, the brilliant character actor from Ireland, was a natural choice for the role of an aging Irish cleric and Frank McHugh that of a priest the same age as Crosby. There remained, however, a serious flaw in the scenario as it was originally conceived. A role for an actress which would provide much needed relief from the essentially all male cast was badly needed. The female angle, however, was thorny since, as a priest, there could not be a love interest for Crosby. When it was decided that the leading lady was to be an opera singer, an old school chum of Crosby's, who once may have been more than just a friend before he was ordained, two of the opera world's biggest names and veteran film personalities, Grace Moore and Lily Pons, were approached unsuccessfully. Both felt their reputations might suffer in appearing opposite a crooner.

Risë's success in *The Chocolate Soldier* coupled with Crosby's having gotten to know and admire her from their appearing together on the Victory Caravan and earlier radio shows, made her a definite possibility. McCarey needed no further recommendation than Bing's and arranged to meet her for lunch at the Brown Derby. When he brought up the reason for the invitation, she was genuinely flattered to be offered a starring part in a Bing Crosby movie but she refused claiming she was through with films. He asked her to reconsider, she said she would have to call Walter at Camp Kohler. McCarey summoned the waiter for a telephone. Camp Kohler was called and Walter paged. When Risë told him where she was, whom she was with and what she had been offered, she heard first a deep intake of breath followed by his telling her to sign on a napkin if she had to. She did. A formal contract was finalized soon thereafter for a role that was equal in importance with Crosby's and Fitzgerald's.

The *Padre*, later renamed, *Going My Way* was a straightforward story of a priest, Father Charles Francis Patrick O'Malley, and his attempt to save a church from bankruptcy and keep the young boys in the parish from becoming delinquents. Risë's role was that of an opera singer, Genevieve (Jenny) Linden [née Tuffle], who is the catalyst for preventing the church from being turned over to creditors and raising funds to rebuild it after it burns down. Father O'Malley, in addition to being a priest, is also a capable composer and when Jenny and his boys choir take it upon themselves to introduce his songs to a music publisher, enough money is earned to pay off the church's debts.

On her first entrance, more than half way through the film, Jenny runs into her old school mate, O'Malley, outside the Metropolitan Opera House and since his coat collar is pulled up she does not realize he is a priest. He, too, does not know that she is a famous opera singer and when she invites him to come backstage to observe her performance as Carmen, he thinks she is fooling. Later, in her dressing room, when she learns he is "Father Chuck", the expression on Jenny's face leaves no doubt that she once loved him and that Risë was the actress Louis B. Mayer envisioned.

Originally, the idea was to have Risë sing "Ave Maria" for O'Malley rather than having him see her in opera. As an alternative, Walter suggested an excerpt from *Carmen* that, by then, had top priority on roles she and Edward Johnson wanted her to do at the Metropolitan Opera. Around the time of *Going My Way*, the "Carmen blitz" began, skillfully engineered by Walter who was again a civilian having been discharged from the army with a case of diabetes later cured by strict dieting. Selections from *Carmen*, included in almost every recital, radio show and concert were either programmed or sung as encores. The "blitz" was such that it prompted retired diva, Geraldine Farrar, who was an acclaimed Carmen earlier in the century, to comment that in her day you had to sing an entire role first before you became identified with it.

Actually, Carmen did return in toto before filming for *Going My Way* began in October of 1943. On July 13, as a pre-Met try out in Cincinnati, it proved the time was right to revive it. "A new Carmen is always an interesting event in the operatic field and such a one occurred last evening. [Her] singing left little to be desired. Her dramatic interpretation is alluring without being too obvious, a distinction few Carmens

159

observe." [1]

On the 21st, Edward Johnson wrote Risë, "heartiest congratulations on your success in 'Carmen'. With the limited rehearsals, it seems to me quite an achievement. As your performances proceed, you yourself will find the spots to emphasize. [We] are counting upon you to carry this opera to the heights during the coming season." [2]

In the meantime, *Going My Way* was foremost on Risë's mind. Her Paramount contract was for one picture only. Unlike at M.G.M., she was not being groomed to be a star and was accorded first class but not preferential treatment. She had agreed to do the film even though Columbia Artists Management had tried to discourage her from having anything to do with it. They, like Grace Moore and Lily Pons, thought it could be detrimental to her career to appear with Bing Crosby. She saw it differently. Risë was fond of Crosby and not only liked his singing but was impressed with his success. Unlike Nelson Eddy who had a background in classical music, Crosby made a career singing popular songs on bandstands and radio. He took as much of a chance in appearing with Risë as she did with him since he was very aware of the voice he would be pitted against. At one taping session in which he sang with Risë, it was obvious that he was outmatched and, frustrated, uttered a very audible expletive heard on the tape, followed by, "She's an opera singer!" The fact that he was obliged to wear shoes with built up heels to match her height added to his frustration but his enthusiasm for appearing with Risë never wavered. It was a congenial cast all round. McHugh was much to Risë's liking and they became friends. As for Fitzgerald, he kept to himself but was easy to get along with. It was obvious to everyone that the film was his.

Paramount ran into a serious problem with Walter's suggestion to use a scene from *Carmen* since in Europe, the copyright was still in effect. That segment in the film, therefore, had to be shot twice, *Carmen* for domestic distribution, and a scene from the *Bartered Bride* with Risë in the soprano role of Marenka. The *Carmen* sequence was filmed in the Shrine auditorium where the stage door, dressing room and facade of the Metropolitan Opera House were recreated. The orchestra, chorus and scenery came from San Francisco opera and Edith Head designed the costume Risë wore as Carmen as well as all the others. The *Bartered Bride* segment was filmed on a studio lot with very little time and money spent on it, whereas, *Carmen* was given a great deal of attention. Armando Agnini, the veteran stage director with San Francisco Opera, however, directed both. *Carmen* offered invaluable publicity for the concept of Risë as the Bizet heroine but while her "Habañera" came off well vocally, the entire scene was too Hollywood, her costume too elaborate.

Fortunately, her performance was not micro-managed as it was in *The Chocolate Soldier*. McCrary told her to be herself and even the look was more Risë whose hair was blond at the time and was told to leave it that way. The role was shorter than in *The Chocolate Soldier* (several of her scenes having been cut in the overly long 130 minute film) but it gave her an incomparable opportunity to be part of a film that went on to become one of Hollywood's classics-something that all her opera star colleagues past or present failed to achieve. That exposure as Carmen went along with the success was no small bonus.

Risë's role is not large but essential to the plot. In the early treatment of the screenplay, she had more to do. An extended scene set in Jenny Linden's apartment where she entertained the three clerics with songs from *The Flamingo and the Rose*, a musical O'Malley wrote when they were in high school, was cut as was a pep talk she gave the choir before they set out on a fund raising tour. The song "April wants to dance again", which she sang in the rectory was also cut. In spite of that, Risë's reviews were as fine as all the veteran actors she appeared with.

Eileen Creelman termed her, "sparkling in a scene from

'Carmen'" [3] and Kate Cameron wrote, "Risë Stevens distinguishes herself in the role of the Metropolitan Opera star. Her personality is one which the screen could use advantageously. [Her] voice is, of course, superb." [4]

Risë learned she was pregnant toward the completion of *Going My Way*. Fortunately, the timing was such that she was in no danger of having to withdraw from the film that was behind schedule (although in one scene she was positioned behind a piano as a precaution against the slightest hint of her condition.) Her recital tour was abruptly terminated, however, after her November 4th appearance in Bozeman, Montana, and she returned to New York on the 12th to prepare for her Metropolitan Opera season that was to start on November 26th. The rigors of touring and the early stages of pregnancy were not compatible but it did not prevent her from fulfilling a number of radio dates and some out of town concerts later on. She had only seven performances with the Metropolitan that season and no contract for the Spring Tour. As it turned out, Carmen had to wait two more years before she felt she was sufficiently ready to sing it at the Metropolitan. In the meantime, Lily Djanel (whom Stevens admired in the role), Jennie Tourel, Irra Petina and the rarely seen, Gladys Swarthout, kept Carmen's ardor burning.

Risë would appear as Octavian and Mignon, only, the two roles that she had made her own but the first would be sung under the leadership of her early benefactor, George Szell, and the second with a new conductor for her, Sir Thomas Beecham.

A less than smooth beginning to her reintroduction to Szell was totally unexpected. At the final dress rehearsal in front of an audience, Szell stopped the orchestra and berated her for a musical error. Risë knew she wasn't wrong but she didn't contradict him. After the act was over, he rushed back stage and apologized, he realized that it was his error.

As for Sir Thomas Beecham, Risë was warned that he was equally well known for his conducting as for his cutting wit. Born into wealth made from the manufacture of liver pills, Sir Thomas had turned his back on trade and went on to earn his laurels as a musician. He made his debut at the Metropolitan Opera on January 15, 1942, conducting a staged version of J. S. Bach's *Phoebus and Pan*. Johnson had sounded Risë out about doing *Carmen* with him but she declined feeling it was still too soon.

Mignon had remained a constant in Risë's repertory since she first sang it in Prague. She knew the role and Beecham appreciated that. However, there was to be a slightly different ending to the opera than the one she was familiar with. Sir Thomas asked Johnson to present the original Opéra-Comique conclusion to the opera which has Philine officially relinquishing Wilhelm to Mignon. In the version the Metropolitan used, the opera ended just before this scene when Mignon and Lothario are reunited. Johnson had his doubts about the practicality of opening this cut and expressed them to Beecham in a letter dated June 21st,

> I must draw your attention to the fact that we cannot obtain orchestral material for the ending of 'Mignon' which you suggest. Do you know where such material could be obtained, or could you estimate approximately what the cost might be? Also can the finale be played in the same room in which the first scene of the last act takes place and, if not, what happens during the change of scene? [5]

Reservations were put aside if Johnson wished to retain Beecham. While there is no specific reference as to where the missing music or where the set for the final scene came from, all was in place for the premiere. The addition provided little new music for Mignon but Philine gained another aria. The "Beecham edition" was presented only once again, in 1945, under Pelletier's direction but for the 1948 revival, the old edition was reinstated.

Beecham and Risë worked together in harmony with only

one misunderstanding arising from her pregnancy. Her stage movements had to be altered depending on how she felt and a particular entrance in Act 1 was changed from stage left to stage right at the last minute, to accommodate her inability to get where she was supposed to be in time without having to run. This did not amuse Sir Thomas and when the act concluded, he stormed back stage ready to reprimand her. Obliged to tell him she was pregnant, a fact she had not acquainted him with before, Sir Thomas was all gracious understanding and apologized for his ignorance in thinking she was just getting fat.

An unusual assignment fell to Risë when she substituted for Jane Froman on Andre Kostolanetz's January 16th program. This wasn't the first time she pinched-hit for Froman but the first time she did so as herself. Early in her radio days, when she was doing back-up singing for stars, she was asked to impersonate Froman when she suddenly became indisposed. No one was the wiser. Her January engagements ended with the Ed Sullivan show on the 31st where during the course of an interview she mentioned that her family had not heard from her brother for two months. As a Private First Class in the Engineers, stationed in England before being shipped to the front, Bud was in the thick of it.

Now that Walter was a civilian again, Lou Wasserman of Musical Corporation of America (MCA) asked him if he would test for *To Have and Have Not*. Warner Brothers, the producers of the film, needed an actor with a French accent. A professional through and through as a result of appearing not only on stage but in several films produced by UFA, the great European film corporation, Walter could transform his Hungarian accent into one of a French cast even though he spoke not one word of the language. At the audition, Humphrey Bogart fed the lines to him while the director, Howard Hawk, observed. The part was his but he was signed not as Walter Szurovy but as Walter Molnar for reasons Jack Warner kept to himself.

Walter soon found that the role he auditioned for was better than the one he actually played which was greatly abbreviated in the final version. Lauren Bacall, who was making her debut, was given much more footage than originally planned. A former model and a Howard Hawk discovery, a combination of talent and beauty not only won for her instant stardom but her co-star, Humphrey Bogart, as well. The very married Bogart at the time had an insanely jealous wife, Mayo Methot. After she heard the rumors about her husband's interest in his co-star, she would arrive at the set unannounced brandishing her revolver intent on using Bogart as a target. All work stopped while everyone ran for cover until the not quite sober Methot left.

Even though his part was brief, Walter's efforts did not go unrecognized when the reviews appeared. He impressed the critics with the *Hollywood Reporter* calling his performance, "intriguing." [6] Unfortunately, Walter saw himself type cast in "Paul Henried parts", Nazis and other heavies with thick accents and ignoble motives. When Bogart suggested him for a role in *The Petrified Forest,* he declined realizing that it would be better if he concentrated on managing Risë's career.

Before he came to that decision, Jules Stein, the founder of MCA wanted Walter to act as an agent for hiring big bands. It was extremely tempting and very financially rewarding but it would have meant the eventual dissolution of his marriage. Risë's involvement in films was virtually over. Even though rumors persisted, with the exception of *Carnegie Hall* in 1947, she was not to make another. She remained in Hollywood because she genuinely believed it would be better to raise a child there than in New York and her pattern for concertizing fit neatly into this set-up. However, she did not see it as a permanent arrangement since deep down she knew that New York would once again be home for her. Had Walter accepted the position, it would have of necessity forced him into a heavy routine of socializing for business reasons, long hours and, of course, permanent residence on the West Coast. The marriage would certainly have come apart and with it the control he had on Risë's career. Theirs was a partnership in more than just marriage and the ending of it would not have been in the best interests of either.

Her April column in *Metro-Lark* kept the members up to date on some future events,

> As you all know, we are waiting the arrival of a third Szurovy who is expected by the end of June. The past few months have been without a doubt the happiest of my life. I have had the opportunity to be just Mrs. Walter Szurovy and Risë Stevens has been obliged to take a back seat. Therefore I hope you won't mind my passing over "Going My Way", plans for next season at the Met, and in concert, and my new picture "The Gypsy Baron" which goes into production in September. [7]

In the midst of all this happiness came the devastating news that Bud had been killed in France. The actual event took place two days after the Normandy invasion on June 6th but due to Risë being on the West Coast along with her parents, they did not learn of the fact until almost a week later. The letter that every relative dreaded receiving was delivered to her parents' home in New York. It lay unopened along with other accumulated mail until Sadie's brother, George, found it and immediately telephoned them in California. Risë, beside herself, was rushed to the hospital to prevent a miscarriage. The events leading up to Bud's death were not entirely clear and it was only after many years that Risë learned what happened from a man who was in the same fox hole with him when he died.

She was receiving visitors backstage after one of her concerts when a stranger approached and told her that he was with her brother when he was killed. He went on to explain that the invasion, one of the bloodiest in the war, proved to be a turning point and Bud and some others wanted to celebrate the victory. They made a foray at night into the nearest town and returned with armloads of liquor and cigarettes. It wasn't long before they were all somewhat drunk and Bud momentarily forgetting that he was in a fox hole within reach of enemy fire, stood up and lit a cigarette. He was shot and killed instantly leaving behind the nurse he had married shortly before entering the service.

Chapter 8

New York 18, N. Y.
July 5, 1944

My dear Risë and Walter:

Thank you for the telegram of June 30th and my warmest felicitations on the happy arrival of Nicolas.

We are all overjoyed as you must be that your first born is a boy and I hope that he will grow up to be the Siegfried for which the world is waiting.

With all good wishes,

Sincerely yours,
Edward Johnson [1]

Nicolas Vincent Szurovy was born in Hollywood's Cedars of Lebanon Hospital on June 30th. Risë's August column in *Metro-Lark* filled in more of the details,

My happiness in Nicky was overshadowed to a large extent by the tragic death of my brother Bud who was killed in action in Normandy two days after the invasion. The news from the War Department was a great shock to my mother, father and myself, as you can imagine, but we are trying our best to deal with being without him. [2]

Professional engagements did not begin in earnest until the end of August with several radio appearances and on the 30th a highly successful Hollywood Bowl concert with the Los

Angeles Philharmonic under the direction of Leopold Stokowski. Risë programmed three selections from *Carmen*, the "Habañera", the "Seguidilla" and the "Chanson Bohème." The reaction of the audience was overwhelmingly in her favor, which did not sit well with the egocentric Stokowski. An opportunity to have revenge occurred years later when he, Risë and Jan Peerce were engaged by RCA Victor in 1954 to record excerpts from *Samson et Dalila*. As part of her contract for the recording, Risë reserved the right to approve the final takes, a stipulation agreed to by Stokowski. When it came time to make the final decisions, unknowingly to Risë, he had the engineers favor the orchestra over the soloists. Both Jan Peerce and she felt that they were singing in another room when they heard the final pressing. In 1958, Risë consented to appear in a second album of excerpts from *Samson et Dalila* for RCA Victor with Mario del Monaco and Fausto Cleva conducting. This time she saw to it that the balance was correct and much to her satisfaction the recording eclipsed the Stokowski version almost entirely.

In reference to her 1944-45 Metropolitan Opera season, Edward Johnson received word from Lawrence Evans that Risë

is hoping you will give her 10 performances next season, especially with 'Carmen' being definitely added to her repertoire. In the meantime, she agrees to be on hand to rehearse and sing her first performance on December 27, and therefore you can send me a contract covering a minimum of 7 performances at the same fee as last season. As previously advised, we had protected the two months of January and February for her opera performances, but she is free and completely willing to sing a performance on March 5. In giving attention to the matter of 'Carmen', I hope you will be able to work out something for Risë on this opera during the months of January and February. She is definitely singing 'Carmen' in California on October 27 and November 1. [3]

On August 28th, the contract was signed committing her to a minimum of seven performances at a fee of two hundred eighty-eight dollars each between December 25th and March 5th. Payment was still low but proportionally not out of line with the fees of other mezzos on the roster. Risë was contracted for seven performances but sang ten. Lily Djanel was paid three hundred fifty dollars per performance but assigned only five *Carmens* and one concert. Bruna Castagna received three hundred each for ten performances in house and one on tour. The addition of Carmen to Risë's repertory would remedy this inequity but that did not occur until December of the following season. In anticipation of the Metropolitan Opera *Carmen*, her coming to grips with the role continued.

"The Standard Symphony Hour" which was broadcast from San Francisco presented highlights from *Carmen* on the 22nd with Risë, Charles Kullman, Virginia MacWatters and Frank Valentino in the leading roles. Although the one hour program allowed her to sing only the "Habañera", "Seguidilla", and the final duet, to many in the audience, when it came time for Risë to step before the microphone she was no longer herself but Carmen.

When she essayed the complete role on the 27th, her success was immediate,

"A new Carmen trod the boards of the War Memorial Opera House last night in the person of Risë Stevens-and what a Carmen! [she] gave us a sophisticated Carmen who had everything except vulgarity. [it] was a personal triumph and she drew the largest crowd on record." [4]

Word got back to Edward Johnson of the very warm reception she received and in a letter dated, November 9, 1944, he said, "May I take this occasion, also, to compliment you on your successful presentation of CARMEN, which I am told was a 'Knock-out'. Certainly the press was most enthusiastic in its praise, and probably even at that did not adequately reflect the enthusiasm of the audience. The progress took a little longer than I anticipated, but I felt confident that you can do it. Bravo!" [5]

Risë wasn't scheduled to appear until one month after the opening of the Metropolitan Opera on November 27th. Cherubino served as her introduction to a season that offered no surprises. The *Der Rosenkavalier* on February 23rd turned out to be the final performance Risë was to sing with Lotte Lehmann at the Metropolitan. It was Lehmann's return to the house after a season's absence and it was her last Marschallin there. At the close, she "received such an ovation after the last act that the outer curtain had to be pulled down before the crowd would stop applauding." [6]

On March 17th, the Metropolitan revived *Fidelio* for Bruno Walter. The incidents leading up to this very much involved Risë and resulted in an artistic rupture between the two. Bruno Walter was not an easy man to deal with and Johnson had a sheaf of notes outlining problems in the past,

The management had offered him "*Norma* in which he was not interested; *Seraglio* for which he could find no bass. He regretted the inability to produce *Don Carlo* and accepted *Ballo* with reservations. He regretted the loss of *Fidelio* but, without a competent Leonore, realized it was impossible. He regretted *Tristan*, was sorry that Johnson offered him *Parsifal* so late." [7]

On January 9, 1945, Bruno Walter finally agreed to conduct two operas during that season, *Fidelio* and *Don Giovanni*. The *Fidelio* needed a Leonore and, the question was who among the current crop would be acceptable to him. To complicate matters, the opera was to be performed in an English translation that added to the difficulty in finding the right person.

Lotte Lehmann invited Risë and Walter for lunch at her home in Santa Barbara along with Mr. and Mrs. Thomas Mann, her companion, Frances Holden and Bruno Walter. After lunch, Lehmann asked Risë to come with her to the music room where Maestro Walter was seated at the piano in front of an open *Fidelio* score. Lehmann was all smiles as she leaned over the piano looking straight at Risë, "The Maestro and I agree that you would be an ideal Fidelio." Risë managed to express her appreciation in their confidence in her but questioned how she could possibly cope with the *Abschulicher* and the ending. Anticipating this, Lehmann said that Maestro Walter would arrange a music line that would not go too high -"Ich werde es punktieren" [I will give you other notes to sing is the way he phrased it]. Without thinking, Risë protested that the critics would kill her if she transposed the music. With that, the Maestro who had been picking out passages from the opera, shut the score. Lehmann, almost in tears, offered to work with her but Risë held firm protesting that parts of the role were manageable but not all of it. The Maestro was livid that she should question his judgment and never forgave her.

* * * *

Having been chosen as the most popular female classical singer on radio the year before in a *Musical America* poll, Risë was a "hot" item as far as the public was concerned. In view of this it was not surprising that she was tapped to be the summer replacement for one of radio's most listened to shows, *Information Please*. A brief notice in the *Toronto Globe and Mail* illustrates the extent to which the popular aspect of Risë's career took over. After it was announced that she would host her own radio show, the article mentioned that the readers would remember her as Bing Crosby's co-star in *Going My Way*. As a trade-off, her recital and concert fees rose because she had become a mainstream entertainer. She had more clout in bargaining opera fees as well since she had achieved stardom. Her face was featured in "ads" for Pacquins hand cream, Rogers Brothers silverplate, Camel and Chesterfield cigarettes, Faberware cookware, and even Texaco Havoline motor oil, among others. People wanted to see her live. When she toured with the Metropolitan, it was she who was immediately recognized on the street, in stores, everywhere, much to the envy of some of her colleagues. In the forties, she was greeted as a movie star; in the fifties, it was as a television star.

Her popularity was such that she was given her own radio program which was broadcast beginning July 2nd for ten weeks on Monday evenings at 9:30 EWT [over NBC]. *Music from Hollywood - The Risë Stevens Show*, with the theme song, "Keep a Song in Your Heart", by Leith Stevens, the producer, was essentially a tribute to the motion picture industry. Each show featured a different motion picture conductor and highlighted songs and orchestral music from one of Hollywood's major studios. Risë was introduced as "the Metropolitan Opera soprano and Hollywood screen actress", thereby, making her vocal range more familiar to the average listener and avoiding being called a screen "star", an appellation she felt she didn't deserve. The show was an immediate hit and the *New York Daily News* wrote, "Names make news...but not entertainment. This became more evident last night when five new shows premiered three featuring movie names - Risë Stevens, Mary Astor and Pat O'Brien - the latter duo failing to twinkle. Miss Stevens, alone, came out unscratched. Her glorious voice was matched by the flawless gems of opera and concert repertoire." [8]

Risë's column in *Metro-Lark* mentions that, "the success of my little show came as a surprise to me. I didn't dare to hope that this show would rate among the best, as proven by the Hooper and Crossley ratings [occupying eighth place in regular programming and first for a summer replacement]." [9]

Rumors speculating on Risë's next venture circulated throughout the summer with Louella O. Parsons prophesying that she was to star in a new film by Leo McCarey, called *Strike a Note*, a musical which would capitalize on her voice and glamour; Hedda Hopper reported that, *My Wild Irish Rose* was being considered by her; Danton Walker commented that Irving Berlin was writing a show especially for her and/or Noel Coward was set to star her in his new musical.

After the last radio show on September 3rd, Risë's next event was opening the twenty-third San Francisco Opera season on September the 25th as Carmen. Marjory M. Fisher reporting to *Musical America* found the proceedings not entirely to her liking, "Risë Stevens sang the title role and acted it with a vengeance à la Hollywood. The result was less satisfactory than it had been last year when she seemed to be inside the role mentally and played it with a conviction not evident on this occasion. Even her singing had some of the exaggeration of the film colony." [10]

The specter of Hollywood was to haunt Risë for many a performance to come. While she had gained in popularity, she seemed to have lost a certain degree of credibility in classical music circles.

Besides Carmen, her San Francisco engagement included Octavian with Lotte Lehmann and Eleanor Steber in their familiar roles. Risë received exceptional notices,

> Once in a very long while one witnesses a musical performance that can scarcely be described and can only be described as having achieved complete and unassailable perfection. Such a performance was that of Risë Stevens as Octavian...For some years past Miss Stevens has been widely acknowledged as the foremost Octavian on the stage today, but with increased experience and maturity her interpretation has grown in stature until, for the first time, the whole work centers in her...[she] was flawlessly magnificent, but the romantic radiance that surrounded her figure throughout the evening was not simply a matter of acting. It was also a matter of easy and beautiful phrasing, nuance and emotional coloring in the music, plus one of the loveliest mezzo-sopranos in the world. [11]

The October 23rd column in *Metro-Lark* found Risë rushed as usual, "Due to the strike in the motion picture industry, all my picture plans have been indefinitely postponed." [12] She made a point of stressing that it was difficult to coordinate film activities with her free time away from opera, concerts and radio appearances. A growing disenchantment with things Hollywood had made deeper inroads by then.

* * * *

The 1945-1946 Metropolitan Opera contract was an improvement over the previous ones in that it guaranteed three hundred dollars per performance in house and five hundred dollars per performance on tour. Two new roles, Laura in *La Gioconda* and Carmen were to be introduced.

Her first performance was to have been as Octavian in Philadelphia on the 27th, but illness forced her to cancel. The November 30th performance of *Der Rosenkavalier* found Risë not in the best of health. In December, the stalemate that existed in her Metropolitan Opera career came to a close. A new role, Laura in *La Gioconda* entered her repertory. A *Seconda Donna* to be sure but one which allows for a solo [the aria, "Stella del marinar", last performed by Marion Telva fifteen years earlier and omitted thereafter until Risë reinstated it], two duets, an entire scene and a final trio. An opera that must be cast from strength, Johnson had assembled an enviable line-up for the 1945-1946 revival. Zinka Milanov, Margaret Harshaw, Richard Tucker, Leonard Warren, and Ezio Pinza, along with Risë, brought it to incandescent if controversial life.

Virgil Thomson, firmly on the side of its virtues, gave it a review atypical of him in its adulation, "There is no denying that Ponchielli's 'La Gioconda' makes a good show when they really sing it...and a brilliant cast gave us [that] last night at the Metropolitan Opera House." [13] The Thomson review seems uncharacteristic for a critic who could be churlish to the extreme. Thomson went on to say, "Risë Stevens has never in my hearing sung half so well. And her voice, when she does sing well, is one of rare beauty." [14]

The key to Risë's success with Laura was her understanding that she is a noble woman and must be played that way. The excellence of the cast, of course, helped. Risë admired Zinka Milanov in the title role and took it in stride when she objected to Laura's glamorous red velvet and gold costume as opposed to her dreary black. She said Laura looked too beautiful and that Gioconda, the leading lady should be in red. Johnson, to appease her, changed hers from black to wine!

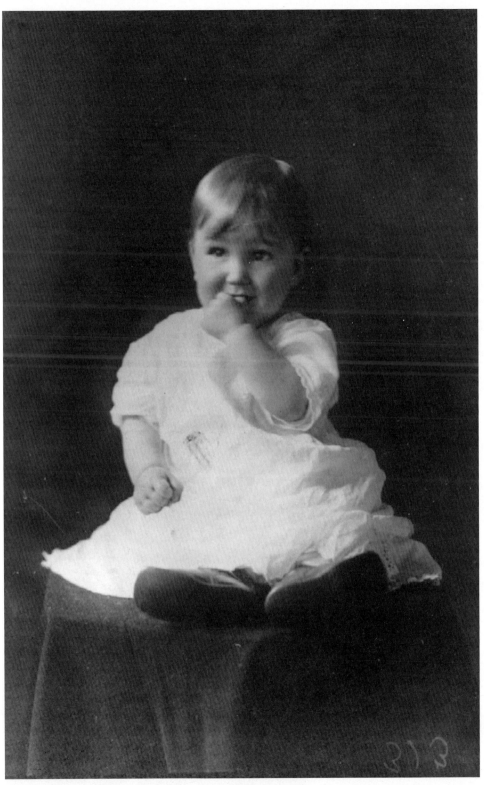

1. *Risë Steenberg*

2. *Risë as* Prince Orlofsky,
Opéra Comique, 1933

3. *Anna Schoen-René*

4. Risë as Orfeo, *Juilliard,* 1933

5. *Marie Gutheil-Schoder*

6. *From L to R: Pat Britton, George Britton, Harriet Henders, Risë, Kurt Prager,* Prague, 1937

7. *Risë and Harriet Henders* "Der Rosenkavalier" Prague, 1937

CREDIT: AUTHOR

8. *"Le Nozze di Figaro" with Risë, Elisabeth Rethberg and Bidú Sayão*, Metropolitan Opera, 1940

CREDIT: METOPERA ARCHIVES

9. *Risë about the time of her Metropolitan Opera debut*

10. *Risë's first Metropolitan Opera debut,* Octavian, *"Der Rosenkavalier",* 1938

11. *Risë's second Metropolitan Opera debut, Title Role,* Mignon, 1938

12. *Herbert Graf rehearsing Risë for Orfeo, 1938*

13. *Risë with Fritz Busch,*
    Glyndebourne, 1939

14. *Fricka, "Die Walküre", 1939* CREDIT: METOPERA ARCHIVES

15. *Risë and Lotte Lehmann*, c. 1939

CREDIT: METOPERA ARCHIVES

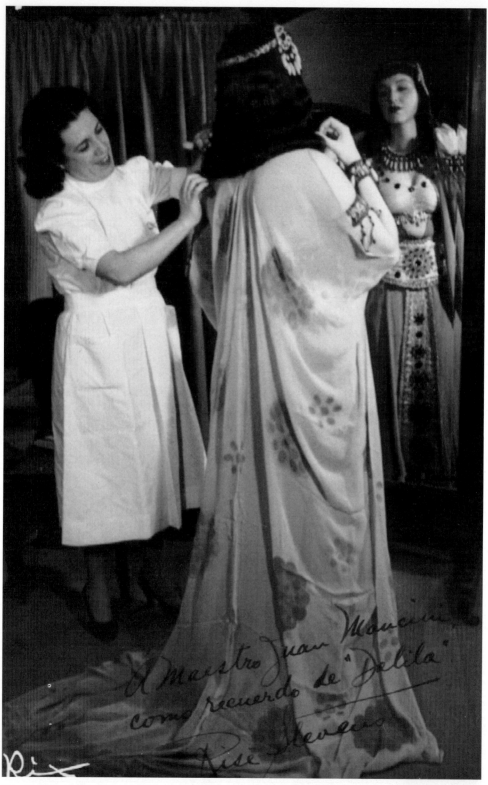

16. *Dalila, Argentina*, 1940

17. *Risë with Edward Johnson, 1940*

18. Risë signs her first recording contract in the presence of Edward Wallerstein, President of Columbia Recordings, and Moses Smith, CRC's Director of Artist and Repertory, 1941

CREDIT: METOPERA ARCHIVES

19. Risë and Nelson Eddy, "The Chocolate Soldier"   CREDIT: AUTHOR

20. *Risë given the*
Hollywood treatment

21. *Risë at leisure after filming* "The Chocolate Soldier"

22. *The third Roosevelt Inauguration. Left to right: Irving Berlin, Risë, Ethel Barrymore, Hans Kindler, Nelson Eddy, Charles Chaplin. Eddie Cantor. Mickey Rooney, 1941*

23. *Risë, Emanuel List, Irene Jessner Metropolitan Opera Tour, Texas, 1946*

24. *Risë with a handful of the stars who
participated in the HollywoodVictory Caravan, 1942*

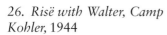

25. *Risë christening the plane
named for her.*

26. *Risë with Walter, Camp
Kohler, 1944*

27. *Risë with Alexander Sved and Walter backstage at the Cincinnati Zoo Opera where she sang her first USA "Carmen", 1943*

28. *Risë and Eleanor Steber broadcasting to the Allied armed forces overseas*

29. "Going My Way", "Carmen" *for the USA*   CREDIT: AUTHOR

30. "Going My Way", "The Bartered Bride" *for Europe*   CREDIT: AUTHOR

31. Walter, Nicky, and Risë, 1944

32. Risë signing autographs on one of her many tours in the 1940's

33. Risë Stevens and Music Club Members c. 1947. Left to Right: Diana Gilmore, June Bancroft, Louise Neumann, Jo and Rita Mottola, Jo Lucchin, Virginia Shaw, Florence Savas, Mary Basile, Florence Peterson

34. Risë with Frank Sinatra, Hollywood, 1945   CREDIT: AUTHOR

35. Stargazing with Atwater Kent. c. 1945   CREDIT: METOPERA ARCHIVES

36. *Nadine Conner, Risë, Herbert Graf, and Claramae Turner rehearsing* "Hansel and Gretel", *1946*

37. *Risë played herself in* "Carnegie Hall"

38. Risë as Carmen, 1940s

39. *The "ad", 1948*

40. *The pre-1952 Carmen, getting ready to make her entrance*

41. "Carmen", *Act I, Metropolitan Opera* 1949 *with Charles Kullman and Marie Savage in a picturesque setting by Joseph Urban*

42. *The Joseph Urban* "Carmen", *Act IV, with Risë and Frank Guarrera, Metropolitan Opera,* 1948

43. "Carmen", *Act IV*, 1949

44a. *Risë with frequent*
     collaborator
     Bing Crosby   CREDIT: AUTHOR

44b. *Risë on one of her*
     many radio
     broadcasts   CREDIT: AUTHOR

45. *Raoul Jobin, Risë and Robert Merrill at the stage door*
    of The Metropolitan Opera, c. 1946
                              CREDIT: METOPERA ARCHIVES

46. Laura, *"La Gioconda"*,
   1945

47. Marina, *"Boris
   Godunov"*, 1946

48. *Marfa,*
    "Khovanshchina",
    1950

49. "Der Rosenkavalier",
    *Paris,*1949, *with Hilde
    Konetzni*

50. *Risë with Walter at the 1950 Metropolitan Opera opening night*

51. *Prince Orlofsky, "Fledermaus", Metropolitan Opera, 1950*

52. Recording "Carmen", 1951. Left to Right: Richard
Mohr, Fritz Reiner, Robert Shaw, Risë, Licia Albanese,
Jan Peerce listening to a playback, Act I

53. Fritz Reiner and Risë
embracing after the
completion of the
"Carmen"
recording, 1951

54. *The* 1952 "Carmen"

55. *Tyrone Guthrie rehearsing Carmen's entrance in Act 1, 1952*

56. *Rehearsing* "Carmen" *Act I, for the* 1952
   premiere

57. *The starkness of the* 1952 *setting is in direct
   contrast to the Urban production*

58. Risë and the boys, "Carmen", Act 1 CREDIT: METOPERA ARCHIVES

59. Risë and Richard Tucker, "Carmen", Act 1. The same scene in sharp contrast with the pre-1952 production CREDIT: METOPERA ARCHIVES

60. "Carmen", *Act I, Risë, Louis Sgarro,*
Richard Tucker, 1958

CREDIT: METOPERA ARCHIVES

61. "Carmen" *Act II, Risë amazed Reiner by*
catching the tambourine every time

CREDIT: METOPERA ARCHIVES

62. *Rehearsing the Quintet, "Carmen", Act II, 1952*
   Left to Right: Risë, Margaret Roggero, George
   Cehanovsky, Alessio de Paolis, Lucine Amara

63. *"Carmen", Act III, c. 1958*

64. *Risë and Richard Tucker rehearsing* "Carmen",
   Act IV, 1952

65. "Carmen", *Act IV, with Risë and Richard Tucker.*
   The setting left Carmen with nowhere to escape

66. *A segment of the final act of "Carmen" was presented on Ed Sullivan's salute to the Metropolitan Opera, 1953. Risë with Richard Tucker*

67. "Carmen", *the final confrontation, Risë and Richard Tucker, Act IV*

68. *Risë as Carmen entwined in the curtain at the end of Act IV*

CREDIT: METOPERA ARCHIVES

69. *Risë triumphant: a "Carmen" curtain call, disheveled but beaming*

CREDIT: METOPERA ARCHIVES

70. *Walter, Risë and Nicky in front of the Schattenstein portrait of Risë as Octavian*

71. *Risë and Nicky in Athens, 1955*

72. *Left to Right: Cesare Siepi, Risë, Igor Gorin, Nadine Conner, James Melton, Charles Kullman join in song to celebrate the 25ᵗʰ Anniversary of Community Concerts, Dec. 1, 1952*

73. *Risë with Ed Sullivan preparing for the* June 7, 1954 *television show*

74. *"Toast to the Met", with Risë and Richard Tucker leading up to the Quartet from* "Rigoletto", 1953

75. "La Figlia del Diavolo", *La Scala*, 1954

76. *Opening night, Metropolitan Opera, 1955-56 season. Martial Singher and Risë, "Les Contes d'Hoffman", Act II*

77. "Orfeo ed Euridice", *Act II, Metropolitan Opera*, 1955

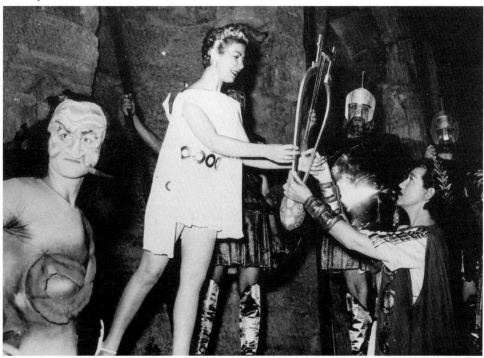

78. *Vilma Georgiou as Amor handing Risë the lyre, "Orfeo ed Euridice", Athens Festival,* 1955

79. *Risë celebrates her birthday at New York's Idlewild Airport June 11, 1957, before boarding for Rome with Nicky*   CREDIT: AUTHOR

80. *Vera Schwarz, Risë and Robert Merrill listening to the playback of "The Chocolate Soldier" recording on RCA, 1957*   CREDIT: AUTHOR

81. Mario del Monaco and Risë, "Samson et Dalila",
Metropolitan Opera, 1958

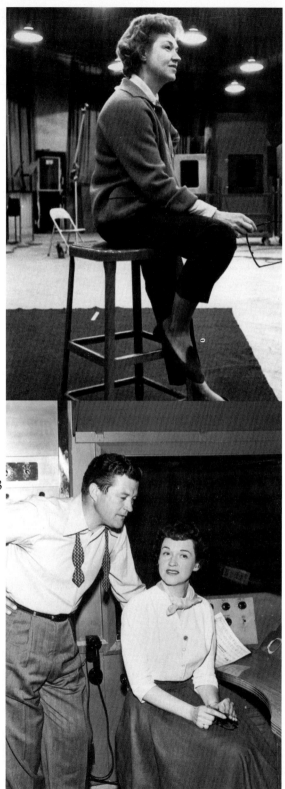

82. *Risë in the Columbia recording studio,* "Lady in the Dark", 1963

83. *Dennis Morgan and Risë who joined voices for* "The Merry Widow" *recording, listening to a playback,* 1963

84. *Rudolf Bing with Risë toasting the opening of the National Company, 1965*

CREDIT: METOPERA ARCHIVES

85. *Michael Manuel, Risë, and Rudolf Bing arriving for the inaugural performance of the National Company, 1965*

CREDIT: METOPERA ARCHIVES

86. *"Shall We Dance", Risë with Darren McGavin in "The King and I", 1965*

CREDIT: AUTHOR

87. *The Metropolitan Opera Archives mounted an exhibit of Risë's costumes in 1988 in honor of the fiftieth anniversary of her debut*

Chapter 9

When asked on a Metropolitan Opera Press questionnaire, "What is your favorite role and why?" Risë answered, "Carmen, because it is interesting dramatically." [1]

After Prague, Carmen remained out of her repertory until the 1943 Cincinnati performances undertaken at Fausto Cleva's suggestion. Living with the role a good year before she sang it, she studied movement with a Flamenco dancer and learned to play the castanets. Flamenco taught her how to hold herself, to walk correctly, to utilize the proper hand movements, everything that would build the character from the outside. Actually, the key for the character was formed over many years. One of the first operas Risë ever saw -it may have been the first- was *Carmen*. Sadie took her to the Hippodrome Theater when she was still in high school and she saw Castagna and even at that early age, thought her too obvious. When at the Met, she saw Djanel's Carmen, which was much more to her liking. Her interpretation was understated, subtle and, indirectly, Risë borrowed from her. So much has been said about the Carmen that she did with Tyrone Guthrie at the Metropolitan in 1952 that many of the virtues of the earlier interpretation are forgotten or discredited even by Risë, herself.

Jo Mottola, *Metro-Lark* reporter, wrote of the cautious approach Risë took before allowing Carmen back into her life, "She did not merely step into the part and give a carbon copy of hundreds of Carmens before her. She gave all parts of it her careful consideration. I remember talking to her about it in the spring of 1943. She said, 'I want to give at least 10 performances of Carmen before I do it at the Met. I want to have the feel of it in me and be able to live it. Carmen means 20 years to me if successful'." [2]

Creating the visual side of Carmen was equally as difficult as forming the character. In Prague, the production leaned toward the somber with costumes that were simple and monochromatic. The Metropolitan's sets for *Carmen* were designed by Joseph Urban in 1923 and the costumes for the ballet by his daughter, Gretel. In 1941, Mary Percy Schenck, the resident designer, reconceived the costumes for soloists and chorus. Urban was a colorist and an architectural designer whose settings were works of art in themselves. His career at the Metropolitan Opera began with a *Faust* in 1917 and his artistry was on view until his *Elektra* was replaced in 1962.

When Risë entered the production in its eighteenth season, it had already served as background for eleven different Carmens, including Maria Jeritza and Rosa Ponselle. As was customary at that time, most leading singers provided their own costumes and in doing so developed a distinct look recognizable even in a distant stage photograph. Risë's Act 1 Carmen is a case in point. There was a very curly black wig with some roses on one side, big earrings and a lot of colored beads and bracelets. The top of the outfit was a white off the shoulder blouse with a wide red belt complemented by a flowered shawl. The bottom half was an ankle length tiered black skirt with each tier bordered in red. The stockings were black net and the shoes red. The entire look became her trademark in advertisements and record covers but one that Risë admits was very artificial.

The staging for the first act required her to enter stage left at the top of a small bridge. Partially obscured by a guardrail, only the top half of the costume could be seen but, even at that, instantly recognizable as Risë's. It was as though her Chesterfield cigarette "ad", which showed her in that guise or her *Carmen* album's cover came to life. She always had the ability to project across the footlights by merely walking on stage but in the glossy trappings of that first act costume everything else evaporated. She was a tall, young, healthy looking Carmen, one who could enjoy a good laugh, seduce a good man, straighten a stocking so that the skirt went dangerously high, brawl, dance and even die because she dared to. The costume of the first act carried out her larger than life approach to the role. It was as eye-catching as the person who wore it and became so identified with her that it changed minimally, if at all, during the five years it was worn.

Conversely, the second act costume went through various modifications. It started out as "bright yellow gown trimmed in red over which [is] worn a red velvet bolero banded in black." [3] This was discarded in 1948-1949 for "a white gown painted with brilliant colored flowers and a shawl to match with green fringe." [4] In 1949-1950, Risë had Elizabeth Montgomery (Motley) design another second act costume which according to *Opera News* had "a black velvet bodice, shocking pink puffed blouse, the skirt of shocking pink net veiled in black net and lined with a turquoise petticoat." [5] Her third act costume originally consisted of a brown leather skirt and bolero jacket, brown suede boots and a bright red kerchief. This, too, was changed in the 1949-1950 season for "black suede boots, a printed waist, black jersey skirt and brown bolero jacket and a bright red bandanna under a black hat." [6]

The last act costume must be elaborate and for four years Risë favored one designed for her by the African-American artist, Julian Dempsey. An off-the-shoulder white tiered dress, it had buttons originally worn on Emma Calvé's third act costume. The black mantilla gave way to a white one in 1948-1949 but the red roses in her hair remained. For the final year of the Urban production, Risë had Motley design a new fourth act costume, which was suggested by a Goya painting. It featured a "black velvet bodice trimmed with net and a huge gold satin skirt opening at the side over a black underskirt covered with a yellow fish net with large yellow pompons." [7] Three large red roses in a black mantilla completed the picture.

Risë's approach to the role may have been somewhat too contemporary to fit in perfectly with an over twenty year old scenic concept. She was influenced by Hollywood, to be sure, but not overwhelmed by it. Her interpretation, although sultry, was never vulgar. Even the stocking-straightening bit of the first act was calculated to be more playful than suggestive. Much of the elegance left over from Prague was still in evidence and it would take Tyrone Guthrie to rid her of it completely. The costumes may have been gaudy here and there but the person in them was not. When she came down the stairs from the bridge in act one and walked to center stage for the "Habañera" the star quality took over. The image on the movie screen, Maria Lanyi and Jenny Linden, the disembodied voice on countless radio shows which had blended with the teen-age and beyond idols, Sinatra and Crosby, the visitor from Hollywood, the face in advertisements, all came down to center stage with her. Risë never entered a scene alone, her popular other self was there right along side of her giving an added degree of glamour to an already glamorous figure.

Her concept of the role was bounded by the confines of a highly traditional production. She could not break out of that since Désiré Defrère's staging, Boris Romanoff's choreography, Mary Percy Schenck's costumes that drew heavily on the expected, saw to it that she did not. In this telling of the story, Micaela had her long blonde braids, José his canary yellow uniform, Escamillo his knee-pants leisure suit, all meant to soften a tale of seduction, desertion, smuggling and murder. There was, however, some leeway for personal interpretations and approaches that were not stale. Even in the pre-Guthrie days, for example, she never allowed the "Card Scene" in the third act to be the high point of the drama as some Carmens see it nor did Guthrie). While it is significant, it doesn't change anything. To some, she is doom-laden from that point on. Risë used to throw the cards in the air in a show of defiance.

She did see the final scene as one of highly charged drama and fought for her independence and life with everything in her. Vocally, the last act was Stevens at her most vivid, reflecting each emotion in varying shades of color and throwing caution aside by singing an alternate high A on the word, "libre", to show Carmen's defiance. The note was eventually omitted but not the scorn that accompanied it. The histrionics in this scene were criticized as being too arcane, especially the scream upon seeing José's knife ("in the best blood-curdling traditions of the New Star Theater back in 1910,") [8] but that, too, would be synthesized eventually into a portrayal that brought the final confrontation to its logical conclusion.

The reviews for her initial Metropolitan Opera Carmen were, on the whole, very favorable, but one in particular stands out. Unlike Dalila, this interpretation, both from a vocal and interpretive standpoint, was almost there from the start, especially Act 1. It did not as yet have the sureness of Octavian that seemed to have been born full-grown but it was in its hot-blooded adolescence.

Carmen is one of the most, if not the most, controversial of all operas, since everyone seems to have a preconceived idea of how the title role should be sung and acted. For this reviewer Calve, at the end of her illustrious career, was the standout performer and Geraldine Farrar was his second love. Since that time, almost a quarter century, there have been many Carmens that have been heard at the Metropolitan and elsewhere, but Risë Stevens' first effort here at the role, was about the best and most promising I have heard since Farrar. This is a broad statement and needs clarification. Miss Stevens voice is neither large in size nor luscious in quality. It is limited in range both at the top and bottom. But with these vocal limitations, she succeeded in creating an illusion which stirred the writer for the first time this season.Her acting was that of an unbridled extrovert; a woman at the height of her sexual prowess and who knew it. This was a Carmen who knew that men desired her for her lovely body and to tame that unquenchable spirit, and it was a Carmen who wanted and desired men, but only to add to her own enjoyment and then to sadistically toss them off when she was finished...[She] secured this effect with a peculiar use of staccato diction, the first Carmen I have heard since Gerville-Reache to do the same. The darkly hued coloring of her voice was frequently employed in a colorless whine, which, combined with a brilliant legato, sent a shiver of anticipation through the audience. A slim youthful body added immeasurably to the effect. That Miss Stevens failed to carry her illusion through to the end of the opera, where the last-act melodramatics were too film-like, is but a minor point in a brilliant performance which will grow with repetition since the intelligence of the artist is too well in evidence not to allow her to do so. [9]

The recorded excerpts provide a vivid document of the command she had of the role at that time. When the album was released in May of 1946, *PM*'s "Hague on Discs" said, "Miss Stevens Carmen, as it emerges on wax is vital and generally convincing. Her singing, though by no means technically flawless, has considerable personality, color and emotional punch. Mr. [Raoul] Jobin's Jose is suitably fervent, his singing impeccable in style and diction...he and Miss Stevens infuse the opera's final duet with intense dramatic fire." [10]

Risë had requested Pinza as Escamillo for that recording. He was very agreeable until he tried out the 'Toreador Song' and found that it was no longer possible. It was disappointing for both of them. There was no time for regrets, the recording was a success anyway and the next year at the Met "looks like an extremely exciting season for me." [11] Several of her old roles were on tap as well as Marina in *Boris*

Godunov. Eboli in *Don Carlos*, not presented at the Met since 1922, was also talked about but it gave way to Hansel in a much anticipated revival of the Humperdinck score.

Films crept back as well. On July 10th, *Variety* reported, "Production of 'Carnegie Hall' by Federal Films, Inc. will get under way Aug. 5 in New York, it was announced here by William LeBaron and Boris Morros. Shooting will be done in Carnegie Hall itself and in the Fox Movietone studios. Musical talent for the picture has been augmented by Jascha Heifitz, Risë Stevens, Burno [sic] Walter and The New York Philharmonic Orchestra, plus Serge Koussevitzky and the Boston Symphony, Jan Peerce and Ezio Pinza." [12]

Louella O. Parsons summed up the entire venture as pretentious but felt the decision to shoot a film about Carnegie Hall in Carnegie Hall was the most sensible aspect of it. For the artists, it meant showing up at Carnegie Hall on the appointed day or days in August when the house was not in use, run through the number they selected with Charles Previn (father of André) and film it. For Risë, it meant a two-week stay in New York since she was in residence in California by then. In essence a personal appearance (she sang the "Seguidilla" and "Mon coeur s'ouvre à ta voix") but one which kept her name active in the film industry. It also earned some added publicity from wearing with her gown by Adrian (which she was allowed to keep) two hundred fifty thousand worth of gems on loan from Van Cleef and Arpels, the Fifth Avenue jewelers.

The Metropolitan Opera contract for the 1946-1947 season that Risë signed on September 27th was a decidedly good one since her stock with the company had risen sharply after the success she had with *Carmen* both in New York and on tour. Promised five hundred dollars each for a minimum of twelve performances, her popularity was rapidly reaching that point where she could virtually write her own contract. With Walter's dogged determination not to have her second to anyone, she had begun her ascent in rivaling the top sopranos and tenors on the roster in fees and prestige.

The Essex House apartment was still to be home away from home. Two suites were reserved for them, one for the family and one for business. The office also served as a practice room for Risë so that she would not disturb Nicky and was converted into a quarantine area when Walter or Nicky had a cold. If Nicky were ill, Walter moved in with him until he posed no threat to his mother. The arrangement worked and surmounting any awkwardness was the fact that she had Nicky with her. As she pointed out in her Metropolitan Opera Press Bureau Artist's Questionnaire, her favorite off-stage activity was playing with her son. However, trading the easy living of Hollywood in a hilltop house surrounded by greenery for cement encased Manhattan was not one they felt beneficial to Nicky at his age. Later, Manhattan would be home, but by then he could appreciate what it had to offer. For now, in a pre-season interview in *Opera News*, Risë indulged in a bit of crowing about her two year old, "Do you know...that after more than nine months away from New York, Nicky has remembered not only my family, but the park, the zoo, and the elevator boys in the apartment house as well? That's my son!" [13]

Eight weeks of concerts were on tap before the opera season's start in November, which would keep her on the road for most of September and October. In addition, she had to learn Marina and reacquaint herself with the score of *Hänsel und Gretel* that she had not looked at since Prague. It was to be performed in an English translation and that added another chore.

The first of her new assignments, Marina, was introduced in the November 21st revival of *Boris Godunov*. Out of the repertory since it opened the 1943 season, Pinza again headed the cast and again it was sung in Italian. Several of the key roles were entrusted to different artists with Risë replacing Kersten Thorborg as the Polish Princess.

Metro-Lark had an anonymous correspondent at the

performance who offered a detailed description of Risë,

> The curtains parted revealing Miss Stevens seated on the chaise in her boudoir, wearing a filmy negligee of blue...her auburn tresses lustrous in the candle light. She sang her taxing music effortlessly with rich full tones, enhanced by the dramatic impact of her fresh interpretation of the role. At the close of the scene, Miss Stevens came before the curtains to the thunderous applause of the audience. When the curtains parted again we were transported from Marina's boudoir to the ballroom...Miss Stevens wore...a glittering crown and long earrings which only accentuated her Patrician features. In this scene she danced the Polish mazurka with such charm and grace that she evoked spontaneous applause from the audience during its performance. [14]

Like Laura, this, too, was a role that was heard briefly at the Metropolitan and not performed elsewhere. Judging by its reception, it is one that should have stayed in her active repertory longer. However, in Rudolf Bing's time, Risë's repertory had been fine-tuned to a handful of starring roles. She also out-priced herself. It became a luxury to cast her in smaller roles when there were others who could perform them for less.

Chapter 10

On December 8th the Prudential Insurance Company of America's radio show, *The Family Hour*, underwent a significant change. Patrice Munsel and Jack Smith gave way to Risë and Jimmy Carroll. In view of the wholesome nature of the program and its Sunday 5 P.M. time slot, when Munsel opted to leave it was essential for the sponsor to have as star a singer who in the mind of the public was equally as wholesome. Identified with the epitome of family viewing, *Going My Way* and countless radio appearances in homes across the country, Risë, an old and admired friend in many households was a perfect choice.

"The present understanding is that I will sing at least one operatic aria each week," [1]

Thereby trying to quell and doubts that she had "sold-out" to the popular sector.

Opera arias did appear on the program approximately once a month, but they were more of an indulgence than a necessity. The singer was far better than a good many of the songs she sang but Risë never let the listener be aware of that. By not condescending to the material, she brought it up to her own standards.

Seemingly wholesomeness bred wholesomeness since Risë's next assignment at the Metropolitan was Hänsel, a model of pre-teen virtue. Last heard at the Metropolitan on December 26, 1938, *Hänsel und Gretel* was to be revived on

December 27th for her and Nadine Conner. Presented previously in German, it was to be performed in an adaptation of the English translation by Constance Bache.

Hänsel was a character that Risë enjoyed doing because in many ways he resembles Cherubino in playfulness but, of course, is totally innocent. Moreover, the role let her play with her voice, use different colors, which was always to her liking. On the down side, however, while it is not difficult to act young, it can be difficult to sound young since the orchestration is very heavy.

In recalling the revival, Nadine Conner said, "Risë and I had great fun as children. We made up our own playful games and dances. I had the flu prior to the matinee broadcast and in the scene where we fall asleep in the forest and the dew fairy and angels descend to protect us, I actually passed out for a few moments. Fortunately it was the end of the scene and Risë, calling for help and blowing on my face, revived me. As we know the show must go on, and it did." [2]

The revival was well received by all the critics who for once found everything to their liking. John Chapmam, "...Risë Stevens, looking like a clean Dead End Kid, made a fine Hansel, and Nadine Conner, looking just like the little girl she is supposed to be, a delightful Gretel;" [3] Irving Kolodin, "...Nadine Conner... and Risë Stevens ...made up the best brother-and-sister act to be heard at the Metropolitan in recent times, with Miss Conner...pert, child-like and clear-voiced...Miss Stevens had the harder task ... Her Hansel, as well as being cleanly and charmingly sung, had a well-studied awkwardness that neatly suited the character, as one who has had the experience, I can attest it was really boyish." [4]

Having committed herself to a weekly radio show, Risë divided her time between broadcast studio and opera house. Subsequent programs featured her singing a variety of songs that appealed to a mixed audience. B. H. Haggin of the *New York Herald Tribune* reviewed the second show on December 15th.

I tuned in all ready and eager for what was announced as 'The New Family Hour' but turned out to be - to my ears at any rate - indistinguishable from the old. After the usual preliminary fanfares, there was Al Goodman's Orchestra and Chorus in 'Midnight in Paris', then, as Miss Stevens contribution of high art to the program, there was a vocal arrangement of the Intermezzo from *Cavalleria Rusticana* - as an 'Ave Maria', no less...then Miss Stevens frenetically introduced by the chorus in the cafe-chanteuse agonies of 'Night and Day', then Miss Stevens and Mr. Carroll in a duet from The Vagabond King and finally everyone in 'Bless this House'...Only one thing was better, Miss Stevens' singing." [5]

Risë had no control over the format of a show that always followed a set pattern since its inception. Basically, it was no different from that of *The Harvest of Stars* with James Melton, *The Treasure Hour of Song* and *The Voice of Firestone*, all of which were to a degree interchangeable.

On February 19th, *Variety* reported, "Metropolitan Opera signed a five-year contract with Columbia Broadcasting Company yesterday to record complete operas from the Met stage, for the first time in Met or U. S. opera history. Recordings will start this season with Mozart's 'Marriage of Figaro' as likely first choice. Diskings will be made at special sessions, without audiences, with Met stars, chorus and orch [sic]." [6]

The same day, the *New York World Telegram* reported, "James W. Murray, vice president of RCA Victor Records, announced today plans for a projected series of recordings of full length operas by leading singers of the Metropolitan Opera Co. to be made in recording studios. Mr. Murray said this method is more satisfactory than attempting to record actual performances." [7]

Edward Johnson was faced with a significant problem, a contract with Columbia Records and a number of his artists contracted to RCA Victor. When RCA announced that it would not allow any of its stars to record for Columbia,

Johnson was obliged to say that he would honor his Columbia Records contract and develop new leading singers.

As it turned out, for Stevens' admirers and fans of the opera itself, the decision to record the Humperdinck was fortunate since it is the only documentation of Risë in that role that was preserved (apart from the Metropolitan Opera broadcast). This was the lone Stevens' recording in the series and the opportunity to commit to disc her Mignon [especially with Pinza as Lothario] and Octavian, unfortunately, lost.

The Metropolitan Opera's spring tour began in Baltimore's Lyric Theater on March 17th with *Boris Godunov* but without Risë. Scheduled for Octavian on the following night, Martha Lipton went on as Marina. The company moved to Boston where Risë opened the season in *Carmen* on the 20th, "Vocally, she was in good form, although she occasionally sacrificed beauty of tone for dramatic accent. She is an excellent actress and makes good use of many Hollywood touches to underline a point in the action". [8]

Hansel and Gretel on the 22nd was a Saturday matinee after which Risë returned to New York for *The Family Hour* on Sunday. She was not scheduled to rejoin the tour until an April 11th *Hansel and Gretel* in Cleveland. The Boston performance went every bit as well as the ones in New York, quite fortunately since H. Wendell Endicott, president of the Boston Opera Association, underwrote the revival of the production. As for Risë, "It says a good deal for Miss Stevens' ability that after her Carmen the other night she could so completely and naturally immerse herself in the role of a peasant lad." [9]

The March 24th performance of Marina which Risë was scheduled to sing in Boston found Blanche Thebom in her place. According to a telegram from Risë to Frank St. Leger on the 23rd, she had sustained an injury, "During Hansel performance Saturday in Boston I was chemically poisoned by the sulphur explosion in the last act, My entire windpipe is inflamed and I am forced to cancel not only my

'Marina'...Monday night but all my engagements for the entire week..." [10] On the 28th, Columbia Concerts vice-president, Kurt Weinhold, wrote to St. Leger acquainting him with the fact that on account of the accident, Risë could not appear in recital in Allentown on the 26th and in a concert in Philadelphia on the 28th. The Philadelphia concert could not be rescheduled but the Allentown recital could be given on April 24th, the first available date that was mutually compatible, "Miss Stevens is scheduled for a performance with your company in Chicago on April 24th, Cherubino in the Marriage of Figaro. Inasmuch as the cause of Miss Stevens' inability to fill the Allentown engagement as scheduled was an accident in line of duty with your company, Miss Stevens requests you to release her from the Chicago performance of April 24th so that she can fulfill her commitment in Allentown and not suffer further financial losses." [11]

Permission was withheld since Chicago was too important a stop on the tour and she was too important a component of it. The tour ended for Risë with *Le Nozze di Figaro* in Rochester, New York, on May 19th. It was close enough in distance for her to arrive in good time after her broadcast on the 18th. After the last broadcast of *The Family Hour,* Columbia Records informed Risë that the recording of *Hansel and Gretel* was scheduled for June 5th and 6th in the Metropolitan Opera House. A vacation that was to have started on the 2nd had to be postponed. On the 5th, looking quite chic in blue slacks, white blouse and red wedgies, she reported to the Metropolitan ready to record her first complete opera and to be a part of the first complete recording of an opera in the United States. Max Rudolf recalled that "the recording was hastily arranged. He had studied the score for a tour performance in New Orleans that was canceled. For the recording there was no rehearsal. The orchestra was in the pit, the singers in chairs in front of the curtain, and the recording equipment was in the boxes and a hallway." [12]

As for the recording, itself, Howard Taubman, declared

it, "a good job...Miss Stevens, whose singing has been un-
even on some occasions, has done Hansel with rich, well-fo-
cused tones." [13]

Risë, Walter and Nicky were ready to try once again to
leave for the coast once the recording sessions were over. This
time, they were successful. The July 24th column in *Metro-
Lark* told of her much needed rest,

> Ever since I can remember, I promised myself that some
> day I would take a vacation - one that would last for
> many weeks - just, simply, to do as I pleased and, be-
> lieve it or not, it happened. [14]

Not quite! On July 31st, she was a guest on Eve Arden's
Seal Test show where she played the part of a singing wait-
ress with Arden as her comedic side kick. Risë did get to sing
the "Chanson Bohème" from *Carmen* straight, but when she
teamed up with Eve Arden for "Ai nostri monti," it was
strictly for laughs with Risë ending it as a solo.

Five recording sessions were also a part of her "total vacation" as was the filing of a petition to legally drop the "z"
in Szurovy. Later in the year when several of the sides recorded were issued as an album called, *Sincerely Yours*, *Billboard* magazine gave it high marks in its own inimitable style,
"The delicate shadings of this canary's richly-colored pipes
applies to this set of universally popular songs, makes for real
lyrical charms. Risë Stevens sings these lovely melodies over
the four 10" records with rare restraint, her mezzo-soprano
voice capturing the delicate melody fabric of each
selection...[an] Autographed portrait of the Metop canary
graces the front cover, her 'sincerely yours' giving the package its merchandising title. Inside cover carries photo and bio
notes of la belle Risë." [15]

When Brooks Smith reentered Risë's life in September, it
was the resumption of a working relationship that began at
Juilliard. Smith recalled,

I played the piano for Schoen-René's classes. When Risë asked me to help her refine her lessons before sessions with Schoen, I agreed because she had great promise. A while later, she asked me to accompany her in recital since we had already appeared on programs together. Her early recitals were planned with Schoen-René and other Juilliard faculty but if I were asked, I made suggestions also. Schoen-René had a particular reverence for *lieder* and she instilled this love into Risë. Wolf and Schubert became staples on her programs as a result of this influence.

I enjoyed the tours. Risë always had an assistant along with us who took care of the business end of traveling. This arrangement left us free for music making. She was wonderful on stage - an immediate hit with the audience. A combination of a splendid voice, beautiful appearance, fine stage manners - she 'wowed' them. What's more, the critics liked her and bad reviews were a rarity. Most of these attributes were there from the start. She always looked to learn from the best. At Juilliard, she went to the Met quite often since students were let in standing room for a reduced price.

We eventually parted ways when outside engagements took over my time to a greater extent. [16]

An event equally significant in Risë's career was her introduction to Vera Schwarz. Originally from Zagreb and in her late fifties by the time she and Risë met, Schwarz became Risë's vocal coach. Around 1947 Risë became concerned that her voice wasn't all that it should be. Her first thought was to ask Irene Jessner if she would work with her since she admired her greatly but Jessner declined saying they were too close. She recommended Vera Schwarz who lived on the West Coast and coached film stars for the Hollywood studios. Nelson Eddy, Jeanette MacDonald and others had benefited from sessions with her. Schwarz had been a famous Octavian and Carmen in Vienna but always had to take second place to the reigning diva, Maria Jeritza. Schwarz worked with Risë in opening up her voice, evening it out by strengthening the top but leaving the middle and lower alone. During their many sessions, she would tell her, "go for it", when she approached a high note, "it's there".

With the coming of September, the Surovys were back in New York and residing in the Essex House. The home on Woodrow Wilson Drive was shuttered for the duration. This marked the last year for a bi-coastal way of life. With Nicky approaching school age, a more permanent and convenient way of living had to be found. The plans for Risë to appear in the Universal International film version of *The Song of Norway* were put on hold indefinitely since it had run into script and casting problems. No contracts had been signed and when Frank Sinatra pulled out, John Dall was chosen to take his place. Dall was not a singer, which necessitated changes in the script, and a second female lead had yet to be cast. Another film project also faltered. Boris Morros wanted to follow-up his successful, *Carnegie Hall*, with a similar treatment featuring the Metropolitan Opera as the setting with Risë as star. This, too, died in the planning stages which made living in Hollywood more and more non-essential.

The Family Hour was, as Risë mentioned in her December 1st column in *Metro-Lark*, "much more to my liking this year...there seems to be much more room for good music." [17] *Variety* agreed,

> As in previous years, the feature of this season is the Met's Risë Stevens, whose versatile and expressive mezzo soprano lends warmth and authority to the [air]. Miss Stevens is equally capable of bringing out the best in either pop or classical renditions. [18]

* * * * * * * * * * * *

The 1947-1948 Metropolitan Opera contract did not raise the in house per performance fee of five hundred dollars but it was equal to Thorborg's. The rate for performances on tour, however, rose to seven hundred dollars each, attesting to her drawing power on the road. Her position at the Metropolitan was becoming more secure and when, earlier in the year, she was asked by a reporter from *Band Leaders and Record Review* why she didn't forsake opera for the more lucrative Broadway, Risë explained that a concert singer could earn very substantial fees between opera performances and in her case on the average of seven to eight thousand dollars a week. She also pointed out that a Broadway show which took in three thousand dollars a week was considered doing very well but that she appeared in a performance of *Carmen* in Cleveland which grossed thirty-two thousand dollars in one evening. Radio shows gave her sufficient exposure in the popular field of entertainment to make appearing on Broadway unnecessary.

The Family Hour of December 7th followed a particularly hair-raising performance of *Carmen* the night before. Risë was thrown roughly to the ground in the third act by an unintentionally heavy-handed Kurt Baum who according to *PM*, was having a difficult time with his first Metropolitan Opera Don José,

> vocally acceptable, his performance was an uncommonly wooden one, and plagued on this occasion by a series of mishaps usually met with only in a René Clair comedy. In the second act, his sabre became so entangled in its harness that struggle as he might he could draw it in time to engage the oncoming Zuniga; in the third act, during one of his less wooden moments, he nearly fell backwards over a large rock; and in the last, as he threw himself down on his adored Carmen's corpse, his toupee came off. Perhaps radio has its good uses, after all, Mr. Baum's Jose should be heard and not seen. [19]

Risë was to remember later that it was the only time Carmen died from laughing.

Chapter 11

The itinerary for the 1948 Metropolitan Opera tour covered thirteen cities in thirteen states. The first stop Boston and *Der Rosenkavalier* on March 15th earned a headline in the *Boston Globe*, "Risë Stevens Acclaimed at Metropolitan Opening." [1] Cyrus Durgin reported, "There was plenteous applause for all concerned from the capacity audience in the Boston Opera House, but every time Miss Stevens appeared alone for a bow the din was terrific. She deserved it, too, for she sang her role admirably." [2]

The next appearance for Risë on the tour was Atlanta, Georgia, on April Fool's Day and nature played a joke on all concerned. The train carrying the costumes and properties to Atlanta for that evening's opening night *Carmen* was delayed by a Virginia landslide. After holding the curtain for several hours in the hope that the train would arrive, the show went on with most of the singers in street clothes. During the evening, which ended at 2 A.M., more and more costumes began to appear. At the start, however, the audience good-naturedly accepted Kurt Baum in business coat and tuxedo trousers, Licia Albanese in a plain black dress and red scarf and Martial Singher in white shirt and tuxedo trousers with a red sash and ribbon tie. Only Risë was in costume since she had hers with her.

Her next stop on the tour was Los Angeles on the 13th, where she would open the two-week stay as Carmen. The Metropolitan's last visit to the West Coast forty-two years earlier met with catastrophic results. The earthquake that devastated San Francisco on April 17, 1906, wrecked havoc on the company and remained a bitter memory. Prior to that, a visit to Los Angeles on April 17 and 18, 1905, was a financial disaster. In theatrical lore, the West Coast was a jinx and the Met avoided it on subsequent tours. Ignoring or ignorant of past history, sixty-five hundred elegantly dressed patrons defied the jinx and filled the Shrine Auditorium to overflowing not only to welcome the company but to honor one of its own, Risë Stevens.

It was not a typical Hollywood opening. There were no searchlights illuminating the sky and socialites outnumbered film stars. The latter were out in force, however, and taking seats in the auditorium were many of the film colony's elite: Greer Garson, Ann Southern, Gracie Allen, George Jessel, Glenn Ford, Kathryn Grayson, George Murphy, Eleanor Powell, and the Met's own, Dorothy Kirsten, among others. Unlike the New York openings, the audience was in place well before the start of Act 1 to witness Risë's "Carmen of undaunted confidence and plenty of movement." [3]

On Sunday, the 18th, instead of being in her customary place before the CBS microphones, popular singer Joan Edwards substituted for her on *The Family Hour*. Missing two programs in a row was unacceptable by the sponsor so Risë had to return to New York by the 25th and then rejoin the tour in Denver on the 27th. Commuting to and from New York continued all through April except for the one program on the 18th when the distance from Los Angeles was too great.

Carmen in Atlanta on the 1st was followed by *The Family Hour* on the 4th, a concert in Baltimore on the 7th, a return to New York on the 11th, *Carmen* in Los Angeles on the 13th, back in New York on the 25th, Denver on the 27th and so on. In May, there was *The Family Hour* on the 2nd and a *Der Rosenkavalier* in Bloomington, Indiana, on the 3rd. The pace was hectic-the monetary rewards substantial but the price steep.

Risë's *Metro-Lark* column of the 24th was somewhat

breathless reflecting the accelerated pace of her activities, "I have just flown in from Los Angeles for the Family Hour and I am leaving for Denver right after the program. I sometimes wonder what concert and opera singers did when they depended on trains." [4]

"The chances are Bizet never saw a 'Carmen' anywhere like Risë Stevens. She is, of course, well known in this part which she does with much force and effectiveness. Her work was up to all expectations and it was her evening all the way." [5] A long sold out performance of *Carmen* concluded the stay in Denver and the Metropolitan's visit for two days netted the company around fifty-seven thousand dollars.

The next city on the tour was St. Louis on the 29th and Risë would not only introduce her Octavian but *Der Rosenkavalier* would have its local premiere as well. After the performance which ran until midnight, she dispensed with backstage greetings and returned to the hotel immediately since she had to catch an early flight to New York for a run-through of her radio show.

The day after, she was in Bloomington, Indiana, and on the 6th, Minneapolis, Minnesota saw her Octavian. The *Minneapolis, Minnesota, Star* ran an item on Risë, "The most traveled person on tour is Risë Stevens. She has almost twice as many miles as any other member of the company. The reason is her Sunday radio program which originates in New York. This means a plane ride east and then back each weekend, twice from California alone. She leaves immediately after her performance tonight to make this Sunday's show." [6] She was back in New York for the radio broadcasts on May 9th and the 16th.

On the 19th, a recital took her to Ritchie College in Washington, DC, and Paul Hume of the *Washington Post* was on hand to review it. "When we reached the final group of Carmen arias...as far as Bizet was concerned, sex was rampant." [7]

The Family Hour the following Sunday, the 23rd, had a

surprise for all of Risë's listeners when she sang "Vissi d'arte" from *Tosca* (albeit lowered a tone). An even bigger surprise occurred before the final show of the season. *Variety* ran the following item, "Risë Stevens is scramming from the Prudential Hour come fall. The Singer will follow through current pact but won't return in September because she refuses to take a salary cut." [8] Meeting the deadlines for the show each week was an exhausting responsibility considering the amount of time she spent away from New York. Traveling expenses, loss of other engagements, maintaining a wardrobe, planning the show, rehearsal time, all figured into a reduction in fees overall. It was not worth her while to do it any longer, even though the exposure was desirable. In addition, Walter knew that the sponsor was not happy with two roles in Risë's repertory, Carmen and Dalila, since they were not wholesome characters. He was told that for Risë to stay with the show, they would have to be dropped. Of course, that was not possible.

Before she could take a well-earned break for the summer, Risë had commitments with the Cincinnati Zoo Opera, which was located quite literally in the zoo. During a performance, it was not uncommon to have the ecstatic Love Duet from *Madama Butterfly* accompanied by honking geese or Roméo wooing Juliette to the roar of a lion. Even the advertising for the operas was colorful, *Der Rosenkavalier* was billed as "Gaily Indiscreet", "A riotous comedy of young lovers and elderly wolves" or *Carmen*, "She lives to love", "Carmen the bewitching vamp who loves all men", "The opera of torrid passions wherein love is dear and life is cheap". If that didn't bring in an audience the promise of, "100 people on stage 100", most assuredly did.

Good fortune was smiling down on the season since the weather was ideal and the opening night's, *Der Rosenkavalier* saw the largest net gross in the history of the company. Risë's reception by audience and critics was as favorable, "Time nor space permits mention of all the 23 members who contributed to the success of this initial opera performance of the summer. But dominating them all was Risë Stevens, both by her singing and her acting." [9]

If *Der Rosenkavalier* caused a mild sensation, *Carmen* went one better. "The greatest throng to turn out for any attraction in the Zoo Summer Opera's 27 years of performances filled and exceeded the park's theater last night for 'Carmen';" [10] Stevens... filled the stands and lined the railings just by being in the cast;" [11] "Opera-Lovers spilled over into the park benches outside the Zoo pavilion...to accommodate everyone who wanted to hear 'Carmen'. The chief inducement, as anyone might guess...was Risë Stevens...She is a cool and calculating Carmen...The singer is a talented actress...with considerable beauty thrown in." [12]

A constant in all of her performances that year was the comments on the better state of her voice. Risë had Vera Schwarz to thank for that. Schwarz was the ideal choice to see Risë back to vocal health since, like Risë, she was at home in the classics and the semi-classics. Risë's musical versatility encompassed popular music as well and was an integral part in the success of her career. While she had extensive training in the classics, no one taught her how to sing popular music. An innate ability to take from the best, an admiration for radio and band singer Connie Boswell's way with music and lyrics in particular helped her to adopt certain of her characteristics without imitating her. Long before Boswell, however, Risë learned how to put over a song when she was on the *Palmolive Beauty Box Theater,* by listening to what Swarthout and others did. Then later *The Family Hour* continued her development in the popular music field since there was almost no opera on the show. When composing a recital program, however, she would never have included a popular song even as an encore as many singers do today. That wasn't the place for it. Semi-classical, yes, but not popular.

Risë's July column in *Metro-Lark* gave every indication that while she was enjoying a vacation that was to extend through the end of September, her thoughts were on upcoming events, "My next season looks very interesting for me, particularly because I will do a rare opera by Moussorgsky at the Metropolitan Opera Company. An opera which was never performed in this country before." [13]

Chapter 12

On July 17, 1948, a disturbing piece of news was issued by George A. Sloan, chairman of the board, and Charles M. Spofford, president, that the Metropolitan had lost two hundred twenty thousand dollars in the past season attributed to an increase in the payroll and costs of new productions. In an admittedly ill-timed gesture, Herbert Graf, less than a week later contacted two of the Metropolitan Opera's top officials; a formal proposal on the necessity for updating productions was sent to Spofford and ideas on repertory and casting for the coming seasons was forwarded to Edward Johnson. His letter to Spofford pointed out that many of the productions for standard fare were over twenty-five years old and in need of modernization. He suggested that this be accomplished over a period of five to ten years and that one hundred and fifty thousand dollars should be set aside each year to implement the changes for three operas.

Among the first group which he felt should be updated and which would affect Risë were, *Boris Godunov*, *Der Rosenkavalier* and *Carmen*; from the second group, *Mignon* and *Hänsel und Gretel* and the third, *Samson*, *Orfeo ed Euridice* and *Le Nozze di Figaro*. His choices for repertory included some novelties and would have presented Risë in several new roles: Eboli, Dorabella, Orfeo, Giulietta, and Orlofsky. When Rudolph Bing took over, three of the five became a reality.

On August 5th, George A. Sloan announced the cancellation of the 1948-1949 season due to a failure in coming to terms with five of the twelve unions over a fair wage scale. Negotiations had been going on since February and while more than half of the unions sympathized with the company's financial state, the remaining five held out for better terms. The artists were formally notified of the cancellation and consequently they were at liberty to accept other engagements.

The *Dallas-Times Herald* commented on the loss of a season to some of its featured singers, "In any event no tears need be shed for such hardy perennials as Lily Pons, Lawrence Tibbett, Risë Stevens, Lauritz Melchior and other name singers who for years have been the glamour and the mainstay of the Met. The real truth is that these stars probably would make the greatest incomes of their lives if there were no Metropolitan Opera season. The reason is that they demand and get as much as five times as much money for a concert appearance as they receive for an entire evening at the Met." [1]

Meanwhile there were those enterprising few who were not going to sit idle while the company died. Lawrence Tibbett in his capacity as president of the American Guild of Musical Artists (AGMA), which represents singers, chorus and dancers, called a meeting of the unions on August 5th to discuss ways to save the season; Newbold Morris, chairman of the board of the City Center of Music and Drama offered his services as a mediator; Billy Rose, night club owner noted for its chorus line, put himself up as the savior of the Met if allowed to manage and streamline it, a prospect which had critic, Robert Bagar, quipping that if that came to pass we could expect *Das Rheingold* to have a bevy of aquamaidens in the cast.

AGMA made the most concrete advance in getting a promise from its members not to accept other engagements until September 6th. On August 24th, the Metropolitan announced that there would be a season after all since agreement had been reached with the holdouts.On the 26th, Eleanor Roosevelt wrote a widely distributed article praising the decision to save the Met. She quite candidly confessed that even though she preferred symphonic music she was very pleased that the Metropolitan Opera would not close.

Risë's 1948-1949 contract was similar to the year before which made her and Thorborg still the two highest paid mezzos. However, Risë's rate per performance on tour remained at two hundred dollars more than Thorborg's. There were no new roles but Mignon, Carmen and Cherubino more than made up for the postponement of *Khovanshchina*. The Mignons would be the last of her career and Cherubino would be all but retired as well. Carmen was steadily becoming her most sought after characterization.

The reviews for Risë's first performance of Carmen on December 14th, however, illustrate that she needed a new point of view, a different approach in order to bring her concept to full maturity. What she had was a tired production and a resident stage director, Desiré Defrère, who could not see her as Carmen to begin with. He thought her too tall and decidedly not French enough in spite of the fact that Edward Johnson always said he heard a French sound in her voice.

"Miss Stevens sang much of Carmen's music with a certain reserve: the tone quality was likable, but the vocal and histrionic interpretation were not particularly persuasive, even with one or two moments of exaggerated stage business." [2]

A young baritone from Philadelphia, Frank Guarrera, made his debut that evening. The twenty-five year old of Sicilian background, was a 1948 Auditions of the Air award winner, and when interviewed said,

> Risë was *the* Carmen of the whole era. I can't remember having too many rehearsals before my debut; the basic staging was gone over, entrances, exits, etc. In Act 2, after I did my aria and got a very big reception from the audience which was full of all my friends from Philadelphia, the men in the Chorus, taking into consideration that this was my debut performance, tried to help me make my exit. They hustled me to the place where I

would leave but forgot that the staging called for Risë to have her back to me and lure me to her with her shoulders. I was supposed to grab her then and kiss her on the back of the neck but the Chorus kept pulling me away to get me off stage. When the act was over, Risë came up to me and said, 'Don't you like me? Where's my kiss?' So I kissed her on the back of the neck and she said, 'That's better'. [3]

The 1948-49 opera season was not long underway when it was made known that there might be another crisis for Risë's admirers. Along with anxiety over the season's near loss and Risë with it, came a new fear she was headed for Broadway to star in *Regina*, a musical adaptation of Lillian Hellman's play, *The Little Foxes*. It was not at all surprising that she might do so since it was rumored that Marc Blitzstein, the composer of *Regina,* fashioned the title role with either Risë or Dorothy Kirsten in mind. Of the two, Risë was certainly the more logical choice to bring to life the strong willed Regina Giddons, for the darker timbre of her mezzo was more suitable to the character than Kirsten's lyric soprano. When casting decisions were made, Risë was the top contender but had second thoughts and her fans at *Metro-Lark* wasted no time to publish Risë's withdrawing from the project,

"Music lovers across the country have been speculating for months whether Risë Stevens, the glamorous mezzo-soprano star of the Metropolitan Opera ...would leave opera and concerts to star on Broadway...All speculation ended when [she] wrote a letter to the producer explaining that she regretfully had to reject the role." [4]

Risë's column in *Metro-Lark* of March 15th explained her position on *Regina,*

In answer to your many letters asking me why I turned down the Broadway production of 'The Little Foxes', I would like to tell you that despite the fact that I loved Marc Blitzstein's score, I did not find it important enough for me to take a leave of absence from my Metropolitan

Opera season and concert activities... [5]

As if to compensate for a voluntary loss of a Broadway debut, a more important phase of her performing career began on Sunday, March 20th, which added immeasurably to her popularity. *Lamb's Gambol*, a comedy show, was on NBC from 8 to 8:30 and Risë shared the stage in her first experience before television cameras with actors, William Gaxton, Bert Wheeler and Guy Kibbee. Costumed as Carmen in her Act I get-up, she played a painting which came to life and sang the "Habañera". Offering an operatic excerpt reinforced her commitment to bring opera to the general public as she had been doing all along on her concert tours. She was one of the earliest classical artists to attempt television in its fledgling stages and she and the medium were compatible from the start.

Jane Bancroft reported in *Metro-Lark*,

The program opened with a quartet singing the Maxwell House Theme. An announcer said; Maxwell House presents Lamb's Gambol with William Gaxton, Risë Stevens of the Metropolitan Opera and then introduced Bert Lahr, Wheeler and Guy Kibbee. Each person stepped before the camera as their names were mentioned and their names were also superimposed on the bottom of the screen. Risë was dressed as Carmen from the first act. A courtroom scene was on first-then Risë's contribution. Two men in evening dress were standing in front of what seemed to be a full length painting of Risë. They were discussing her singing voice when Bert Wheeler approaches them trying to sell opera programs. The two men leave and Bert began talking to the picture. He said he often dreamt of singing with Miss Stevens on the stage of the famous Metropolitan. The picture comes to life with Risë moving and saying to the surprised Bert Wheeler, 'Are you Bert?' He helps her step down with Risë thanking him. A few more words and then Risë was alone on stage singing 'The Habañera'. Risë's personality came over very well. She looked beautiful with not too much make-up. [6]

The Metropolitan's spring tour opened in Baltimore on March 21st with *Otello*. Fritz Reiner gave a vivid interpretation of *Le Nozze di Figaro* the following evening with a stellar cast headed by Risë singing Cherubino for the last time with the Metropolitan. As the tour progressed, her reception became more and more intense. To Risë, the steady compliments on her voice, especially in *Mignon*, were of particular satisfaction, "from the yearnings of 'Connais-tu le Pays'...to the dreamy child-like prayer near the end, she gave pleasure with the sustained beauty of her sounds." [7]

The performance of *Mignon* in Atlanta on the 19th went over in a big way with both audience and critics. The opera turned out to be surprisingly popular and the cast with Stevens, Giuseppe di Stefano, Patrice Munsel and Jerome Hines enthusiastically received. By any standards, the tour was a personal success for Risë and for the company as well.

The heady atmosphere vanished with the morning headline of the 21st, "Find 'Met' Opera Tenor Slain in Atlanta Alley." [8] The body of John Garris, the Laërte in *Mignon*, was discovered early in the day by a passer-by. Shot in the chest and apparently dumped in an alley already dead or where he was left to die for some still inconclusive reason.

In New York, Walter was shocked when he saw the headline, "Murdered Star in Last Performance", over a photograph of Risë flanked by di Stefano and Garris. He immediately thought the worst until he read the account of what happened. Later in the day, Licia Albanese's husband, Joseph Gimma and he, had the task of breaking the news to their wives who had flown to Dallas without any knowledge of the murder.

The end of the Met tour on May 20th and her debut as Octavian in Paris on the 30th, with rehearsals in between, precluded a leisurely crossing to France. Risë and Nicky flew over and Walter, given his aversion to traveling by air, went by ship. Although she had sung the Strauss score with Hilde Konetzni and Emanuel List before, Julia Moor, the Sophie, was unknown to her. The conductor, Louis Fourestier, was not very inspiring when he led *Carmen* at the Metropolitan so there were qualms about how he would fare with *Der Rosenkavalier*. Had she known what was transpiring behind the scenes at the Metropolitan, she might have had qualms about the future there as well.

The letterhead read, "Edinborough Festival Society, Ltd.," and the date, May 27, 1949. The letter was addressed to Professor Bruno Walter, 68 N. Bedford Drive, Beverly Hills, CA. and in it, Rudolf Bing informed him that the board of the Metropolitan Opera had named him Johnson's successor.

On June 1st, Dr. Walter responded: "Dear Friend, Without doubt you are aware that not one, but whole hordes of dragons spitting fire and belching fumes are waiting for you". [9]

While Risë was in Paris, the news of Rudolf Bing's appointment as General Manager of the Metropolitan Opera made headlines. She reacted favorably to the appointment since he was a very experienced manager with a solid background in opera. He had, after all, brought her to Glyndebourne, which was a great boost to her career, even though negotiating with him was difficult. It was only after he came to the Metropolitan that she found out as good a manager as he was, he was also a very strange man. He could be very cold and distant to her, something Walter felt she imagined. He actually liked Bing, which was fortunate, since it was he who dealt with him on Risë's behalf. He knew how to get around Bing's Machiavellian mind and Prussian attitude, an invaluable knack few others had.

On June 28th, Risë, who was in Cannes, wrote her column for *Metro-Lark* updating her fans on her European adventure,

> The very first day in Paris of course, meant rehearsal. Several of the singers I had known previously and [we] talked over some happy times. The second day we were called for orchestra rehearsal and from then on we were on the stage rehearsing with full orchestra until opening night. The three Rosenkavalier performances went very well. The public [response] was very exciting and I was asked to return next year as Carmen, Orfeo and again Rosenkavalier.[10]

Risë almost lost the Paris engagement due to a full calendar both with the Metropolitan Opera on the spring tour and her own recital appearances. The opening performance was to have been on May 23rd but Risë's contract with the Met ended on May 20th with her St. Louis *Carmen*. Therefore, the premiere was moved to the 30th and the two subsequent dates to June 3rd and 6th. Since by now, she was the Octavian of choice, Dorothy Kilgallen revealed in her *Voice of Broadway* column that the Vienna State Opera postponed its trip to Paris Opera for one week so that Risë could honor her commitments in New York. Her contract was not with the Paris Opera but with the Vienna State Opera for their appearances in the *Salle Garnier*. However, based on her reception, the Paris Opera wanted her for the year after, which was what she was alluding to in her column. She was very interested in appearing with the Paris Opera in *Carmen* but when she was told that it would be at the *Opéra-Comique*, she declined. The *Opéra-Comique's* version interpolated dialogue heavily laced with topical political allusions with all the spoken recitatives aimed at making comments about the then current regime. Raoul Jobin invited her to a performance hoping she would change her mind but it only reinforced her decision. Undoubtedly, if they had offered her *Carmen* for the *Garnier*, she would have accepted. As it turned out, her refusal left both Jobin and the conductor, Georges Sebastian, very disappointed over not being the ones to introduce her Carmen to Paris.

When the reviews for *Der Rosenkavalier* came out Risë garnered high praise, "Miss Risë Stevens easily carries off the pants role of Octavian and sings this difficult role with rare brio, emotion and subtlety." [11]

Predictably, there was some comment by the French Press on the engaging of non-French singers, especially Risë,

> The principal roles are taken by foreign artists (six from Vienna, and two from the New York Metropolitan). Miss Hilde Konetzni (the Marschallin) has a magnificent voice, and she is marvelous particularly in the melancholy monologue of the aging woman which ends the first act. Octavian...is Miss Risë Stevens who sings very well...Let's not forget while we're on the subject that we have a great artist who premiered the role of Octavian here, and who played it in other places more than 100 times. She is Miss Marisa Ferrer*. who we will have the pleasure to hear again in 'Rosenkavalier' in October. [12]

Due to unprecedented interest in the Vienna Opera's *Der Rosenkavalier*, two more performances were added on September 7th and 9th. When the news broke that Strauss died on September 8th, the day before her final appearance at the *Opéra*, a moment of silence was called for before the curtain went up, and Risë paid tribute to Strauss with a performance that paid full honor to his memory,

Risë Stevens, a glory of the Metropolitan Opera, is one

---

* Marisa Ferrer had debuted with the Paris Opera in 1924 and built her career mainly in France. By 1949, she had entered the beloved artist stage of her career and enjoyed a large following. Parisian by birth, she was in her early fifties at the time of the *Der Rosenkavalier* performances. A 1947 recording of *Les Troyens* in which she sings both leading roles, Cassandra and Dido, under the baton of Sir Thomas Beecham, reveals that she had a much leaner sound than Risë's more refulgent mezzo.

of the most famous mezzo-sopranos in the world. The warmth of her timbre and the range of her voice alone would be enough to make her reputation, but what can one say of her beauty and her talent as an actress? Not for an instant are we looking at the splendid creature that she actually is, but rather a noble young man, courageous knight and passionate lover, or that bumbling false chambermaid jammed into her skirts. [13]

Her Marschallin on this occasion was Maria Reining, her Sophie, Lisa della Casa. It was a privilege to appear opposite Reining and della Casa was one of the best Sophies she ever sang with, on a level with, her favorite, Steber in that part. Fourestier was another matter. He didn't have the right tempi or feeling for the score. It was doubly disappointing since it had been hoped that Richard Strauss would conduct the performances and it was on that basis that Risë accepted the engagement. When it became obvious that Strauss was too ill to appear, Forrestier was engaged instead.

Risë's agent, Kurt Weinhold, contacted Frank St. Leger at the Metropolitan on August 1st expressing her eagerness to begin studying the role of the prophetess, Marfa, in Modest Moussorgsky's, *Khovanshchina*. The Metropolitan Opera premiere for the opera was in the planning stages and Risë was handed one of the most problematical characters in opera to interpret. He requested that the score with the English translation and cuts be sent to her in care of Walter's mother in Vienna. On the 16th, Max Rudolf reached Risë at the Hotel Alte Post in Zell an See, Austria, assuring her that she would receive a score even if he had to send her St.Leger's. He did not have the cuts since the conductor, Emile Cooper, was still in Paris and had not as yet given them to him. He suggested she write directly to Cooper for further information.

Arrangements were made to meet in Paris on the 28th with

rehearsals scheduled for the 9th of September. Risë left for the States on the 12th on the "America."

Under Johnson, contracts were not concluded very far in advance and on September 18th, Kurt Weinhold of Lawrence Evans & Weinhold, Inc. represented Risë at the signing since she had not yet arrived from Paris. The fee per performance rose to six hundred fifty dollars in New York, which made her the highest paid mezzo on the roster. Very few artists commanded the top fee of one thousand dollars since sopranos and tenors were more likely to Risë to that level than lower voice singers. Helen Traubel and Lily Pons were two who were paid at the highest level. With this contract, however, Risë, broke a fee barrier for mezzos by getting one thousand dollars on tour.

After their return from Paris, Risë and Walter decided to move back to New York for good. Both of them knew that the center of their lives would not be Hollywood. Her career at the Metropolitan had blossomed beyond their expectations and Walter had found his niche as her manager. The house on Woodrow Wilson drive was put up for sale and a bid by popular radio actress, Lillian Randolf, accepted. When word got out in the community, unidentified members threatened to ruin Risë's career and do physical harm to Nicky if the sale went through. Upon learning of the hostility against her, the African-American, Miss Randolf, withdrew her offer saying she would not live where she was not wanted. The house eventually sold to Lex Barker of *Tarzan* fame. When they returned to New York to stay, they took up residence again at the Essex House but soon thereafter rented an eleven room duplex in 130 East 67th Street, a colorful block that housed a Police Station, a Fire Station, a Synagogue and the Russian Embassy.

Risë's second television show was on the October 10th edition of *The Voice of Firestone*, a program she was particularly fond of on account of her warm regard for Harvey and Betty Firestone. It was a reciprocal feeling, one that prompted Risë to devote a 45 rpm disc to the songs of Harvey's mother, Idabelle, who wrote, "If I Could Tell You" and "In My Garden," the opening and closing theme songs of the program.

The Voice of Firestone was typical of early television in that it was presented live. Rehearsals were limited to one on the morning of the show. The lighting was primitive and since the studios were not air conditioned, they had to be turned on and off to prevent over-heating. Risë soon learned it took getting used to. The conductor, Howard Barlow, was mediocre at best but he was distinguished looking, photographed well and had great charm. Entire changes of costumes for specialty numbers were difficult to manage given time limitations. Bits and pieces of costumes were added to an evening dress, a shawl and a flower for the ladies or a sash worn with a tuxedo for the gentlemen. Sometimes, in later shows, complete costume changes were attempted but were nerve-wracking. Risë needed Walter's assistance in buttoning the costume, fastening a wig, adjusting anything that needed it, all in the space of the time it took Barlow to get the orchestra through a brief musical interlude. The exposure the show provided was invaluable, however, and helped make her even more popular when she toured.

Now with television added to her already full calendar of opera and tour dates, free time became increasingly scarce. In spite of that, Risë did not neglect her responsibilities to her fans and her customary *Metro-Lark* column appeared as usual,

> As you know, this is Mr. Edward Johnson's last season at the Metropolitan and I am especially interested in making his last season a memorable one. He has been one of the most important people in my artistic life since I was a student at the Juilliard School of Music. His advice and guidance have been important to me. [14]

Der Rosenkavalier was selected as the opening opera of Johnson's final year, a first for the rambunctious Strauss score. It was to have been a tribute to the composer but in view of his recent death became instead a memorial.

Like the previous season's *Otello*, it was telecast over ABC under the sponsorship of Texaco to an audience larger than the year before. Viewers in Detroit, Chicago, Washington, Philadelphia and Baltimore, who never thought it possible, could now witness a Metropolitan Opera opening. The telecast began at a quarter to eight with curtain time set at eight-fifteen, which enabled commentators, Gene Hamilton and Pauline Frederick, to conduct pre-opera interviews in the lobby. Milton Cross was in the broadcast booth, as usual, and Edward Johnson gave a backstage tour after the first act. During the second intermission, retired diva, Mary Garden, and composer, Deems Taylor, interviewed guests.

Prominent in Edward Johnson's box was Rudolf Bing and his wife, the retired ballerina, Nina Schelemskaya-Schelesnaya. The standees, were reduced in number due to television equipment. Seats were at a twelve-dollar high for the orchestra and the total receipts for the evening added up to twenty-three thousand dollars. The opening was part of the Monday night subscription series, Society Night, as it was sometimes called, and was by far the most heavily in demand. Bing would change this by making opening nights non-subscription, thereby, placing emphasis on the opera and not on the audience.

The Metropolitan Opera opening on November 21st was attended by the usual cadre of reporters among whom was the irrepressible gossip columnist, Cholly Knickerbocker, who found the social end of it rather unremarkable unlike others in the recent past, "nobody stood on his head or came barefoot or [socialite] Betty Henderson didn't prop her leg on the table or drink champagne from her shoe." [15]

Rudolf Bing was to comment years later, "Opening night in 1949 was depressing in the extreme, not so much the performance...as the audience. I had never seen such antics in an opera house." [16] What he observed in the audience was decidedly mild in comparison to other years and what he saw on stage was a mixed affair if Virgil Thomson's review is accurate,

> it should have been a better show than it was. Actually, the second act almost jelled. The first failed to produce an ensemble between stage and pit [the third was unheard due to a deadline] Both acts witnessed had the advantage of Stevens' vocal beauty and admirably studied boyish movements in the role of Octavian. [17]

Frieda Hempel, the Metropolitan Opera's first Marschallin, attended the performance and paid Risë a very high compliment when she said, "Of the several singers who have essayed this role, perhaps Risë Stevens most closely approximates the true Octavian as Strauss conceived him." [18]

Four days after the opening, Risë reintroduced her Dalila on a Saturday matinee broadcast that, by then, reached over 235 stations. It was eight years earlier that an initial encounter with the role did not please most of the New York critics. In the meantime, she had restudied it and was able to bring to it greater vocal opulence through her on-going work with Vera Schwarz.

Motley designed new costumes but again, the critics were less than impressed. Francis D. Perkins recognized the problems inherent in the opera, "To represent Dalilah with irresistible persuasiveness, yet without exaggeration, is difficult. Miss Stevens avoided this pitfall, but was dramatically persuasive only at intervals." [19]

Chapter 13

Apart from observing the workings of the opera company during Johnson's last year, Bing was determined to firm up repertory and artists early, both to ease himself into the top spot as smoothly as possible and to show the type of opera company he planned to run. When it came time to meet with Bing to discuss her next season, he was all formality, ignoring the fact that they knew one another since Glyndebourne. There was no attempt at any pre-discussion informality. He informed Walter and Risë that he had no intention of presenting *Mignon* ever or *Carmen* for the foreseeable future. He could offer only two performances of *Der Rosenkavalier* and the part of Prince Orlofsky in *Die Fledermaus*. Risë was insulted. Orlofsky was a role she had done at the Brooklyn *Opéra-Comique* when she was eighteen and, typically, she was just about to make her feelings known in no uncertain terms and walk out when Walter kicked her leg signaling her to be silent. He knew what Risë was thinking but instead of getting on the wrong side of Bing, Walter told him they would be very happy to consider what he told them. When they left the office, Risë was furious but Walter convinced her that if she helped Bing out now, he would consider her for other things in the future. Placated, she agreed and accepted the contract on Bing's terms with one important proviso, that it would be for no more than six Orlofskys.

Bing was grateful although he did not express it directly to Risë. In a letter to her agent Kurt Weinhold, he not only confirmed her continued association with the company but also raised her performance fee for *Der Rosenkavalier* to seven hundred fifty dollars. With her consent, Orlofsky would be one hundred dollars less considering it was in essence a cameo appearance. There was no tour option, therefore, the one-thousand dollar fee she was given by Johnson as of February 1, 1950 for each performance outside of New York was not a factor. A very important point was confirmed that she would be given first nights and broadcasts. He concluded his letter of March 6th with his asking Weinhold to tell Risë how much he was looking forward to working with her once again. It would have made her feel much better had he told her that himself at their first meeting.

* * * *

Producing *Khovanshchina* in Johnson's last season, was a case of bad timing. It soon became apparent that Rudolf Bing was not interested in the work for his opening season and that all the effort invested in it would be short-lived. As it turned out it received only four performances and disappeared along with its conductor, Emil Cooper, who was one of Bing's first casualties.

John Chapman offered the most positive review after its premiere on February 16th, "[the] opera is jammed with strange and often exhilarating music and is alive with color. The sets and costumes by somebody christened Mstislav Dobujinsky, are highly effective theatrically. Under the direction of Emil Cooper, the orchestra sounded fascinatingly Russian...For me the triumphant figure of the performance was Risë Stevens...It seemed that never before had she sung with such warmth and range and beauty, or with such effectiveness in the portrayal of a character." [1]

"Khovanshchina was not a success", stage director, Dino Yannapolis commented almost fifty years later in conversation with the author. "The sets were disappointing, too old-fashioned. I thought Risë was excellent and Jerome Hines, too, but Cooper was heavy handed; he did too much explaining of what the music should sound like. He had an affinity for the work and conducted the world premiere in Paris for Diaghilev. Tibbett was another problem, he was miscast. He was a sweet and lovely man but his voice couldn't carry it." [2]

The work was done as a gift to Johnson in his last season and replaced Prokofiev's *War and Peace* which was originally planned. Worsening relations with Russia prompted the Met to distance itself from an opera by a contemporary composer identified with the Soviets. The casting was variable and, sadly, Lawrence Tibbett's career was pretty much over by then. He could not carry the pivotal role of Prince Ivan Khovansky, leaving a gaping whole in the center of the work. Cooper was a competent conductor but not great. He was able to transfer his love for the score to Johnson who in turn agreed to its being presented by the Metropolitan opera. It was Cooper, also, who talked Risë into doing Marfa even though it didn't have the depth of characterization that she always looked for. Marfa is down-trodden from beginning to end, one-dimensional, and difficult to bring to life. However, the second act's, "Divination Scene", in which Marfa foretells the downfall of Prince Galitzin is one of its highlights and one of the most powerful scenes in opera. Apart from the difficulty of realizing the character, the tape of the broadcast on February 25th reveals another problem, much of the score is too low for Risë causing her to lose vocal color, a rarity in her performances.

The 1949-1950 Metropolitan Opera season was a particularly heavy one for Risë and it was the focus of an article in the February 20th issue of *Life* magazine. Titled, "Work Horse of the Met", [3] it described Risë as one of the busiest artists on the Metropolitan Opera roster and was illustrated with an array of photographs by Walter Sanders showing her in several different roles. Behind the article was Edgar Vincent who had been writing publicity for Risë while employed by the Muriel Francis Agency. When he was encouraged to strike out on his own by Walter, he became the third in Risë's immediate group of advisors, along with Walter and Vera Schwarz. At times, Nicky was included in these sessions, which made him an unofficial fourth.

It was their custom to sit down regularly to plan her next move. In essence, they served as the governing body for her career but she always retained the right to veto any of the suggestions. They knew the matter was settled once Risë said "no". While she quite often deferred to Walter on every day domestic matters, the turns her career would take were not his to control. Walter may have shaped her career but it was she who held the reins. She would not give up opera and he knew that. She did Hollywood at his urging but she could have resisted had she wanted to. Radio and television were part of his "stretching" but again she chose to go along with it and reaped the benefits. She took great pride in her accomplishments and had become very popular as a result of her own talent, hard work and luck. She knew that once a certain level of fame is achieved by public figures, there will be those who try to cut them down. It is this threat to her career that both she and her advisors had to guard against.

* * * *

The Summer Edition of *Metro-Lark* carried Risë's column dated July 28th, from her vacation rental on Southhampton, Long Island, she wrote,

> I would also like to tell you that I have decided to go with RCA Victor Records. I have been with Columbia Records for many years and I would say that they have been one of the most important factors in my life and I did not mean to upset them by leaving them. The interesting plans RCA Victor have in mind are complete recordings of my operatic repertoire. That will mean that within the next few years, I will be able to record complete: 'Carmen', 'Der Rosenkavalier', 'Mignon' and

'Samson and Dalila'. [4]

The move to RCA was not an easy decision since Columbia's Goddard Lieberson had taken very good care of Risë. He guided her through all of her albums, many of them best sellers. It was he who said that she made love to the microphone when she sang. According to the head of the Red Seal label's Artists and Repertoire activity, Alan Kayes, Risë's being lured away from Columbia was engineered by Manie [Emanuel] Sacks, who had resigned from Columbia Records some time before Risë's decision to switch labels. Shortly after he joined RCA as vice president in charge of the corporation's Record Division. Sacks was also instrumental in bringing Ezio Pinza and Frank Sinatra to RCA. Risë's attorney at the time was Harold Stern, a prominent lawyer in the entertainment industry, and his contract negotiations with Sacks on behalf of Risë involved intensive discussions about repertoire which Columbia had not proposed to Risë during her affiliation with them.

RCA was actively engaged in making full length operatic recordings at the time but Kayes, when interviewed, could not attest to verbal recording commitments made in the course of contract negotiations between Sacks and Risë's attorney. He also did not know whether any assurances might have been given for recording *Mignon*, *Carmen*, *Samson et Dalila* and *Der Rosenkavalier* for RCA. If indeed such commitments were made they were made without his knowledge.

Another factor in the decision to leave Columbia was that unlike RCA, they would not give Risë a ten thousand-dollar guarantee for twenty years. The guarantee was Walter's idea, and when Frank Sinatra and Dinah Shore heard about it, they requested the same arrangement and got it. The timing of the move, however, was awkward since the recording industry had suffered a loss in income with a slight falling off of sales and in moving to RCA when she did, she missed out on Columbia's recording of the Metropolitan Opera's version of *Die Fledermaus*.

219

Chapter 14

While Risë's involvement with *Die Fledermaus* was a footnote to her career at the Metropolitan Opera, the planning of the production by Rudolf Bing is indicative of how he operated and is worth studying. Johnson could not have handled the ins and outs of negotiations to get the production on the boards as Bing did, since his successor was a born administrator and he, always a tenor, in spite of his position. Risë and Johnson went back a long way and she was as genuinely fond of Johnson as he was of her, but with Bing it was different. She disliked and resented him for being cold and indifferent to her, for looking the other way when roles were distributed instead of looking at her. Importing Italian mezzo, Fedora Barbieri, to sing Eboli in his opening night, *Don Carlo*, while she was given a nothing role like Orlofsky, was an insult to her as an artist and could diminish her standing in the company. Johnson had promised her Eboli on two occasions and given her success as Laura and Marina a few years earlier, she should have done them. That Bing chose Robert Merrill to sing the Marquis di Posa over Leonard Warren, *the* Met's Verdi baritone, for his opening night was understandable. Warren and he could not come to terms on his contract. In spite of his assuring the Press that American artists would not be neglected in his administration, the opening *Don Carlo* raised doubts. With a cast that included, besides Barbieri, Italian bass Cesare Siepi as Philip I, Argentinian soprano Delia Rigal as Elisabetta and Swedish tenor Jussi Björling as the eponymous hero, the difference between what

Bing said and did was disturbing.

Johnson had to nurture a number of native born singers because World War II prevented European artists from coming to the States. If there had been no war, many of the American artists who developed under his aegis may not have had the opportunity to do so. The Metropolitan was always an international house but Bing sent out the wrong signals when the second cast for his opening were the Americans, Blanche Thebom, Jerome Hines (who did appear as the Grand Inquisitor in the opening cast), Eleanor Steber and Richard Tucker. In the minds of some observers this clearly meant trouble ahead for the Americans. Fortunately, choosing Robert Merrill in the lead cast over the fine Italian baritone, Paolo Silveri, who was assigned second place, offered some assurance that Bing would make good on his statement. From the start he wanted to show that it was his Metropolitan Opera now and not Johnson's. Introducing singers who had not appeared under the past administration, attempting to give productions a leaner Broadway look, seeking out the best in designers and directors, would be his way of doing things.

No one could argue against the merits of Bing's grand plan. Barbieri deserved the success she had on opening night. The more established Stevens, however, would have been equally impressive, but Bing did not see it that way. It is an entirely plausible assuption that Risë and Walter did not see it that way either. She had progressed beyond *seconda donna* roles which Eboli is, and there is no assurance that she would have consented to do it at that stage of her career. It would have presented her with the dilemma of turning Bing down whereas Walter's advice on accepting Orlofsky was a lesson in how to deal with the autocratic General Manager. As it turned out, Orlofsky was a personal triumph for its originality, which made Bing look good as well. Eboli would have been the greater risk and might have been picked apart by the critics, thereby, diminishing her in his eyes. Warren no doubt took umbrage at losing the opening but had he not insisted on doing things his way contractually, it would have been his. When Bing suggested he sing Posa in a subsequent revival, he refused. It is the only major baritone role in a Verdi opera presented by the Metropolitan Opera during his twenty-two seasons that he did not sing.

Perhaps, featuring Johnson veterans in his opening might have tied Bing too much to the former General Manager. New faces of 1950 were what he wanted and certainly introducing Cesare Siepi to Metropolitan Opera audiences from day one of his tenure made a good impression. That Siepi was called in virtually at the last minute to replace Bing's original choice, the Bulgarian bass, Boris Christoff, who was denied a visa, was a stroke of good luck. The Italian proved to be a sound investment in the future, returning for twenty-three seasons thereafter, whereas Christoff would never again agree to Bing's terms for making a debut.

Bing, however, was not without constraints. His success was tied to audience approval as shown in box office receipts and it took that body of overseers to confirm Warren's stature in the Verdi repertory. He didn't need to be told of Risë's importance to the company. His first season's line-up of operas included only one role in her active repertory, Octavian. He gave it to her and a new role as well. In the eleven years she sang during his reign, Carmen was the only one of her major roles that received a new production and he gave her that also*. Orlofsky did not compensate for other new assignments he might have chosen, but it is less a comment on his respect for her, than how he saw her as an artist. He had promised her *Carmen* in Glyndebourne ten years earlier and he picked up the thread the following year in New York. She may not have been Eboli in his opinion or her own but she definitely was Carmen. Between then and now, however, Risë was still saddled with that infernal Prince Orlofsky.

Samson et Dalila of 1952-53 and *Der Rosenkavalier* of 1955-56 were revised productions.

The *Fledermaus* Affair and Risë's Triumph Against All Odds

Viennese born Bing, unlike Risë, had a special affinity for *Die Fledermaus*. While she might have aborted plans to present it if she could, or at least her involvement in it, he wasted no time in securing Fritz Reiner as musical director early on in the planning stages. That Bing wanted Joseph Mankiewicz to direct was a shrewd move on his part if the Metropolitan Opera were to be brought into modern times. He had been turned down by his first choice, Rouben Mamoulian, when he committed himself to the ill-fated Kurt Weill musical, *Huckleberry Finn*. Danny Kaye was also high on Bing's list of talent he wanted associated with the production and when the Press heard about it they went to no ends to point up the novelty of the idea.

Bing's next step was to sell Reiner on the idea of both Mankiewicz and Kaye. In a letter dated March 28, 1950, Bing apprised Reiner that Danny Kaye was entertaining the offer to perform Frosch in the Strauss operetta. He also revealed to Reiner that Joe Mankiewicz was a possibility as stage director but that Rolf Gerard was definite as production designer. Concentrating next on the cast, he mentioned Charles Kullman as suitable for the second or third covers for the lead tenor role of Gabriel von Eisenstein and Lawrence Tibbett as first choice for the prison warden, Frank.

Reiner answered on March 30, 1950,

...Re: Danny Kaye - After hearing him on the Radio last Sunday night I am not convinced that he is the right man for Frosch. Did you check on Bobby Clark?
Your description of Mr. Mankiewicz certainly makes him sound eligible for the difficult task of staging the Fledermaus.
Kullman - Eisenstein definitely better than [Set] Svanho[l]m - Why not the first cast? Also Dorothy Kirsten - Rosalinde better than the Bulgarian bombshell [Ljuba Welitsch]. Frankly I do not see Welitsch in the

part. Tibbett for Frank, ausgezeichnet [first rate]...

This is followed by a P.S.,

> I have been thinking over the Mankiewiez idea - I have
> had experiences in working with non-operatic stage di-
> rectors and learned a lesson. [1]

As it turned out, Mankiewiez was not agreeable to directing *Die Fledermaus*. When he withdrew, Bing's second choice,
Tyrone Guthrie, recommended Garson Kanin. In a three-page
letter to Bing, dated May 5th, Kanin made clear that he did
not take it lightly that the control of the production would
not be in his hands but Bing's.

The powers of persuasion on Bing's part and a lessening
of his grip on the production brought Kanin around to accepting the contract. That John Gutman was relieved of his
responsibility for the adaptation of the book and Howard
Dietz hired in his place was mainly due to Reiner's dissatisfaction with the Gutman version. This was good news to
Kanin and Dietz, who had been only concerned with the lyrics up to that point.

On September 16th, Bing contacted Reiner relating his
distress over the "'Fledermaus' business". [2] Reiner was engaged by RCA Victor to conduct a highlights album of *Die
Fledermaus*. Columbia Records had an agreement with the
Metropolitan to record an abridged version in December of
1950 with Columbia Artists but since Reiner was with RCA,
contractually, he could not conduct the Columbia cast recording. Bing was not happy about his recording it for Victor nor was Columbia. Apart from the arrangement the Metropolitan had with Columbia, the record company had promised to back a long tour of *Die Fledermaus*. Any false move
on the opera company's part could jeopardize both the future of the Met on records and the tour. To add to the deli-
cacy of the situation, the RCA Victor album was due to appear before Columbia's.

Max Rudolf apprised Bing of the *Die Fledermaus* recording *via* house memo dated September 1, 1950, which both RCA and Columbia were intent on doing. In it he informed Bing that RCA had scheduled rehearsals for September 5th and that their casting of the featured roles could conflict with the Met's new production. Victor wanted Marguerite Piazza who had already signed a contract to appear with the Met but did not have an existing contract with RCA. Her contract forbade her to make any recording commitments without the consent of the Metropolitan. Under the circumstances, approval was denied and the role went to Regina Resnik. Since Stevens and Munsel already were Victor artists, the Met could not prevent them from doing the recording although Risë had reservations at first. She did not want to strain relations with Bing in particular and the Met in general. As it turned out, she did neither. Hugh Thompson signed with RCA before the Met could stop him and he was allowed to do the new production but not the Columbia recording. The remainder of the RCA cast did not concern Bing. Robert Merrill [Falke], Jan Peerce [Alfred] and James Melton [Eisenstein] were not scheduled to appear in the staged version. The RCA highlights would be sung in the Ruth and Thomas Martin translation since the Dietz lyrics went to Columbia.

On September 18th, Reiner did the unforgivable and commenced to record *Die Fledermaus* or *Fledermaus* as it was called at the Met. Unknowingly, it meant the beginning of the end of his involvement with the production. On the same day as his letter to Reiner made known his distress over the recording, Bing contacted Danny Kaye confirming that September 25th must be the deadline for his accepting or rejecting the Metropolitan's offer of Frosch. Realizing that the chances for signing Kaye were getting slimmer, Bing was open to suggestions. On the 18th, Kanin wrote "R. B." ("This is how we address tycoons in America")[3] that Buster Keaton had commitments elsewhere but Bert Lahr and James Barton were possibilities. Gutman liked the Lahr idea but rejected Barton since as an actor for years in *Tobacco Road*, he felt he was not for them. He suggested Henry Morgan since as a radio and television personality outside commitments would not be a factor.

In the meantime, Bing started looking around for another conductor for *Fledermaus* since Reiner had seriously jeopardized the opera house's contract with Columbia. He needed one who could direct both production and recording and his attention turned to his long-time friend, Bruno Walter. He contacted him at the Schloss Hotel in Berlin by telegram on September 21st offering him *Fledermaus* in a new production with a cast headed by Ljuba Welitsch (Rosalinde), Patrice Munsel (Adele), Risë (Prince Orlofsky), Set Svanholm (Eisenstein), Richard Tucker (Alfred), the recording for Columbia Records (with different principals) and ample rehearsal time.

On the 22nd, Spyros Skouras, President of Twentieth Century Century-Fox Film Corporation gave Bing the latest update on Danny Kaye. Filming for his current movie, *On the Riviera*, would run into the time he would have to report for *Fledermaus* and, therefore, he could not accept the engagement. Skouras was all apologies but it left Bing with two important components not in place.

On September 24th, Dr. Walter answered, "Deeply regret cannot accept Fledermaus." [4]

Not one to give up easily, Bing sent a second telegram on the 25th, recalling Walter's *Die Fledermaus* in Salzburg with great fondness, stressing that his doing it at the Met would be a highlight of the season.

At the same time, Bing wrote to Kanin and wanted to know if Lahr responded or if Bobby Clark was still interested after all the publicity about Kaye. He also suggested Eddie Cantor but expressed doubts about Fred Allen's suitability. A second letter to Kanin on the 27th, found Bing still hopeful of securing Lahr or Clark but expressed ignorance of Zero Mostel whom Kanin suggested in his letter of the 26th.

On September 28th, Walter reiterated his earlier feelings,

"Please do not doubt my wish to help you as much as possible but cannot conduct Fledermaus for compelling artistic reasons." [5]

A month passed with no breakthrough on either the conductor or comedian front and to relieve the tension, Kanin wired Bing on October 30th, "I wonder why you don't engage Toscanini at this propitious moment." [6]

Without realizing that he was on a very shaky ground with Bing and the production might be taken away from him, Reiner wrote to Kanin on October 31st and voiced objections over several directorial suggestions,

"...Re - Conducting the Overture facing the audience; sorry for various reasons not feasible.

"Re - Repeat of 'Dui-Du': I prefer not to tamper with the original score.

"Re - 'Acceleration Waltz' - I will play 'Southern Roses' because I like it better", etc., etc. [7]

However, on November 1st, Reiner in a letter to Kanin, expressed his complete delight with Rolf Gérard's sets. Bing responded to Reiner the same day in a letter that was a polite slap on the wrist for the conductor who had to be dealt with cautiously until a replacement was securely in place. He thanked Reiner for sending him a copy of his letter to Kanin but pointed out that it did not have his accustomed charm. Bing's acerbic wit (when dealing with all but the members of the board) would become better and sharper as time went on.

Two telegrams were exchanged between Bing and Kanin. Bing to Kanin on November 2nd alerted him to the fact that Milton Berle was not interested, but Groucho Marx and Eddie Cantor were still possibilities. Kanin responded on the 3rd that he was to see Marx but Cantor was not suitable. Bing sent a telegram to Kanin on the 7th as well, asking if he preferred Jack Gilford to Jimmy Durante or else Jimmy Savo who might be willing to play Frosch. An answer came back immediately, "Please sign Gilford." [8]

The comedian problem solved, Bing still had every inten-
tion of replacing Reiner and was negotiating with Eugene
Ormandy. Bing informed Reiner on November 24th, that
Ormandy was agreeable to conducting both the new pro-
duction and the complete recording. He also thanked Reiner
for his volunteering to stay on until everything was finalized.
Ormandy's appointment was announced on the 25th giving
Reiner's heavy workload at the Metropolitan as the reason
for his stepping aside. The reports also mentioned that since
Reiner was with RCA, Ormandy would conduct the
Fledermaus recording for Columbia.

As the date drew nearer for her to take Prince Orlofsky
off the shelf where she had stored him without regrets over
twenty years ago, Risë found that the costume created for
her by Rolf Gérard would not do. Baggy Russian style trousers stuck in boots worn under a blouse with flowing sleeves
was not the look she wanted. If she was going to bring
Orlofsky to life, it had to be according to her own show-stop-
ping design. She was determined to make the role bigger than
it is by visually making Orlofsky dominate his surroundings.
Recalling how Walter looked in one of his films, she insisted
on a similar costume, a military jacket, straight trousers and
to add to her height, built up men's shoes (which she herself
purchased from a store near the opera house). A combed
back wig (later restyled and used for Orfeo), a pencil mus-
tache (supposedly modeled after Edgar Vincent's), a monocle
(her own invention), a few medals and a foot long cigarette
holder completed the outfit. As she did with Octavian, she
planned to wear Walter's cologne to make the "masculine"
illusion complete for those around her.

Loren Hightower, a leading dancer with the Metropolitan, recalled his *Fledermaus* experience, "Risë was marvelous in a role [Orlovsky] that can be a bore. She is theatrical
by nature and when she played a man she looked like one." [9]

Patrice Munsel added to the *Fledermaus* saga, "Risë's
Orlofsky was very chic and you couldn't get near her with

that cigarette holder. Welitsch was a delight to work with but she made it to the top by fighting for it. Bing had the notion that solo bows were out, so we took curtain calls in groups. When Ljuba, Risë and I went out Ljuba was in the middle and we were on either side of her. Before we knew it, she grasped our arms and pushed herself forward to receive the applause. Now Risë and I weren't about to let her get away with this so we did the same thing when we came out again and we held her arms and pushed ourselves forward. Ljuba was a good sport and we all had a big laugh over it." [10]

That *Fledermaus*, turned out to be the hit of the season took everyone connected with it by surprise. The critics, while generally in accord with praising most of the production, still had a few qualms about this or that.

Virgil Thomson's review of Risë, in particular, eased any ill-feelings she had about doing Orlofsky but he was not terribly kind to the rest of the players. He threw a few wilted flowers at Welitsch and several brickbats at Gilford, reserving his highest praise for Ormandy and Risë, "As actor, only Risë Stevens seemed to this observer distinguished. Playing the role of an adolescent and fabulously rich Russian prince, she had style, elegance, carried conviction." [11] While he admired the scenery, he felt "An easy going spirit, indeed, dominated the action and left a stamp of amateurishness on the whole stage." [12]

Harriett Johnson to the relief of all found much to admire, "As staged by Mr. Kanin, it's far from being a dull show or a 'high-brow' one. On the musical side...The Metropolitan was fortunate in securing the services of Eugene Ormandy. Patrice Munsel was superb...Risë Stevens was riotous as the slick monocled dandy. Streamlined and decorated with a Russian accent she made the audience hilarious." [13] The representative from *Musical America* was no less positive, "Her portrait of the bored prince was a masterpiece of bloodless languor...she delivered her principal song with the greatest aplomb, ending it leaning against the proscenium arch and flirting with the occupants of the stage box." [14]

The remainder of the reviews were equally as positive aside from major reservations about the ballet choreographed for Act 2 by Anthony Tudor to the *Roses from the Waltz*. Taking the criticism to heart, Bing asked Zachary Solov to create new choreography. The problem with the Tudor version was that it had nothing to do with the time or mood of the piece. Bing insisted on something more Viennese. He wanted waltzes. Solov gave him waltzes.

The best was saved for the New Year's Eve performance of *Fledermaus* and in the tradition of anything goes on that particular day of the year, impresario Bing became the center of attention. Risë as Prince Orlovsky stepped forward to serenade the General Manager in Box 23 with interpolated lyrics to "Chacun à son goût" penned specially for the occasion by Howard Dietz.

> "The op-er-as that must be your choice -
>   If you like plays that sing -
> Are solely dependent on one voice -
>   The voice of Rudolf Bing.
> If he is in a Wagnerian mood -
>   We're forced to strain a lung -
> To serve the ponderous musical food -
>   of Götterdämmerung.
> But if he feels the surge of an urge
>   To charm the op'ra house
> With Viennesy tunes that emerge
>   As light as Fledermaus,
> The spring in Bing can turn off a dirge
>   And turn on a Johann Strauss.
> Mister Bing is the king uncrowned here
>   Though he rarely is on view
>   And we do
>   Just what Bing
>   Tells us to.
> The expression is never found here
>   'Chacun à son goût'.

There is only one 'goût' around here
And you all know who! [15]
[copyright 1998 Howard Dietz's daughter, Liza Gard.
Reprinted with her permission]

At the conclusion, she pointed her long cigarette holder at Bing prompting a hearty round of applause from a delighted audience.

When the two recordings of *Fledermaus* were issued, Arthur Bronson in *Variety* felt, "RCA has the double-barreled advantage over Columbia of youth and intelligibility. The RCA 'Fledermaus' is a sharp, incisive performance, done with clarity, pace and spirit under Fritz Reiner. Singers are first rate, and chorus and orchestra are good." [16] His criticism of the Columbia album centered on the unintelligibility of Ljuba Welitsch and Lily Pons. The fact that they could not be understood defeated the purpose of recording the work in English.

Variety reported that *Fledermaus* was the, "Hottest B.O. Prospect in Years; B'way Slant a Factor." [17] Arthur Bronson added, "'Fledermaus' probably has caused more excitement than any other production this season said one official, 'every homesick Viennese in N.Y. wants to come'." [18]

Halfway through her *Fledermaus* assignment, another aristocratic male, much more to Risë's liking, entered her life, but this time Octavian had an entirely new Marschallin to romance. As part of her appeasement package, Helen Traubel was given one complete *Ring* cycle and one new role to help take away the sting of Kirsten Flagstad's return. Why anyone, including Traubel, would envision her in this most Viennese of roles, is difficult to fathom for Traubel was very American. There was no question of her having the voice for Marschallin but having the style for it remained to be seen.

The most startling of [Bing's] innovations was to cast Helen Traubel as the Princess von Werdenberg. This was not a wholly successful innovation, for Miss Traubel in appearance cannot provide the illusion of a woman inspiring a passionate love in a young man. Moreover, her voice is a little too heavy and too slow for the light and dancing Strauss music. Nevertheless, she was surprisingly effective in her own arias. [19]

The reviewer for the *Wall Street Journal* went on to say, "Risë Stevens as Octavian was in good voice, and she performed with conviction once she got over the first act obstacle of trying to dash Miss Traubel off her feet." [20]

Fortune didn't smile on the next two performances of *Der Rosenkavalier*. An indisposition caused Risë to cancel the Philadelphia appearance on the 9th and on the 11th she was injured on stage.

John Chapman reported the incident, "On Thursday night, Risë Stevens got sore at Fritz Kreen [sic, as Baron Ochs] and, in a well-bred fury, dashed a wine glass to the floor, to show her displeasure [as Octavian]. A splinter of the glass bounced up and hit her in the eye-and she bravely carried on to the end." [21]

Apart from emergency first aid during a long intermission, she returned for the final act. The sliver of glass was removed later and she was able to appear as Orlofsky on the 13th. After that there were only two performances to go before she bid farewell to the bored Russian Prince on the Saturday matinee broadcast of January 20th. That also marked the end of her engagement and she would not be seen again at the Metropolitan for over a year.

What could have been a disappointing season for her turned out to be one of the best. Even she had to admit that Orlofsky was successful beyond belief. Her stock of recordings at RCA was constantly increasing and another month-long recital tour would occupy her in February. At home, Nicky was enrolled in New York's prestigious Browning School on East 62nd street and would remain there until eighth grade. In addition, rumor had it that Bing had relented on producing *Carmen* and the possibility of its return to the Metropolitan as early as the following season was mentioned by Arthur Berger in the February 25th edition of the *New York Herald-Tribune*. Few knew, however, that Risë had already been approached by Bing and was assured that if a new production came about, it would be hers. Walter was right, she helped Bing out in his first season by consenting to do a role she had no interest in and in return, as a thank-you, she would get the one which meant a great deal to her.

The Metropolitan Opera contract for 1951-1952 was signed March 24th for ten performances of *Carmen* at seven hundred fifty dollars each in New York and one thousand dollars each for out of town performances. The following December, she agreed to sing an additional thirteen Carmens on tour, thereby, increasing her Metropolitan Opera income by thirteen thousand dollars.

In anticipation of the new Metropolitan Opera production, RCA Victor planned to record a complete *Carmen* starring Risë with Jussi Björling, Licia Albanese, Robert Merrill and Fritz Reiner conducting. It was one of Risë's and Björling's hopes that someday they would be featured together either on stage or on a recording. *Werther* was suggested as a joint vehicle for them in the 1940s but did not materialize and the *Carmen* recording with Björling went awry also much to her disappointment. *Jussi*, a biography of Björling co-authored by his widow, Anna-Lisa, and Andrew Farkas, provides an explanation for the tenor's absence, "With an endless string of engagements in the months ahead, Jussi realized that in spite of his fabled memory and his capacity for concentrated work he wouldn't be able to learn Don José in time to absorb and do justice to a role in French he had never rehearsed or sung on stage. On 25 April Jussi cabled RCA that it was impossible for him to make the *Carmen* recording in June; he proposed that the recording be postponed. Alan Kayes [commercial manager for RCA] replied by return mail that too was impossible; the recording was announced for an October release, and 'we were so far committed in our arrangements as regards orchestra, chorus, rehearsal and recording studios that we found it necessary to go forward with the project by securing a replacement for you in the role of Don José'." [22]

Richard Tucker was a logical choice but had a contract with Columbia. Jan Peerce, however, was a Victor artist and the role of Don José fell to him. He learned the part on very short notice and proved musically efficient.

Alan Kayes said, "The casting of Peerce as Don José and Albanese as Micaela was a decision I made along with Dick Mohr [Richard Mohr, Artist and Repertory Representative] for contractual as well as artistic considerations and Fritz Reiner certainly did not object to the casting. The highlights of *Die Fledermaus* which had been recorded with Reiner as conductor had been successful and he was completely satisfied with the casting of *Carmen*." [23] Mohr later recalled that Peerce was aware that his voice was not large and compensated for it by trying to always be very close to the microphone creating problems of balance.

The orchestra Reiner led was comprised of musicians from various orchestras including the Metropolitan Opera. The timpanist, Richard Horowitz, a veteran member of the Metropolitan Opera Orchestra, when asked about the recording, waxed enthusiastic about Risë but remembered some disagreement over tempi. Robert Merrill had the same recollection,

> I spoke to Dick Mohr about Reiner having to listen to us singing. He was too involved with the orchestra. A good opera conductor is involved with both. If he respected your tempi, he went along, otherwise they were too fast. Toscanini would accommodate a singer, Reiner would sometimes. After I talked to Mohr, Reiner did slow the tempi down a little. It wasn't a one take recording, I remember doing the 'Toreador Song' two or three times.

We had a little trouble with the fight scene and it had to be redone. With recordings, the people in the control booth run it. When recording an opera, the conductor is much closer to you. It's a different deal than when he's in the pit. Reiner was easy to talk to though in spite of all that. [24]

When the recording was issued, evaluating it with two others, Harold D. Rosenthal said, "To give Risë Stevens her due, she does contrive to create a real Carmen-she has the sultry type of voice that one usually associates with the part, and is far more successful than either [Suzanne] Juyol or [Solange] Michel on the other complete sets." * [25]

* * *

Rudolf Bing's second season promised to be even more an artistic success than the first. Three of the most popular operas in the repertoire, *Aida, Rigoletto*, and *Carmen* were to be restored in new trappings. *Così fan Tutte*, not heard at the Metropolitan since 1928, was scheduled for a long overdue return.

Bing had been stunned by the adverse reception accorded the updated Horace Armistead *Cavalleria Rusticana* and *Pagliacci* the season before, therefore, three of the new productions of 1951-1952, as a result, followed a conventional, albeit well-designed path which aimed to please a conservative audience. The fourth and last of the new productions, *Carmen*, had, as it turned out, the distinct advantage of being inadequately financed. It was badly in need of an infusion of fresh ideas. The awareness that it was the riskiest undertaking of the four restudied works did nothing to calm Bing's anxieties.

* Suzanne Juyol with Albert Wolff, Conductor, Orchestra and Chorus of the Opéra-Comique, Paris and Solange Michel with André Cluytens and the Orchestra and Chorus of the Théatre National de L'Opéra-Comique.

Chapter 15

A stage director must be found, new backgrounds built, the mise-en-scène restudied, some of the leading roles redistributed. Artistic success for Bizet's opera lies in complete rehabilitation. I believe it can be accomplished. Robert Lawrence, "On Doing 'Carmen'." [1]

It wasn't sheer perversity on Bing's part that he did not immediately restage *Carmen* his first year as General Manager. If it were to be done right, the production team had to be chosen with great care in order to restore the work to a pristine state. In *5000 Nights at the Opera*, Bing wrote, "Not having a French conductor for *Carmen* I was extremely anxious to get a French director, specifically René Clair, whom I had come to know in London; and when Clair proved impossible I tried Jean-Louis Barrault, who was also unavailable." [2]

As early as January of 1950, while negotiating unsuccessfully, as it turned out, with Rouben Mamoulian to stage *Don Carlo* and, perhaps, *Fledermaus*, Bing mentioned that he was not yet ready to tackle *Carmen*. By the following November, however, Bing contacted Mamoulian by letter dated the 18th that he was seriously considering *Carmen* along with *Aida* and *Rigoletto*. While he did not specify which he would like Mamoulian to direct, he was opening the way for him to take his pick. The offer came with the hope that he would not be let down again at the last minute as he was with *Don Carlo*. He also was wary about engaging someone involved in films since he was having a great deal of trouble securing a "yes" or "no" from Danny Kaye at that time. Mamoulian would have to give him a firm commitment or he could not realize his hope of bringing him to the Metropolitan. The elusive director answered early in December that he would be interested in *Carmen* and that Bing's willingness to do it meant that he had found a Carmen. However, since Bing's plans would not be finalized for at least two months, he could not commit himself until the project was more definite.

This, of course, was not an answer that Bing wanted or could live with. He needed a definite commitment. In January of 1951, he approached his fourth choice, Joshua Logan, who was offered *Carmen* outright based on past discussions with the director concerning his desire to work at the Metropolitan. Bing cautioned him, however, that he would face a lower fee than he was accustomed to on Broadway and far fewer rehearsal hours. The date for the premiere was now firmed up for the end of January of the following year.

Logan expressed an interest in the offer since he was very fond of the work but made a counter-offer that it be performed in English. Bing dismissed this suggestion immediately on the basis that some of the leading singers would be foreigners and could not cope with the text. In his experience, he pointed out that Covent Garden, which at that time did all opera in English, faced the problem of incomprehensibility of non-English speaking singers. He also could have mentioned that most native born singers in England and America were quite often incapable of being understood when singing English. Logan quickly bowed out when he could not get his way saying he would feel strange doing an opera in a foreign language in America. He did suggest he might be available for *Faust* in the future if he could rewrite the libretto.

While he was still in a quandary about where to turn next for a director, Bing secured Rolf Gérard as designer for three of his four new productions. *Carmen* would in all probability be his also but Bing cautioned Gérard that it might have to be postponed for a year. In February, Bing tried Mamoulian once more and this time, he had definite plans to present to him. The work would be done in French; there would be nine rehearsals with piano and four with orchestra; two lighting rehearsals; working with the artists away from the main stage could be arranged to his satisfaction; the time frame would be all of January. In addition he apprised him of the fact that Reiner would conduct and Gérard design.

At that time, Risë was in place as the first Carmen and Fedora Barbieri as the second [as it turned out, Risë was sole interpreter of the role that season]. Richard Tucker was to be the first Don José and [although this was not mentioned], Mario del Monaco as the second if he ever learned the opera in French [he did]. Bing could offer Mamoulian no more than two thousand dollars for his services and considering he gave Gérard five thousand dollars for each of his three operas, this was low for a director of Mamoulian's stature. Mamoulian declined again citing schedule conflicts.

In March, Bing wired Gian Carlo Menotti about directing *Carmen*. Menotti wired back that he would be in Europe January of 1952 so it was not possible. Soon after, Bing contacted Tyrone Guthrie and Guthrie was most amenable to the idea of taking on the assignment. Moreover, since Gérard would be in Europe, he could see him and discuss plans almost immediately. Bing was ecstatic. He wired Guthrie that the production should be in keeping with contemporary style but retain a French flavor.

As for the cast, the first Carmen would be Risë who he added was most attractive, with a good figure and very intelligent. Moreover, she was very anxious to work with an outstanding director in order to restudy the role. With a typical Bing barb, however, he added that he did not think her voice was as he remembered it from Glyndebourne twelve years earlier. Don José would be Richard Tucker, also an American, and the best tenor around according to Bing.

On May 10th, Guthrie signed a contract, which would run

from January 1ˢᵗ to the 31ˢᵗ of 1952 for a fee of one thousand dollars, plus one thousand five hundred dollars towards travel expenses. Tyrone Guthrie was fifty-two when he arrived in America to work on *Carmen*. A native of Kent, England, the 6' 4" director had extensive experience in opera with Sadler's Wells [*Carmen, The Barber of Seville*, *Falstaff* and *La Traviata* and Covent Garden [*Peter Grimes* and *La Traviata*]. Originally trained as a cymbalist, his career as a musician came to an abrupt end when as he explained, "deputizing, without rehearsal, for an inebriated cymbal player with the Belfast Philharmonic Orchestra. I counted 197 bars and made a sensational and confident entry 11 bars late." [3]

At the end of May Guthrie wrote to Gérard that he was delighted to be working with him since he remembered his Edinborough *Così*. Above all, he assured him that he did not want to inflict a concept on him that would go contrary to his own feelings. He wanted them to work together as one in formulating the stage picture. Guthrie had directed *Carmen* once before and this would eventually play an important part in the final shape the Metropolitan Opera production would take. He had definite ideas about the entire undertaking and in a lengthy letter to Bing on July 25ᵗʰ, he acquainted him with them. First, he mentioned that after meeting with Gérard he was confident they could work well together. Moreover, the designer enlightened him on daily life at the Metropolitan and what he would encounter. He then went on to stress the importance for adequate time to rehearse the chorus since they would have to act and not stand around as though they were singing an oratorio. He also suggested that some attractive looking extras be mixed with the chorus to improve the overall appearance.

Guthrie had to know who would be cast as Escamillo, Micaela and Zuniga. For Escamillo, he wanted a baritone who looked like a toreador and was sexually appealing; for Micaela, he stressed voice over looks and for Zuniga, handsome but rough. He did not stress physical appearance for

Don José but rather voice. Both director and designer wanted the third and fourth acts played as two scenes without an intermission. Guthrie suggested the chorus could be placed before a drop cloth depicting the front of the arena while the scenery was being changed. The suggestions became more and more detailed as he became more involved. The boys' chorus in Act I could be dispensed with or abbreviated since it went on too long [both Bing and Reiner were appalled at that notion and vetoed it immediately] and that extra lighting should be installed to brighten the front stage. He also hoped that Reiner would agree to eliminate the ballet, which by tradition was interpolated in the last act, on the grounds that it held up the final denouement.

As for casting, Bing assured him that he would not be disappointed. He mentioned that Nadine Conner [always a favorite with Bing] would be in the first cast and that she was both attractive in voice and appearance. Victoria de los Angeles would sing the role later in the season and the same could be said for her. Hilde Güden, who was second in the cast, had not made her debut as yet and, therefore, Bing refrained from mentioning her. Escamillo, he admitted, was a problem. Robert Merrill was no longer with the company having been fired by Bing for breaking his contract at the end of the preceding season to try his luck in Hollywood by co-starring with Dinah Shore and Alan Young in the immediately forgettable film, *Aaron Slick From Punpkin Crik*. Renato Capecchi was mentioned as a possibility but his patrician good looks did not agree with the raw sex appeal Guthrie demanded. Paolo Silveri, another young and personable Italian, was under consideration [and was chosen as second in the cast] as was the Metropolitan's own Frank Guarrera who beat out the competition with his voice, stage presence and appearance.

Mario del Monaco had been requested to learn Don José in French. At the same time, it was rumored that Maria Callas would make her Metropolitan Opera debut as Norma.

Del Monaco was Bing's choice to appear opposite her as Pollione, a role he did not know. When he objected that he had too many new roles to study including the French Don José, his complaints and Callas' waffling killed *Norma,* but fortunately not *Carmen.* He considered Don José to be one of his best roles but he also found it difficult to relearn in French. In February of 1951, he wrote to Bing informing him that he was withdrawing from *Carmen.* The determined General Manager persuaded him otherwise giving him a veiled threat that his entire contract might be in jeopardy if he reneged on *Carmen.*

Although Reiner was seemingly in place from the very beginning, rumor had it that Bruno Walter was Bing's first choice to conduct the new production. However, the condition under which he would accept the offer was that Elena Nikolaidi would be cast in the title role. Bing wanted Risë and, as with *Fledermaus,* he chose another conductor. When interviewed for this book, Elena Nikolaidi said that if Bruno Walter wanted her for *Carmen* that was news to her. He had never mentioned it and, moreover, when she told friends that she was about to sign a contract with the Metropolitan, they warned her that she would never sing Carmen or Dalila there since Risë owned those roles. George Darden, a member of the Metropolitan's Music Staff and close friend of Nikolaidi elaborated on the *Carmen* inquiry. Nikolaidi perceived Carmen as a flirt, not the near whore that the Guthrie version turned her into. Guthrie's way was not Nikolaidi's but it was just what Risë was looking for, a reinterpretation which would see her in a totally new light.

It was fortunate that Bruno Walter did not consent to conduct if Herbert F. Peyser's review of his Vienna *Carmen* in 1937 is accurate, "Bruno Walter may be whatever you will, but he is not a 'Carmen' conductor. He adopted some singular tempi..., yet the most conspicuous failing of his performance was its prevailing flabbiness. He lacked acuteness and edge. He seemed largely insensitive to the bite, the tang and the piercing vitality of this score, which is immensely red-blooded theatre rather than fragile chamber music, to which state he appeared eager to convert." [4]

Reiner had first conducted the Bizet score at nineteen in Hungary and it eventually became one of his most performed operas. For Risë, Bing's choice was a godsend because she genuinely admired him. It wasn't easy to like him, however, a fact which veteran Metropolitan Opera mezzo, Herta Glaz, brought out, "Once I had to take over for an indisposed colleague and as a result Reiner never once looked at me from the pit nor gave me cues. He was angry that there was a substitute whom he had not previously worked with. The director had to tell him if he didn't act correctly with me and give me the usual cues, there would be no performance. He was a magnificent musician but a terrible human being." [5]

As for the ballet, Bing felt the one in Act 2 should be a spontaneous occurrence with one or two girls and boys beginning it and more joining in as the frenzy increased. Guthrie was in agreement but for the ballet in the last act, Bing wanted a formal dance that was contrary to what Guthrie had in mind. As for his other suggestions, Bing assured him that adequate time was set aside for working with the chorus; that Zachary Solov, the choreographer, and Reiner were to discuss the ballet; that additional lighting would be considered as far as money allowed and that the boys' chorus stayed.

Bing wanted Guthrie in New York shortly after Christmas to prevent any delay in the start of rehearsals. Since the new production of *Così Fan Tutte* was to open on December 28th, he extended an invitation to Guthrie to join him in his box to see what director, Alfred Lunt, made of the opera. Guthrie responded that the 28th arrival would be the earliest he could arrange since his involvement with *A Midsummer Night's Dream* at the Old Vic would occupy him until the 26th and accepted the offer to attend *Così*. Also, he had heard nothing from Gérard about the designs. Bing wired Guthrie at the beginning of December that Gérard followed his instructions on scenic concept and that replicas were being sent to him for all acts but the final one. Gérard approved the scenery with minor alterations and construction began on December 10th on the third act as per Guthrie's suggestion. He had still yet to see the costume designs.

A shortage of money played an important part in the final form the production would take. There was quite simply none for an elaborate fourth act. A procession with all the pomp and trimming, a full ballet, massive scenery were all out of the question. As luck would have it, Guthrie faced a similar problem when he staged *Carmen* for Sadler's Wells in 1949. The economy of post-war Britain was still unsettled with money for a small opera company not forthcoming. There was no attempt at a procession in the final scene; Act 4 was set in Escamillo's dressing room in the amphitheater with a balcony that overlooked the approach to the arena from which the procession could be imagined without actually being seen.

In his autobiography, *A Life in the Theatre*, Guthrie discussed the Sadler's Wells' *Carmen* and said outright that he conceived the central character as, "the vulgar, violent slut which the story demands...In this production we made some small, unimportant, but I think sensible, innovations. The first act was set in quite a squalid sort of environment and the factory girls looked like factory girls, not like operatic choristers whose sole concession to the warm South is to sling embroidered Spanish shawls over themselves, as if they were suburban grand pianos." [6]

The last act set in the vast empty space before the arena seemed implausible to him, "The situation seems to demand that José edges Carmen into some position from which she cannot run away, and from which if she screams for help she will not be heard. Most of the problems, I thought, could be solved if the scene were transferred from outdoors to some interior...a room at an inn maybe, or a dressing room behind the arena. We did this: the acting was much more plausible and, so far as I am aware, no violence was done to the story and certainly none to the score." [7]

The concept was received for the most part favorably by the British Press which pointed out that the opera came across as though it were new.

When the concept was transferred to the Metropolitan, it was the fourth act that was causing trouble for the opera house's technical staff. There was not enough space on stage to have a dressing room positioned in such a way so that the faulty sight lines of the theater would not prevent a good many ticket holders from missing the most crucial of scenes. Originally space was reserved for a procession and a ballet which interfered with the dressing room taking center stage. Bing realized that this problem should have been worked out sooner but took the blame for putting too much on Gérard's shoulders. Three productions all in the first half of the season were too much and the delay in getting final stage and costume designs to Guthrie was the result. Furthermore, Bing pointed out that some of the old costumes would have to be used. Most of the first act and the entire fourth act costumes would be new, but the other two acts would have to make do with hand-me-downs.

The ballet in Act 4 was easy to eliminate since Reiner intended to present a *Carmen* that was free of interpolations. The music used for the dances was traditionally borrowed from the composer's *L'Arlésienne Suite* and *La Jolie fille de Perth*. The decision to dispense with the spectacle of the procession was one that Bing consented to while realizing both the public and press might revile him for doing so.

The second and third acts were not radical departures from traditional design, whereas the first and last were. Gone was the picture postcard look of Joseph Urban's 1923 setting for the first act with its sand colored buildings, picturesque bridge and, of course, the Urban blue sky. Instead, Gérard had dirty gray buildings set at the top of a steep staircase and clothes drying on a line. The last act, as Guthrie wished, was not in a public square but in a room which was dominated by a huge window with ratty drapes, a round table with a candelabra and a cheap lace cloth, some chairs, a mirror, packing crates and otherwise virtually bare. Admittedly it was a huge space for a dressing room but the blank areas between objects tended to give it an almost surreal quality. The bareness focused the attention on the two protagonists.

The costumes were also a departure. Risë's old ones had a Hollywood glamour about them. The new ones, with the exception of the last act, were simple in design. Originally, Risë's first act costume as visualized by Gérard was more along traditional lines. A peasant skirt and blouse in the drab colors Guthrie favored for this act. When Risë showed up at rehearsal wearing a simple sweater and skirt, Guthrie found the look he wanted. To him, she was sexier in that outfit than the one that was designed for her. He created the costume which was, "a short sleeved black linen and jersey blouse and skirt, tied at the waist with a dirty rose draped apron [and] two pink carnations in her hair." [8] *Opera News* described the second act costume as "a faded red shawl, its shabbiness emphasized by a slashed fringe, over her orange skirt. At the hem, her dress is flared to give movement to her dance." [9] The third act's was her old costume of leather with high boots. The last act costume was "gleaming white velvet, fitted in a high molded bodice and overlaid at the shoulders with jet fringe and mesh scrollwork. A single, huge scarlet velvet rose crowns several tiers of black net ruffles which taper at the floor to a long sweeping train." [10] In place of the traditional mantilla, she wore a rose in her hair which was caught up in a snood.

As far as the musical values were concerned, Risë felt she had to work on the high voice, the low and middle were there. Vera Schwarz, as she had done with Dalila, stressed that she had the high notes but not the confidence to produce them. She helped her to feel more secure by evening out the scale so that the voice did not favor the middle and low registers.

Reiner had a tremendous effect on her Carmen musically - shaping phrases, tempi that were on the fast side, the *Chanson Bohème* and even the last act moved at a clip. Normally, he conducted with minute movements but in dramatic passages the arms would open up into wide arcs illustrating the effect he wanted. As for Guthrie and Reiner, there was a contest of wills. Guthrie wanted certain pauses not in the score, Reiner said, 'no'. Guthrie wanted Carmen to be stabbed sooner and stagger around the table before collapsing and dying, Reiner was adamant that it would go against the music and he would not give in. Reiner was never difficult with Risë but he usually said 'no' first until she showed him what she wanted to do. In the second act there is a pause after the 'Flower Song' but Risë wanted to make it three times as long to play with the 'nos' which Carmen sings when José is finished. When Reiner heard how it sounded, he agreed to it.

Risë's first discussion with Guthrie about his concept took place in a bar across the street from the old Met. Sitting opposite her and Walter, he ordered an orange juice and a large tumbler of vodka, mixed the two, drank some and then said, "It must be sensuous, very, very sensuous!" He expanded on that when interviewed by Douglas Watt, "We're going to turn a respectable house into something not far removed from a bordello." [11]

The preliminary rehearsals took place on the roof stage and none of the cast had seen the settings. When they did, it was the dramatic possibilities of the last act that captured Risë's imagination. There was only one door in the room, leaving Carmen with no means of escape. She was trapped. In the final act of the old production, staged according to tradition outside the bullring, Carmen could have run anywhere but she does not. Her fatalism precludes running away. If she was meant to die, she would. In Guthrie's, it turned into a cat and mouse situation with a highly effective *coup de theatre*. With the only means of escape blocked, Carmen tried to save herself but could not. In this version she defied fate -

or tried to. Making her way toward the window to call for help, José grabbed her, pinned her to the wall and stabbed her. Carmen hung onto the drape to support herself. It ripped, fell and enveloped her like a shroud as she sank to the floor. It was a tricky ending to bring off since after Carmen was backed into a corner and stabbed, she had to stagger to the window to call for help, grab hold of the drape which would rip, turn her body and the curtain in the same direction and fall with the curtain around her. It was choreographed more than staged and each movement had to be carefully timed with the music. Nothing could ease Risë's or Bing's qualms about her getting it right on opening night.

To make sense of Carmen's remaining in Escamillo's dressing room and not leaving with him, Guthrie had her linger in order to put on a necklace he had given her. She sees Don José in the dressing room mirror and says, 'C'est toi'. When José entered, Guthrie had him take his knife and plunge it into the trunk. Del Monaco objected to this piece of business since he felt José should have the knife with him. Without it, he looked too weak. The Guthrie staging called for José to grab the knife just prior to killing Carmen to stress that he had not planned to do so. Del Monaco remarked that not only Carmen but he also felt trapped by the setting and that's exactly what Guthrie wanted to hear.

As for developing her character, Guthrie did not tell Risë how to go about it. At the beginning, it made her uneasy since she felt she needed direction but wasn't getting it. Desperation set in until she was advised by Walter to follow her own instincts. Doing what *she* felt was right was exactly what Guthrie had in mind. He wanted the role to emerge from inside of her. However, once in the second act when she wasn't certain what Carmen's next move should be, Guthrie told her to go over to the pillar and rub her body against it; an erotic gesture that helped bring out Carmen's sensuousness, the need for her body to be touched, to be aroused. Moreover, he wanted her movements to be suggestive, insinuating, therefore, Risë made her cat-like in her walk. It was obvious that this Carmen loved her body, it is important to her. Her body was her life as was love. She is constantly in love with love but never serious. "Je suis amoreuse" in the second act is accepted by the others as a joke. They knew her all too well. She is a free soul. Guthrie, who wanted a light touch, underscored this aspect of Carmen.

The third act is the most difficult to bring off. Guthrie told Risë never to think of the card scene before it occurred. Carmen must approach the cards as though what they foretold could not happen to her. At the end of the act in the old production she always threw the cards in the air in defiance of fate. Guthrie liked that. He wanted Carmen to believe she would never die. This was further developed in the last act. Seeing José in a weakened state, Carmen felt she could walk out of that room unharmed. During the 'laissez moi passez' business, Carmen tried to escape but José barred her path. She was trapped as Risë envisioned when first seeing the setting, and then impending doom manifests itself. She realizes the cards did not lie. She would die - but not passively.

Both Reiner and Guthrie were amazed that she was willing to enter the production with few preconceived notions since her old concept was not unsuccessful. Tucker had no previous conceptions; he had never performed Don José before. He was not an actor but Guthrie manipulated him. If he overacted, he would tell him to just let it happen. He picked up on Tucker's characteristics on stage, wide eyes, jerky movements and worked them into the characterization. Guthrie jokingly referred to his having a Norwegian Carmen and a Jewish José. He grew to admire both of them inordinately.

Stairs, especially in the first act where almost all of the action took place on different levels, compensated for the difference in Risë's and Tucker's heights. Walter saw that Risë was having trouble with the width of the stairs since they were narrow. He told Bing that he was willing to pay the two thousand dollars for a new staircase and since it didn't entail spending any of the company's money, he approved. For the "Habañera", Guthrie wanted the men who surrounded Carmen to lift her and hand her from one to the other, symbolizing her being passed around by men for sex. There were three of these lifts and when Bing saw them he told Guthrie to eliminate them because they could be dangerous and distracting. He relented for the premiere, but unaccountably left them in for some time thereafter.

When asked his opinion of the production, Frank Guarrera said, "I liked some things - the handling of the crowds - standing on tables or on different levels. My Escamillo became much more athletic than before. In the last act, I missed entering with Carmen in a carriage as we used to in the old production. I missed taking Risë by the arm, walking around   the stage with her, showing her off, going down stage to sing our duet. In Guthrie's version, we sauntered in and sang.

It was always a privilege to work with Risë. Her performances of Carmen were exciting and had great theatricality. The torn sleeve in the last act when José grabbed her, for instance, or when the top of her dress accidentally slipped down in the first act. That wasn't part of the show but it would have been great to have kept it in!" [12]

Loren Hightower, principal dancer in the last act with Janet Collins, had definite opinions on the production and Guthrie, "I hated him! He announced he didn't like dancers and didn't like ballet. He, himself, was big and clumsy. There was supposed to be a ballet danced to *L'Arlésienne*, though not included by Bizet in the opera, it was often interpolated. He cut it. The stage set for the last act had a balcony with arches, a railing, pillars, the entire chorus crammed onto it supposedly watching the parade. All Janet Collins and I did were a few steps to the "Dancez, Dancez" music and you could barely see us.

"Risë was a consummate professional, tough when she had to be. There was one time when we had a stage dress rehearsal of the first act and she was wearing a pair of shoes made of the same fabric as her costume skirt. Obviously she had them custom made, maybe because her feet were sensitive, maybe because they looked better. A very self-important stage manager stopped the rehearsal and pompously demanded that she wear the shoes that were issued. He was a tedious man who liked to throw his weight around. There was dead silence for a minute, than Risë looked him straight in the eye and said, something to the effect of, you know, I have worked very hard for a very long time to be in a position to tell off people like you. The shoes stayed. Risë was never pretentious. Reiner certainly was, but what a fabulous conductor. He would think nothing of stopping a rehearsal just because he could. There was one time when Risë and he were having different thoughts about tempo and she walked down to the footlights and said, 'Fritz!' There was stunned silence on stage because we had never heard anyone address the 'Maestro' in such a manner." [13]

Assistant Conductor, Walter Taussig, had the same memory, "during a rehearsal of *Carmen*, Risë and Fritz Reiner had some differences about tempo-she walked to the footlights and addressed the generally very fear-inspiring conductor (whom everyone called Maestro, or more daringly, Dr. Reiner) in her most charming way, 'Fritz'...You could hear the walls of tradition come down! Reiner, not averse to beautiful ladies, took it very well though." [14]

Loren Hightower continued, "I never thought much of Gérard's designs in *Carmen* or his designs in general. The costumes were unimaginative. That last act, what an enormous dressing room with a sixteen-foot window! The death scene was very effective though. In that act, Risë was very earthy, she conveyed disgust exceptionally well. Her rejection of Don José was extraordinarily effective." [15]

In Tyrone Guthrie's autobiography, *A Life in the Theatre*, he has some trenchant remarks on the *Carmen* experience,

...Fritz Reiner conducted-a martinet who expected the singers to watch the beat, every single second...We had one or two skirmishes on this topic. I felt that, here and there, dramatic tension was seriously diminished if the singers could not look one another in the eye, and that, if everyone had to rigidly face front, any lively or expressive choreography was impossible to achieve. Reiner was adamant and I gave way. Stevens was delightful. A beautiful and intelligent woman at the top of her particular tree, it would have been understandable if she had felt a bit disgruntled about altering a performance which had been greatly admired...On the contrary she was delighted to welcome a new approach and would interpret suggestions with the enthusiasm and humility of a neophyte, but also with the accomplishment of a star. [16]

William Hawkins, a reporter from the *World-Telegram & Sun*, was one of the few who were allowed to visit during rehearsals. His article appeared the day prior to the opening,

...Watching the British director at work is in its way as interesting as many theatrical performances intended for public consumption. Guthrie is a head taller than most of the people who work for him...He walks with the spicy swiftness of a boxer and his deep crisp voice penetrates any hubbub...'In the dark auditorium, Risë Stevens, waiting for her cue spoke...of the character of Carmen which she is singing...'[Guthrie] makes her aggressiveness so tantalizing...For instance, he carefully leads the characters up to a kiss, then something interrupts. The Seguidilla is done with a banister between them. When Jose finally becomes aggressive, Carmen withdraws. It's so much more dramatic. Developing an entirely new approach to the closing scene. Guthrie has Tucker, knife in hand, cornering Miss Stevens, in a climax that comes off like a cross between 'Angel Street' and 'Medea'. [17]

Even if Reiner thought the production worked, crowing to the newspapers that all the music Bizet wrote would be heard, Bing was on edge when the night of the premiere drew closer. He did not like the staging and, convinced that Guthrie's concept would be trashed, barred the press from the final dress rehearsal, not wishing any comments to be made by the critics until the first performance.

On the 24th, he issued a memo banning all outsiders from the two rehearsals of *Carmen* on Monday, January 28th and Tuesday, the 29th,

> ...NOBODY - will be admitted to the two rehearsals...The only exceptions will be members of the company, but without friends or relatives and one friend or relative for the principal members of 'Carmen': that means to say that Mrs. Reiner will be welcome...and Miss Stevens' husband and Mrs. Tucker - but without guests or friends. Please make that as clear as possible so that we can avoid embarrassing scenes at the rehearsals when I will have the auditorium cleared of everyone who has no business to be there. [18]

On the night of the premiere, once inside her dressing room, Risë was visited by wardrobe mistress, Jennie Cervini, who made sure her costumes were in order. Vera Schwarz arrived and reviewed parts of the score with her. To look like a Gypsy, Risë had to apply two coats of dark body makeup and since there was much physical action, it had to be applied all over. She then put on the black top and skirt Carmen wore in the first act, the net black stockings and high-heeled shoes. A scarf was tied around her waist and flowers fixed in her hair. The "on-stage" call was given. Walter spat on her shoulder three times-a superstition-and she made her way to the spot backstage where she would make her entrance.

For those who last saw Risë as Carmen in her highly decorative first act get up it was quite a surprise to see this black clad figure making her way down a grimy staircase. Enthusiasm grew as each act followed but the crucial one, the fourth, had everyone back stage holding their breath. Would the audience accept it? By the time the mortally wounded Carmen staggered to the window, tore the drape down and the crazed Don José stood lamenting over his dead mistress, the audience was totally involved. When the last chord died away at eleven forty one, there was an outburst of applause and bravos, stamping and cheering for what had just taken place. When the cast and conductor came out for bows, the excitement grew in intensity. Guarrera, Conner, Tucker, Reiner received shouts of approval but the greatest demonstration was reserved for Carmen, herself. Risë with arms upraised in a deep curtsy, hair disheveled, one sleeve of her dress hanging ripped from its mooring, accepted the audience's adulation. Not even her debut in Philadelphia surpassed the reception she received that evening. At the bottom of the stage manager's "performance time sheet" on file in the Archives of the Metropolitan, is written, "Opening Performance Excellent".

For most of the evening, Risë was unconscious of what was going on but her natural theatrical instincts made her determined to give her best. Enveloped in Carmen's sordid world, she thought she sang well but that details of the acting could have been better. Guthrie had said it would all fall into place by the third performance. Of the four acts, she was pleased most with the second. The first and last worried her because she wasn't sure how they would go over with the critics. The third act bothered her because it was the old one redesigned to look new.

Even after the ovation she had just received, she was convinced that her performance had failed. Walter and she went home in silence. She was too dazed and tired to speak. When they arrived home, Risë, Edgar Vincent, his friend, John Stephen, and Walter broke open a bottle of champagne. Risë did not join them. After a warm glass of milk to quiet her down and several baths to remove the body makeup, she went to bed and was sound asleep in a matter of minutes.

Walter and the others went to Times Square around 2

A.M. to buy all the papers they could. They each took one and started reading the reviews and were amazed at the positive reaction. Virgil Thomson concluded his assessment of the production by calling it "the most convincing I ever saw." [19] Miles Kastendieck was no less enthusiastic, "What the Metropolitan did for Bizet's 'Carmen' last night is little short of sensational. The new production makes the opera a wonderful theatre piece. In the title role, Risë Stevens gave the finest performance of her career. Outstanding as an actress, she lived the part with fire and conviction last night. This 'Carmen' qualifies as a first-class Broadway show." [20]

On February 3rd, Risë wrote to Fritz Reiner expressing her gratitude to him for making the premiere of *Carmen* the exciting and successful event that it was,

> My respect for you has always been of the highest degree but after Thursday night's performance I don't think there is anyone who can come anywhere near you. Our success was one I shall long remember. My work with you in the past has always been great experiences for me but our Carmen was the greatest thrill of all. The way you waited for me at precisely the right moments, the way you let me breathe after difficult phrases - you seemed to live the whole part with me. I cannot thank you enough, Fritz. With you on the podium I felt confident for the first time in Carmen...

[In a post script, she added] "...Walter goes around Town telling everyone that a job like that could only be done by a Hungarian." [21]

With one exception, the cast was the same when *Carmen* opened in Philadelphia on February 12th. Paolo Silveri, the young Italian baritone who made his debut in November as Don Giovanni, replaced Frank Guarrera. Max de Schauensee, who had seen Risë's "old" interpretation, commented, "Carmen herself as portrayed by Risë Stevens last night, is a far cry from what Miss Stevens' Carmen used to be. This...is a dangerous, vicious girl, cheap and sloe-eyed." [22]

The fifth performance on February 19th introduced two major cast changes. Reiner was scheduled for only the first four performances but he would join the spring tour to conduct a dozen more. Kurt Adler, the Metropolitan's chorus master and Risë's sometimes accompanist, took over the directorial chores from Reiner. Mario del Monaco with his newly learned French, replaced Tucker and "used his remarkable voice to good vocal and dramatic effect." [23]

Carmen on March 17th had Risë again paired with Mario del Monaco who could get carried away on stage. That night, pushing her harder than usual, she tripped on her skirt, fell on her hand and almost broke her wrist. In his autobiography, *La Mia Vita e i Miei Successi*, del Monaco remembers the incident somewhat differently and much more colorfully,

> During a rehearsal, I had immersed myself in my role so much that Risë, seeing my eyes glaze over with jealousy, began to watch me carefully. It was probably she who suggested to the stage director that the knife be the safest possible. So I was given a navaja with a wooden handle and a rubber blade painted silver. Everything went smoothly until the fourth act, when Don José is supposed to pull out the knife to kill Carmen. At that moment I realized that I had in my hand what looked like a pickled herring that wobbled back and forth. A moment of rage came over me....I threw away the fake navaja and I grabbed a very sharp sword that was in Escamillo's dressing room...Faced with that unexpected change...Stevens panicked...An absolutely realistic sequence then took place, with the beautiful Risë Stevens trying to get away from me...It was her misfortune that she tripped over the lace of her skirt... she cried out...I 'ran her through' with the sword and the audience was left breathless. [24]

For Risë the New York opera season was drawing to a close. On March 25th, the company presented *Carmen* in

Baltimore. The performance was played before the largest audience in years. As luck would have it, Risë was again injured. This time it was at a point when del Monaco shoved her away in the first act and she fell against the staircase. The audience was relieved when she got up smiling. One member of the Baltimore audience had older opera goers recalling her performances as Carmen. Rosa Ponselle was there to see for herself what all the fuss was about. After it was over, she went back stage to meet the cast. Greeting Risë, she told her that if she had a production like that, she would have been a success also. Her less than successful Carmen still bothered her. Risë didn't know whether she meant what she said as a compliment to her or a reflection on herself.

Chapter 16

All three of us had a wonderful summer overlooking the Atlantic Ocean from our new home at Oneck Point in Westhampton Beach. We have bought a very old house and are in the process of remodeling it which is a great thrill for me. As it looks right now we shall be able to have Thanksgiving in our new home. [1]

Prior to the start of her semi-annual recital tour, Risë agreed to appear on television's *All Star Review*, starring her neighbor from Hollywood days, Martha Raye. They used to run into one another all the time and chat about Nicky and her daughter, Melanie. Martha would always say that they should do a show together some time and, of course, Risë told her that would be wonderful, never thinking that it would happen - but it did.

In her *Metro-Lark* column, Risë also confessed to looking forward to singing Dalila since the role proved to be a challenge to her. Little did she know that a bigger challenge was just around the TV corner.

Metro-Lark reported on what went on the evening of September 27th,

This was a hilarious one-hour comedy show, starring Martha Raye, who had as her guests for the evening: Risë Stevens, Caesar Romero and Rocky Graziano. After some clowning about a picture being filmed in her apartment, a take-off on Dr. Jekyll and Mr. Hyde, the script finally called for Caesar Romero to invite Miss Raye and Rocky Graziano to a benefit dinner given by Miss

Stevens. Since Rocky and Martha were pretending to be uncouth characters who had never been to such a 'swank' affair before, they agreed beforehand that they would observe the behavior of Risë and Cesar and imitate them at the dinner table. To put her guests at ease, Risë told Caesar that she thought they'd feel better if Martha's and Rocky's manners at table were copied. So the fun began! With each couple trying to imitate the other, the waiter who took their order was a bit confused, to say the least. He mentioned, however, that the grapefruit was already on the table. Risë started to eat hers, the usual way. Martha, however, picked hers up and squeezing it hard tried to get the juice onto her spoon. Everyone followed suit, and you can imagine how the grapefruit juice was squirted around! Rocky squeezed the juice right into his mouth...Finally, Miss Stevens said that she would like to prepare her own tossed salad. That's all she had to say. The salads were TOSSED up into the air by the 'peasants' who presumably didn't know any better, until it became a free-for-all. At which point Miss Stevens beat a hasty retreat. [2]

For Risë, the opening of the Metropolitan Opera's 1952-1953 season had the added significance of reaching the highest level in the fee structure for principal artists. For every performance of *Carmen* she would receive one thousand dollars (but lowered to seven hundred fifty dollars when she appeared in other operas). On tour the one thousand-dollar fee held firm for all performances. Risë expressed her thoughts to Rudolf Bing in a letter written on November 19th, thanking him for the part he played in her early career and now making her the only mezzo in the history of the Metropolitan Opera to receive the highest fee paid to artists. In gratitude, she donated the first check to the Metropolitan Opera Fund Drive.

Relations with Bing were not all positive, however, since this season the broadcast *Carmen* would go to Fedora Barbieri. Bing made known this decision to Kurt Weinhold late in February stating he was obliged to distribute plum assignments equitably among his stars. He also informed Weinhold officially that Risë in attaining the highest fee level had in effect priced herself out of *seconda donna* parts. Walter wanted Risë free of these anyway but it reduced her repertory to only a handful of starring roles.

The loss of the broadcast did not matter as much after Risë learned the December 11th performance of *Carmen* would be televised in select theaters across the country on a pay per view basis. It was a joint venture of the Metropolitan Opera and Theatre Network Television (TNT) and would be a benefit for the Opera. The artists who were scheduled to appear were all from the original cast with the exception of Robert Merrill who replaced Frank Guarrera. When asked how he reacted to this, Guarrera explained, "It is my feeling that Merrill was chosen for the television performance because of the drawing power of his name, his popularity, his recordings. When I was at the Met, I was up against two great voices, Warren and Merrill." [3]

Theatre Network Television (TNT) was instrumental in relaying sports events to movie houses where they could be seen on large size screens. The Rocky Marciano-Joe Walcott championship bout of September 23rd was seen on a pay-per-view basis by one hundred twenty thousand viewers and was one of TNT's biggest successes. Agreeing to televise an opera performance was, like the radio broadcasts, a major step forward in bringing opera to the masses. Bing saw the endeavor as an important method for making the Metropolitan Opera truly national in scope.

On the whole, the *Carmen* telecast received mixed support from the Press. The *Daily News'* John Chapman offered one of the more positive reviews, "At the Met I've seen several performances of this 'Carmen' with its vigorous staging...and its matchless playing and singing by Risë Stevens. Yet, last night in a movie house...I saw that Miss Stevens was an even better actress than I had thought.

There were some faults in the production...In the long camera shots the picture was indistinct...But the medium shots and close-ups were superb." [4]

Due to the altering of the lighting that had to be increased, the house was lit by a brilliant glare found to be disturbing by many in the audience. In March, Theatre Network Television issued a press notice lauding their foray into opera, however, the profit was certainly not on the level of the Graziano-Walcott fight. TNT quietly withdrew from future opera presentations chalking it off as an interesting experiment.

It was with a great foreboding that Risë allowed Walter to talk her into her next television adventure, *The Colgate Comedy Hour* on the 21st with virtuoso hoofer, Ray Bolger, in his TV debut. Risë had studied dance while apprenticing with the Little Theatre but she was, by no means, a professional dancer. She moved well in the second act dance in *Carmen* but there the situation is more important than the steps. As long as Carmen befuddles the vulnerable soldier by suggestively moving her body, that is all that is important. Dancing with Ray Bolger, however, was the real thing.

As it turned out, *Billboard*'s Bob Francis rated Risë's contribution to the Bolger outing most favorably,

> Around the superlative Bolger stepping, they built a Christmas toy store theme, not only pointing Ray up as a comedian but giving guest star Risë Stevens a painless introduction into an excellent Carmen aria [the Gypsy song]...Incidentally that Met songbird is amazing. She teamed up with Bolger subsequently for an hilarious stepping session, comprising everything from Black Bottom to Rhumba. A reporter had no idea Rudolf Bing had included that in the Met curricula. [5]

In the immediate future, the customary spate of recitals was upcoming. When she visited Atlanta, Georgia, in January, prior to her recital, The *Atlanta, GA. Constitution* ran an article called, "Met's 'Hussy' Risë Stevens is Really a Homebody." The article assured readers that basically she was no different from themselves, maybe,

> ...Miss Stevens was resting up here for her concert in a housecoat and hair curlers. The housecoat was a swishy red damask one, more like Hollywood than Main Street. 'I don't have time for PTA's and mother's clubs as I'd like', complained the singer...Home is not so humble to the Met's famous 'hussy'. Two maids help in her duplex apartment in New York...She does most of the house-keeping in her country place...She made the curtains for her house and loves to cook up Wiener Schnitzel and Hungarian Goulash for dinner guests. Her friends are used to finding the opera siren at home in blue jeans or a shirt and sweater. [6]

While Risë was away on tour, Fedora Barbieri took over the role of Carmen. The veteran of over one-hundred "Italian" Carmens, the mezzo was known more for Verdi than Bizet when interviewed by *Opera News* prior to the broadcast on January 31st, she explained,

> I am not preparing the opera under Mr. Guthrie...all my scenes are under [Dino] Yannopoulos' direction...I expect to rely on a minimum of movement and large gestures. [7]

Unfortunately, her approach didn't work, and not being directed by Guthrie put her at a disadvantage from the start. "Singing the title role in 'Carmen' last night...Fedora Barbieri made a surprisingly placid and uninteresting heroine....there was no passion in her work...Miss Barbieri looked out of place in the role, especially in Tyrone Guthrie's briskly staged production ...a little fire would have helped...", thought Douglas Watt. [8]

Loren Hightower added a personal evaluation, "I liked Barbieri a lot in other roles and in a conventional *Carmen* she probably was very good. She seemed old fashioned in the

Guthrie production. She tried to adapt herself but it didn't come off. After Risë's real dramatic performance, Barbieri's didn't have the range of color. It didn't have the punch...she was kind of tubular, she didn't look as good...and Stevens did have that lusciously voluptuous voice so well suited to a seductress." [9]

For Barbieri, the last act costume was changed from white to maroon a color more flattering to her figure, otherwise, they were as originally designed. If there was a flaw in the Guthrie production, its being built around Risë made it not an easy concept to adapt for someone else. Bing, however, was adamant about maintaining a uniform look to new productions throughout their run and would relent only if circumstances obliged him to.

Dino Yannopoulos, who took over the staging from Guthrie, when interviewed for this book, expressed strong feelings on the production, "I didn't try to change anything Guthrie did although I didn't like everything he did. For instance, I thought the huge staircase in the first act was good up to a point but it dominated too much -it dictated the movement. I did not like Carmen being carried down the stairs in the 'Habañera'. That is originally a very slow Cuban dance that builds slowly.

> I thought Risë's costume in the first act was too sophisticated, too elegant, it wasn't earthy enough. Risë was a marvelous actress though...she could be demanding and difficult if there were uncertainties. If something worked for her, it stayed. Guthrie did not try to change her concept; he worked with her concept that was already in place.
> The fourth act had problems. When Don José enters, he tells Carmen he is not going to harm her, how much he still loves her, etc. but the first thing he does is bang his knife into a crate. Now to get the knife to stick in wood, it had to be a sharp knife. Risë rightly objected to using a sharp knife...once in the end, the knife didn't hit the

mark on the wall beside her when she is supposed to be stabbed but went into her hand. She was bleeding profusely. But Bing adored Guthrie so everything had to stay the way he wanted it. [10]

By mid-January, Risë was back in New York to prepare for *Der Rosenkavalier,* which was to reenter the repertory on the 22nd. She had developed a viral infection and there was a possibility that she might not be able to appear in the opening performance. However, if Harriet Johnson's review is any indication of how things went that evening, her condition cleared up in time, "Risë Stevens outdid herself...acting with more vitality than many male members on the Met roster manifest as operatic lovers." [11]

The Marschallin in that performance was Astrid Varnay, "Risë and I were on the same wave length...[she] brought her own European studies to bear on an interpretation so authentic in its old world tradition that our Viennese colleague, Erich Kunz, who sang Faninal...thought of her as a neighbor, an opinion later confirmed by Austrian soprano, Hilde Güden...And yet there was also a healthy component of the adolescent in her performance, something any Manhattan or Brooklyn teen-ager could directly relate to as a contemporary." [12]

Dalila came back into her life once again and the question whether she would be more successful this time remained to be seen.

"There was no money for a new production", recalled Dino Yannopoulos, "so Ellen Meyer, a designer in the Technical Department, utilized the 1936 one but eliminated all the old-fashioned elements. She designed a series of platforms and lighting for the first act. For the second act here was no house but a tent with a big canopy borrowed from *La Gioconda* and a Lion which changed allegiance from St. Mark to Judah. The second scene of the third act was dominated by two large pillars." [13]

"Risë asked me to work with her on the first act", Zachary Solov said. "She wanted to dance with the priestesses. She asked for extra rehearsals so that we could perfect the dancing. She wanted to look good. She would study the legs and gestures of the ballet girls to get hers right." [14]

Her efforts were not wasted in coming to terms with a role that had been elusive in the past. "Miss Stevens...has not sung with such smoothness and beauty of tone in a long time. She was careful never to push her voice, and the results were most gratifying. So, too, was the commanding style of her acting, an effective combination of seductiveness and malice." [15]

With the approaching 1953-1954 season, Risë was faced with the loss of Brooks Smith who had decided to play exclusively for Jascha Heifetz. Fortunately, Edgar Vincent came to the rescue by introducing her to James Shomate who quickly became a valuable addition to the Stevens' retinue. They took to one another immediately. Luck played a part in their meeting since Edgar Vincent, aware of Smith's departure, thought of Shomate as a replacement while attending a recital at Town Hall that featured mezzo, Lorna Sydney. At the same time Brooks Smith left, Risë was also faced with the loss of her secretary, Melanie Romano. Shomate, much to Risë's surprise that he would want to be bothered with such things, offered to serve as both accompanist and secretary. Assuming Romano's responsibilities meant announcing to tour cities that they had arrived; inspecting the hall where they were to perform; making sure the piano was tuned and that a spotlight was available; stating the ground rules, that is, if they were on a tight schedule, a post-recital party was out; discouraging any offers for Risë to tour the city on the day of the recital since she had to rest at the hotel. Unlike Brooks Smith, Shomate worked exclusively with Risë, traveling to cities even when she gave concerts which didn't include him. This was important since Walter did not accompany Risë on the tours. Unlike her, he disliked flying and always feared for

Risë's safety. He insisted that she telephone him immediately upon arrival after every flight, a request she sometimes forgot. Later, while greeting her hosts, she would remember and make a dash for the nearest phone.

As it turned out, neither Risë nor Shomate ever regretted the arrangement they had. Shomate recalled "selecting material and rehearsing the program for the coming season at Risë's home on Long Island. Those summers were especially memorable with her, Walter, Nicky and Sadie. They all had big personalities. Sadie was the real performer. She was a bit like Momma Rose in *Gypsy*. Risë was much closer to her father whom she adored. We enjoyed a good relationship. We were relaxed with one another." [16]

Since her 1953-1954 season at the Metropolitan was an unusually abbreviated one with only seven *Carmens* in the offing, her time away from the house was even greater. Both Weinhold and Walter expressed their concern about the Metropolitan's not coming up with new roles for Risë. If the tour had materialized, she would have again been scheduled only for *Carmen*. Walter, acting on Risë's behalf, rejected outright a suggestion that she consider Herodias in *Salome* for the 1954 season even though it meant a higher fee than the role warranted. Apart from it being essentially a character role, the vocal line is very harsh and Risë thought it could be injurious to her voice. Ironically, she did eventually play Herodias but not in the Richard Strauss opus.

On the 12th of December, *Carmen* was back on the boards at the Met and Risë returned to Bizet's Seville to give her seventy-sixth performance of the wayward Gypsy. Pierre Monteux, her new conductor, had last led *Carmen* at the Metropolitan in the 1918-1919 season with Geraldine Farrar in the title role. He was not to appear again in the house until 1953 when his contract called for twelve performances of *Faust* and *Pelléas et Mélisande*. *Carmen* would be extra and the budget could not sustain his conducting all of them, therefore, he only did the first two which was just as well since

Risë and he did not agree on the interpretation of the score.

For Risë, who had become used to Reiner's brisker tempi, he was too slow and she found herself always rushing ahead. There were too many pauses in the pacing of the music where everything would come to a full stop when it should have flowed. At the dress rehearsal two days before the opening, singer and conductor were at such odds that Monteux laid down his baton, left the pit, went to Bing and offered to step aside for another conductor. Bing would not hear of it and a modicum of harmony was achieved for the performances but for both of them it was a rocky collaboration.

The day prior to her last *Carmen* with Monteux, the *New York Herald-Tribune* reported, "Risë Stevens will be the first American-born Metropolitan Opera singer to create a role in a new Italian opera. She said yesterday that she had accepted the invitation of La Scala to appear as Herodias...in *La Figlia del Diavalo*. Although she was invited nearly a month ago, Miss Stevens was scheduled to go on a recital tour during March and she also wanted to see the score before giving her decision. Her fourteen scheduled recitals will be postponed to April." [17]

The fifty-one year old composer of *La Figlia del Diavolo*, Virgilio Mortari, was known more for orchestral and piano compositions. However, he also composed a number of vocal works and an earlier opera based on a libretto drawn from Moliere's, *L'Ecole des Femmes*. Corrado Pavolini, the librettist, based the scenario for the Mortrai opus on the John the Baptist legend with one perverse twist. In his version, Salome tries to save John and it is Herodias who, as the devil incarnate, teaches Salome to dance in order to destroy him. The orchestration called for three choruses, one in the pit, one on stage and one backstage.

All of the action transpired in one act, which necessitated two other one-act operas to round out the evening. *La Gita in Campagna*, a new work by Mario Peragallo and Gian Carlo Menotti's *Amelia al Ballo*, new for La Scala, were added but not even the frothy Amelia could save the evening.

Chapter 17

La Scala had just witnessed an American invasion of sorts. Leonard Bernstein, the first American conductor to be engaged by La Scala, had made an impressive debut on December 10, 1953 conducting Cherubini's *Medea* with Maria Callas in the title role. In addition, on December 17th, Leonard Warren became the first American to sing Rigoletto on that stage and enjoyed a personal success. Risë faced stiff competition because of them. She had to prove to a very demanding audience that she deserved her reputation as much as the two Leonards did theirs, but unlike them she had to help create a new work. The pressure on her was great but singing in the world's capital of opera, La Scala, meant more to her than the risk involved.

It was an honor to be invited to sing in that fabled theater and the fact that Mortari wrote the score with her in mind added to her determination to appear there, if only once before she retired. However, when she first heard about the nature of the character she would play, the devil himself in the guise of Herodias, she had serious reservations as to whether she wanted to take on such a bizarre role.

As was her custom, she discussed her reservations with Walter and it was his encouragement that triggered her acceptance. Walter realized that it would be best if she made her debut at La Scala in a role no one had done before, thereby, avoiding comparisons with past favorites. Certainly Carmen or Orfeo would have made her a prime target for sniping, especially since she was an American and a very prominent personality.

When she was given a copy of the score for the Mortari opera, surprisingly, she could find nothing in it that she wanted altered. It seemed custom made to suit her voice and temperament. How Mortari could have fashioned such a perfect fit without working directly with her was astonishing. But then Bizet could have written *Carmen* for her, Gluck, *Orfeo and* Strauss, *Der Rosenkavalier,* since, they too, found in her a definitive interpreter. February was devoted to learning the score thoroughly under the guidance of an assistant conductor at the Met, Victor Trucco. All outside activities were shelved and, unlike certain of her colleagues, as she would discover, she knew her role in its entirety before she left for Milan.   To add to the pressure she was under, Bing insisted that she had to be back at the Metropolitan for the broadcast of *Carmen* on April 3rd. If she missed it, her contract could be canceled and future relations with the Metropolitan terminated. That remained unsaid but the implication was clear. Her relations with Bing remained tenuous at best and it was not within his nature to overlook indiscretions. Even after her success as Carmen, he was cool toward her. It was as though he never forgave her for driving such a hard bargain at Glyndebourne.

On March 1st, Risë, Walter, Edgar Vincent and Vera Schwarz, flew to Milan since rehearsals for the March 24th premiere of *La Figlia del Diavolo* were scheduled to begin early in the month. It was only natural that she and Walter thought that all opera houses were run along the lines of the Metropolitan. Walter assured Bing that nothing would prevent Risë from singing on the broadcast since the entire trip was carefully planned to get her back on time. At the Metropolitan, if a premiere were scheduled for a particular date, it was relatively certain that it would occur. At that time, however, things at La Scala were vastly different. Schedules were not kept to the letter and it was not uncommon for opening dates for operas to be moved forward by days, weeks or postponed indefinitely.

That rehearsals did not start when they were supposed to was the first indication trouble lay ahead. Time was passing and there was talk of delaying the opening for how long no one could say. When rehearsals did begin, Nino Sanzogno, the conductor, was not entirely comfortable with the score, the tenor, Eugenio Fernandi, had not learned his part, the very dense scenic design had to be reconsidered at the last minute since it proved unworkable and Risë's costumes had to be redesigned as well, at her insistence.

Just when their morale was at its lowest, the reigning queen of La Scala, Maria Meneghini Callas, was introduced to them. Earlier in the season, Callas had triumphed as Medea and now she was next scheduled for *Alceste*, the premiere set for April 4th and *Don Carlo* on the 12th. Acting as the gracious host for the theater, she made a point of walking the stage with Risë pointing out the best places to stand in order for her voice to be heard to optimum advantage.

With nerves at the breaking point for everyone concerned, the evening of the premiere arrived and it offered a good opportunity for the Milanese audience to express itself,

> *La Patria*'s, Giulio Confalonieri reported, Mortari...has composed an opera learned but not heavy, intelligent without being cerebral, a score which is modern yet substantial. The orchestration, very successful, can sometimes be faulted for excessive loudness. Mme Stevens turned out to be an actress of great class and a steady vocalist as well, even though a little hollow in the middle register. [She] brought the opera to life with an intense variety of contrasting expressions, with her appropriate gestures and her excellent musicality...'La Figlia del Diavolo' was, as people say, an unqualified success with a total of seven curtain calls for the [composer] and the interpreters. [1]

The remainder of the program did not fare as well,

'La Gita in Campagna' was put to death by unanimous verdict. The performance went on among ironic laughter and pleasant audience conversations unwittingly abetted by the pale orchestral interludes. At the end there was a near riot, especially when Peragallo appeared to take a bow and stood there with the look of a misunderstood Messiah. Menotti's opera was a moderate success. [2]

Years later, Angelo Mercuriali, who played the Eunuch in the Mortari opera, commented to the author, "the rehearsals were many and tiring [but] Miss Stevens was a lovely colleague, a model of serious professionalism. After the first rehearsal, the orchestra applauded her." [He continued], "the opera was very well received, thanks to and above all to her magnificent interpretation. In addition, she proved to be an excellent singer with a remarkable vocal technique. To complete the picture, she was, and probably still is, a most beautiful woman." [3]

La Scala expressed interest in a return engagement and offered Smetana's rarely performed, *Dalibor*, a very odd choice but Risë's years in Prague may have been the reason behind it. Evading a definite commitment, in order to review the score first, she decided the part did not suit her and declined the invitation.

Getting back to the Metropolitan in time for the April 3rd broadcast was an adventure in itself deserving of its front-page coverage by the *New York Herald Tribune*,

Risë Stevens sang Carmen at the Metropolitan Opera House yesterday, thirty-six hours after she had sung the leading role in a new Italian opera at La Scala...On Thursday evening, Miss Stevens sang in La Scala...On Friday at 1 p.m. she boarded a plane for New York...She was in Zurich in mid-afternoon and in Paris at 7 p.m. Friday evening. She was in Iceland at 2:30 a.m. yesterday and landed at Idlewild Airport a few hours later. She had a bath at her home...before reaching the Met at noon...". [The same reporter went backstage to determine how she felt,] 'I didn't know if I could make it. My ears kept popping. When this is over, there's one thing I know I can do-sleep'...She described the plane trip as 'fairly restful' and said she had been able to sleep during most of it... [4]

And how did the performance go?

"...The singer must be stronger than most of us; neither she nor her voice showed a sign of fatigue- they were both as lovely as ever- and the role of Carmen calls for an outstanding amount of energy." [5]

The question of how to best utilize that energy around the Met was nagging at Risë, Walter, Kurt Weinhold, but not Bing. The wily General Manager had found for her the perfect vehicle in Carmen. She was *the* Met's Carmen. He had given her that opportunity to fulfill a long-standing desire to conquer Bizet's elusive creation. Of course, Bing realized it was her own abilities that made it the success it was. That it also made him look good was a fact he no doubt knew but never once expressed to her.

Her contract for the 1954-1955 season was being drawn up and first and foremost Bing insisted she make the tour. Not scheduled for the current one, her presence was necessary to keep out of state backers happy and missing two years in a row would not do. Her box-office draw was undeniable and while he left it up to her, he also said she must do it. Bing could be very persuasive in having you come around to his way of thinking and making it seem like it was your decision all along. The second item of importance was finding another vehicle for her. Weinhold, the previous year, had suggested Rosina in *Il Barbiere di Siviglia* but no one thought it a good idea and, at that time, the role was still associated with coloratura sopranos. Bing suggested one of two works by Jacques Offenbach, *La Périchole* or *La Grande-Duchesse de Gérolstein* done in the manner of *Fledermaus* which was still entertaining Met patrons. Actually, Oscar Hammerstein had already been considered for adapting *Gérolstein* and with the right approach, it would have been perfect for Risë's comedic talents, insightful way with words, and that something French in her voice. She was very interested in it but both Weinhold and Gutman felt it hopelessly outdated which was all Bing had to hear. *Gérolstein* was put aside in favor of *La Périchole*, which had a success with Patrice Munsel in the leading role and Cyril Ritchard as actor and director.

Walter tried to interest Bing in having a new work commissioned for her but the idea, while tempting, was not feasible. Bing left the door open for other suggestions and he was careful to assure Risë that not finding anything new for her did not mean a lack of interest on his part. Rather his putting an emphasis on rescuing standard operas from the disrepair they had fallen into kept him from spending money on new works. He didn't even mention the periodic problems he had with the standees, claques, various unions, the latest one occurring in March when the stagehands walked out leaving him to help work the lifts. All of these had an effect on his focusing on new vehicles for her. When the broader picture is considered, there were very few artists in Bing's regime who were given a production to rival "her" *Carmen*. If he gave her nothing further, it still assured her popularity for the next dozen years.

Towards the end of January when Weinhold sat down with Bing to discuss the details of Risë's next season, he confronted him with the rumor that *Orfeo ed Euridice* was to be revived. Bing admitted that what he heard was true and added that Giulietta Simionato would sing Orfeo. Weinhold reminded Bing that it was a role Risë wanted to do and that by rights it should have been assigned to her. Bing was adamant. He had made up his mind that Simionato would be given the revival much in the same way he stood by his decision to cast Risë in *Carmen*. *Orfeo vis á vis* Simionato was conceived early in 1954 when Bing notified his European contact, Roberto Bauer, that a revival was planned in either French or Italian, that Pierre Monteux had alredy been engaged to conduct and that Simionato was the first choice for the title role. When Simionato's contract was being negotiated in the spring of 1954, Bing ignored Simionato's wish to make her debut in one of three operas, *Aida, Il Barbiere di Siviglia* or *Cavalleria Rusticana*, all of which showed off her voice to better advantage than *Orfeo*. Bing saw no reason to be concerned at that time since between her arrival in America in January of 1955 and the opening of *Orfeo* late in February, she could make her debut in a role of her choice.

However, other reservations on the Italian mezzo's part surfaced which should have given a man of Bing's experience serious doubts about her engagement: Simionato expressed great concern about the air conditioning in American trains since she was scheduled for the tour and the arrival date of January 17th for *Orfeo* rehearsals did not sit well with her from the start; also, most importantly as it turned out, her debut role would be Orfeo.

The Crichton biography offers an explanation for the reason behind Risë's exclusion from the revival– Monteux did not want her based on the differences of opinion with *Carmen*. More likely, however, the reason was that Bing did not see her in what is essentially a *bel canto* role. He felt she could not do justice to it at that time of her career. During the Glyndebourne years, he would not have hesitated to offer it to her, but he felt that her voice had changed in the interim.

Risë had toyed with the idea of reviving Amneris and Max Rudolf was having difficulties casting the February performances of *Aida*. With Bing's consent, February 16th was earmarked for the second Amneris of her career. Both he and Rudolf were in agreement that it could only be advantageous to the box office. That it did not take place was due to Risë's being cast in the role she wanted more than anything else the Metropolitan could offer.

At that time, however, there still remained the question of *Géroldstein* that had not been resolved. With the loss of Orfeo,

Risë still hoped that the Offenbach would materialize and Rudolf pointed out to Bing that they were faced with a delicate situation. One more rejection of her request for a new role and they were in danger of losing her permanently. The financial loss attached to this was a definite consideration - one that needed the vacationing Bing's immediate attention upon his return to America.

On September 28th, Christian Steenberg died at age seventy. At the time of his passing much of the older generation had gone. Only Sadie, Aunt Tina and Sadie's brothers, George and Ben were still living. It was a depressing end to what otherwise was an idyllic summer, especially for Risë, who, in spite of an occasional difference of opinion, was very close to him. For those who knew them best, there was at least on the surface a hint of competition between mother and daughter for center stage. The warm, outgoing, Sadie who loved to play cards was quite unlike the more reserved Chris who was remembered as always being conservatively dressed in shirt and tie, smoking a cigarette. The family made its way back to the city for funeral services at Riverside Memorial on the 29th.

February 24th was to be the premiere of *Orfeo ed Euridice* and Giulietta Simionato's debut with the company in a role she had performed with great success in Europe. Without a doubt it would have created as much interest in a season that witnessed Marian Anderson's historic debut on January 7th as well as that of Renata Tebaldi's, three weeks later. Bing had acquiesced to Simionato's wishes and planned the revival in the Italian version as opposed to an English translation as had been done with Gluck's *Alceste* in 1952. Although it would not be a new production, the Harry Horner sets of 1938 were still quite serviceable and with the company in financial straits, would have to do.

On December 4th, a lawyer representing Simionato informed Bing that his client had taken ill with an attack of nerves while rehearsing *La Forza del Destino* in Rome and on the advice of her doctor could not come to America as planned. This in itself was a legitimate cause for cancellation but it was subsequently discovered that Simionato had sung a *Forza* performance in Rome and that she had entered into the contract in October which overlapped her New York dates. Through its lawyers, the Metropolitan filed a complaint against her with the American Guild of Musical Artists (AGMA) which in effect barred her from appearing in the United States during the extent of her contract with the Metropolitan. Other American opera houses were persuaded, notably Chicago and San Francisco, to respect the Met's position and not engage her.

In her own defense, Simionato explained that in her condition traveling a long distance to America and making a debut in a house that was not familiar to her was different from singing near her own home and doctors. She offered to compensate in part any money the Metropolitan may have lost as a result of her cancellation. While the legal implications did not clear up for well over a year, it was eventually decided to drop the matter since the Met could not bar her from singing in America once the date of the breached contract was up and the money lost was not even a couple of thousand dollars.

Several questions should be clarified concerning this incident particularly since rumor had it that Simionato canceled because Monteux, who was to conduct, did not want to abide by her suggestion to interpolate the very florid aria, "Amour viens prendre à mon âme" (intended for the French version of 1774 in which much new music was added), at the end of the first act. Simionato was contacted to shed some light on the matter. In a letter to the author, she denied insisting on an interpolated aria, moreover, she was not even aware that there was one. Also, she reiterated her claim that she did not feel physically up to the strain of making her debut at the Metropolitan.

Whatever the reason for Simionato's non-appearance, Bing was left with a very serious casting problem. He had bypassed Risë and no other mezzo on the roster had the same star quality that she had. Barbieri was a consideration but Bing doubted that she would agree to it. More importantly he felt she could not possibly do Orfeo overlooking the fact that she had sung the role successfully in Europe. If Monteux had a say, he no doubt would have suggested Jean Madeira with whom he had a special rapport and a great success in *Orfeo* in Brussels earlier that year,but giving it to her could have further alienated Risë.

When Bing told Walter of the problem, he couldn't have been happier. Bing was aware that he had hurt Risë by not offering her the role from the beginning, but Walter assured him that she was not too proud for her own good and accepted without even asking her. In strict confidence, Bing informed Roberto Bauer that he had persuaded Risë to sing Orfeo. He felt she was not the best vocal choice but stressed the fact that she had outstanding artistry and box office appeal. He was deeply grateful that she would come to the rescue and in essence extricate him from a very difficult position with both the public and the board.

The cast for *Orfeo* is quite small and the opera has a great deal of dancing in it. In Solov, Bing had his choreographer and leading male soloist to partner the celebrated English ballerina, Alicia Markova. Monteux, of course, was the conductor. This time, Risë and he worked well together. Monteux had great feeling for the score, everything flowed, the recitatives and arias were of a piece. There was a mutual respect on both their parts and at the first rehearsal, Risë made a point of telling him that she was in his hands.

As successful as her Carmen was, the evening of February 24th was, for her, the high point of her Metropolitan Opera career. Orfeo was by her own admission her favorite role, and through Schoen-René, she was a direct descendent of Pauline Viardot Garcia who had triumphed in the revival of the original Italian version in Paris in 1859. While she had a great respect for Octavian and was intrigued by Carmen, it was Orfeo that meant the most to her. She had much to thank Simionato for canceling and Bing for giving her a second chance. But then again she always credited luck for everything that happened to her. Standing on the stage she loved best before Euridice's tomb ready to sing the music which had been in her since Juilliard, she gave "a magnetic performance." [6]

Chapter 18

On June 15th, Risë, Walter and Nicky boarded the ocean liner, Queen Elizabeth, for an extended stay in Europe. Their itinerary included visits to England, France, Switzerland, Austria, Italy and Greece. Typically, this was not to be a complete vacation for Risë. For ten-year-old Nicky, part of it would be spent in a French camp and part in company with his parents. The first stop on the tour was Glyndebourne. Risë and Walter had not been back since 1939 and it was with a great sense of nostalgia and an awareness of all that happened to the world and themselves in the meantime. Glyndebourne had been restored to its former beauty and the three of them delighted in walking in the gardens. It was like old times for them and for Nicky it was a broadening new experience. HMV was responsible for the visit since a projected recording of *Le nozze di Figaro* conducted by Vittorio Gui was to feature her as Cherubino.

Risë had not appeared as Cherubino since 1949 and, in a sense, was competing with her younger self in a role she no longer sang. It was not an altogether pleasant experience since the role did not suit her as well as it once did. The performance of July 2nd gave the Maestro time to familiarize her with his tempi and for her to become acquainted with her colleagues. Maestro Gui did not know her voice, so she agreed to sing for him when she arrived and to appear in two performances of *Nozze* in order to work herself into the production. RCA planned to release the recording in America and wanted her name in the cast to sell records in the United States.

Frances Bible, who was scheduled for all the Cherubinos, stepped aside for these two performances.

Career choices had taken her beyond the miniature that is Cherubino both in voice and acting. The softer-grained voice of the thirties and forties was exchanged for more presence and richness. The palette of colors was always there but the colors were now more vivid. The qualities in her voice that were womanly and warm were necessary for Carmen and Dalila. The quality for Octavian and Orfeo is richer than that needed for Cherubino. The Mozart is a role that was relinquished at the right time and would best have been left in the past. If Crichton is accurate, the experience was one of frustration since she felt trapped in too small a place, like Alice in Wonderland after having drunk from the bottle and grown ten feet tall.

When Sena Jurinac was contacted to learn from her some of the details of the Glyndebourne *Nozze*, the letter was answered very graciously soon after, "It was in 1956 [sic] that I sang with Risë Stevens at Glyndebourne. I appreciated her very much, she was a nice colleague I loved to work with. Please excuse that I can't give you more details about this production that took place 40 years ago!" [1] Evidently, it was not one of her more memorable experiences either.

With the Glyndebourne "mistake" behind them, Risë and Walter traveled through Europe eventually arriving in Rome. Ahead of them was the prospect of journeying to Greece with Nicky where Risë would sing Orfeo in the opening opera of the first international festival since ancient times.

"The festival was my creation", Dino Yannopoulos said. "It seemed only natural that Greece with its rich history should celebrate its heritage. The theme of the first festival was Greek influence on works of art. For example, we presented *King Oedipus* by Sophocles and *Oedipus Rex* by Stravinsky. *Orfeo* was chosen as the first opera in the Festival and even though there was an effort to have Nikolaidi sing the title role, Risë was engaged on my insistence. Cognizant of the honor that was bestowed upon her, she accepted a fee of only three hundred dollars for each performance, far below what she would normally get.

In the *Orfeo* we presented, we used an alternate ending from the one at the Metropolitan. In my version, it was one of the few times that *Orfeo* ended on a tragic note. In standard versions, when Euridice dies again and at the moment Orfeo is about to kill himself, Eros appears and restores Euridice to life. In mine, Orfeo does kill himself followed by a return to the music of the Furies who tear him limb from limb. Orfeo is buried with Euridice. It is my feeling that this was the way the opera was to have ended originally, but it was first presented on the name day of the Emperor and the opera had to end on a happy note. Therefore, it was changed and both Orfeo and Euridice are alive at the end of the opera. When Risë was to have done *Orfeo* in San Francisco, she insisted that it be my version. It was arranged but then she had to cancel that season. [2]

The inaugural program was a concert by the Greek State Orchestra under Theodore Vavayannis with Elena Nikolaidi as soloist. *Orfeo ed Euridice* followed on the second evening with King Paul and Queen Frederika in attendance and Risë, "not only displayed the qualities of an exceptional singer, but must be considered today as unsurpassed in the interpretation of this particular role." [3]

> It was the magic of the Acropolis, that made that evening unforgettable", recalled former Metropolitan Opera soprano, Vilma Georgiou, Amor in the production. "I had never seen Stevens do it like that before. She was affected by the magic. We all were. The theater was not only full but also on the rocks beyond, hundreds of people were seated.
>
> Stevens understood you don't have to scream to be heard. In 'Che farò' she really cried for her Euridice. When she finished, the audience was silent for a moment and then

thunderous applause. That voice gave you chills. She saw the Acropolis before her, she stood still and she sang - beautifully. [4]

When her part in the Festival was over, the Surovys flew back to Rome and visited Verona a short time later. They left Italy on September 22nd on the Andrea Doria and arrived in New York on the 30th. By October 11th, Risë was back on the road where, in Knoxville, Tennessee, she appeared with the Symphony under David Van Vector. Her first number on the program was "Che farò" sung with the applause in Athens still resounding in her ears.

For the sake of doing something different, Risë agreed to sing Giulietta, one of Hoffmann's four loves, in *Les Contes d'Hoffmann.* which would open the 1955-1956 season. Even though the role was virtually a cameo, it had the hit tune of the show, the "Baccarole" to make it worthwhile. Bing was genuinely pleased that she would be giving the Met a large percentage of her time and, most importantly, go on tour with the company in the spring.

Giulietta's music had been carefully reviewed with James Shomate while they were playing recital dates so she was already well versed with the musical values of the score. There were some troublesome passages, however, for a mezzo. Max Rudolf was instructed by her to point out to Monteux sections of the septet that would have to be transposed to tailor her voice to a soprano part.

As she had done with Orlofsky, Risë rejected Rolf Gérard's original design that consisted of little more than net and flowers. She saw Giulietta in more elegant attire, a ball gown similar to what she wore in recitals. Keeping in mind the nature of the character she was to play, a courtesan, the dress was comprised of black tulle over a lighter underskirt, the arms bare, the neckline cut quite low. A tricorn hat with a veil to add a hint of mystery, jewels around her neck, wrists and hair created an illusion of decadence. She also insisted that the new design be shown to her for her approval by the end of May before her trip to Europe. That she declined to accept her full fee for so brief an appearance was gratefully accepted. The opening on November 14th was typical of the Met under Bing, a business as usual night, but Risë "gave to her Giulietta the attraction of her most convincing stage personality plus the benefit of her sumptuous voice." [5]

While *Hoffmann* was treated to a new production, *Der Rosenkavalier*'s scenery was a thing of rags and patches dating back to 1913. Although she had a sentimental attachment to it since it served as her debut, it was her fondest wish to appear in a new rendering of the opera much as she had done with *Carmen*. Bing did not have the funds to scrap the old production entirely but he commissioned Rolf Gérard to use what he could of it and concoct a revised production.

The framework of the Kautsky originals was retained but Gérard jettisoned the coverings and replaced them with his own designs. When Risë asked for new costumes for Octavian to compliment the new scenery, Bing assured her that the ones from Prague were perfectly beautiful. She countered that the revised production needed different costumes but Bing pleaded poverty so Karinska was commissioned to design new ones for which Risë paid one-thousand dollars of her own money.

On the whole, the critical consensus was that there was much to admire in this production and that Risë "outdid herself both singing and acting wise- high praise since this is a part in which the mezzo-soprano has always been first class." [6]

"Indeed, I had many times the pleasure to sing with Risë Stevens whom I think to have been one of the finest Octavians of my time", Otto Edelmann, the Baron Ochs, recalled. "Her voice was very much appropriate for this difficult role and the acting full of humor was outstanding." [7]

This was the time she should have recorded a complete *Der Rosenkavalier* for RCA Victor. Her voice was at its lushest and she had become pre-eminent as Octavian, but George

Marek vetoed it. There was no suitable Baron Ochs available since Edelmann was with EMI and had just recorded the role with Herbert von Karajan, Elisabeth Schwarzkopf and Christa Ludwig, in what has become a classic interpretation of the score. The other possible choice, bass, Kurt Böhme, was with Deutsche Grammophon and would commit his Baron Ochs to disc in 1958 with Karl Böhm conducting and Irmgard Siefried in the title role. RCA did have Leinsdorf, della Casa and Peters in their stable to round out a cast but the absence of a bass was critical. To make matters worse, in Marek's opinion record sales were another stumbling block since *Der Rosenkavalier* had limited buyer appeal and with EMI issuing its recording in 1956 and one on Decca since 1954 with the formidable Erich Kleiber conducting Maria Reining, Sena Jurinac and Hilde Güden, prospects for yet another recording of a marginally popular work were not encouraging.

Carmen was Risë's only role in the 1956-57 season, Dimitri Mitropoulos would conduct. The sixty-year-old music director of the New York Philharmonic was best known for his way with the moderns but he proved himself first-rate with Bizet as well. Risë and he got along from the start and during one stage rehearsal with piano, he sat on stage and watched her perform much to their mutual satisfaction. "This was the maestro's first encounter with the score here, and for many in the house it must have sounded like their first too. The performance had the freshness and impact of a wholly new experience." [8]

"I was very new at the Metropolitan when I was asked to direct the 1956 revival of *Carmen*", Nathaniel Merrill recalled. "The Guthrie production needed freshening up but I could not change the basic outline. It was essentially getting the action to flow more smoothly by eliminating little pieces of stage business and adding others. That was over forty years ago so I no longer remember in detail what the changes were since they weren't major. As far as Risë was concerned, she made suggestions for herself and I made mine, we talked it over and some of her ideas but not all were used. She was willing to try new ideas. She was a very good actress with great musicality.

Risë always had a very strong personality on stage. It was especially hard for the tenors who appeared opposite her because all eyes were on her. She could literally take over with that combination of voice and looks- remember she was very tall with a wonderful figure- which was phenomenal." [9]

The 1957-1958 season at the Metropolitan was one of the longest for Risë. Scheduled for twenty-seven performances of her four biggest roles, Octavian, Carmen, Orfeo and Dalila, she was at the peak of her career and an invaluable member of the company. Behind the scenes, Weinhold was already sounding out Bing about his plans for Risë in the season following. Her services were much in demand on the road and Weinhold needed to know how to schedule around the Metropolitan's dates. He also reminded Bing that her fees for out-of-town recitals and concerts were four times as much as the Met paid.

Karl Böhm had made his debut at the Metropolitan on October 31st when the Eugene Berman and Herbert Graf production of *Don Giovanni* was unveiled. Apart from his way with Mozart, Böhm was what some would call the definitive interpreter of the works of Richard Strauss, which created some friction at the very beginning. Quite simply, he did not trust Americans with Strauss. Problems with Risë over tempi threatened to bring the rehearsals to a halt until one evening, assistant manager, Robert Herman invited Risë, Böhm and his wife to dinner in hope of bringing about some rapport between the two. At the end of the evening, quite unexpectedly, Böhm made a toast to Risë, "To the best Octavian I ever worked with."

Next on Risë's agenda at the Metropolitan was, by now, an annual encounter with Carmen. When it premiered on December 4th, the main difference this season was the presence of the twenty-seven year old Thomas Schippers in the pit and, later, Carlo Bergonzi's first Met, Don José. Working with two new conductors presented problems but, whereas Böhm was well versed in the Strauss, Schippers had never conducted the Bizet. It became embarrassingly obvious that it was too soon for Schippers to be conducting *Carmen* at the Metropolitan Opera since the incisive understanding of the work was missing. However, Bing was very fond of him, which created a protective shield around everything he did.

From the first rehearsal, chaos reigned. He threw out ideas as to how things should go and the singers told him why they would not work. The cast coached him, not the reverse. Tempi were slowed down and speeded up for no reason. The "Quintet' in Reiner's version, for example, was very fast but Schippers took it twice as slow in the one orchestra rehearsal allotted to him. In performance, however, to the relief of everyone in the cast, "his tempos were steady but had the breath of life." [10]

One of the most anticipated events of the Metropolitan's spring tour was the pairing of Risë and Mario del Monaco in *Samson et Dalila*. In January, Bing received a request from the *Teatro Colón* to release del Monaco from his spring engagement so that he could appear in a special anniversary season at their theater. Bing refused since he was not about to lose his Samson. To anticipate the tour, three performances including a broadcast were scheduled for New York and met with considerable success.

In conjunction with this revival RCA Victor planned a recording of highlights from the opera in Boston's Symphony Hall. The Metropolitan Opera Orchestra was contracted to play for it and since the company opened its spring tour in Boston on the 14th and Risë was due to sing Octavian on the 16th, scheduling was tight. Necessity worked to its advantage since the acoustics in Symphony Hall are among the best anywhere, which augured well for a superior sound on the recording.

In spite of a this being a down period in relations between Bing and del Monaco (who was using his star power to extract future contractual concessions and who would depart permanently from the Met in 1959), the recording was done quickly and with telling results in the skilled hands of Cleva. Here was a conductor who was not out to glorify himself as Stokowski did in the earlier recording of *Samson et Dalila*, but had the utmost consideration for the singers. The only casualty was Leonard Warren who was originally thought of as the High Priest but who haggled so on terms that Clifford Harvuot was signed instead.

Scheduled to appear in a television version of the Grimm Fairy Tale, *Hansel and Gretel*, on April 27th, Risë, who was on tour with the Met, flew back to New York on the 25th. The show had nothing to do with Humperdinck's opera, which under the circumstances was its chief flaw. Among the story line's misguided efforts was a broom garage for the Witch's favored means of travel and a forest that moved about threateningly. Risë was cast as the mother and Rudy Vallee the father of Red Buttons and Barbara Cook, two obviously over-aged children. It was a dismal failure and on top of it, Risë's throat was affected by an accidental inhalation of a chemical that was used to create smoke. Scheduled to sing Octavian on the evening of the 28th in Washington, D.C., Walter sent a 7:00 A.M. wire to Max Rudolf sending regrets for Risë. Management had a dim view of cancellations as a result of outside activities, especially for tour performances, and Risë went on after all and "looked the same radiant, passionate youth she has since her first singing the part twenty-two years ago." [11]

After the Met tour and another leisurely summer in Westhampton, Risë was due to report to the Metropolitan on November 13[th.] Negotiations leading up to the contract for this season were momentarily bogged down when it was made known that she was not anxious to go on the spring tour two years in a row. Management held fast to their position that if she were to get the first New York performance of *Carmen* and the broadcast, she must tour the production. However, if another artist were to go on tour as Carmen then she should by right get the first New York performance and the broadcast. The matter was settled when Risë gave in on the tour. Her reluctance stemmed in part from the ability to earn a higher fee in recitals and television, the production of *Carmen* offered nothing new to the tour cities and an increasing awareness that Bing was not about to offer her anything she had not already done. Otherwise the terms of her contract were essentially the same as the year before, only a five hundred-dollar per performance tour bonus was added.

The 1958-59 season at the Metropolitan Opera introduced Jean Morel's *Carmen* on November 21ˢᵗ. Morel, an authority on French opera, pleased the critics only some of the time. The consensus was that the opening performance did not come as alive as it should under his baton. For Risë, he was too French in manner, too *Opéra Comique*, a style she did not like. He did not approve of the sung recitatives and wanted them spoken. Risë insisted they remain as they were and they did. She also felt there was little continuity in his approach to the score. It didn't flow. Robert Merrill recalled that he had tempi all his own – very fast.

Television again offered the greater novelty, this time, on the new *Bell Telephone Hour* over NBC on February 10ᵗʰ. The *New York Times'* critic, John P. Shanley, found "Miss Stevens appealing as she sang an excerpt from the seldom-heard Victor Herbert operetta, 'Natoma'." [12]

Originally she and her Metropolitan Opera colleague, Giorgio Tozzi, were scheduled to sing two excerpts from *Regina* but the sponsor felt the subject matter and lyrics were not appropriate for television. It was unfortunate since Risë had decided not to create the title role on Broadway and performing a selection from it would have been of interest. The director, Herbert Ross, had to make a quick decision on what she would sing, so when an aria from *Natoma* was suggested, she accepted even though the music is very thin. The glamorous costume designed for her by Reuben Ter Arutunian for *Regina* could not be used and the replacement consisted of a nondescript Indian outfit and heavy braids. Risë was not happy about the change visually or musically but she overcame both as a videotape of the program reveals. Her ability to make the music sound more important than it would be in less skilled hands is the most striking feature. She makes the scene riveting through rich vocal delivery, unwavering concentration and seemingly total belief in what she is singing.

The Metropolitan Opera began its tour in Boston on April 13th with Samuel Barber's *Vanessa. Carmen* was presented on the afternoon of the 15th and critic, Kevin Kelley, commented, "In the last decade, Risë Stevens has assumed virtual control on the role of Carmen. It is probably her most vivid portrayal, a taut and perceptive projection of character ...In voice and gesture, she is Carmen, intense, fractious, insolent." [13]

Risë was invited to appear at the groundbreaking ceremony for Lincoln Center for the Performing Arts on the 14th. After President Dwight D. Eisenhower turned a symbolic shovel of earth to inaugurate the undertaking, the musical section of the program opened with the "National Anthem" sung by the Juilliard Chorus. Sandwiched between speeches, Leonard Warren sang the "Prologue" from *Pagliacci*, followed by Risë's "Habañera". Bernstein acted as Master of Ceremonies and led the New York Philharmonic in the "Egmont" Overture, the "Hallelujah" Chorus from Handel's *Messiah* and Sousa's "Semper Fideles". Of the three performers, only Leonard Bernstein performed inside the actual theater destined for the New York Philharmonic. As for Risë and Warren singing in the new Metropolitan Opera House, by 1966 when it was completed, Risë was retired from a stage career and Warren was dead.

Chapter 19

During August, Ed Sullivan moved his popular Sunday evening television show, *Toast of the Town*, to Russia for a series of shows sponsored by the U. S. State Department to foster better relations between the two countries. The troupe was booked for two weeks in Moscow and one in Leningrad. Risë, one of his favorite guests, was scheduled to appear as were the Hawaiian tenor, Charles K. L. Davis and the American soprano, Margaret Tynes. They represented the classical field as did the prima ballerina, Nora Kaye, and her partner, Scott Douglas. The remainder were from all walks of theatrical life. Everyone on the trip had to have a job title in order to get a work permit to appear in Russia, Walter of course, was Risë's manager but since they wanted to take Nicky along, a job title had to be made-up for him so he became their "baggage handler".

When they arrived, Risë was asked to record arias from *Carmen, Samson, Figaro*, and others, for a Russian recording company. Escorted in a private car to a recording studio in an undisclosed location, she recorded the selections the government requested without ever learning what became of them or how they were used.

The television shows were filmed in Gorki Park, Gum Department Store, a gymnasium and on a boat on the Volga under heavy surveillance of the whole troupe the entire time they were there. Everyone could feel they were being watched even in the hotel where they knew someone was listening to everything they said and making note of everywhere they went. If they commented to one another when they were in their room that there was no soap, when they reached the lobby, they were handed soap without having asked. Only prescribed areas could be visited and as for dining, the hotel offered a billboard size menu that listed numerous items but when any were asked for, none were available. Omeletes or chicken Kiev were omnipresent and became the staple morning, noon and night.

Any inconveniences were made bearable because the audiences wholeheartedly embraced the efforts of all the entertainers. The show was part of the American Exhibition in Moscow with the congenial Sullivan introducing the acts in less than fluent Russian, a courtesy thought well of by those who attended. Gasps of surprise, mixed with delight and shock, greeted the Barry Sisters when they entered the stage in what could have been painted on white dresses. Risë had a less obvious way of pleasing an audience and her rendition of "Getting to Know You" from the *King and I* with several measures in Russian went over in a big way. Otherwise it was a Sullivan show, the format pure vaudeville. To compensate for language differences, the American acts were combined with Russian artists, the Soviet Army and Air Force dancers, the Obratsov puppets and even a brown bear from the Moscow Summer Circus.

Upon their return home, the feeling of good-will from Russia was overshadowed by a pending law suit. A San Francisco engagement in September and October during which Risë would have sung Carmen and Orfeo ended with bitter feelings on both sides. Walter, protecting their interests and Risë's professional standing, objected to foreign singers, notably Mario del Monaco and Leonie Rysanek, receiving higher fees. Insisting that Risë be paid more, even if by one dollar, Walter had not expected to deal with an intransigent administration. Refusing his request to rewrite her contract, they threatened a law suit if she did not fulfill it as written. When Walter made the same threat, Risë's contract was abruptly canceled. A heated no win situation had time to cool off while the Surovys were in Russia. When they returned, the suits were called off and the matter resolved with no one emerging the winner. It might have been the best turn of events for Risë since the new *Carmen* production had costumes that were extremely heavy in design whereas she had become used to the more natural fit of the Metropolitan's.

The 1959-1960 season at the Metropolitan offered four Carmens and one Octavian with no commitment for the tour. Morel was again the conductor for *Carmen* and the only novelty was that she was not in the first two performances. Madiera sang these since Risë was spending more time concertizing as her operatic career was winding down. The last week in February found her in Ft. Lauderdale with the Miami Opera. With San Francisco fresh in her mind, she opted to wear the Metropolitan Opera's costumes. The production was very old fashioned and when they were rehearsing Walter noticed that all during Risë's "Habañera" there was a man walking a mule behind her. It was very distracting and as soon as he could he complained to the Manager, Arturo di Filippi. He was told that the man with the mule was underwriting Risë's fee. The mule stayed.

Her annual concert tour was interrupted mid-way through March since her Octavian at the Met was scheduled for the final *Der Rosenkavalier* on the 17th. As it turned out, it was her farewell to the role. That she could have kept it with her a bit longer was brought out by Miles Kastendieck, "Miss Stevens remains the finest Octavian since this opera was restored some 20 years ago. She not only looks the part, but carries herself remarkably well as a young man...Vocally, she may have seen her prime when she sings forte but in half voice the quality remains lovely. She floated some beautiful tones throughout the evening." [1] This was one of the rare times that Bing actually complimented her for when she mentioned to him that it would be her last Octavian, he appeared astonished and said, "After a performance like that?"

April 20th brought with it the news that Edward Johnson died in Guelph, Canada. Risë and Walter, in company with Lucrezia Bori, were three of the few of his former New York associates who attended the funeral. On the flight back, when the captain introduced himself as "Edward Johnson", Bori turned pale under her makeup.

Two performances of *Carmen* were all that Risë could fit into the 1960-1961 season at the Metropolitan. To make up for her absence, a brace of new Carmens was brought in a futile attempt to satisfy the Metropolitan Opera audience: the Swedish mezzo, Kerstin Meyer, and French soprano, Jane Rhodes. Of the two, Rhodes was better received even though she violated the original concept of the Guthrie production by wearing her own ornate costumes and not tearing the drape in the last act. Meyer's chief handicap was that her voice was too small for a theater the size of the Met. Otherwise, the critics thought her efforts veered between striking and unexciting.

The first of Risë's two Carmens was to have been on December 16th but due to an indisposition, Blanche Thebom went on in her place. A month later she was in Hawaii for what she thought was a much-earned rest. Risë and James Shomate were overdue for a vacation so Walter proposed they use some free days on the tour to go to Hawaii. Unknown to them, he had arranged a recital in Honolulu. Since she had no intention of using her voice, Walter's suggesting she vocalize puzzled Risë. He kept insisting but when she continued to refuse, he confessed what he had done and Risë and Shomate found themselves on stage trying to forget they were on vacation. Professionalism won out over any feeling of resentment since the *Honolulu Star-Bulletin* reported, "Miss Stevens will long be remembered in Honolulu for her beauty of sound, her mastery of color and diction and her artistry of interpretation." [2]

Carmen on Wednesday, April 12th was Risë's only performance at the Metropolitan. The house was sold out far in advance for this non-subscription performance. A large contingent of fans was in the audience and gave her a tremendous ovation when she stepped out on stage. Their enthusiasm was contagious, inspiring Risë to give one of her strongest performances in this decade old production.

Irving Kolodin, who had been one of her unkindest critic through the years, was equally won over and paid tribute to her by now definitive portrayal of Carmen,

> Risë Stevens is still by much the best Carmen the theatre commands, not only in action (which could be anticipated) but also in voice (which couldn't). Perhaps because of a rest from the rigors of opera (this was her only Metropolitan appearance in a winter devoted mostly to concertizing), this performance looked as much to the future as to the past- which is to say that her sound had warmth, nuance, and color, all under vocal discipline. There were some suggestions that Miss Stevens has been thinking about the role even though she hasn't been performing it, for it was played less for the easy, superficial sexy 'glamour' of her past Carmen, more for a hardened, calculating kind of amorality.   Such certainly can be found in the role, and it is worth noting that Miss Stevens's instinct for change and development is still with her. [3]

After the performance, with the customary ritual of autograph signing, hand shaking, kind words and compliments completed, unknowingly, she said good-bye to all that.

While Risë was officially on leave from the Met in the 1961-62 season, Bing approached Walter about having her appear in two performances of *Orfeo* in March. Walter's reply was affable but to the point in a letter to Bing dated September 6, 1961:

> It is the second time that you offer this part to her because *Simionato* cancelled. As I told you the first time, Risë's pride cannot be hurt because she has so much of it. She never thinks of herself as a replacement. She simply feels that it was an error on the managements part not to have asked her in the first place...Unfortunately, this time I have to turn you down, for one reason only; the dates you have

given to me are solidly booked in concert. [4]

The Metropolitan, however, was faced with the threat of closing its doors permanently due to a crippling strike brought on by the musicians' salary demands and the endemic intransigence of Rudolf Bing in dealing with Unions. When an impasse was reached, Bing threatened to cancel the 1961-1962 season, a ploy he always used.

The seriousness of the situation was exacerbated by the end of July when all artists were released from their contracts. On August 7th, the Board of Directors officially announced the cancellation of the 1961-1962 season. Bing then left New York for his annual vacation in the Dolomites. Risë, all too aware of the seriousness of the situation, sent a telegram to President John F. Kennedy, the same day the season was canceled, appealing to his sense of national pride in saving a cultural organization that was esteemed world wide.

With Secretary of Labor, Arthur J. Goldberg, acting as mediator at Kennedy's request, the impasse was breached and the season saved. "Soprano Risë Stevens, who had been the most active artist in seeking Presidential intervention declared: 'Isn't it exciting...I'm happy of course and so grateful the President stepped in...This is the American way. If you want to get something done, go directly to the President'." [5]

Risë's column in her "Music Club" journal updated her fans on recent activities,

> Nicky is in his last year at Choate, and the choice of a college is foremost in his mind. Walter is very busy with his various clients*. This has a great advantage for me

* Walter had entered the artist management field as Risë's career was winding down, numbering among his clients, Anna Moffo and Mary Costa. While it was a satisfying occupation when working on behalf of Risë's interests, he found it less congenial and frustrating to work for others. With Risë, they would discuss things at home and come to a mutual understanding, with the others, it was across a desk with the results not always to his liking. Eventually, he stepped away from management and entered the real estate field as a broker.

because now he takes me to the opera, which we have so rarely attended before. There is some talk about my recording LADY IN THE DARK. I am looking at the score right now and it sounds interesting. [6]

When Columbia records approached Risë to record *Lady in the Dark*, she readily agreed. Her affection for the Kurt Weill score resulted in one of her best recordings. In particular, the pivotal song, "My Ship", in her hands, is an excursion into a land of fantasy, the rendering of which parallels the wistful yearning of Judy Garland's classic, "Over the Rainbow". The recording is a good example of how Risë colored her voice to suit the music- a feature of her approach to a popular song or an aria that some critics could not understand right from the start. For the Weill song, the resonance in her voice is drained out to give the semblance of a childlike remembrance of a dream. It is Liza Elliott coming to terms with her past and is light years away from the belted out "Poor Jenny" necessarily brazen in tone.

Risë's recording was the first that contained most of the Weill score. Gertrude Lawrence had recorded six numbers from the show as did Danny Kaye [Kaye's are included in the 1997 reissue] but neither aimed for completeness. *Variety* was quick to point out in its assessment of the recording that Risë was handed a tough assignment since anyone following Gertrude Lawrence was at a disadvantage. That she handled it with great aplomb and gave to it her own special qualities was to her credit. She had, of course, the advantage over Lawrence in voice. Her co-star, Adolph Green, had an equally tough job in trying to keep up with memories of Danny Kaye. *Variety* admitted that Kaye's frenzy was missing but Green brought to the roles of Beekman and the Ringmaster his own considerable talent for comedy.

In 1997, *Lady in the dark* was reissued on the Sony label [which took over Columbia] to general praise from the critics. The *Kurt Weill Newsletter* welcomed its return and *Gramophone* gave it a thumbs up all the way, "Risë Stevens makes no attempt to imitate Gertrude Lawrence and her rich operatic mezzo sounds suitably tough- after all she is meant to be the Editor-in-Chief of a glossy magazine, a woman succeeding in a predominantly male world."[7]

Jean Dalrymple wanted her for a revival of *Lady in the Dark* to be presented at New York's City Center theater, but by then Risë was too involved with the National Company to consider it.

Part 3:

1963 and Beyond

John Pennino

Chapter 1:
The National Company

It was an enormously taxing undertaking but, God, we loved that Company. [1]

An Overview

While Risë was in Vienna's *Sofiensaal* recording highlights from *Die Fledermaus* for RCA Victor in June of 1963, preliminary discussions were taking place in New York concerning a National Company which would present opera under the auspices of the Metropolitan Opera and the National Cultural Center of Washington. After President John F. Kennedy declared on October 8, 1963, that a National Company would indeed become a reality, the position of co-manager was offered to her. The person behind Risë's appointment was the Met's General Manager, Rudolf Bing, who earlier had made known to Anthony Bliss, President of the board, that when Risë retired from singing she would be a good candidate for an administrative position with the main company. He thought of her in terms of Edward Johnson who was, in his opinion, an affable manager rather than a hard driven administrator. Bliss originally voiced doubts due to her lack of experience behind a desk, but realized that her public appeal would go far in promoting the company. Bing was named overseer of the entire project and by the beginning of 1964, Robert La Marchina had been named principal conductor and stage director, Michael Manuel, the second co-general-manager.

On January 28, 1964, the *New York Times*, published a statement that Risë would continue giving recitals which were already planned through the 1965-1966 season, however, she would revise the schedule to fit around her responsibilities with the Metropolitan Opera National Company. Risë's assignment required her to be almost constantly on the road, visiting each city of the tour prior to the company's arrival. She was obliged to speak to local sponsors, grant interviews, appear on radio and television advertising the company, reiterating its purpose and, in general, be a good will ambassador. In addition, supervising the company, chartering the progress of singers and productions and looking after the personal well being of the company fell under her aegis. She was not obliged to coach but advised on interpretation if asked. Her only involvement with production values occurred when she felt that the best interest of the work was not being served.

In April, the two co-managers and the music director left for a brief audition tour in Germany and Switzerland, Dusseldorf, Munich, and Zurich. The general feeling of good will about the new company was somewhat dimmed, however, by a report from the board questioning the timing. The Metropolitan faced a move into a new opera house in 1966 and plans to televise operas were being seriously considered. There were those who felt the formation of the company should be delayed until the Met was in its new home and in a stronger financial position.

Anthony Bliss played down that the Company was being formed at the worst possible time, but not Bing. Against it from the start, he felt that it would saddle his two top administrators, Robert Herman and Herman Krawitz, with added responsibilities and, moreover, be in competition with the main company for funding. In a letter to Bliss, Bing voiced doubts about the entire enterprise including the inability to attract good singers and outstanding directors. Tension between Bliss and Bing began to mount over what Bliss felt was

Bing's lack of true interest in anything beyond 39th and Broadway.

Susannah was chosen to inaugurate the company on September 20, 1965, and met with excellent reviews. Momentarily suppressing his animosity for the National, Rudolf Bing commented that it was one of the most dramatic performances he had ever seen.

The National's repertory for the second season was announced in February, and ever the public relations arm for the company, Risë exuded pure optimism when she said the first year was "'tremendously successful. I think the company has proved itself to nth degree'." [2]

On June 30th, a special meeting of the Executive Committee of the Metropolitan Opera Association was held in the offices of Anthony Bliss in 1 Rockefeller Plaza. The National Company was the chief topic on the agenda. Bing had made certain changes in the reporting structure of the company. Reginald Allen would now be the senior member of Management responsible to Bing for the National. It was stressed that this did not diminish Risë's and Michael Manuel's roles, it meant that Allen would now be final authority on questions concerning the Company.

The Committee for the National Company submitted a report to the Board of Directors of the Metropolitan Opera Association which stated that the company should continue beyond the second season. Rudolf Bing sent his own recommendations to the board demanding, unequivocally, that it should be liquidated at the end of the current season, basing his decision on a variety of issues: that it was drawing top management's attention from the considerations of the main company to an excessive degree; taking care of the new house was top priority; the deficit of the National Company was 30% higher than predicted and by the end of a third season could be two million dollars in the red; the National Company owed the main company one million dollars which created a near financial crisis; the pool from which outside funding could be obtained was only so large and pledges to the National could mean fewer pledges for the main company.

On December 5th, Anthony Bliss notified the board of the Metropolitan Opera at an informal meeting of officers and committee chairman that contrary to popular opinion he intended to vote against suspending operations of the National Company. Moreover, he voiced opposition to picking up the option on Rudolf Bing's contract for the 1969-1970 season. The Bliss stand was voted down. Bing's option was exercised and operation of the National Company was suspended after the second season. A letter was drafted that would be sent over Risë's and Manuel's signatures to break the news of the company's demise and the reasons for it.

Risë called the company together to tell them the news before they read it in the papers. At the same time, she sent a wire to Royall Victor, Chairman of the National Company Board requesting it be read to the board. In essence she asked not be paid for the remainder of her contract since she realized the financial burden the Metropolitan Opera was faced with due to its move to Lincoln Center.

On December 17th, Risë and Michael Manuel are given formal notice that their association with the National Company would not exceed June 30, 1967. This was followed up by an informal letter from Bing reminding them that he was against establishing a second company but "I saw with pleasure the enthusiasm that you both have given this Company and you have every reason to be proud of your achievements. I know the present decision must be heartbreaking after all the work you put in..." [3]

A Closer Look

The offer to run the company came as a complete surprise to Risë. In November 1963, Anthony Bliss invited her to lunch at the Hemisphere Club and brought up the National Company. He asked whether she would be interested in helping form a company that would tour the United States, Mexico and Canada and introduce opera in small towns and encourage larger cities to start their own companies. "Show them how it can be done," was the way he put it. She told him that she would be interested only on condition that there was a full orchestra and chorus and as much support help as necessary. Nothing was decided right then, and Risë was non-committal on whether she would agree to it or not until she discussed the matter with Walter. Truthfully, she was not keen on accepting since touring would take her away from home once again, however, the possibilities it offered to educate people in opera appealed to her.

Walter thought it was a great idea and encouraged her to accept but before doing so, he went to Bing to ask what Risë's title would be. When he was told, "director", Walter suggested, "general manager". Bing said no at first but later came around. Walter knew that she would not have accepted with a lesser title. As it turned out, the title became, co-general manager, since Michael Manuel was appointed to head the company along with her. Prior to their appointments, Bing had engaged Robert La Marchina as music director, thereby cutting them off from offering any recommendations on a vital position. Robert La Marchina recalled both his appointment and his subsequent, at times, troubled dealings with the co-general managers: "Rudolf Bing hired me while I was conducting at the Menotti Spoleto Festival. At that time, he appeared very much for the National Company. I can't say that Risë, Michael and I were always in agreement. Risë had definite ideas on how things should be done and I had mine. Michael was in the middle, the *consigliere*." [4]

"I first heard from Reginald Allen and Herman Krawitz," Michael Manuel, former Executive Stage Manager of the Metropolitan, said of his involvement with the company, "that there was something in the wind, a National Company. Allen had worked out a budget for it. Bing asked me to review the budget which I did and I estimated that it should be two million dollars plus. Evidently, he was impressed with what I did. He asked me if I might be interested in co-managing the National Company with Risë. I admired her greatly so I jumped at the chance. I would not have shared management with anyone else.

We were essentially appointed at the same time. My responsibility was to structure the Company and hers to provide the talent. She was a well-known person, I was not. She handled the public end of things and very capably." [5]

Herman Krawitz recalled:

The idea for the National Company was in the air so to speak. Herbert Graf, ever a champion of American artists, suggested a company of young singers. Anthony Bliss and members of the National Council lent support to the concept. I was instrumental in planning the organizational framework for the company.

The National Company was conceived as a touring group for non-Metropolitan tour cities, with talented young artists who might one day be cast at the Met. This was compatible with Rudolf Bing's position that the main company was not and should not be a training ground for singers.

Bing was *never* an advocate of the National however. He considered it an unnecessary distraction of his team which, at that time, was also planning the move to Lincoln Center. Robert Herman and I were enlisted to oversee the new company. Although we exercised caution so as not to undermine the efforts of Risë and Michael, our involvement was necessary. [6]

At the same time Risë was becoming more involved with the National Company, an offer was made to appear in a musical not on Broadway but as the opening attraction in the newly built State Theater in Lincoln Center. It came about as a result of Richard Rodgers asking her to sit in on auditions for *The King and I*, which he was producing as part of a musical comedy series for Lincoln Center. What he didn't tell her was it was she who would be auditioned. Walter, of course, knew of Rodger's intentions and suggested she vocalize before her meeting with him. After the auditions were over, Rodgers asked Risë to sing some songs from the show for his own pleasure. She obliged and when she finished, he offered her the part. Ever the pragmatist, she told him that first of all she had unofficially retired from staged performances, that she had a contract to form an opera company and, moreover, she had to go to Europe to audition singers. When Rodgers assured her that the show would run for five weeks only and practically begged her to accept, she agreed to do it subject to Bing's approval. When she told him of Rodgers proposal, Bing was very surprised that she would want to do it. However, he released her from her contract for the run of the show, when he heard that it would inaugurate the Music Theater of Lincoln Center and play for a limited time.

The show was very successful and proved quite profitable an undertaking for Risë. Through Walter's skillful negotiations, her fee was based on 10% of the box office receipts, earning her eight thousand dollars a week, three thousand dollars more than the straight fee of five thousand dollars a week originally offered. Rodgers wanted her to tour the show when it closed but her Metropolitan Opera obligation would not allow it. It was just as well. Annamary Dickie commented, "I was asked to be the 'stand-by' for her. I've never forgotten how humbled Risë was by the demands of the role. She said it was the most difficult of any she had ever done." [7]

When asked about her memories of *The King and I*, Patricia Neway, who played Lady Thiang, said,

> I remember *The King and I* as a lovely experience. It was the first in a season of musicals at the State Theatre in Lincoln Center in 1964. Dick Rodgers was the direc-

tor that year and he told us once it was the most pleasant company he had ever worked with in all forty-three
years he had been in the theatre. Of course, Risë and
Darren largely set the tone for that. Darren's characterization of the King was softer than Yul Brynner's on
Broadway and in the film, but strong nevertheless. Risë's
Anna was dignified and elegant, characteristics Risë
possessed in abundance in real life.

There was little socializing among the cast so I didn't
get to know Risë well personally, but I was very aware
that she was a consummate professional, even giving
me full stage in the one scene we had alone [by keeping
her back to the audience], a courtesy many singers did
not extend readily. I had been an admirer of hers, particularly of her beautiful Octavian which I saw many
times, and I am grateful that I had the opportunity to
work with her on stage. [8]

The *King and I* opened at the State Theater on July 6th,
and Risë was, "Happily cast as Anna...Vocally she adjusted
well to the music, sang the familiar tunes with the right emotional inflection and built an artistic entity of characterization." [9]

*****

On October 30, 1964, while still concertizing, Risë formally announced that she would not sing in opera again.
There is an old saying that singers die twice, once when they
stop singing, and again when they stop breathing. It was not
an easy decision to make but she was never one to deceive
herself. No doubt she discussed it with Walter; no doubt he
agreed. It was time to move on. Being involved with the National Company helped remove the sting of leaving opera,
also second thoughts about continuing with the Met helped
ease the transition from performer to administrator. The 'second thoughts' arose over Risë's having signed a contract which
she later canceled for the 1962-1963 season with the Metro-

politan Opera. She was scheduled to sing Octavian in the first performance of *Der Rosenkavalier* on November 19th in recognition of her 25 years with the company. Directed by Lotte Lehmann with Régine Crespin making her debut as Marschallin it was to be a gala event. Prince Orlofsky in the New Year's Eve *Fledermaus* was added on although she had vowed never to perform the role again. For the latter, invitations were printed with Risë and Jack Gilford, the only two holdovers from the original 1950 cast (although Bing claimed that he tried, unsuccessfully, to sign Patrice Munsel for Adele), Elisabeth Söderström (Rosalinde), Roberta Peters (Adele) and Frank Guarrera (Dr. Falke), among others. As it turned out, Herta Töpper was the Octavian and Jean Madeira the Orlofsky in these performances.

The reasons Risë had for withdrawing pale beside the fact that it was a wise decision. Her last appearance at the Met was the much praised Carmen in April of 1961. It was best that she left it at that and not try to compete with herself as Octavian or resurrect, yet again, Orlofsky. She would have sung both operas with conductors that were new to her, Lorin Maazel in *Der Rosenkavalier* and Silvio Varviso for *Fledermaus*. That in itself might have been troublesome since she had definite ideas about the Strauss opera that might have been at variance with Maazel's. Then there was Lotte Lehmann, a novice stage director, albeit sharing her responsibilities with the seasoned Ralph Herbert. What could Lehmann or anyone tell her about Octavian? As for *Fledermaus*, it would be difficult to work with a better conductor than Eugene Ormandy or repeat the success she had with him.

Risë was not through with Orlofsky just yet, however, since as much as she disliked the role, her post opera career had her cast in both highlights and a complete recording of *Die Fledermaus*. *Musical America* reviewed the complete set quite favorably and reported, "Risë Stevens contributes a rather frightening vignette of that neurotic adolescent, Prince

Orlofsky." [10]

In addition to her new career as opera administrator, and success in the *King and I,* Risë had another reason to feel pleased with the way things were going. Following in the footsteps of his father and, in a way, her own, Nicky was making his local debut as an actor in *Helen,* a play by Wallace Gray based on the Helen of Troy legend due to open on December 9th at the Bouwerie Lane Theater. Prior to that, the sad news that Vera Schwarz died in Vienna on December 4th, reached Risë, as if to balance the happiness.

Underscoring these events was Bing's growing antipathy for the National Company. His attitude toward "Bliss's Baby", and Risë's association with it came to a head when towards the end of the second season, he called her into his office and said, "What are you trying to do? Take my job and be General Manager of this Company?". Risë was stunned. The notion was so farfetched that it was laughable but he evidently believed rumors that Risë would replace him when he retired. In addition, Bing's admitting that the performance of *Susannah* was one of the finest he ever heard doomed the company from that moment. He saw the entire enterprise as a threat to him.

"Apart from Bing, the Hurok Organization also proved troublesome", Michael Manuel said, "since its representative, Walter Prude, was not skilled in booking. He created too many short stays, did not consider the logistics very well. What operas we should open and close with to get us from stop to stop with the most ease. He did not consider if we could get there in time.

On the plus side, Risë was very level-headed and we respected what each other had to do. Her interests were singers, mine operations although I did sit in on auditions, however, the final choice was made by her and La Marchina. Bing chose the directors and designers. One director he couldn't get was José Quintero. He never returned Bing's calls. I suggested I try but Bing instructed me to figure out a budget to close down the company since he felt without Quintero there was no point in having it. He did not like having the Met's name attached to what he thought of as a second rate company. I called Quintero anyway and when I explained that we wanted him for an American opera, *Susannah*, with a cast of young singers whom he could choose and who would benefit by his training, he came around. When I told Bing of my success, I could tell it was not received very well since he lost his excuse to terminate the company.

As far as the choice of opening in Clowes Hall in Indiana," Manuel continued, "it chose us not the other way around. It was a new facility and needed attractions. Risë and I both agreed that when we formed the company, it should open away from a big city like New York. When we inspected Clowes, we both were sold on what it had to offer but, it distressed Bing to have us working out of town since he could not keep an eye on us. The opening was a big success and I have heard that Bing was very proud of it but that he resolved to kill us because of its success.

The first indication we had that the company was to close down was half way through the second season. The move to Lincoln Center blew the budget and since Bing didn't want the Company anyway he prevailed. The board with the exception of Roger Stevens and Royall Victor were all in Bing's pocket. It was, however, never meant to be a permanent entity. Its purpose was to sow the seeds of opera where it did not exist. I am very proud of the fact that the budget I worked out came in within one percent of projected cost. This having been figured with no guiding precedents. We were let down by Hurok in bookings, that's where we fell down. Otherwise pricing was fair as were guarantees of ten thousand dollars."
[11]

Lila Wallace came into the picture when she heard the company was going to be disbanded. During the second season in New York, Risë and Reginald Allen were in the City

Center and Mr. and Mrs. Wallace came to a matinee performance of *La Bohème*. At the end, they remained in their seats. Both Allen, who was now the person the co-general managers reported to and Risë were sure they were disappointed in what they had seen. Before the performance, however, Lila Wallace had asked Risë what it would take to keep the company running and was told one million dollars. When Allen and she joined the Wallaces where they were sitting, Mrs. Wallace invited them to be their guests for dinner. Towards the end of the evening, she turned to Risë and said the one million dollars was theirs.

As soon as he could, Allen called the Chairman of the National Company's Board and told him about the money. He, in turn, scheduled a meeting with Bing and the Met Board. When Bing was told of the Wallace gift, he said, "I do not believe it!" The Chairman said, "You mean Risë is a liar?" Reginald Allen knew that the Wallaces would not want to be in the middle of a messy situation between Bing and the National Company but whether Risë was bluffing about the gift was still a question. She asked Mrs. Wallace to make a statement to the Press that the offer was legitimate but was told she would do so only through a press release. Even after it was announced in the papers, Bing refused to believe it was true or did not want to believe it since it meant saving the company.

In the meantime, Risë received a phone call from Peter Mennin who was the President of Juilliard asking for Lila Wallace's telephone number. She told him she could not disclose it. He found out the number through another source and as a result of his call, Mrs. Wallace donated the one million dollars to build the Juilliard's new library.

"I feel that we accomplished two very important things," Krawitz said, "the first is that we created a place in America for the American singer and the second that we helped desegregate areas in the South. We followed Bing's ideas on racial discrimination that no invitations based on segregation could be accepted. We had Black soloists and Chorus members so it was an important consideration that the entire company was treated equally." [12]

For soprano Mary Beth Peil, the company provided a gateway to career choices that were not preordained,

> "Risë looked after my well being. She was careful about what roles I should sing and interested in what I was doing technically. She didn't coach any of us but she did offer advice to the mezzos doing Carmen. I sat in on those sessions. Her Carmen was of another period. The young singers could not begin to emulate her grandness, her persona. The way she could use a fan. Her inner fire. She was fascinating to watch.
> "With the National, I had tender, loving care. The singers were all hand-chosen. Risë and Michael were good partners. She was charming, warm, protective, made everyone feel great. Michael looked after business and his 'Englishness' made everything more palatable. He was with us practically all the time. La Marchina was an incredible musician. He and the orchestra understood one another. [13]

"The demise of the National Company cannot be attributed to economics," Krawitz contended. "The one million dollars offered by Mrs. Wallace would have sustained it. It was Bing who persuaded the Met's Board to turn down the offer because of his overall antipathy to the project. Bob Herman and I, among many, were saddened by the turn of events because we felt that the National provided an important and exciting adjunct to the Met." [14]

"The value of the company," mezzo Joy Davidson said, "was summed up by Risë when she told me after my fifteenth Carmen that it took her thirteen years to do that many." [15]

For La Marchina, "on a personal level, the company did little to further my career outside of giving me the opportunity to conduct several operas over and over." [16]

In retrospect, the negative aspects of the National Company were the heavy schedule the singers had and the constant traveling with the variables of theater size and acoustics. The positive side was the start of regional companies. Atlanta Opera built an Opera Center which was headed by Blanche Thebom; Houston and Dallas were both influenced by it. For Risë it was a learning experience but very frustrating and tiring.

After the National Company disbanded, Risë and Walter lived quietly in the Virgin Islands. All reminders of her career were stored away in their house on a bluff one hundred fifty feet above the Caribbean on St. Thomas. None of her photographs decorated the walls. Not even a piano was in evidence. The existence was ideal but the social unrest on the Island was of real concern.* Of even greater concern, Nicky was in the army, flying missions in Vietnam, and that, too, did nothing to mitigate an all pervasive sense of disquiet.

Of course, Risë being Risë, she could not be forsaken by old friends no matter the distance. In a letter addressed to the Metropolitan Opera but forwarded to 303 East 57th Street, an apartment they maintained in New York, Tyrone Guthrie reminisced on October 11, 1967 in a letter from his home in Ireland,

> Have been listening repeatedly to your splendid recording of *Carmen* with Reiner. I've been asked to direct it again next Spring in Düsseldorf-hence the brushing up. I cannot [begin] to tell you what immense pleasure your singing gives- so free and strong and gutsy, yet controlled [and] (ghastly word) tasteful. The last scene, especially, is superbly done - Jan Pierce [sic] is marvelous too. Indeed the whole recording is a very Special effort. Sad that Reiner is no longer with us. As you know, he [and] I didn't just get along like two loving brothers; I'd liked to have been able to say how - then as well as now - I admire (tho didn't always agree with) his work. [17]

When they returned to New York for good, having sold their property in the Virgin Islands,* and Nicky had finished his tour of duty in Viet Nam, life was returning to normal. It was a relief to have Nicky with them again and it provided a great feeling of satisfaction for Risë in particular when he informed his parents of his decision to study at Juilliard. Although he was older than the average entering student, John Housman, the director of the Drama Division, sympathized with his wanting to develop his speaking voice so that he could broaden his repertory. For Risë, of course, Juilliard was special and so was Tyrone Guthrie. Hearing from him across the distance of more than a decade brought back many memories of their unique collaboration. Memories can be deceiving, however, and if Risë could have been warned that her next venture was to be as frustrating as was the outcome of the National Company, she might have avoided it all together. But she did not.

.

---

* A letter addressed to Risë in St. Thomas from Lila Wallace in May of 1969 speaks of the sale of the house. A subsequent newspaper item confirms that it was sold in July of 1969.

Chapter 2:
Mannes College of Music

Peter Mennin approached Risë early in 1975 with an offer to teach at Juilliard. The idea was appealing since she always enjoyed working with young singers but did not want to accept students on a regular basis (although she did teach interpretation privately). Unexpectedly, another more challenging prospect opened up after she agreed to join Juilliard.

In March, John Goldmark, President of New York's Mannes College of Music, died suddenly, leaving behind a bankrupt institution. A search was on for a successor who could breathe life into the moribund school and restore confidence in its future. David Tcimpidis, Dean of the College, suggested Risë as a possible candidate to Hubert Doris, the acting President, who in turn presented it to the board. With her background as a major figure in the Arts, Risë was deemed ideal for the position. It is certain that the problems the school had were outlined to her before accepting the offer, but the idea of heading what was in essence a conservatory, like the *Mozarteum*, was too tempting to resist.

The official contract dated July 29th and signed July 31, 1975, was for an appointment which commenced September 1st that same year and ran through the 1977-1978 semester. As part of the contract it was stated that Risë could continue teaching privately as she had been doing and any remuneration for that would remain hers. Apart from this, she was not to engage in any activities that would take her away from her duties as President of Mannes. Membership on the board of the Metropolitan Opera Guild and acceptance of the nomination as an advisory member on the board of the Metropolitan Opera Association in February of 1976 did not violate the agreement since they were not activities that occupied a substantial amount of her time.

Apart from the financial problems the school was having, the morale of the faculty and students was very low. The orchestra was not good and Risë walked into a very difficult situation where she was forced to retire the conductor, Carl Bamberger, whom she knew since the Egypt tour in 1937. To replace him, she appointed a student of his, Sung Kwak, as Music Director and Semyon Bychkov as Associate Conductor.

Bychkov had left Leningrad three months before, graduating as a conducting major in the Leningrad Conservatory. When he came to America, he applied and was accepted at Mannes. When he arrived without funds in 1975, Mannes was not in the best of shape, but he was excused from paying tuition. About two months later, after conducting the student orchestra in Dvorak's *New World Symphony*, Risë asked to see him and offered him the appointment as conductor of the student orchestra the following year. Thrilled, he was hardly three months in the country and already had his own orchestra to conduct.

The orchestra was quite weak and the level of the individual students not high. The school always offered a well-rounded musical education. It was, however, a theoretical approach and when it came to performing it was not strong. Risë as a performer wanted to change this. For her, theory was there to support performing. If you want to perform-perform. The board wanted to keep the school as it was. It might have been a question of funds which eventually caused friction between them because the changes Risë had in mind cost money.

It was Bychkov's task to reorganize the orchestra, which wasn't easy, since he had no say in admitting students to the school. When the orchestra started playing regularly, the level improved. The Faculty also improved when Risë, with her celebrity status, was able to add Vladimir Horowitz to the roster. He had very few students but having his name connected with Mannes was important.

When, in an effort to revitalize the voice department, Risë decided to present a fully staged opera, Bychkov suggested Tchaikovsky's *Iolanta*. She liked the idea of presenting something different. Equally important, there weren't singers who could handle the familiar repertory. Lacking one of their own, they leased the Marymount College Theater and once the right singers were found, Risë was totally involved in every aspect of the production. The choice of the director and designer was hers. She made every costume decision and sat in on rehearsals but apart from advising not to take the recitatives too fast, she did not try to be the conductor, stage designer or director. It was extremely modest of her not to interfere but only to suggest.

Iolanta, in an English adaptation by Robert Hess, was presented on the evenings of March 24th, 25th and 26th and the matinee of the 27th. Since the main roles were all double cast, the close scheduling was not damaging to young voices nor was the vocal line. Harriett Johnson of the *Post* commented that, "President Stevens had captured a 23-year old recent Soviet emigre, Semyon Bychkov, to lead the work and he must be admired for conducting a tightly-knit performance that moved consistently and never split at the seams." [1]

On the surface everything seemed to be going well but half way through her third term, Risë notified the Faculty, Administration and Student Body that she had handed in her resignation effective June 30, 1978. She made known to them her pride in her three years as President, during which she eliminated the deficit and tapped new sources of revenue. Moreover, she had brought new blood into the faculty and revitalized the orchestra. The production of *Iolanta* was the first step toward expanding the opera program, a concept dear to her but opposed by members of the board. It was this opposition which triggered her decision to leave. She was the musician, the professional being dictated to by musical amateurs

Outstanding among the problems was the absence of fund raisers on the board. Shortly after Risë arrived, she discovered that some of the Rockefeller family went to Mannes and as a result of approaching them, Mannes received a $100,000 donation. Another handicap, equally as daunting, was tenured professors who were inadequate but who could not be replaced. The board was upset that she engaged Horowitz for master classes given in his home. They resented his request that he would accept only those students selected by Nadia Reisenberg, thereby ignoring recommendations by other faculty members. In addition, the need for stronger voice teachers and the opposition of the board to expanding the opera program, all played their part in her decision to leave.

Charles Kaufman who joined the faculty in 1975 as a Professor of the History of Music and became President of Mannes in 1980 was one of Risë's most loyal supporters,

Risë Stevens served the college well. She was, of course, a first-rate artist and had a broad knowledge of music and a personal view of how music should be taught. Early in her tenure she recognized that the voice and opera departments, as well as the orchestra program, needed restructuring and revitalization. It was no coincidence that the voice and opera programs were in direct support of opera at Mannes.

Her contacts and her personality made her a successful fund raiser, and she brought to the college a number of fine faculty selections, not the least of which was Vladimir Horowitz and her appointment of Semyon Bychkov to the post of orchestra director, the latter being among the earliest recognition of a conductorial talent that soon was to be very public. Risë's relationships with faculty were generally quite good, but the same did not hold true as far as the Board of Trustees was concerned.

It should have been obvious that one of the great opera artists of the century was going to have a strong interest in strengthening the opera program and would seek means to do so. It also was somewhat unrealistic to expect that Risë would be as virtuosic an administrator as she was an artist. She should have, but did not have sufficient staff to free her from the mundanities of day-to-day operations and problems, thus allowing her to focus on those areas in which her experience and expertise would have been most productive and at which she was most proficient.

Regrettably, her relationship with the board deteriorated. The then board had neither the means nor the management skills to see to the progress and maintenance of the College; nor did they have an understanding that Mannes was and is a community of musicians pursuing a common goal - making music together under optimum artistic and academic conditions. This judgment was validated a few years after Risë's precipitous resignation, when the New York State Board of Regents ejected the board after a disastrous attempt to merge the College with the Manhattan School of Music. Had such an attempt been made during Risë's tenure there is little doubt that she would have stood in strong opposition. She understood the College and its unique qualities too well to have accepted such a proposal. The brevity of her stay at the College was the College's loss. [2]

As Kaufman pointed out, subsequent to her departure, there was an attempt to merge the College with the Manhattan School of Music. At hearings before the Board of Regents of New York in 1979, ostensibly with the aim to point out the deficiencies of the Mannes Board by concerned Faculty, Risë's tenure was examined. After it was determined that all fund-raising had practically ceased subsequent to her departure (resulting in a deficit of four hundred thousand dollars in 1979), Risë's efforts in development were reviewed. At the close of her first year there was a net profit of forty-five thousand dollars; in 1977 a deficit of fifty-two thousand dollars was erased almost immediately and in 1978, a shortfall of one hundred thirty-five thousand dollars. Fund raising netted three hundred thousand dollars in 1975-1976; three hundred thousand dollars in 1976-1977; two hundred fifty thousand dollars in 1977-1978 and practically nothing in 1978-1979.

When it became apparent that she was not getting the support she needed either from the board or certain administrative areas under her, Risë opted to resign. She left in April although her contract ran through June. An Acting President was in place by May of 1978. Risë was well out of it. Her record of fund-raising cannot be contested. Her attempt to strengthen the performance opportunities of students was unappreciated in certain quarters but successfully launched with *Iolanta*. Above all, the morale of the College was enhanced by her presence. She was attracted to Mannes because when she first entered it, the aura brought back memories of the *Mozarteum*. As it turned out, memories can be deceiving.

Chapter 3:
A Metropolitan Opera Encore

Risë's appointment as Advisor to the Young Artist Development Program and Executive Director of the Metropolitan Opera Regional Auditions in the fall of 1980 returned her to the organization that had played a central role in her professional life. The Auditions under the aegis of the National Council were the successor to the Auditions of the Air that was the catalyst for sending her to Europe over sixty years earlier.

In 1954, the old format was put to rest by Rudolf Bing and a new means of choosing competitors took its place that provided a wider pool of talent. The National Council was asked to step in to establish regional centers for auditions. Under the first chairman, Howard J. Hook Jr., the Auditions network which consisted of sixty districts and sixteen regions throughout the United States, Australia and Canada, came into being as a result of his organization, tireless efforts and financial support. The National Council, itself, was founded in 1952 by Mrs. Belmont and had as its primary function the granting of a say in the running of the Metropolitan by members across the country. In effect, it made the Metropolitan Opera national in scope. Through its audition's program, regional winners receive cash awards and first place winners are brought to New York to participate in the National Semi-Finals and Finals at the Opera House.

In her new appointment, Risë worked closely and effectively with General Manager, Anthony Bliss, then Music Director, James Levine and Assistant Artistic Administrator, Lawrence Stayer. In the Board of Directors minutes for April 16, 1981, the following statement was read,

> The auditions Finals concert on Sunday, April 5th, under the directorship of Miss Risë Stevens in the Opera House was a great success and was widely felt to represent the highest professional level in many years. [1]

Risë's involvement with the program came about when she was approached by the President of the National Council, Louise Humphrey, who said she would appreciate it if she headed the Auditions. Having already refused once before because of the amount of work involved when Mrs. Humphrey's predecessor, Alexander Saunderson, asked, Risë made known that if she did accept, it would have to be a salaried position. Anthony Bliss wanted it to be on a volunteer basis but even though Risë was an Advisory Director on the board she still felt strongly about not volunteering her services. Mrs. Humphrey wanted her and used her considerable influence to get Bliss to attach a salary to it. He relented and Risë accepted.

Her first priority was to review the selection process in preparation for the 1982 auditions with the help of assistant manager, Joan Ingpen, Lawrence Stayer, Theodor Uppman, John Alexander and, assistant conductor, Joan Dorneman. The audition format was in place so she was relieved of that aspect of planning, but she did have to travel throughout the country to hear the candidates [A memo in the Metropolitan Opera Archives lists Risë's itinerary for January through March of 1981: January 16, Minneapolis; January 25, Detroit; January 30, Sarasota; February 7, Cleveland; February 13, San Antonio; February 18, Dallas and March 7, Toronto. It was her annual concert tours and the National Company all over again].

To assist her in the audition process, she had the invaluable help of Licia Albanese, Rose Bampton and Anna Moffo, to name three among others. They were sent to the various regions listening to the young hopefuls and choosing those who would come to New York for the finalists' concert held at the Opera House.

The audition process worked to the advantage of the Young Artists Program, which was founded by James Levine in 1980 and organized by Stayer. It is an effort, and a very successful one, in training the most promising young singers in all aspects of their profession. They receive an annual stipend for the up to three years they are in the program enabling them to devote all of their time to their studies, private coaching in voice, interpretation, stage craft and, if ready, the chance at essaying roles with the company. The program also monitors all outside engagements determining whether the role and venue are appropriate.

When Risë took over, one of the significant changes was the engaging of a full orchestra for the Finalists' concert and rehearsals for the concert. She felt strongly that the piano accompaniment generally used in the past did not give the artist optimum support. The format of the concert was also redesigned with the finalists chosen before hand, eliminating the selection of the winners at the concert. The tradition of awarding a Metropolitan Opera contract to the winner (a holdover from the original Auditions of the Air) was in effect ended in 1976 since Bing was against having a company member forced on him.

Disillusionment began to set in when Risë grew increasingly annoyed that some members of the National Council who were not musically sophisticated but were very vocal in telling her what to do. Also, on a more personal level, acclaimed soprano, Judith Raskin's death was a great loss to the Program. Her input meant a great deal to Risë who respected her judgment in choosing and developing young artists. Feeling she had done as much as she could, she stepped down effective July 31, 1988. Subsequently, she was nominated to the highest level of board membership, a Managing

Director of the Metropolitan Opera Association. Risë was named an Honorary Director with the 2005-06 season. A distinction very few achieve.

Risë has been associated with the Metropolitan Opera for over sixty years and during that time has witnessed many developments. When she was first approached to do *Orfeo* in 1936, the Metropolitan Opera was still a nineteenth century run house and it remained so until Edward Johnson retired. Bing brought it into the twentieth century and now Joseph Volpe is guiding it in the new millennium. In spite of her many accomplishments and the honors bestowed on her, the prestigious Kennedy Center being only one, her association with the Metropolitan Opera must surely override all.

In June of 2003, Risë entered the tenth decade of her life. She is now without her life's companion since Walter Surovy died on November 4, 2001, ending a marriage and business partnership that endured for sixty-four years. Nicky, his wife and daughter, visit New York whenever his professional commitments allow. By necessity, if not necessarily by choice, the family resides in California since much of Nicky's work is centered there. He has continued the theatrical line started by his parents and appearances on stage, television and films, attest to the scope of his career.

John Pennino

Coda:
APPRAISING THE STEVENS' CAREER:

When dealing with Risë Stevens' career, it is interesting to speculate on what might have been had she made different choices. Situations arose which forced her to make decisions that altered the course of her life. Significant among them was having the opportunity to study with Schoen-René and, subsequently, rejecting an offer to join the Metropolitan Opera right after Juilliard, a decision that opened the path to not only a greater career than she would have had, but affected her personal life as well. As a member of the Metropolitan Opera with very little experience, regardless of the merits she had, and she had many, her first years would have been devoted to supporting roles or roles that may have been beyond her means. Whether she made an independent choice or Schoen-René made the choice for her is a moot point overridden by the impact of the decision itself.

It was under the influence of Schoen-René that opera rather than Broadway became her professional goal. Her teacher's ambition to see her reach the top soon became her own. Her exceptional voice was her entrée to that career since she was gifted with an instrument that had an identifiable sound, an even range that extended from G below middle C to high C and a sensuous texture. In the early days, she did not have the personal glamour that she acquired later on, which became a vital component of her career. What she did have was an uncanny ability to communicate with her voice. Since she had appeared both on radio and in concerts from

325

an early age, in spite of an innate shyness, she learned how to use a microphone to her advantage and to charm an audience. Her musical knowledge may have been acquired in Schoen-René's studio and Juilliard but her natural talent was her own.

Going to Europe when she decided against the Metropolitan for the time being, was the second most important decision since it led to perfecting her craft in Prague and meeting Walter Surovy. In the *Neues Deutsches Theater*, she was cast immediately as Mignon, Octavian, Orfeo and Carmen, among other roles, which gave her the experience she needed to arrive at the Metropolitan a seasoned professional,

> When you became a member of an opera house in those days, you not only sang leading roles, but you had to sing everything in the repertoire. I went from Octavian to Flower Maiden and back again. You started in September and went through the end of June. You were singing night after night, I was always on stage, always rehearsing, always having something to do with music at all times. That's how you learn. By singing with the same group of people you become an ensemble where you can really build a characterization. After you've been there a few years, you and they see in what direction you're growing. Then they start concentrating and putting you in certain roles that would be advantageous for the growth of your career. [1]

Then Walter Surovy entered her life and changed its course, not immediately, but eventually his concept of what type of career she should have became hers as well.

What if she had not married Walter? She was engaged to a wealthy investment banker who saw her continuing in a career in opera which would be European based and built along traditional lines, some opera, some recitals, concerts and recordings reflecting all three. She would have reached the top but as an artist in a purely classical venue and not as the classical singer/popular entertainer that Walter encouraged.

Was his managing her career and "stretching" that career beneficial or detrimental to her in the long run? The answer is, "both". In an article published in *Opera News*, Walter is quoted as saying, "As Risë's manager, it took a five year struggle for me to win her respect. Often I'd give in because I didn't want to quarrel." [2] Risë added her own take on their partnership, "A few years ago when I dislocated my shoulder singing Carmen, he first called the *New York Times*, then the doctor. As a wife I felt insulted, but as a client I had to bow to him." [3]

On the plus side, Walter gave her the incentive to appear on many radio and television programs which she most likely would not have done on her own, and branded her name on the public's mind. Tapes of Jack Haley's radio show, for example, illustrate the funny and enduring type of comedy that cast him as pure lowbrow. He enjoyed the adulation of a faithful following and Risë's participation in his show cast her as a good sport, willing to kid herself, opera in general or Haley in particular as the script dictated. In this mode, she was Risë Stevens, popular entertainer, willing to take a symbolic pratfall but always with style. Walter rejected an offer made by Harpo Marx for Risë to appear with him in a night club show in Las Vegas. While he admired the comedic talents of the silent harp-playing Marx brother and had nothing against nightclubs, Walter did not approve of the part Risë would play in a skit with Harpo. As Harpo described it to Walter, Risë would be wearing an evening gown and while she was singing, Harpo would snip away at her dress working his way upward.

On September 24, 1950, Fred Allen, a comic of a more intellectual bent, had Risë on the premiere of his television show. Apart from roasting television, itself, and a few of its revered stars, the old radio veteran devised a skit that gave his guest a chance to partake in an alternate version of

Carmen. Jean Wax described the occasion in *Metro-Lark*,

> In character with her surroundings, she gave every evi-
> dence of enjoying the Fred Allen comic version of
> 'Carmen' in which she assumed the role of the typical
> Farmer's Daughter to Allen's Traveling Salesman. With
> Bizet's familiar music and (we presume) Allen's lyrics,
> we saw a delightful 'take-off.' In a yellow peasant dress,
> black velvet bodice, and tightly wired pigtails with yel-
> low daisies pinned to either end and in a exaggerated
> handle-bar effect, which constantly tickled Mr. Allen's
> nose when he tried to get close to her, Miss Stevens was
> a real caricature. Her farmgirl appearance was height-
> ened by an effected, nasal twang. In keeping with the
> role, the drollest part of the skit came when Carmen
> told her papa that in spite of his objections she was go-
> ing to marry the traveling salesman. Mr. Allen, how-
> ever, would have none of this, because he said that if he
> set a precedent by marrying her, it would ruin all the
> traveling salesman jokes. [4]

Milton Berle, a pioneer on early television, was the star of
one of its most successful shows, *Texaco Star Theater,* but
when he had Risë as a guest, she flatly refused to appear in
the parody of *Carmen* his writers devised. Unlike Fred Allen's
corny but harmless spoof, Berle's crossed the line of good
taste. It was not a parody but rather a trashing of the opera
which made all the difference between the two versions. Allen
was never vulgar nor were other comedy shows she appeared
on, but they were light years away from presenting a recital
in Carnegie Hall.

Films were something else she would not have attempted
without Walter. She never became a "movie star" and when
she had her own radio show in the 1940s she billed herself as
opera singer and movie actress, avoiding the "star" designa-
tion. *Going My Way* may not have put her on equal footing
with Katharine Hepburn, Bette Davis or other Hollywood
deities but it did present her as Carmen, her ticket to becom-

ing a legend in opera.

Carmen became an obsession and pursuing it was her third most important decision. There were those singers in the past, Rose Bampton for example, who avoided the role even though it was offered. Bampton recognized the pitfalls in bringing Carmen to the stage and in more recent times, Maria Callas recorded the role but never took it beyond that. Risë, after her own dissatisfaction with an early attempt in Prague, claimed Carmen as her own through a combination of will power, hard work, public relations and reinvention. During the period when Carmen was reemerging, she dyed her hair black to make herself less Nordic and more "Gypsy-like", she was Carmen in a cigarette "ad", she sang excerpts on recitals, orchestra concerts, radio, television, recordings and films. On radio appearances during the 1940s, either the "Habañera" or the "Seguidilla" was almost always regularly programmed for her. Her early renditions of the "Habañera", in particular, are particularly enticing for what could be best described as fatal playfulness. She toys with the words and imparts knowing inflections to the meaning, cajoling Don José into the web she is weaving. The microphone is her accomplice; with it she achieved an intimacy the vast reaches of an opera house would not allow. Carmen became her most performed role with the Metropolitan Opera, one hundred twenty-four repetitions over fifteen years in two productions and eleven broadcasts.

The other most important role in her career was Octavian in *Der Rosenkavalier*. Both Carmen and Octavian are borderline roles, that is, sopranos and mezzos can sing them. Risë, when turning down Leonore in *Fidelio*, never considering Marschallin in *Der Rosenkavalier*, side-stepping Tosca (or Eva in *Die Meistersinger*, her favorite, but impossible), recognized the hazards of pulling her voice out of shape to accommodate the strain on her upper register each of these roles would impose. The notes were there but not the ability to sustain them over long stretches of music. Risë was a true mezzo as

Marian Anderson pointed out to her in the early days, not a contralto as Anderson, herself, was. Schoen-René pegged her as a mezzo and never tried easing the voice into a higher range, which would have been ruinous.

Much of Risë's career was spent on the road. Recital tours with long stretches of one-night stands, punctuated by train or plane rides, hotels and restaurant eating are difficult. Living this type of life for more than twenty weeks a year, while fulfilling opera, radio and television commitments may have contributed to the changes in her voice. Rudolf Bing was in a position to notice the difference from how she sounded at Glyndebourne, three years into her career, and what he heard at the Metropolitan, a dozen years later. She still possessed a first rate instrument but for him some of the bloom had gone. She never spared herself and when doing Carmen or Octavian, Dalila or Orfeo, she threw herself into them without caution. No one could ever accuse Risë of being boring even if they found vocal or interpretive flaws.

An inevitable question arises as to how she compared with her contemporaries as far as voice was concerned. Eschewing body language, which she had in abundance, the voice taken alone could hold its own against any of her mezzo colleagues through the individuality it had by nature. In the 1940s and 50s, the period of Risë's big career, at one time or another, there were at the Metropolitan Opera, among others, Karin Branzell, Bruna Castagna, Gladys Swarthout, Kerstin Thorborg, Lily Djanel, Blanche Thebom, Cloe Elmo, Jean Madeira, Elena Nikolaidi, Fedora Barbieri, Nell Rankin, Marian Anderson and Giulietta Simionato, who were on equal footing with her in status. Of these, Branzell's and Thorborg's voices were of a more heroic bent, more suited for Wagner than Mozart or Bizet. Thorborg's Orfeo was by all accounts formidable but one can only conjecture that Risë in the 1940s would have compared favorably with her through her musicality and tonal beauty. Castagna, Elmo, Barbieri and Simionato belonged to the late lamented "Italian mezzo" species that seemingly has gone into a decline from which it may never recover. The darker hued timber, full throated delivery, volume, all characteristics of this breed, were not Risë's. Nikolaidi belonged more to this group than did Thebom or Rankin, Americans both, possessors of first rate if less refulgent voices.

Marian Anderson was past her best by the time she arrived at the Metropolitan in 1954 and was a cultural icon in a class by herself - beyond comparisons. Swarthout's career closely paralleled Risë's in the emphasis on mixing opera with more popular forms of entertainment. The Swarthout voice was darker in color, throaty, and lacked Risë's luminous quality but her persona radiated the same glamour as did her younger colleague. Her career at the Metropolitan Opera was winding down as Risë's was taking off and her success as Carmen effectively put an end to it since it was virtually the only role Swarthout still did. A history of poor health hastened her premature retirement, but had her career and Risë's been more of the same time period she of all the others would have offered the most competition.

This leaves Djanel and Madiera to be considered but Djanel like Jarmila Novotna (who shared Octavian and Cherubino with Risë) was a soprano who at times sang borderline roles. Djanel's Carmen (the role that makes one think of her as a mezzo) was much admired by Risë and Novotna's Cherubino judged by her to be better than her own.

On the other hand, Madiera was a true contralto, richly endowed with a mahogany colored low and middle register but with a top that while it retained its color did not go very far (a high "G" and "A" were beyond her range). Her Amneris, in particular, suffered from this flaw but her Carmen was another story. During Risë's involvement with the Tyrone Guthrie production, Madeira was Risë's cover from the very beginning and had the advantage over those who followed to have worked with Guthrie directly. However, while Madeira was very good in the role, she did not have that indefinable ingredient which was Risë's alone and which made her unique among her colleagues, that is, vocal allure. A story circulated that once when Risë decided to cancel a performance of Carmen after arriving at the opera house, Walter informed the management and Madeira was told to get into costume. The transformation completed, Walter took her to Risë's dressing room and when she left, Risë seeing how beautiful she looked decided to sing. By nature, Madeira was a beautiful woman and by acquired artistry, a first-rate actress but the voice did not have a unique sound, as did Risë's.

To define a voice is difficult but Edward Johnson was not wrong in hearing a "French" quality in Risë's- leaner than the Italians, less covered than the Germans and Scandinavians. It was a lyric mezzo for sure but one which could be lightened or darkened to suit a role. She had the flexibility of a true *bel canto* singer (witnessed by her 1940 recording of "Che farò"), and attention to the text that made each word meaningful in itself.

Over forty years have passed since Risë last performed in public and her reputation today rests with her recordings, several videos and off-the-air tapes. Hänsel, Carmen, Cherubino, Orfeo and Prince Orlofsky are preserved in complete commercial recordings, Dalila and Octavian only in excerpts. Tapes of live performances are available; some committed to CDs, which help to give a more rounded picture of her artistry. A complete *Der Rosekavalier* is a major loss but in her duets with Erna Berger, her silken mezzo blending seamlessly with the pure soprano of Berger, has been preserved. There are tapes of her Metropolitan Opera broadcasts of Octavian and they, too, bear out the command she had of the role. The best was issued by the Metropolitan Opera as one of its first Historic Broadcast recordings of a 1939 performance, but today is out of print. The recording recalls her legendary partnership with Lotte Lehmann and hearing those two voices together illustrates how much Risë learned from Lehmann. Phrasing, in particular, gives the impression that they are reacting to one another in a very real way – that the lines are spontaneous not preordained.

As Dalila, the dusky quality of her voice vibrates sensuously against the *macho* Samson of Mario del Monaco in the second RCA Victor recording. Their voices compliment each other, hers languorous in the moments of seduction, furious in frustrated anger at his resistance, his, aggressive at first and pleading in helpless blindness before a cry of triumph at the end. A complete recording of her Dalila taped live in New Orleans in 1960, in what was to be her last appearance in the role, shows her in full command of her vocal and interpretative resources, more so than her partner, Ramón Vinay, who regrettably has lost it by then.

There are three versions of Risë's Orlofsky to listen to, one complete in German and two highlight discs in English. It is ironic that the role she liked the least was preserved the most, if only the main aria in the highlight albums. All three are done to a turn and only lack the visual dimension of what must have been a unique portrayal.

Of the complete recordings, Hansel is a welcome reminder of the light-hearted way she approached juvenile roles. There is laughter in the voice and would have been there for Cherubino as well had it been recorded sooner. The "laughter" is too mature, the voice unable to wrap around the scherzo quality of "Non so piu" with as much ease as before.

Orfeo is an example of dedication overriding realization. Had she recorded it ten years earlier, it would have eclipsed all her recordings. By the mid Fifties, the flowing line so necessary in this opera is not always hers to command. It is more jagged than ideal. She wills the role to life because it is her love for it that supports it where her voice cannot. As such, it is a flawed jewel, but a jewel none-the-less.

Carmen is, therefore, the recording that best exemplifies what Stevens was all about. Made just prior to her success at the Met in the same role, she has Fritz Reiner who conducts a reading of the score that literally throbs with excitement. He carries the cast along with him in a performance that has both authority and passion. It is not a perfect recording, however. Jan Peerce is an outstanding artist and equally outstanding musician but not ideally cast as Don José, a role he never did outside of the studio. His characterization is sound but vocally he operates too much at one level. As with the excerpts of *Samson et Dalila* he recorded with Risë, he lacks the vocal colors needed for French opera. He is too stentorian, but it is a solid piece of work. There is something about the role of Don José that drives tenors a little bit mad in the last act. Peerce remains in control, killing Carmen because the libretto says he must. Licia Albanese as Micaela is her usual impassioned Italianite self and imparts to her one big aria in the third act great feeling. Robert Merrill as Escamillo, like Peerce, emphasizes voice over characterization.

Risë leaves little to be desired. True, the results might have been even better had she recorded *Carmen* one year after the Guthrie version altered her views on the role, but it is a superb rendering of the score as is. She and Reiner operate as one in spite of rumored disagreements in tempi. The required seductiveness is there in her vocal colors, the arch inflections, the playing with lines all come together to create a Carmen that is uniquely her own. Remarkably, it is not overdrawn. She eschews any attempt to grandstand by making her performance a star turn. It fits neatly into the whole and gives her colleagues a fighting chance.

The highlight album of *Carmen*, recorded five years earlier for Columbia, is not eclipsed by the RCA complete recording. Raoul Jobin, Nadine Conner and Robert Weede are arguably better suited to their roles than their RCA counterparts and Risë's interpretation reveals the differences from her later version. The "Habañera" in the earlier recording is a case in point. It is the way she sang it on numerous broadcasts and in complete stagings, like a *chanson* rather than an aria. It is more insinuating than outright seductive; more come closer than stay away. The voice is fresher without the richness acquired later and, therefore, presents a notably youth-ful Carmen. This Carmen would be no match on a one to one basis with the hard-boiled whorish Carmen that was to come. Both are valid interpretations, however, and document Risë's development in a role.

An off the air tape of the January 12, 1957 Metropolitan Opera broadcast of *Carmen*, preserves to even better advan-tage than the commercial recording, a performance of the opera that lacked nothing. No one would classify Mario del Monaco as a French tenor but the macho sound of the voice, the intensity with which he approached everything he sang made his Don José the perfect foil for Risë. The chemistry between this Carmen and Don José is felt without being seen. Del Monaco is at his most exciting overindulgent and Risë, excellent singing actress that she is, plays off his passionate outbursts and manic ravings. Five years into the Guthrie ver-sion by the time of this broadcast, she had honed the charac-terization to razor sharp incisiveness. Dimitri Mitropoulos is the conductor and he is a propulsive interpreter of the score, which he realizes in flashes of color. Although Frank Guarrera lacks the vocal opulence of Robert Merrill, his Escamillo has the requisite flair even on the blind medium of a recording. The Micaela, Lucine Amara, does not have the dramatic in-stincts of Licia Albanese, but her voiced is girlishly pure, vir-ginal and, therefore, more in keeping with the character.

As with every performer, there is always a wish list of roles or music that they never attempted. With Risë, it is regret-table that she did not record more *lieder*. While her way with Cole Porter is treasurable, Mahler's *Das Lied von der Erde* or *Kindertotenlieder*, for example, would have shown her in a totally different light. Arias from oratorios, her specialty in her early days, should also have been committed to disc and much more welcome than songs set to familiar symphonies.

On stage, it is unfortunate that Eboli, Adalgisa, Leonora in *La Favorita*, Cenerentola, Isabella, Charlotte, Alceste, Regina and even the Grand Duchesse were missing from her active repertory. One would have traded some performances of the roles she did for any one or all of these. Recordings of selections from them would have been a welcome reminder of what was lost by her not having the opportunity to perform the roles in their entirety (as illustrated with her first-rate renditions of "O Mio Fernando" and "Divinites du Styx"). Her repertory became limited to a handful of operatic roles and a group of songs that were augmented on rare occasion by excursions into the less familiar.

Singing with Liberace on the Ed Sullivan Show, dancing with Ray Bolger or clowning around with Eve Arden on radio made her a recognizable entertainer, but Risë never wanted the term "entertainer" after her name. She was by her own design an opera singer who strayed from the classics once in a while, but was she in fact only that? Walter and she differed over the use of the "entertainer" term, she denied it, he supported it. In many ways, she grew up professionally at a time when opera singers wanted to be accepted by the general public and with Walter's encouragement she succeeded. The biggest names in opera, Lily Pons, Grace Moore, Lawrence Tibbett and Gladys Swarthout, were all, in today's terminology, "cross-over artists".

Risë followed their lead and in doing so became a popular entertainer. She admired Connie Boswell's way with a song and learned, either consciously or unconsciously, from listening to her on the radio, how to find the heart of a song. Boswell's recordings illustrate her way with coloring a word, emphasizing a phrase, playing with a note much the same way Risë did with a popular song. While Jane Froman, another popular singer of the Thirties and beyond, did not influence Risë as much as Boswell, she had a voice that was more of a classical bent. A mezzo range, a smoky coloring echoes Risë's voice and it is not surprising that with a bit of calculated imitation Risë could pass herself off as Froman as she did once.

An example of what Risë could do in a recording studio

to achieve the effect of a popular singer is found in her RCA recording of excerpts from Jerome Kern's, *Show Boat*. Portraying Julie La Verne, the downtrodden *seconda donna* created by Helen Morgan when the operetta premiered in 1927, she sings "Bill", "Can't help lovin' dat man of mine" and "Dance away the night." Throwing caution to the wind as well as her operatic voice, she employs tones drained of resonance. Similar to her early broadcast arias from *Carmen*, she again uses the microphone as if it were an ear into which she whispered her innermost feelings. The listener is drawn in and taken on an emotional ride with her. It is a night club voice for sure and oh so right for the material at hand. It was to be used again in "My ship" when she recorded *Lady in the Dark*.

Helen Morgan took an entirely different approach to the same numbers. Using her pure soprano, she sang in the manner that was expected thirty years earlier when she went before the microphone to record the excerpts. Her more operatic voice takes one by surprise. To the uninitiated, the name, Helen Morgan, conjures up a *chanteuse* along the lines of Marlene Dietrich at her most baritonal. That is not the case. Risë could have recorded the selections using more resonance and it would have worked but on a different level. Hers is the way one expected Morgan to do them but didn't. It is a fresh interpretation and one that added another dimension to her interpretive palette. She always maintained that her voice changed with the material, as did the colors in creating a mood. "Bill" and "Can't help lovin' dat man of mine" are perfect examples of her many voices. Soprano, Mary Garden, always described herself as not having one voice but a voice for each character she portrayed. All great singing actors have that ability. It is a remarkable achievement to create a character in only a few songs, but Risë does that. She was a chameleon as Astrid Varnay points out in the Introduction and that quality extended to her non-operatic side as well. What she could have done with the role on stage is anyone's guess but based on the recording, it would have been as far away from opera as she dared to go.

She could have forsaken opera all together with Walter's blessing but both knew that it was all-important to her. He firmly believed that she had the makings of a film star but it is doubtful that he would have been right. Of the three roles she played in the movies, Maria Lanyi, Jenny Linden and Risë Stevens, the last is her most successful. In *Carnegie Hall*, she is seen at her best because she is herself at her most natural. Although the dark hair she had at the time was adopted as a concession to her Carmen period, it is becoming, as is the Carmen-like gown of black net and large roses. She is not required to act but she does, subtly, her shoulders and arms moving to the rhythm of Carmen's, "Seguidilla", while the orchestra plays behind her. It is Risë as she was on the concert stage, beautiful, committed, communicative.

Her look for the first of her films is generic Hollywood. This is not to imply that she does not look good, she does, but it is not Risë. The wig changes her appearance to make her fit the mold of what a Hollywood star looked like at that time. Comments were made that she resembled Jeanette McDonald. There may have been a conscious effort on the part of M.G.M. to have her appear so in order to make the break between Eddy and McDonald less painful for their fans. Maria Lanyi, the operetta star she portrays in the film, comes to life in her spirited and insightful reading of the script. She is best in the scenes that take place off-stage. Both her acting and singing are much more at ease than when she is in the operetta portions of the film. The main problem is that she is not used to looking at a camera and the narrowing of her eyes betray her. Her speaking voice comes across well, mellow with a musical lilt to it. She colors her words as if they were musical notes. She acts well, she sings well in these scenes but she looks uncomfortable in close-up as though she is trying to do what the director has told her but can't.

By the time she filmed *Carnegie Hall*, she had overcome

this awkwardness and was well on the way to doing so in *Going My Way*. As Jenny Linden, a role modeled somewhat on her own persona, she portrays an opera singer who is down to earth and willing to help a friend in need. Her look is more her, although the blond hair is an affectation, but attractive. She is more of the "girl next door" type unlike the lacquered Maria Lanyi. She gives a sincere reading of her lines and appears quite at home with the situation but she is more of a straight actress in this than she is in *The Chocolate Soldier*. That is, apart from the singing, it is a role that could have been portrayed by any number of Paramount's contract players.

M.G.M. needed a singer first and an actress second to appear opposite the non-actor Eddy. *The Chocolate Soldier* is a musical with a story tacked on. With Crosby and especially Barry Fitzgerald, excellent actors both, and a story that comes first, the opposite is true. It is why Risë's success with her role is more significant. She has enough to sing but she is equally effective in her non-singing scenes with Crosby.

For Risë, the film experience may not have been for her, but it trained her to be at ease before a camera, which proved invaluable when television came along. She was lucky to have been cast in *Going My Way* regardless of its merits or defects since it still has an audience. But then again, she always said she was lucky.

Luck was on her side with Carmen in the Tyrone Guthrie version. It allowed her to remain in Bing's good graces and to continue her career at the Metropolitan until she chose to leave. Without that success, it is doubtful that she would have remained for very long under his aegis. After Prague, hers was not a career built on the European stages and without the Metropolitan her operatic career might very well have languished soon after Bing's arrival. He gave her a production of *Carmen* that stood by her for ten years but he did not suggest many new roles after that. In part Walter's stand that she be cast only in operas that had her character's name in the title (translated to mean the staring role) imposed its own limitations. Bing could not deny her box office appeal, her popularity on the tour and her way with the roles she did sing. During the time she was at the Metropolitan, she virtually owned Octavian and Dalila from the beginning and, eventually Orfeo, but it was Carmen everyone wanted, including Bing who could hear the cash register ringing every time she sang it.

If reports about her in the early days are to be believed, Walter gave her the glamorous appearance that became her personal trademark. One radio executive described her at the time of her back-up singing on shows as not being very stylishly dressed. Of course, she did not have the means and, perhaps, the interest to be overly attentive to such things at that time. Later, when she was under Walter's influence and she was able to afford the best designers, her style emerged- a reflection of how Walter wanted her to look. At times, he chose her outfits without consulting her and more often than not his taste was unerring. The bouffant evening gowns for the stage, the requisite "star" day ensembles, placed her on the best-dressed list. The public relations articles printed at his suggestion, got her talked about and kept her name in the public's mind.

The nature of the times forced her to forge a career in America since the War prevented continuing European and South American appearances. After the War she had too big a career in radio and touring at home to consider picking up the foreign operatic thread to any great extent. Plainly stated, it would not have been cost effective as was proven when she accepted the La Scala engagement at a personal financial sacrifice. Much of the career had to be governed by financial considerations as opposed to idealism. She did not give recitals in New York, as did almost every major artist of the time, because according to Walter her repertory was limited and he did not want her overexposed. Her performances in opera, confined almost exclusively to the Metropolitan, were limited in number also, again because of the paucity of roles. However, it was to their financial gain to keep the career on the road where fees were higher than in opera and the constant change of locale permitted and even encouraged repetition of familiar material.

In this, both she and Walter were realistic as to what she could do in the classical field. Hers was not a voice that was suited to heavy Verdi or Wagner roles. She attempted Wagner with some success but without personal enthusiasm and Verdi's Amneris was put on hold after one outing. Walter wanted her cast in star roles and for lyric as opposed to dramatic mezzos, once past Carmen, Orfeo, Octavian, Dalila, Mignon and a handful of others, (all of which she did) the selection is thin. Risë would have succeeded as Eboli in *Don Carlo*, Leonora in *La Favorita*, Charlotte in *Werther*, Isabella in *L'Italiana in Algeri* and *La Cenerentola*, but they were not presented at the Metropolitan in the forties and, therefore, eluded her. When *Don Carlo* was done in the fifties, Bing looked elsewhere.

Whether appearing in recital in New York would have appreciably contributed to her standing is debatable. In theory, she should have attempted it even once every decade to reinforce the classic side of her career but doing so would have meant exposing her to the New York critics and the inevitable comparisons with other recitalists. She was eminently suited for radio since her voice took to the medium and on television, her personality, looks and style, made her a viewer's delight. The same was true of films but she did not have a commitment to the medium. In a sense, Risë's career was Walter's as well, but it was she who received the acclaim no matter how much he contributed to it. On the stage, it was she who was the star and at home, her professional needs had always to be considered. Risë was no Trilby, however, and Walter owed her as much as she did him. But he has to be given a great deal of credit for the part he played behind the scenes. For both of them, his "stretching" worked. Without it, she would have had a very respectable career, but with it, Risë's fame surpassed even her mother's dreams.

Footnotes

Part I Chapter 1

1. *Providence Sunday Journal*, Margaret McManus, 23 December 1962.
2. *Collier's*, Mona Gardner, 14 March 1942.
3. Radiogram and Guide, April 1927.
4. Scrapbook, unidentified article, Risë Stevens Collection, Boston University Special Collections.
5. Scrapbook, unidentified article, Risë Stevens Collection, Boston University Special Collections.
6. Scrapbook, unidentified article, Risë Stevens Collection, Boston University Special Collections.
7. Metropolitan Opera Archives
8. Scrapbook, unidentified article, Risë Stevens Collection, Boston University Special Collections.
9. Scrapbook, unidentified article, Risë Stevens Collection, Boston University Special Collections.
10. Scrapbook, unidentified article, Risë Stevens Collection, Boston University Special Collections.
11. Scrapbook, unidentified article, Risë Stevens Collection, Boston University Special Collections.
12. Scrapbook, unidentified article, Risë Stevens Collection, Boston University Special Collections.
13. *New York Times,* 6 December 1927.
14. *New York Times,* 30 September 1930.
15. Frederica von Stade letter to author, undated, c. 1996.
16. *Musical America,* 14 December 1931.

Part I Chapter 2

1. America's Musical Inheritance: Memories and Reminiscences, Anna Schoen-René, Putnam, 1941. 10
2. Ibid. 15
3. Ibid. 43
4. Ibid. 226
5. Juilliard Archives.
6. Juilliard Archives.
7. Juilliard Archives.
8. New York Times, 1 December 1932.
9. New York Herald Tribune, Francis D. Perkins, 9 February 1932.
10. New York Times, 8 May 1932.
11. New York Times, 5 April 1932.

12. Subway to the Met, Doubleday & Co., 1959, 41-42
13. Ibid.
14. *Great Singers on Singing,* Jerome Hines, Limelight Editions, New York, 1984. 318
15. *Opera News,* "Miss Margaret's Way," James van Sant, 21 March 1996.
16. *Great Singers on Singing.* 321-322
17. *Great Singers on Singing.* 321
18. *America's Musical Inheritance: Memories and Reminiscences.* 206
19. Ibid.
20. Margaret Harshaw interview by author, 5 November 1996.
21. *Opera News,* "Miss Margaret's Way.
22. Margaret Harshaw interview
23. Juilliard Archives.
24. Ibid.
25. Ibid.
26. Ibid.
27. *Worcester Telegram & Gazette*, 3 October 1934.
28. Scrapbook, unidentified article, Risë Stevens Collection, Boston University Special Collections.
29. Annamary Dickey letter to author, 4 March 1996.
30. Juilliard Archives.
31. *New York Sun,* W. J. Henderson, 8 December 1934.
32. Ibid.
33. *Brooklyn Eagle*, Winthrop Sargent, 8 December 1934. Courtesy of the Brooklyn Public Library, Brooklyn Collection.
34. *Musical America,* A. Walter Kramer, 10 December 1934.
35. *New York World Telegram,* Pitts Sanborn, 6 December 1934.
36. *New York Herald-Tribune*, Francis D. Perkins, 31 January 1935.
37. *Brooklyn Times Union,* Harold Strickland, 31 January 1935.
38. *Musical America,* R. F. E., 10 February 1935.
39. *New York Herald-Tribune,* Lawrence Gilman, 3 February 1935.
40. *Denver Post,* 16 March 1935.
41. *New York Times,* Howard Taubman, 9 April 1935.
42. Ibid.
43. *New York Sun,* W. J. Henderson, 9 April 1935.

Part I, Chapter 3

1. Metropolitan Opera Archives
2. Metropolitan Opera Archives
3. *Subway to the Met.* 52
4. *San Francisco Opera Magazine,* "Our First Octavian", Arthur Kaplan, May, 1978.
5. *Musical America*, August 1935.

6. *Subway to the Met.* 53
7. *The Story of the Metropolitan Opera*, Irving Kolodin, Knopf, 1966. 385.
8. Scrapbook, unidentified article, Lindon Martin Collection, New York Public Library.
9. Rose Bampton interview by author, 31 July 1996.
10. Natalia Bodanya interview by author, 12 June 1996
11. Juilliard Archives, A. Schoen-René to Dean Hutcheson, 15 March 1936.
12. *New York Daily News*, Danton Walker, 23 April 1936.
13. Metropolitan Opera Archives
14. *New York Times*, Olin Downes, 23 May 1936.
15. *New York Daily News*, Danton Walker, 23 May 1936.
16. *San Francisco Opera Magazine*, op. cit.
17. *Musical America*, March 1938.

Part 1, Chapter 4

1. *Musical America*, Paul Stefan, August 1936.
2. Ibid.
3. Carmen Mayer letter to author, 1 November 1996.
4. Carmen Mayer letter to author, 28 November 1996.
5. *New York Daily Mirror,* "Only human", Sydney Field, 25 November 1955.
6. *Opera News*, "Risë", Martin Mayer, 24 December 1988
7. *Musical America*, James Lyons, 15 February 1955.
8. *Subway to the Met*, 58
9. *Opera News*, 29 November 1948.
10. Carmen Mayer, letter to Risë Stevens, undated.
11. *Prager Tagblatt*, 14 December 1936.
12. *Musical America*, Gerth-Wolfgang Baruch 3 June 1937.
13. *Prager Tagblatt*, 11 January 1937.
14. *Musical America*, 25 February 1937

Part 1, Chapter 5

1. *Egyptian Gazette,* 1 February 1937.
2. Ibid.
3. Ibid.
4. *Egyptian Gazette*, 2 February 1937
5. *Egyptian Gazette,* 11 February 1937.
6. Ibid.
7. Ibid.
8. Ibid.
9. *Prager Tagblatt*, 7 May 1937.
10. *Prager Tagblatt*, 8 May 1937.
11. *New York Times*, 13 June 1937.
12. Metropolitan Opera Archives.

13. Carmen Mayer letter to author, 1 November 1996.
14. *Opera News*, "Risë Stevens Discusses Carmen", 2 February 1948.
15. *Prager Tagblatt,* std, 8 September 1937.
16. *Prager Tagblatt*, std, 14 September 1937.
17. *Prager Tagblatt,* mb, 21 September 1937.
18. Metropolitan Opera Archives.
19. Metropolitan Opera Archives.
20. Metropolitan Opera Archives.
21. *Prager Tagblatt,* 31 December 1937.
22. *Musical America*, H.H.Stuckenschmidt, 10 February 1938.
23. *Opera News,* Robert Lawrence, 16 December 1937.
24. *Prager Tagblatt*, std, 11 January 1938.
25. *Musical America*, H.H.Stuckenschmidt, 10 January 1938.
26. Carmen Mayer letter to author, 1 November 1996.
27. *Prager Tagblatt,* H.H.Stuckenschmidt, 16 December 1937.
28. *Prager Tagblatt*, mb, 6 March 1938.
29. *Musical America*, 16 May 1938.
30. *Prager Tagblatt*, 5 September 1936.
31. *Prager Tagblatt*, mb, 26 September 1936.
32. *New York Daily Mirror*, 20 March 1938.
33. *New York Times,* Herbert F. Peyser, 3 April 1938.
34. *Musical America,* H.H.Stuckenschmidt, September 1938.
35. *Prager Tagblatt,* 28 September 1938.

Part 2   Chapter 1

1. *Providence Sunday Journal,* Margaret McManus, 23 December 1962.
2. *La Prensa,* South American edition, 3 September 1938.
3. *New York Times,* Olin Downes, 9 October 1938.
4. *Opera News,* 28 November 1938.
5. Ibid.
6. *Philadelphia Evening Bulletin,* 23 November 1938.
7. *New York Times,* 23 November 1938.
8. *Philadelphia Record,* 23 November 1938.
9. *Philadelphia Evening Bulletin,* Henry E. Pleasants, 23 November 1938.
10. *Philadelphia Evening Public Ledger,* Samuel L. Lacier, 23 November 1938.
11. Natalia Bodanya interview
12. Lucielle Browning interview by author, 11 June 1996
13. *Music Lovers Magazine,* vol. 1, no. 4, undated.
14. *New York Times,* Olin Downes, 18 December 1938.
15. *New York Herald-Tribune,* Francis D. Perkins, 18 December 1938.
16. Ibid.
17. Metropolitan Opera Archives.
18. Metropolitan Opera Archives.

19. *Staats Zeitung,* 20 December 1938.

Part 2 Chapter 2
1. Unidentified source, John Selby, 18 December 1938.
2. *New York Word-Telegram,* Louis Biancoli, 26 January 1939.
3. *New York Sun,* Irving Kolodin, 26 January 1939.
4. *New York Herald-Tribune,* Lawrence Gilman, 10 February 1939.
5. *New York Sun,* Oscar Thompson, 10 February 1939.
6. Ibid.
7. *New York Herald-Tribune,* Lawrence Gilman, 17 February 1939.
8. *New York Sun,* Oscar Thompson, 17 February 1939.
9. *New York World-Telegram,* Pitts Sanborn, 17 February 1939.
10. *New Yorker,* Robert A. Simon. (Reprinted by permission; @ 1939. *The New Yorker Magazine, Inc., All rights reserved.*

Part 2 Chapter 3
1. Juilliard School of Music Archives.
2. Juilliard School of Music Archives.
3. *Daily Telegraph,* Richard Capell, 2 June 1939.
4. *Daily Mail,* Edwin Evans, 2 June 1939.
5. Ibid.
6. Ibid.
7. *Evening News,* W. McN., 2 June 1939.
8. *Glasgow Herald,* 3 June 1939.
9. *Southern Weekday News*, 3 June 1939.
10. *Sketch,* 28 June 1939.
11. *Daily Telegraph,* Richard Capell, 21 June 1939.
12. *La Prensa,* 23 September 1939.
13. *La Prensa,* 4 October 1939.
14. *Youngstown Vindicator,* L.R.Boals, 14 November 1939. [Reprinted in the Monday Musical Club, Inc., *Newsletter*, October 1981]
15. *New York Post,* Samuel Chotzinoff, 7 December 1939.
16. *New York Herald-Tribune,* Francis D. Perkins, 21 February 1940.
17. *New York Journal American,* Grena Bennett, 21 February 1940.
18. *Evening American,* Leo Gaffney, 29 March 1940.
19. *Boston Evening Transcript,* Edward Downes, 29 March 1940.
20. Ibid.

Part 2 Chapter 4
1. *Arkansas Democrat*, 26 January 1942.
2. *Daily Sun*, Charlton Gunther, 3 March 1940.
3. *Opera News*, 7 October 1940.

4. *La Prensa,* South American edition, 24 July 1940.
5. *Argentinisches Tagblatt,* 24 July 1940.
6. Metropolitan Opera Archives.
7. Metropolitan Opera Archives
8. *San Francisco Chronicle*, 8 October 1940.
9. *San Francisco Chronicle*, Alfred Frankenstein, 13 October 1940.
10. Ibid, 18 October 1940.
11. Metropolitan Opera Archives
12. Metropolitan Opera Archives
13. Metropolitan Opera Archives

Part 2 Chapter 5

1. *New York Post,* Irene Thirer, 10 February 1941.
2. *New York World-Telegram*, 12 February 1940.
3. *New York Post,* Henry Beckett, 5 December 1940.
4. *New York World-Telegram,* Pitts Sanborne, 7 December 1940.
5. *New York Herald-Tribune,* Francis D. Perkins, 12 July 1940.
6. *New York Post,* 9 February 1941.
7. *Morning Telegraph*, 4 February 1941.
8. Ibid.
9. Ibid.
10. *New York Herald-Tribune,* Jerome D. Bohm, 8 December 1940.
11. *Washington Daily News,* Helen Buchalter, 20 January 1941.
12. *Washington Post,* Norman B. Bell, 20 January 1941.
13. *New York Herald-Tribune,* Jerome D. Bohm, 12 April 1941.
14. *The Record,* John O'Connor, 30 July 1942.
15. *Baltimore News Post,* Helen A. Penniman, 25 March 1941.
16. *Boston Traveler,* Rudolf F. Elie, 28 March 1941.
17. *Boston Daily Globe,* Marjory Adams, 27 March 1941.
18. Ibid.

Part 2 Chapter 6

1. *Los Angeles Examiner,* Louella O. Parsons, undated.
2. *An Empire of their Own,* Neal Gabler, Crown Publisher, 1988, 214.
3. Ibid., 217.
4. *Metro-Lark,* May 1941.
5. Metropolitan Opera Archives.
6. *New York Daily News,* Kate Cameron, 1 November 1941.
7. *New York Post,* Archer Winston, 1 November 1941.
8. *National Enquirer,* Marcus Griffen, 3 November 1941.
9. Metropolitan Opera Archives.
10. *Los Angeles Daily News,* Bruno David Usher, 7 November 1941.
11. Metropolitan Opera Archives

12. *New York Daily Sun*, 18 November 1941.
13. Ibid.
14. Ibid.
15. *Los Angeles Examiner,* Louella O. Parsons, 2 July 1942.
16. *Star-Ledger,* 27 April 1941 @ 1942, the *Star-Ledger.* All rights reserved. Reprinted with permission.
17. *Dallas Morning News,* 12 May 1942.
18. *Metro-Lark,* Anniversary Issue, 1942.
19. Ibid.
20. Metropolitan Opera Archives.
21. *Metro-Lark,* Concert Edition, 1942.
22. Ibid.
23. Metropolitan Opera Archives.

Part 2 Chapter 7

1. *Cincinnati Post*, 14 June 1943.
2. Metropolitan Opera Archives
3. *New York Sun,* Eileen Creelman, 3 May 1944.
4. *New York Daily News,* Kate Cameron, 3 May 1944.
5. Metropolitan Opera Archives.
6. *Hollywood Reporter,* 11 October 1944.
7. *Metro-Lark,* April, May June 1944.

Part 2 Chapter 8

1. Metropolitan Opera Archives.
2. *Metro-Lark*, Fall, 1944.
3. Metropolitan Opera Archives.
4. *San Francisco News,* Marjorie M. Fisher, 28 October 1944.
5. Metropolitan Opera Archives.
6. *New York Post,* Harriett Johnson, 24 February 1945.
7. Metropolitan Opera Archives.
8. *New York Daily News,* 3 July 1945.
9. *Metro-Lark,* Marc Botts, August-October 1945.
10. *Musical America,* Marjorie M. Fisher, October 1945.
11. *San Francisco,* Alfred *Frankenstein*, 4 October 1945.
12. *Metro-Lark,* November 1945 to January 1946.
13. *New York Herald-Tribune,* Virgil Thomson, 22 December 1945.
14. Ibid.

Part 2 Chapter 9

1. Metropolitan Opera Archives
2. *Metro-Lark,* February-April 1946.

3. *Opera News,* 17 February 1947.

4. Ibid., 28 February 1949.

5. Ibid., 30 January 1950.

6. Ibid.

7. Ibid.

8. *New York Herald-Tribune,* Jerome D. Bohm, 29 December 1945.

9. *Musical Digest,* December 1945-January 1946.

10. *PM,* "Hague on Discs", 26 May 1946.

11. *Metro-Lark,* 2 July 1946.

12. *Variety,* 10 July 1947.

13. *Opera News,* 18 November 1946.

14. *Metro Lark,* November 1946-January 1947.

Part 2   Chapter 10

1. *Metro-Lark,* November 1946-January 1947.

2. Nadine Conner letter to author, 25 January 1997.

3. *New York Daily News,* John Chapman, 28 December 1946.

4. *New York Sun,* Irving Kolodin, 28 November 1946.

5. *New York Herald-Tribune,* Sunday edition, B. H. Haggin, 22 December 1946.

6. *Variety,* 19 February 1947.

7. *New York World-Telegram,* 19 February 1947.

8. *Boston Traveller,* Doris Sperber, 21 March 1947.

9. Ibid., 23 March 1947.

10. Metropolitan Opera Archives

11. Ibid.

12. *The Metropolitan Opera on Record*, Frederick P. Fellers, comp., Greenwood Press, 1984.

13. *New York Herald-Tribune,* Howard Taubman, 19 October 1947.

14. *Metro-Lark,* Summer edition, 1947.

15. *Billboard*, review, reprinted in *Metro-Lark,* Holiday edition, 1947.

16. Brooks Smith interview, 23 August 1996.

17. *Metro-Lark,* Holiday edition, 1947.

18. *Variety,* 17 September 1947.

19. *PM,* 19 December 1947.

Part 2   Chapter 11

1. *Boston Globe,* Cyrus Durgin, 16 March 1948.

2. Ibid.

3. *Hollywood, California, Citizen News,* 14 April 1948.

4. *Metro-Lark,* Seventh Anniversary edition, 1948.

5. *Denver Post,* 28 April 1948.

6. *Minneapolis, Minnesota Star,* Cedric Adams, 6 May 1948.

7. *Washington Post,* Paul Hume, 19 May 1948.
8. *Variety,* 25 May 1948.
9. *Cincinnati Times Star,* Louis John Johnson, 28 June 1948.
10. *Cincinnati Enquirer,* 3 July 1948.
11. *Cincinnati Post,* Eleanor Bell, 3 July 1948.
12. Ibid.
13. *Metro-Lark,* Summer edition, 1948.

Part 2   Chapter 12
1. *Dallas Times Herald,* James Powers, 15 August 1948.
2. *New York Herald-Tribune,* Francis D. Perkins, 15 December 1948.
3. Frank Guarrera interview by author, 29 May 1996.
4. *Metro-Lark,* Eighth Anniversary edition, 1949.
5. Ibid, Summer edition, 1949.
6. Ibid.
7. *Cleveland Press,* Arthur Loesser, 6 April 1949.
8. *Rome, Georgia, News Tribune*, 21 April 1949.
9. New York Public Library, Special Collections.
10. *Metro-Lark,* Summer edition, 1949.
11. *Le Figaro,* Clarendon, 1 June 1949.
12. *L'Epoque,* Maurice Ballant, 1 June 1949.
13. *Dernière Heure Musicale,* R, B. _1949.
14. *Metro-Lark,* Holiday edition, 1949.
15. *New York Journal American,* 22 November 1949.
16. *500 Hundred Nights at the Opera,* Rudolf Bing, Doubleday & Co., 1972. 133
17. *New York Herald-Tribune,* Virgil Thomson, 22 November 1949.
18. *My Golden Age of Singing,* Frieda Hempel, Amadeus Press, 1998, 123
19. *New York Herald-Tribune,* Francis D. Perkins, 27 November 1949.

Part 2   Chapter 13
1. *New York Daily News,* John Chapman, 17 February 1950.
2. Dino Yannapoulos interview by author, 30 October 1996.
3. *Life,* 20 February 1950.
4. *Metro-Lark,* Summer edition, 1950.

Part 2   Chapter 14
1. Metropolitan Opera Archives.
2. Metropolitan Opera Archives
3. Metropolitan Opera Archives
4. Metropolitan Opera Archives
5. Metropolitan Opera Archives

6. Metropolitan Opera Archives
7. Metropolitan Opera Archives
8. Metropolitan Opera Archives
9. Loren Hightower interview by author, 19, 21 August 1997.
10. Patrice Munsel interview by author, 13 June 1995
11. *New York Herald-Tribune,* Virgil Thomson, 21 December 1950.
12. Ibid.
13. *New York Post,* Harriett Johnson, 21 December 1950.
14. *Musical America,* Cecil Smith, 15 January 1951
15. Liza Gard permission statement.
16. *Variety,* Arthur Bronson, 28 February 1951.
17. Ibid.
18. Ibid.
19. *Wall Street Journal,* V. R., 9 January 1951.
20. Ibid.
21. *New York Daily News,* John Chapman, 13 January 1951.
22. *Jussi,* Anna-Lisa Björling and Andrew Farkas, Amadeus Press, 1996, 207-222.
23. Alan Kayes letter to author, 2 December 1998.
24. Robert Merrill interview, 5 September 1997.
25. *Opera,* H.D.R., May 1954.

Part 2   Chapter 15

1. *New York Herald-Tribune,* Robert Lawrence, 19 April 1942.
2. *500 Nights at the Opera.* 170
3. Metropolitan Opera Archives.
4. *New York Times,* Herbert F. Peyser, 23 December 1937.
5. Herta Glaz interview conducted by Jack Rokahr for the author, 4 April 1998.
6. *A Life in the Theatre,* Tyrone Guthrie, McGraw-Hill Book Co., 1959. 259
7. Ibid. 250-251
8. *Opera News,* 2 November 1952.
9. Ibid.
10. Ibid.
11. *New York Daily News,* Douglas Watt, 15 January 1952.
12. Frank Guarrera interview
13. Loren Hightower interview.
14. Walter Taussig interview by author, 26 November 1996.
15. Loren Hightower interview
16. *A Life in the Theatre.* 253
17. *New York World-Telegram and Sun,* William Hawkins, 30 January 1952.
18. Metropolitan Opera Archives.
19. *New York Herald-Tribune,* Virgil Thomson, 1 February 1952.
20. *New York Journal-American,* Miles Kastendieck, 1 February 1952.

21. Fritz Reiner correspondence, Northwestern University.
22. *Philadelphia Bulletin,* Max de Schauensee, 13 February 1952.
23. *New York World-Telegram and Sun,* 20 February 1952.
24. *La Mia Vita & I Miei Successi,* Mario del Monaco, Rusconi, 1982. 74

Part 2   Chapter 16

1. *Metro-Lark,* Summer edition, 1952.
2. Ibid., Jean Wax.
3. Frank Guarrera interview.
4. *New York Daily News,* John Chapman, 12 December 1952.
5. *Billboard,* Bob Francis, 3 January 1953.
6. *Atlanta Constitution,* Jean Rooney, 9 January 1953.
7. *Opera News,* Mary Jane Matz, 26 January 1953.
8. *New York Daily News,* Douglas Watt, 21 January 1953.
9. Loren Hightower interview.
10. Dino Yannapolis interview.
11. *New York Post,* Harriett Johnson, 23 January 1953.
12. Astrid Varnay interview by Donald Arthur for the author, 30 April 1998.
13. Dino Yannapoulos interview.
14. Zachary Solov interview by author, 18 June 1996
15. *New York Post,* Harriett Johnson, 3 April 1953.
16. James Shomate interview by author, 8 July !1996.
17. *New York Herald-Tribune,* 17 December 1953.

Part 2   Chapter 17

1. *La Patria,* Giulio Confalonieri, 26 March 1954.
2. Ibid.
3. Angelo Mercuriali letter to author, 31 July 1996.
4. *New York Herald-Tribune,* John Molleson, 3 April 1996.
5. Ibid., T.M.S. 4 April 1954.
6. *International News Service,* Paul R. Allerup, 24 February 1955.

Part 2   Chapter 18

1. Sena Jurinac letter to author, 18 March 1996.
2. Dino Yannopoulos interview.
3. *Ta Nea* reprinted in *Metro-Lark,* translation by Florence Savas, Fall 1955.
4. Vilma Georgiou interview, 18 November 1996.
5. *Musical Courier,* Dr. Henry W. Levinger, 1 December 1955.
6. *New York Herald-Tribune,* R.B. 28 December 1955.
7. Otto Edelmann letter to author, 6 November 1996
8. *New York World-Telegram and Sun,* Louis Biancolli, 28 December 1956.
9. Nathaniel Merrill interview by author, 16 November 1996

10. *New York Herald-Tribune,* Howard Taubman, 6 December 1957.
11. *Washington Post,* Paul Hume, 30 April 1958.
12. *New York Times,* John P. Shenley, 11 February 1959.
13. *Boston Globe,* Kevin Kelley, 16 April 1959.

Part 2   Chapter 19
1. *New York Journal-American,* Miles Kastendieck, 18 March 1960.
2. *Honolulu Star-Bulletin,* Marian J. Kerr, 3 February 1961.
3. *Saturday Review,* Irving Kolodin, 29 April 1961.
4. Metropolitan Opera Archives.
5. *New York Daily News,* Nancy Randolph, 24 October 1961.
6. *Risë Stevens Music Club Journal,* 1962.
7. *Gramophone,* Patrick O'Conner, September 1997.

Part 3   Chapter 1
1. Michael Manuel interview by author, 28 June 1996.
2. *San Diego Union,* 25 February 1966.
3. Metropolitan Opera Archives.
4. Robert La Marchina interview by author, 26 June 1996.
5. Michael Manuel interview.
6. Herman Krawitz interview by author, 25 June 1996
7. Annamary Dickie letter to author
8. Patricia Neway letter to author, 4 January 1999.
9. *New York Journal American,* Miles Kastendieck, 7 July 1964.
10. *Musical America,* P. D., October 1964.
11. Michael Manuel interview.
12. Herman Krawitz interview.
13. Mary Beth Peil interview by author, 6 January 1998
14. Herman Krawitz interview
15. Joy Davidson Interview.
16. Robert La Marchina interview.
17. Tyrone Guthrie letter to Risë Stevens, 11 October 1967.

Part 3   Chapter 2
1. *New York Post:* Harriett Johnson,
2. Charles Kaufman interview by author, 16 August 1996.

Part 3   Chapter 3   A Metropolitan Opera Encore
1. Metropolitan Opera Board Minutes. 16 April 1981.

Coda: Appraising the Stevens' Career

1. San Francisco Opera Magazine: 1978.
2. Opera News: 3 July 1964.
3. Ibid.
4. *Metro-Lark,* Jean Wax, Holiday edition, 1950.

CHRONOLOGY
1923-1932

KEY: (LTOC) Little Theatre Opera Company, B) St. Felix Street Theatre, Brooklyn, (M) Heckscher Theatre, Manhattan; (J) Juilliard; (CH) Carnegie Hall; (WMF) Worchester Music Festival; (NDT) Neues Deutsches Theater; (C) Cairo; (VO) Vienna Opera; (TC) Teatro Colon; (MO) Metropolitan Opera: (GFO) Glyndebourne Festival Opera; (SF) San Francisco Opera; (CZO) Cincinnati Zoo Opera; (PO) Paris Opera
NB: Only selections sung by RS are listed for any given program. For some operas only principal roles are given.

NON-PROFESSIONAL PERFORMANCES

1923-1927	Radio, *The Childrens hour*, 9 a.m., WJZ, New York.
1927-1928	
26 Jan.	PS127, Queens, New York, Graduation Exercises ("I dreamt I dwelt in marble halls", "Stille wie die nacht, The song is ended*")*.
1930-1931	
10-13 Dec.	*Orpheus in Hades*: Unspecifed role. Performed in English. (LTOC, B)
15-20 Dec.	*Orpheus in Hades*: Unspecified role. English. (LTOC, M)
1 March	Recital, Hotel Astor, New York. Presenting Pupils of Orry Parado ("I am fate", Martha "Ah,so pure,with Florence Hines).
19-22 March	*The bartered bride*: Ludmilla. Performed in English. (LTOC, B)
24-28 March	*The bartered bride*: Ludmilla. English. (LTOC, M)
1931-1932	
9-14 Nov.	*The poacher*: Countess von Eberbach. Performed in English. (LTOC, B)
16-21 Nov.	*The poacher*: Countess von Eberbach. English. (LTOC, M)
9-12 Dec.	*The blonde donna*: Ensemble. Performed in English. (LTOC, B)
1931-1935	
14-19 Dec.	*The blonde donna*: Ensemble. English. (LTOC, M) (Substituted for Sonia Essin in one performance)
6-9 Jan.	*La vie Parisienne*: Metella. Performed in English. (LTOC, B)
11-16 Jan.	*La vie Parisienne*: Metella. English. (LTOC, M)
3-6 Feb.	*The chocolate soldier*: Aurelia. Performed in English. (LTOC, B)
8-13 Feb.	*The chocolate soldier*: Aurelia. English. (LTOC, M)
2-5 March	*Orpheus in the underworld*: Public Opinion. Performed in English. (LTOC, B)
7-1 March	*Orpheus in the underworld*: Public Opinion. English (LTOC, M)
30-4 March	*The bat*: Prince Orlofsky. Performed in English. (LTOC, B)
4-9 April	*The bat*: Prince Orlofsky. English. (LTOC, M)
13 May	Trinity College, Senior Ball (Led Grand March with William C. Boeger).
1933-1934	
1 May	Bach, "Thou guide of Israel", "Jauchzet Gott" and "Strike the hour": with Roland Partridge, Harold Bogess, George William Volkel (organist), Josephine Antoine, William Vacchiano (trumpet), Inga Hill, Martha Dwyer, Martha Erein. (J)
5 May	Bach, *St. Mathew Passion* and *Cantata* #53 (J)
1934-1935	Radio, *Palmolive beauty box theatre*, with Gladys Swarthout.
1 Oct.	Honneger, *King David*: Gean Greenwall (Narrator), Jeanette Vreeland, Frederick Jagel, Albert Stoessel, Cond. (WMF)
2 Oct.	*Tristan und Isolde*, Act 3: (Brangäna); Elsa Alsen (Isolde); Frederick Jagel (Tristan); Julius Huehn (Kurvenal); Gean Greenwell (King Mark); Robert Crawford (Helmsman); Roland Partridge (Shepherd/Melot); Albert Stoessel, Cond. (WMF)
3 Oct.	Concert for Children, Albert Stoessel, Cond: "O mio Fernando", "Che farò". (WMF)

6 Oct.	*Madama Butterfly*: (Kate Pinkerton); Suzanne Fisher (Butterfly); Frederick Jagel (Pinkerton); Joan Peebles (Suzuki); Robert Crawford (Sharpless); Warren Lee Terry (Goro); Gean Greenwell (The Bonze); Roland Partridge (Prince Yamadori); Samuel Rea (Registrar); Albert Stoessel, Cond. (Performed with scenery and costumes) (WMF) Lanny Ross log cabin program, New York.
18 Nov.	Recital, Monday Afternoon Club (see H-T 11/17/35)
5, 7 Dec.	*Ariadne auf Naxos*: (Dryad). Performed in English. (J)
30 Jan.,1 Feb.	*Orfeo ed Euridice*: (Orfeo). Performed in English. (J)
15 Feb.	The Literature of the Concerto Series, Bach, *Cantata* #53, "Strike, thou immortal hour"; Lambert, *The Rio Grande,* with Judith Sidorsky (piano) (J)
8, 10 April	*Maria Malibran*: (Cornelia Bayard). (J)
27 June	Recital, American Consulate, Berlin.
1935-1936	
30 Jan.	Recital, Altoona Senior High School, Altoona, Pennsylvania ("Habañera", "In the silence of the night", "I came with a song", "By a lonely forest pathway", "Love went a riding").
21 22, 25 Feb.	A. Honneger, *Le Roi David*, John Barclay (Narrator), Agnes Davis, Joseph Bentonelli, The Mendelssohn Club Chorus, Fritz Reiner, Cond. Philadelphia Orch, Philadelphia, Pennsylvania. n.d. Lanny Ross log cabin program, New York.
3 March	Oratorio Society, Bach, *B Minor Mass.* with Winifred Cecil, Dan Gridley, Robert Crawford, Albert Stoessel, Cond. (CH)
22, 24 April	*The merry wives of Windsor*. Mistress Page. Performed in English. (J)

PROFESSIONAL CAREER

1936-1937	
13, 17 Dec., & 5 Jan.	*Mignon*: (Mignon); Rose Book (Philine); Kurt Préger (Wilhelm Meister); Theodor Scheidl (Lothario); Fritz Göllnitz (Laërte); Walter Szurovy (Frédéric); Fritz Rieger (Cond). Performed in German. (NDT)
31 Dec.	*Die vertauschte oper, "Two American Girls"*, with Harriet Henders; entire company. (NDT)
10 Jan., & 4 June	*Der Rosenkavalier*: (Octavian); Zdenka Zika (Marschallin); Josef Schwarz (Baron Ochs); Harriet Henders (Sophie); Josef Hagen (Faninal); Fritz Göllnitz (Valzacchi); Lydia Kindermann (Annina); Kurt Baum (Singer); Fritz Zweig (Cond). (NDT); June 4 Marta Cuno (Marschallin).
30 Jan., & 12 Feb.	*Der Rosenkavalier*: (Octavian); Zdenka Zika (Marschallin); Pavel Ludikar (Baron Ochs); Pia Bolla (Sophie); Friedrich Ginrod (Faninal); Walter Herbert (Cond). (C)
9 Feb.	*Orfeo ed Euridice*: (Orfeo); Hadzik (Euridice); Fanny Cleve (Amore); Walter Herbert (Cond.) Performed in German. (C)
23-15 Feb.	RS sang either Octavian or Orfeo in Alexandria during this period.
12 March, 5, 12 April	*Orfeo ed Euridice*: (Orfeo); Harriet Henders (Euridice); Herta Rayn (Amore); George Schick (Cond). Performed in German. (NDT)
16 March	*Der Rosenkavalier:* same as 10 Jan. except Hilde Konetzni (Marschallin); Josef Hagen (Faninal). (NDT)
27 March	*Parsifal*: (Zaubermädchen); Josef Schwarz (Amfortas); Paolo Marion (Parsifal); Magnus Andersen (Gurnemanz); Rose Merker (Kundry); Julius Gutmann (Klingsor); Georg Szell (Cond). (NDT)
3 April	*Der Rosenkavalier:* same as 10 Jan. except Hilde Konetzni (Marschallin); Josef Hagen (Faninal); Erich Kleiber (Cond).
10 April	*Parsifal:* same as 27 March except Flecher (Parsifal); Alexander Kipnis (Gurnemanz); Rose Pauly (Kundry)..
6,11,19 May	*Der Corregidor*. Frasquita; Jaro Libal (Corregidor); Harriet Henders (Mercedes); Magnus Andersen (Lopez); Fritz Göllnitz (Pedro); George Schick (Cond). (NDT)
22 May	*Parsifal*: same as 27 March except Adolf Fischer (Parsifal); Alexander Kipnis (Gurnemanz); Rose Pauly (Kundry).

Chronology

5 June — *Der Rosenkavalier*: same as 10 Jan. except Hilde Konetzi (Marschallin); Julius Gutmann (Baron Ochs); Josef Hagen (Faninal); Erich Kleiber (Cond).

1937-1938

7, 15 Sept. — *Carmen*: (Carmen); Kurt Préger (Don José); Lotte Medak (Micaela); Josef Schwarz
8, 11,25 April — (Escamillo); Hans Paweletz (Zuniga); George Britton (Morales); Rose Book (Frasquita);
18 June — Elisabeth Wanka (Mercedes); Fritz Göllnitz (Remendado); Jaro Libal (Dancaïro) Karl Rankl (Cond). Performed in German. (NDT); April 8, 11, 25, June 18 Herta Rayn (Frasquita).

12 Sept. — *Die Walküre*: (Fricka); Adolf Fischer (Siegmund); Vane (Sieglinde); Magnus Andersen (Hunding); Josef Schwarz (Wotan); Marta Cuno (Brünnhilde); Karl Rankl (Cond). (NDT)

19, 23 Sept., — *Oberon*: (Fatime); Harriet Henders (Oberon, Titania); Elisabeth Wanka (Puck); Marta
& 19 Oct. — Cuno (Rezia); Kurt Baum (Huon); Fritz Zweig (Cond). Sung in German. (NDT)

22 Sept. — *Der Rosenkavalier*: same as 10 Jan. except Hilde Konetzni (Marschallin); Josef Hagen (Faninal); Elisabeth Wanka (Annina).

27 Oct. — *Die Zauberflöte*: (Dritte Dame); Kurt Baum (Tamino); Harriet Henders (Pamina); Rose Book (Königin der Nacht); Magnus Andersen (Sarastro); Fritz Göllnitz (Monostatos); Josef Schwarz (Sprecher); Josef Hagen (Papageno); Herta Rayn (Papagena); Else Fink (Erste Dame); Elisabeth Hafenbraedl (Zweite Dame); Karl Rankl (Cond). (NDT)

28 Oct. — *Die Walküre*: same as 12 Sept. except RS (Fricka and Schwertleite); Else Fink (Sieglinde).

14 Nov. — *Carmen*: same as 7 Sept. except Adolf Fischer (Don José).

5, 9, 17 Dec. — *Der König von Yvetot* (*Le Roi d'Yvetot*): (Gazette); Harriet Henders (Eine Walse); Hans
& 1 Feb. — Paweletz (König); Adolf Fischer (Der Glöckner); Julius Gutmann (Ventron); Jaro Libal (Mulgron); Magnus Andersen (Der Doyen); Costa (Méderic); Karl Rankl (Cond). Performed in German. (NDT)

14, 19 Dec. — *Hänsel und Gretel*: (Hänsel); Herta Rayn (Gretel); Josef Hagen (Peter); Fine Reich
17 Jan., 14 Feb. Dörich (Gertrude); Elisabeth Wanka (Die Knusperhexe); Fritz Rieger (Cond). (NDT)

8 Jan. — *Carmen*: same as 7 Sept.except Nicola Cvejc (Escamillo); Alexander Zemlinsky (Cond).

14 Jan. — *Der Rosenkavalier*: same as 10 Jan. except Hilde Konetzni (Marschallin); Josef Hagen (Faninal); Erich Kleiber (Cond).

21 Jan. — *Das Rheingold*: (Wellgunde); Josef Schwarz (Wotan); Josef Hagen (Donner); Kurt Baum (Froh); Adolf Fischer (Loge); Julius Gutmann (Alberich); Fritz Göllnitz (Mime); Hans Paweletz (Fasolt); Magnus Andersen (Fafner); Lydia Kindermann (Fricka); Lotte Medak (Freia); Elisabeth Wanka (Erda, Floshilde); Harriet Henders (Woglinde); Karl Rankl (Cond). (NDT)

23 Jan. — *Die Walküre*: same as 12 Sept.except RS (Schwertleite); Hans Grahl (Siegmund); Frederich Destal (Wotan); Hilde Konetzni (Sieglinde); Anni Konetzni (Brünnhilde); Lydia Kindermann (Fricka).

4 March — *Aida*: (Amneris); Maria Nemeth (Aida); Todor Mazaroff (Rhadames); Josef Schwarz (Amonasro); Josef Hagen (König); Magnus Andersen (Ramphis); George Schick (Cond). Performed in German. (NDT)

8 March — *Der Rosenkavalier*: (Octavian); Hilde Konetzni (Marschallin); Fritz Krenn (Baron Ochs); Margarita Perras (Sophie); Wolfgang Martin, Cond. (VO)

19 March — *Der Rosenkavalier*: same as 8 March except Esther Rethy (Sophie); Hans Knappertsbusch, Cond.

24 March, — *Die hochzeit des Figaro* (*Le nozze di Figaro*): (Cherubino); Hans Paweletz (Figaro);
30 April, — Herta Rayn (Susanna); Josef Hagen (Count); Harriet Henders (Countess); Julius
& 13 May — Gutmann (Don Bartolo); Elisabeth Wanka (Marcellina); Fritz Göllnitz (Don Basilio); Jaro Libal (Don Curzio); Karl Rankl (Cond). Performed in German. (NDT); April 30 Fink (Countess).

29 March — *Die hochzeit des Figaro*: same as 24 March except Boraka (Marcellina).

4 April — Kodály, *Te Deum*, Lisa Frank-Swoboda, Hans Grahl, George Britton, Dr. Heinrich Swoboda, Cond. (NDT)

6 April — *Die hochzeit des Figaro*: same as 24 March except Lydia Kindermann (Marcellina).

10,12,20 April *Ariadne auf Naxos*: (Dryde); Julius Gutman (Musiclehrer) Harriet Henders

(Komponist, Najade); Kurt Baum (Tenor/Bacchus); Rose Book (Zerbinetta); Anni Konetzni (Prima Donna/Ariadne); Josef Hagen (Harlekin); Herta Rayn (Echo); Magnus Andersen (Truffaldin); Fritz Göllnitz (Brighella); Karl Rankl (Cond). (NDT)

26 June *Die gärtnerin aus liebe (La finta giardiniera)*: Ramiro; Fritz Göllnitz (Don Anchise; Elisabeth Wanka (Arminda); Kurt Baum (Graf Belfiore; Harriet Henders (Marchesa Onesti); Hans Paweltz (Nardo); Herta Rayn (Serpetta); J Jaro Libal (Ein Medikus); George Schick (Cond). Performed in German. (NDT-Waldsteingarten)

1938-1939

26, 30 Aug. Bruckner, *Te Deum*, Anni Konetzni, Koloman von Pataky, Emanuel List, Erich Kleiber, Cond. (TC)

2, 4, 7, 15 Sept. *Der Rosenkavalier*: (Octavian); Anni Konetzki (Marschallin); Emanuel List (Baron Ochs); (Faninal); Erich Witte (Valzacchi); Karin Branzel (Annina); Koloman von Pataky (Singer); Erich Kleiber (Cond). (TC); Sept. 15 Ingerborg Schmidt Stein (Sophie).

25 Sept. Bach, *St. John Passion*, Margarita Perras, Koloman von Pataky, Emanuel List, Herbert Jassen, Erich Kleiber, Cond. (TC)

4, 8, 12, 14 Oct. *Siegfried*: (Erda); Max Lorenz (Siegfried); Erich Witte (Mime); Herbert Janssen (Wanderer); Hermann Wiedemann (Alberich); Emanuel List (Fafner); Anni Konetzni (Brünnhilde); Margarita Perras (Forest Bird); Erich Kleiber (Cond). (TC); Oct 8, 14 Ingerborg Schmidt Stein (Forrest Bird).

22 Nov. *Der Rosenkavalier*: (Octavian); Lotte Lehmann (Marchallin); Emanuel List (Baron
19 Dec., Ochs); Marita Farell (Sophie); Friedrich Schorr (Faninal); Karl Laufkötter (Valzacchi);
7, 25 Jan. Doris Doe (Annina); Nicholas Massue (Singer); Artur Bodansky (Cond).
(MO-Philadelphia, Pennsylvana); Jan. 7 (MO-Broadcast); Jan. 25 Grete Stückgold (Marschallin); Julius Huehn (Faninal).

17, 28 Dec., *Mignon*: (Mignon); Richard Crooks (Wilhelm Meister); Josephine Antoine (Philine);
& 3 Feb. Ezio Pinza (Lothario); Alessio de Paolis (Laërte); Helen Olheim (Frédéric); Wilfred Pelletier (Cond). (MO-Broadcast); Feb. 3 Charles Hackett (Wilhelm Meister).

1 Jan. Radio, *Metropolitan Opera auditions of the air* w. Edward Johnson. WJZ 5 p. m.

8 Jan. Concert, Fausto Cleva, Cond: *Mignon*, Act 3: Marisa Morel, John Carter, Nicola Moscona, John Gurney; Che farò. (MO)

27 Jan., *Die Walküre*: (Fricka); Lauritz Melchior (Siegmund); Elisabeth Rethberg (Sieglinde);
& 16 Feb. Herbert Alsen (Hunding); Friedrich Schorr (Wotan); Kirsten Flagstad (Brünnhilde); Erich Leinsdorf (Cond). (MO)

29 Jan. Concert, *Mignon*, Act 3 excerpts: John Carter, Nicola Moscona, John Gurney, Fausto Cleva, Cond. (MO)

5 Feb. Concert, Pietro Cimara, Cond. ("Connais-tu le pays"). (MO)

9,18 Feb. *Das Rheingold*: (Erda); Friedrich Schorr (Wotan); Julius Huehn (Donner); Erich Witte (Froh); René Maison (Loge); Adolf Vogel (Alberich); Karl Laufkötter (Mime); Herbert Alsen (Fasolt); Emanuel List (Fafner); Karin Branzell (Fricka); Hilde Burke (Freia); Thelma Votipka (Woglinde); Lucielle Browning (Wellgunde); Doris Doe (Flosshilde); Erich Leinsdorf (Cond). (MO); Feb. 18 Arnold Gabor (Donner); Paul Althouse (Froh); Norman Cordon (Fasolt); Douglas Beattie (Fafner)..

26 Feb. Concert, Armand Tokatyan, Ezio Pinza, John Gurney, Pietro Cimara, Cond: *Mignon*, Act 3 excerpts. (MO)

4 March *Siegfried*: (Erda); Carl Hartmann (Siegfried); Erich Witte (Mime); Friedrich Schorr (Wanderer); Adolf Vogel (Alberich); Herbert Alsen (Fafner); Kirsten Flagstad (Brünnhilde); Natalie Bodanya (Forest Bird); Erich Leinsdorf (Cond). (MO)

1, 3, 9, 14, *Le nozze di Figaro*: (Cherubino); Mariano Stabile (Figaro); Audrey Mildmay (Susanna);
17, 25, 27 John Brownlee (Count); Maria Markan (Countess); Salvatore Baccaloni (Don Bartolo);
June; 5, 10, Constance Willis (Marcellina); Eric Starling (Don Basilio); Maldwyn Thomas (Don 11, July Curzio); Irene Eisinger (Barbarina); Fergus Dunlop (Antonio); Fritz Busch (Cond). (GFO); June 17 Alberto Erede (Cond).; June 25 Irene Eisinger (Susanna); Rose Hill (Barbarina); Alberto Erede (Cond).; July 5 Irene Eisinger (Susanna); Rose Hill (Barbarina)

20, 22,23, 28 June; 3, 9, 15 July	*Così fan tutte*, (Dorabella); Ina Souez (Fiordiligi); Irene Eisinger (Despina); Ginodel Signore (Ferrando); Roy Henderson (Guglielmo); John Brownlee (Don Alfonso); Fritz Busch (Cond). (GFO)
1939-1940	
22, 24, 27 Sept.; 5, 15 Oct.	*Der Rosenkavalier*: (Octavian): Rose Pauly (Marschallin); Emanuel List (Baron Ochs); Janine Micheau (Sophie); Andrés Boehm (Faninal); Rogello Baldrich (Valzacchi); Lydia Kindermann (Annina); Koloman von Pataky (Singer); Erich Kleiber (Cond). (TC)
3, 7, 12 Oct.	*Orfeo ed Euridice*: (Orfeo); Isabel Marengo (Euridice); Janine Micheau (Amore); Erich Kleiber (Cond). (TC)
12 Nov.	Recital Debut Youngstown, Ohio, George Schick, acc. ("Dove sei amato bene", "Quelle fiamma che m'accende", "Bois epais", "Lachen und weinen", "Sonntag", "Im dem schatten meiner locken", "Cacilie", "Connais-tu le pays", Dvorak "Gypsy songs").
14 Nov.	Tuesday Musical Club, Akron, Ohio, joint recital with Zino Francescatti, violin solo, George Schick, acc. ("Lachen und weinen", "Sonntag", "In dem schatten meiner locken", "Cacilie", "Gypsy songs", "A Christmas folk song", "Roving in the dew", "The nightingale", "To a messenger", "Pilgrim's song").
16 Nov.	Recital, Washington Village, New York, George Schick, acc.
30 Nov., 30 Dec	*Mignon*: (Mignon); Richard Crooks (Wilhelm Meister); Josephine Antoine (Philine); Nicola Moscona (Lothario); Alessio de Paolis (Laërte); Helen Olheim (Frédéric); Wilfred Pelletier (Cond). (MO)
4, 29 Dec., 31 Jan., 10 Feb. 26, 28 Mar.	*Der Rosenkavalier*: (Octavian); Lotte Lehmann (Marschallin); Emanuel List (Baron Ochs); Marita Farell (Sophie); Julius Huehn (Faninal); Kark Laufkötter (Valzacchi); Doris Doe (Annina); John Carter (Singer); Erich Leinsdorf (Cond). (MO); Dec 29 Harriet Henders (Sophie); Feb 10 Alexander Kipnis (Baron Ochs); Nicholas Massue (Singer); Mar, 28 Alexander Kipnis (Baron Ochs). (MO-Boston, Massachusetts)
6 Dec., 19 Jan.	*Die Walküre*: (Fricka); Eyvind Laholm (Siegmund); Lotte Lehmann (Sieglinde); Norman Cordon (Hunding); Julius Huehn (Wotan); Marjorie Lawrence (Brünnhilde); Erich Leinsdorf (Cond). (MO); Jan. 19 Lauritz Melchior (Siegmund); Emanuel List (Hunding); Friedrich Schorr (Wotan).
10 Dec.	Concert, Frank St. Leger, Cond. (*Mignon*, "Légères hirondelles", with Ezio Pinza, "Voiche sapete"). (MO)
17 Dec.	Concert, Frank St. Leger, Cond. (*Mignon*, Act 3: John Carter, Nicola Moscona, John Gurney). (MO)
24 Dec.	Radio, Christmas Eve carol program, WABC, 12 a.m. to 1 a.m.
17 Jan.	Concert, Junior League, New York, Julius Huehn, Erich Leinsdorf, Cond. (*Die Walküre*, scene, Wotan and Fricka; *Siegfried*, scene, Wanderer and Erda).
23 Jan.	Lecture Tea, New Weston Hotel, New York, Hugh Ross on *Mignon*, Josephine Antoine, Wilfred Pelletier in conjunction with Vassar College benefit on 26 Jan.
26 Jan.	*Mignon*, same as 30 Nov. except Armand Tokatyan (Wilhelm Meister); Jean Dickenson (Philine); Norman Cordon (Lothario). Preceded by Luncheon at Waldorf-Astoria Hotel, New York, in honor of RS hosted by Vassar College).
28 Jan.	Musicians Emergency Fund Benefit, Waldorf-Astoria Hotel, New York, Grecian tableau and scene from *Orfeo ed Euridice* with Jarmila Novotna.
2 Feb.	MO Guild Luncheon, "A Galaxy of Stars". Waldorf-Astoria Hotel, New York.
5 Feb.	Recital, Richard Crooks, Mayflower Hotel, Washington, DC, Mrs. Lawrence Townsend's "Morning Musicale", George Schick, acc. ("Dove sei amato bene", "Voi che sapete", "Il mio bel foco", "Che farò", "Die Post", "Verschweigene liebe", "Roving in the dew", "Christmas folk song", "Little Jack Horner", "Love went a riding").
14 Feb.	Recital with Richard Crooks, Hotel Statler, Boston, Massachusetts, "Morning Musicale" (included scenes from *Mignon*).
20 Feb.	*Le nozze di Figaro*: (Cherubino); Ezio Pinza (Figaro); Bidú Sayão (Susanna); John Brownlee (Count); Elisabeth Rethberg (Countess); Virgilio Lazzari (Don Bartolo); Irra Petina (Marcellina); Alessio de Paolis (Don Basilio); Giordano Paltrinieri (Don Curzio); Marita Farell (Barbarina); Louis d'Angelo (Antonio); Ettore Panizza (Cond). (MO-new

	production)
Recitals	26 Feb. York, Pennsylvania; 29 Denton, Texas; 1 March Corsicana, Texas; 4 Topeka, Kansas; 6 Lincoln, Nebraska; 8 La Crosse, Wisconsin; 12 Omaha, Nebraska.
31 March	Radio, *So you think you know music*, Eva Gauthier, John Carter, Mrs. H. V. Kaltenborn. WABC, 10:30 P.M.
11 April	Recital with Simon Barer, piano solo, George Schick, acc, Haarlem Philharmonic Society, Waldorf-Astoria Hotel, New York. (Lotus Club, New York, 70th anniversary dinner, James Melton).
23, 28, 31 July, 7 Aug.	*Samson et Dalila*: (Dalila); René Maison (Samson); Felipe Romito (High Priest); Vittorio Bacciato (Abimélech); Jorge Danton (Old Hebrew); Albert Wolff (Cond). (TC)
23, 25, 28 Aug. 5 Sept.	*Die Walküre*: (Schwertleite); René Maison (Siegmund); Irene Jessner (Sieglinde); Emanuel List (Hunding); Herbert Janssen (Wotan); Marjorie Lawrence (Brünnhilde); Lydia Kindermann (Fricka); Erich Kleiber (Cond). (TC); Aug. 25 RS (Fricka and Schwertleite); Judith Hellwig (Sieglinde); Aug. 28 Jorge Danton (Hunding); Sept. 5 RS (Fricka and Schwertleite); Judith Hellwig (Sieglinde); Jorge Danton (Hunding).
30 Aug., 8 Sept.	Beethoven, *Missa solemnis*, Judith Hellwig, Koloman von Pataky, Emanuel List, Erich Kleiber, Cond. (TC)

(In addition to the recitals listed above, RS also appeared through Community Concerts in La Crosse, Wisconsin; Lincoln, Nebraska; Topeka, Kansas)

1940-1941

2 Sept.	Recital, Teatro Nacional de Comedias, Buenos Aires, Roberto Locatelli, acc. ("Bois epais", "Voi che sapete", "Che farò", "Gypsy songs", "Little Jack Horner", "Love went a riding", also lieder by Brahms, Wolf and Strauss).
12, 15 Sept.	*Salome*: (Page); René Maison (Herod); Lydia Kindermann (Herodias); Marjorie Lawrence (Salome); Herbet Janssen (Jochanaan); Kurt Baum (Narraboth, also a Jew as R.Gonz); Erich Kleiber (Cond). Preceeded by final scene from *Daphne* with Judith Hellwig. (TC)
12 Oct. 8 Nov.	*Le nozze di Figaro*: (Cherubino); Ezio Pinza (Figaro); Bidú Sayão (Susanna); John Brownlee (Count); Elisabeth Rethberg (Countess); Gerhard Pechner (Don Bartolo); Irra Petina (Marcellina); Alessio de Paolis (Don Basilio); Robert Ballagh (Don Curzio); Mari Monte (Barbarina); George Cehanovsky (Antonio). Erich Leinsdorf (Cond). (SF)
16, 27 Oct. 9 Nov.	*Der Rosenkavalier*: (Octavian); Lotte Lehmann (Marschallin); Alexander Kipnis (Baron Ochs); Margit Bokor (Sophie); Walter Olitzki (Faninal); Alessio de Paolis (Valzacchi); Suzanne Sten (Annina); Francisco Naya (Singer); Erich Leinsdorf (Cond). (SF)
3 Nov.Radio,	*The Sunday evening Ford hour*, Wilfred Pelletier, Cond., Detroit, Michigan. WABC, 9-10 P.M. ("Connais-tu le pays"; "Songs my mother taught me"; Dvorak, "Gypsy song"; "Pilgrim's song"; "O Lord they will be done".
26 Nov.	Recital, James Melton, Buffalo, New York (incl. *Il Trovatore*, "Ai nostri monti").
6, 28 Dec.	*Samson et Dalila*: (Dalila); René Maison (Samson); Julius Huehn (High Priest); Norman Cordon (Abimélich); Nicola Moscona (Old Hebrew); Wilfred Pelletier, Cond. (MO)
7, 18 Dec. 23 Jan. 7, 17 March	*Der Rosenkavalier*: (Octavian); Maria Hussa (Marschallin); Emanuel List (Baron Ochs); Eleanor Steber (Sophie); Walter Olitzki (Faninal); Karl Laufkötter (Valzacchi); Doris Doe (Annina); John Carter (Singer); Erich Leinsdorf (Cond). (MO); Dec. 18 Lotte Lehmann (Marschallin); Irra Petina (Annina); Jan. 23 Lotte Lehmann (Marschallin); Irra Petina (Annina); Mar. 7 Lotte Lehmann (Marschallin); Irra Petina (Annina); Raoul Jobin (Singer); Mar 17 Lotte Lehmann (Marschallin); Marita Farell (Sophie); Irra Petina (Annina); Raoul Jobin (Singer)
20 Dec.	Tuberculosis Assoc. Benefit Christmas Tree Auction, Lily Pons, Alfred E. Smith, Plaza Hotel, New York.
24 Dec.	Radio, "Christmas Carols", Juius Mattfield, organ, Howard Barlow, Cond. Columbia Concert Orch & Chorus, WABC, N.Y., 12 to 12:55 A.M.
5 Jan.	Musicians Emergency Fund Benefit, Giovanni Martinelli, Waldorf-Astoria Hotel, New York (*Il Trovatore*, "Ai nostri monti").
9 Jan.	Radio, "Musical Americana", The Delta Rythm Boys, Raymond Paige, Westinghouse Radio Orch, NBC, N.Y., WEAF, 10:30-11 P.M.

11 Jan.,	*Le nozze di Figaro*: (Cherubino); Ezio Pinza (Figaro); Bidú Sayão (Susanna); John
5 Feb.	Brownlee (Count); Elisabeth Rethberg (Countess); Salvatore Baccaloni (Don Bartolo);
20, 24,	Irra Petina (Marcellina); Alessio de Paolis (Don Basilio); George Rasely (Curzio); Marita
27 March	Farell (Barbarina); Louis d'Angelo (Antonio); Ettore Panizza (Cond). (MO); Mar. 24
14 April	Licia Albanese (Susanna). (MO-Baltimore, Maryland); Mar. 27 Licia Albanese (Susanna); Irene Jessner (Countess). (MO-Boston, Massachusetts)
17 Jan.	Radio, Committee for the Celebration of Franklin D. Roosevelt's Birthday, WQXR, N.Y.
20 Jan.	Franklin D. Roosevelt Third Inaugural Gala, Ethel Barrymoore, Irving Berlin, Eddie Cantor, Nelson Eddy, Raymond Massey, Micky Rooney, Robert Sherwood, Dr. Hans Kindler, Cond. Constitution Hall, Washington, D.C. ("Habañera", "My hero", "National Anthem" and "God bless America", with entire cast).
26 Jan.	Concert, Fausto Cleva, Cond. ("Mon coeur", "Pilgrim's Song"). (MO)
12 Feb.	Masters of Viennese Music", Oscar Straus, Cond., Philharmonic-Symphony, Carnegie Hall, New York ("My hero").
18 Feb.	Radio, *Women's page of the air*, Interview, Adelaide Hawley, CBS, N.Y., 8:45-9 a.m.
23 Feb.	Radio, *The pause that refreshes: the Coca-Cola hour*. André Kostelanetz, Cond., WABC, N.Y., 4:30-5:00 P.M., with Albert Spalding, violin. ("Vilia", "High on a windy hill", "Flow gently sweet Afton").
9 March	Radio, *The Sunday evening Ford hour*, The Toronto Orchestra, Reginald Stewart, Cond., Detroit, Mich. WABC. 9-10 P.M. ("Mon coeur" in English, "Habañera", Brahms "Lullaby", "The blacksmith").
March 18	Radio, *I know what I like* with Philip Stahl, host. WQXR, 9 P.M. (discussed favorite music played through recordings: Schumann, "Die karterlegerin"; Brahms, "Wie lieblich sind"; Wagner, Fricka's monologue; *Schwanda*, Polka and fugue).
22 March	"Fashion Academy Awards", from Waldorf-Astoria Hotel, 12 P.M.
4 April	Recital, Toronto, Canada.
16 April,	Recitals Indianapolis, Indiana; 21, Davenport, Iowa.
2 May	Filming began for *The chocolate soldier*, Metro-Goldwyn-Mayer, Hollywood, California. *The chocolate soldier*, (Maria Lanyi); Nelson Eddy (Karl Lang); Nigel Bruce (Bernard Fischer); Florence Bates (Madame Helene); Dorothy Gilmore (Magda); Nydia Westman (Liesel); Max Barwin (Anton); Charles Judels (Klementor). Music by Oscar Straus, Gus Kahn, Camille Saint-Saëns and Richard Wagner. Victor Saville (Producer). Roy Del Ruth (Director). Released, October, 1941.
1941-1942	
5 Oct.	Recital, Paul Ulanovsky, acc., Denver, Colorado.
14 Oct.,	*Der Rosenkavalier*, (Octavian); Lotte Lehmann (Marschallin); Alexander Kipnis (Baron
6 Nov.	Ochs); Margit Bokor (Sophie); Walter Olitzki (Faninal); Karl Laufkötter (Valzacchi); Irra Petina (Annina); Leslie George (Singer); Erich Leinsdorf (Cond). (SF); Nov. 6 Anthony Marlowe (Singer). (SF-Los Angeles, California)
30 Oct.	Radio, *Kraft music hall*, Hollywood, California, with Bing Crosby, William Frawley and Warner Baxter, WEAF, 9 P.M.
24 Nov.	*Le nozze di Figaro*, (Cherubino); Ezio Pinza (Figaro); Bidú Sayão (Susanna); John
6, 20 Dec.	Brownlee (Count); Elisabeth Rethberg (Countess); Salvatore Baccaloni (Don Bartolo); Irra Petina (Marcellina); Alessio de Paolis (Don Basilio); George Rasely (Don Curzio); Marita Farell (Barbarina); Ettore Panizza (Cond). (MO)
27 Nov.	*Der Rosenkavalier*, (Octavian); Lotte Lehmann (Marschallin); Emanuel List (Baron
17 Dec.,	Ochs); Eleanor Steber (Sophie); Walter Olitzki (Faninal); Alessio de Paolis (Valzacchi);
3, 12 Jan.	Irra Petina (Annina); Kurt Baum (Singer); Erich Leinsdorf (Cond). (MO); Dec. 17 Irene Jessner (Marschallin); Karl Laufkötter (Valzacchi); Jan. 12 Karl Laufkötter (Valzacchi).
30 Nov.	Radio, *The pause that refreshes: the Coca-Cola hour*, André Kostelanetz, Cond., WABC, N.Y., 4:30 P.M. "My heart at thy sweet voice", "My hero").
3, 9, 13 Dec.	*Samson et Dalila*, (Dalila); René Maison (Samson); Leonard Warren (High Priest); Norman Cordon (Abimélech); Nicola Moscona (Old Hebrew); Wilfred Pelletier (Cond). (MO)
7 Dec.	Radio, *Keep 'em rolling*, New York. (Pearl Harbor) "National Anthem" substituted for

	original selections; Morton Gould (Cond).
14 Dec.	Recital, Lawrence Tibbett, Brooklyn Jewish Center, New York; 14 Eve. Concert, Hans Breisch, Cond. ("Connais-tu le pays", "Mon coeur"). (MO)
15 Dec.	Radio, "Bill of Rights Day", Helen Hayes (Bill of Rights), Mayor of N.Y., Fiorello LaGuardia, City Hall, New York ("National Anthem"),
18 Dec.	Radio, "MO Guild Opera Preview", Nozze Broadcast, "Boys and Girls Together", NBC, Blue Network, New York.
28 Dec.	Radio, *The Sunday evening Ford hour*, Reginald Stewart, Cond. Detroit, Mich.
7 Jan.	Radio, "Eddie Cantor Show", New York
10 Jan.	Recital, Minneapolis, Minnesota.
Recitals	15, 17 Jan. Toronto, Canada; 19, Rock Hill, South Carolina; 23 Kansas City, Missouri; 25 St. Louis, Missouri; 27, Beaumont, Texas; 29 Lubbock, Texas.
22 Feb.	Radio, *Treasury hour of Song*, Hollywood, California.
Recitals	3 March, Seattle, Washington; 6 Theodore Saidenberg, acc., Victoria, Canada.; 5 April Radio, Easter Sunrise Service, Hollywood Bowl, 6 a.m. Hollywood Victory Caravan 30 April Washington; May 1 Boston, Massachusetts; 2 Philadelphia, Pennsylvania; 6 Cleveland, Ohio; 8 St. Louis, Missouri; 9 St. Paul, Minnesota; 10 Des Moines, Iowa; 11 Dallas, Texas; 12 Houston, Texas; 19 San Francisco, California ("Mon coeur s'ouvre à ta voix" sung in English; "My hero")
NB:	The company was categorized by types of material presented. Comedy Spots: Bob Hope, Claudette Colbert, Jerry Colonna, Joan Blondell, Cary Grant, Charlotte Greenwod, Bert Lahr, Laurel and Hardy, the Marx Brothers and Frank McHugh. Dramatic Spots: Joan Bennett, Charles Boyer, Spencer Tracy, Pat O'Brien; Olivia De Havilland; James Cagney and Merle Oberon. Vocalists: Risë Stevens, Frances Langford, Desi Arnaz and Ray Middleton. During the course of the tour, stars left and other stars came aboard, notably, Bing Crosby, The Andrews Sisters, Marie McDonald, Abbott and Costello, Dinah Shore, Eddie Cantor and Milton Berle, among others. Risë's spot on the program was preceded by Burt Lahr, Cary Grant and Ray Middleton in their Income Tax skit and followed by Joan Blondell, Joan Bennett and Olivia De Havilland as the Women's Motor Corps in "How to Dismantle an Automobile".
29 May	Radio, *Treasury hour of Song*, Hollywood, California.
12 June	Navy Relief Society Ball, Ambassador Hotel, Los Angeles, California ("National Anthem").
13 June	Douglas McArthur Day, Westchester Park, Los Angeles, California ("National Anthem").
29 June	Radio, Decoration Day Celebration.
14 July	Concert, Hollywood Bowl, Los Angeles, California.
20 July	Radio, *Telephone Hour*, Donald Vorhees, Cond. ("Habañera", "Songs my mother taught me", "My hero", "Mon coeur").
28, 31 July	*Mignon*, (Mignon); Jacques Gerard (Wilhelm Meister); Jean Dickenson (Philine); Nicola Moscona (Lothario); Giuseppe Cavadore (Laërte); Marion Selee (Frédéric); Fausto Cleva (Cond). (CZO)
9 Aug.	Radio, *The pause that refreshes: the Coca-Cola hour*, André Kostelanetz, Cond., CBS, N.Y. Short wave radio, *Command performance*, precorded "My hero" for the service men in Australia.
16 Aug.	Central Park Mall Band Concert for Pepsi-Cola, New York.
18 Aug.	Concert, Central Park Mall, Laszlo Halasz, Cond., N.Y. ("When I am laid in earth", "Mon coeur" in English, "I love thee", "I'm falling in love with someone", "My hero").
23 Aug.	Recital, Forest Meadows, Theodore Saidenberg, acc., San Rafael, California.
28, 29 Aug.	Concert, Erich Leinsdorf, Cond., Hollywood Bowl, Los Angeles, California ("When I am laid in earth", "Air de Lia", "Adieu, forêts", "Mon coeur", "Songs my mother taught me", "Seguidilla", "My hero"). Tommy Dorsey Show, New York (between late February to late May).

1942-1943

Recital Program: Purcell, *Dido and Aeneas*, "When I am laid in earth", and, *The Indian queen*, "I attempt from love's sickness to fly"; Bizet, *Carmen* "Habañera"; Schumann, "Widmung"; Wolf, "In dem

Schatten meiner Locken"; Brahms, "Sonntag" and "Meine Liebe ist gruen"; Saint-Saëns, *Samson et Dalila*, "Mon coeur s'ouvre à ta voix"; Tchaikovsky, "Pilgrim's song"; Weinberger, "Conversation" and "Olympia" (written for RS); Dvorak, "Tune thy fiddle, gipsy"; Rachmaninoff, "In the silence of the night"; Butterworth, "Roving in the dew"; Diack, "Little Jack Horner; Kingsford, "Command". Paul Ulanowsky, accompanist.

NB:	A standard feature of each season's recitals was solo pieces for the accompanist mid-way through the program.
Recitals	5 Oct. Denver, Colorado; 8 Boise, Idaho; 10 Portland, Oregon; 13 Vancouver, Canada; 16 Oakland, California; 19 Claremont, California; 21 Bakersfield, California; 23 Fresno, California; 29 Pasadena, California; 31 San Diego, California; 10 Nov. St. Paul, Minnesota.
15 Nov.	Radio, *The pause that refreshes: the Coca-Cola hour*, André Kostelanetz, CBS, New York ("All the things you are", "Be careful its my heart").
19 Nov.	Concert, Reginald Stewart, Cond., Baltimore Symphony, Lyric Theater, Baltimore, Maryland.
26 Nov.	Radio, *Stage door canteen*, Joan Fontaine, Brian Aherne, Milton Berle, New York ("My hero", "Night and day", "Praise the Lord and pass the ammunition", with group).
3 Dec.	Radio, *Women can take it*
7 Dec.	Recital, Rudolf Firkushny, piano solo, Paul Ulanovsky, acc., Waldorf-Astoria Hotel, New York. Radio 20 Dec. *Texaco star theater*, Fred Allen, New York ("Ave Maria" sung to "Intermezzo" from *Cavalleria Rusticana*); 27 Ballantine show, New York; 28 Owens-Illinois show, and, Salute to youth, New York.
5, 8 Jan., 4 Feb.	*Der Rosenkavalier*: (Octavian); Irene Jessner (Marschallin); Emanuel List (Baron Ochs); Marita Farell (Sophie); Walter Olitzki (Faninal); John Garris (Valzacchi); Helen Olheim (Annina); Elwood Gary (Singer); Erich Leinsdorf, Cond. (MO-Philadelphia, Penn); Jan. 5 Lotte Lehmann (Marschallin); Karl Laufkötter (Valzacchi); Doris Doe (Annina). (MO) Feb 4 Lotte Lehmann (Marschallin); Eleanor Steber (Sophie); Julius Huehn (Faninal); Karl Laufkötter (Valzacchi); Irra Petina (Annina). (MO)
17 Jan.	Recital, Civic Opera House, Chicago, Illinois.
21 Jan. 27 Feb.	*Le nozze di Figaro*: (Cherubino); Ezio Pinza (Figaro); Bidú Sayão (Susanna); John Brownlee (Count); Eleanor Steber (Countess); Salvatore Baccaloni (Don Bartolo); Herta Glaz (Marcellina); Alessio de Paolis (Don Basilio); John Garris (Don Curzio); Marita Farell (Barbarina); Bruno Walter (Cond). (MO); Feb. 27 Gerhard Pechner (Don Bartolo); Irra Petina (Marcellina).
Recitals	26 Jan. East Carolina Teachers College, Greenville, North Carolina; 29, Columbia, South Carolina; 1 Feb. Havana, Cuba.
14 Feb.	Concert, Paul Breisach, Cond. ("Connais-tu le pays", "Mon coeur"). (MO)
21 Feb.	Radio, *The pause that refreshes: the Coca-Cola hour*, Albert Spaulding, violin solo, André Kostelanetz, Cond., CBS, New York ("The song is you", "I'll follow my secret heart").
28 Feb.	Concert, Paul Breisach, Cond. ("Divinités du Styx", "Seguidilla"). (MO)
3 March	Recital, Theodore Saidenberg, acc., University of Washington, Seattle, Washington.
Recitals	15 March Winnetka, Illinois; 18, Phoenix, Arizona; 30 Los Angeles, California.
6 April	Concert, San Francisco Symphony, Pierre Monteux, Cond. ("When I am laid in earth", "Divinites du Styx", "Adieu, forêts", "Mon coeur", "Seguidilla"; encore: "Habañera").
11 April	Radio, *Standard symphony hour*, San Fancisco, California.
12 April	Radio, *Treasury hour of Song*, San Francisco, California.
28 April	Camp Kohler Benefit, Sacramento, California.
5 May	Recital, St. Paul, Minnesota.
12 May	Radio, *Cresta bianca carnival*, Morton Gould, with Brad Reynolds. WNCN, New York.
16 May	"I am an American day", Lawrence Tibbett, Jan Peerce, Marjorie Lawrence, Bidu Sayao, Frank Sinatra, Gregor Piatigorsky, Alexander Brailowsky, Nathan Milstein, Central Park Mall, New York. ("America the beautiful", "My hero", "Habañera")
14 June	Recital, London, Ontario.
16 June	Radio, *Cresta bianca carnival*, Morton Gould, with the Deep River Boys. WNCN, New York. ("Vilia", "At dawning")
20 June	Radio's Biggest Show, Bing Crosby, Abbott and Costello, Paulette Goddard, Andrews

	Sisters, Rochester, Don Wilson. 40th Anniversary of Walgreens Drug Stores.
23 June	Radio, *Cresta bianca carnival*, Morton Gould, WNCN, New York.
30 June	Concert, Rudolf Ringwall, Cond. Cleveland Summer Orchestra, Cleveland, Ohio ("Seguidilla", "Mon coeur", "My hero", "Songs my mother taught me"; encores: "Why do I love you", "I love thee", "None but the lonely heart").
3 July	Radio, *Records for fighting men*, with Frank Sinatra, Oscar Levant, Kate Smith, Benny Goodman, Xavier Cugat, Capt. Glenn Miller. WNYC. Broadcast concert from the Central Park Mall
4 July	*Samson et Dalila*: (Dalila); Harold Lindi (Samson); Alexander Sved (High Priest); Lorenzo Alvary (Abimélech); Nicola Moscona (Old Hebrew); Fausto Cleva (Cond). (CZO)
8, 16 July	*Mignon*: (Mignon); Eugene Conley (Wilhelm Meister); Christina Carroll (Philine); Nicola Moscona (Lothario); Giuseppe Cavadore (Laërte); Eleanor Knapp (Frédéric); Fausto Cleva (Cond). (CZO)
13, 22 July	*Carmen*: (Carmen); Kurt Baum (Don José); Marita Farell (Micaela); Alexander Sved (Escamillo); Lorenzo Alvary (Zuniga); Wilfred Engekman (Morales, Dancaïro); Giuseppe Cavadore (Remendado); Maria Orelo (Frasquita); Mildred Ippolito (Mercedes); Fausto Cleva (Cond). (CZO); July 22 Harold Lindi (Don José); Christina Carroll (Micaela); Carlo Morelli (Escamillo).

(In addition to the above, recitals and/or concerts were scheduled for Philadelphia, Pennsylvania; Birmingham, Alabama; Knoxville, Tennessee; Atlanta, Georgia; Oklahoma City, Oklahoma; San Antonio, Texas; Chapel Hill, North Carolina; Munneapolis, Minnesota; Milwaukee, Wisconsin; St. Louis and Kansas City, Missouri; Paterson, New Jersey)

1943-1944

Recital Program: Handel, *Rinaldo*, "Lascia ch'io pianga"; Arnold, *The Maid of the mill*, "Hist! Hist!"; Bizet, *Carmen*, "Habañera"; Brahms, "Von ewiger Liebe" and "Ständchen"; Wolf, "Und willst du deinen Liebsten" and "Mausfallensprüchlein"; R. Strauss, "Zueignung"; Saint-Saëns, *Samson et Dalila*, "Mon coeur s'ouvre à ta voix"; Tchaikowsky, "Pilgrim's song"; Weinberger, "Conversation" and "Olympia"; Dvorak, "Tune thy fiddle, gypsy"; Rachmaninoff. "In the silence of the night"; Butterworth, "Roving in the dew"; Diack, "Little Jack Horner"; Kingsford, "Command". Paul Ulanowsky, Accompanist.

8 Oct.	Biltmore Hotel, Hollywood, California, Joe E. Brown.
16 Oct.	Radio, *Command performance, Hollywood victory caravan*, Bette Davis, Gary Moore, John Charles Thomas.

(Filming for *Going my way* scheduled for this period) *Going my way*, (Genevieve 'Jenny' Linden); Bing Crosby (Father O'Malley); Barry Fitzgerald (Father Fitzgibbon); Frank McHugh (Father O'Dowd); James Brown (Ted Haines); Gene Lockheart (Mr. Haines); Fortunio Bonanova (TomassoBozanni); Robert Tafur (Don José); Martin Garralaga (Zuniga); Robert Mitchell Boychoir; Robert Emmett Dolan (Cond). Songs by Johnny Burke and James Van Heusen. Leo McCarey (Producer/Director). Paramount. Released, May 3, 1944. ("Going my way", "Ave Maria", "Habañera" [American distribution], *Bartered bride* Aria [European distribution], "Holy God, we praise thy name", "Way down upon the Swanee River").

Recitals	28 Oct. Seattle, Washington; 4 Nov. Bozeman, Montana; 15 Providence, Rhode Island; 21 Nov. Radio, *The pause that refreshes: The Coca-Cola hour*, Edward Johnson, Vronsky & Babin, duel pianists, CBS,N.Y. (Celebrating Met Opera Diamond Jubilee season; "Habañera", "When you're away").
26 Nov. 15 Dec.	*Der Rosenkavalier*: (Octavian); Irene Jessner (Marschallin); Emanuel List (Baron Ochs); Eleanor Steber (Sophie); Walter Olitzki (Faninal); John Garris (Valzacchi); Herta Glaz (Annina); Kurt Baum (Singer); Georg Szell (Cond). (MO)
29 Nov.	Radio, *Bright horizon* (Demonstrated how to trill and smoothe a legato).
4, 25 Dec. 3, 28 Jan. 5 Feb.	*Mignon*: (Mignon); James Melton (Wilhelm Meister); Patrice Munsel (Philine); Norman Cordon (Lothario); Lucielle Browning (Frédéric); Donald Dame (Laërte); Sir Thomas Beecham (Cond). (MO); Jan. 3 Mona Paulee (Frédéric), Alessio de Paolis (Laërte).; Jan 28 Nicola Moscona (Lothario). (MO-student performance); Feb 5 Nicola Moscona (Lothario).
5 Dec.	Radio, *Texaco star theater*, James Melton. 9:30-10 p.m.
8 Dec.	*Carmen*: Carmen; Armand Tokatyan (Don José); Dorothy Kirsten (Micaela); Alexander Sved (Escamillo), Connecticut Opera, Palace Theater, Cond.

18 Dec.	Appeared as intermission guest along with Mrs. August Belmont and Assistant Secretary of State, Dean Acheson, on the Metropolitan Opera broadcast of *Rigoletto*. RS Chairman of Victory Rally.
Radio	27 Dec. *Broadway show time*, *A Connecticut Yankee*, Bill Gaxton (RS played herself in gaged up version); 28 *Broadway matinee*, Jim Ameche, WABC, 4:00 p.m., ("Zieguinen", Skit with Ameche); 28 "Good Year Program", NBC (Replaced Nadine Conner, "My dreambook of memory", "When you're away")
10 Jan.	Radio, Ed Sullivan, 7:15 p.m.; *Broadway show time*, "Roberta", Bill Gaxton, 10:30-11:00 p.m.
15 Jan.	Concert, Max Reiter, Cond., San Antonio Symphony.
16 Jan.	Radio, *The pause that refreshes: The Coca-Cola hour*, André Kostelanetz (cond); CBS, N.Y. (Sub'd for Jane Froman, Songs from the film, *Cover Girl*, ("Speak low", "Sure thing" and "Long ago and far away").
24 Jan.	March of Dimes, "Wishing Well Parade", Times Square, N.Y. (WNYC), Mayor of N. Y., Fiorello La Guardia; Allen Jones, Kenny Baker.
31 Jan.	Radio, Ed Sullivan, "Interview", CBS.
6 Feb.	Recital, West Point, N.Y.
26 Feb.	Douglas Air Craft Show, Lorraine Day
29 Feb.	Motion Picture Red Cross Drive, Don Wilson, Roosevelt Navy Band, Hollywood, Caliornia ("National Anthem").
8 March	Radio, Eddie Cantor Show, 9:00-9:30 p.m., Los Angeles, California ("Chanson Bohème"; helped select typical GI Joe who would receive $5000 when War is over).
16 May	"I Am An American Day", Jan Peerce, Lawrence Tibbett, Frank Sinatra, Central Park Mall, New York ("National Anthem", "America", "My hero", "Habañera").
17 Aug.	*Going My Way* Pre-opening broadcast, Basil Rathbone, Hollywood Paramount, California ("National Anthem").
23 Aug.	Radio, Frank Sinatra Show, Eileen Barton, Los Angeles, California (Songs from *Carmen Jones*).
25 Aug.	Radio, *People are funny*.
30 Aug.	Concert, United Nations Tribute, Orson Wells, Leopold Stokowski, Stokowski Symphony Orchestra, University of California, Hollywood, California ("Habañera", "Seguidilla", "Chanson Bohème").

NB: during this period RS recorded a radio show transcription for the Armed Forces radio service, War and Navy Departments, for broadcast only. #711 ("Moonlight madonna", "All of my life", "You belong to my heart", "Together")

1944-1945
Recital Program, same as 1943-1944. Robert Payson Hill, Accompanist.

28 Sept.	War Chest Rally, Los Angeles, California.
29 Sept.	Radio, *Duffy's tavern*, Los Angeles, California. ("Seguidilla").
22 Oct.	Radio, *Standard hour*, Charles Kullman, San Francisco, California (*Carmen* highlights).
27 Oct.,1 Nov.	*Carmen*: (Carmen); Charles Kullman (Don José); Virginia MacWatters (Micaela); Frank Valentino (Escamillo); Lorenzo Alvary (Zuniga); George Cehanovsky (Morales, Dancaïro); Thelma Votipka Frasquita); Alice Avakian (Mercedes); Alessio De Paolis (Remendado); Georges Sebastian, (Cond). (SF)
Radio	23 Nov. *Kraft music hall*, Los Angeles, California ("Last rose of summer", "Through the years"); 16 Dec. Christmas carol; 24 *Texaco star theater*, James Melton, N.Y. ("Homing", "People will say we are in love", with Melton, Brahm's, "Lullaby").
25 Dec.	Radio, "Christmas Day Program", Lawrence Tibbett, NBC, New York ("Habañera").
27 Dec., 8 Jan., 2 Mar.	*Le nozze di Figaro*: (Cherubino); Ezio Pinza (Figaro); Bidú Sayão; John Brownlee (Count); Eleanor Steber (Countess); Salvatore Baccaloni (Don Bartolo); Herta Glaz (Marcellina); Alessio De Paolis (Don Basilio); John Garris (Curzio); Marita Farrell (Barbarina); Louis d'Angelo (Antonio); Erich Leinsdorf, Cond. (MO); Mar. 2 Frances Greer (Susanna); Anna Kaskas (Marcellina); Mimi Benzell (Barbarina).
31 Dec.	Radio, *Texaco star theater*, James Melton, Alec Templeton, NBC, New York ("Long ago and far away", with Melton, "More and more", "Is you is or is you ain't my baby", with Melton, Templeton).

5 Jan.	Radio, *Stage door canteen*, New York ("Habañera", "Irish lullaby").
6 Jan.	Radio,Intermission, *Lucia di L*ammermoor broadcast, "Victory Rally", Ezio Pinza. (MO)
15 Jan.	Radio, *Voice of Firestone*, Howard Barlow, Cond., NBC, New York ("Love has wings", "Printemps qui commence", "Sweetest story", "Ciribiribin"). All *Voice of Firestone* shows opened with Idabelle Firestone's, "If I could tell you", and closed with her, "In my garden".
17, 27 Jan. 9, 27 Feb.	*Mignon*: (Mignon); James Melton (Wilhelm Meister); Mimi Benzell (Philine); Ezio Pinza (Lothario); Lucielle Browning (Frédéric); Donald Dame (Laërte); Wilfred Pelletier (Cond). (MO); Feb. 9 Nicola Moscona (Lothario); Feb 27 Jacques Gérard (Wilhelm Meister); Josephine Antoine (Philine); Mona Paulee (Frédéric). (MO-Philadelphia, Penn.)
21 Jan.	Radio, *Texaco star theater*, James Melton, Alec Templeton, NBC, New York ("Habañera", "I'll follow my secret heart", with Melton, "Don't fence me in" aranged by Templeton according to Gilbert and Sullivan, with Melton, Templeton).
24 Jan.	Recital, Western Reserve University, Cleveland, Ohio. (Handel, *Semele*, "Where'er you walk", replaced "Lascia"; Tchaikovsky, *Jeanne d'Arc*, "Adieu, forêts", replaced "Mon coeur"; encores: "I love thee", "None but the lonely heart", "Songs my mother taught me", "Irish lullaby"). Paul Ulanovsky, Accompanist in place of Hill.
30 Jan.	Opening ceremonies of the Lewis J. Stevens Post 959, Bronx, New York ("National Anthem", Address).
1 Feb.	Radio, Paula Stone, New York; Radio, *Going my way* Interview, CBS, New York.
4 Feb.	Radio, *Metropolitan Opera presents*, Edward Johnson, Host, Wilfred Pelletier, Cond., Milton Cross, Announcer, Sponsored by Sherwin-Willias. Blue Network, New York, 5:30 p.m. ("Habañera", "Che farò", "When Irish eyes are smiling", "Through the years"). The program also featured an auditionist.
Recitals	5 Feb. Greenwich, Connecticut; 7 Columbus, Ohio.
11 Feb.	Radio, *Texaco star theater*, James Melton, Alec Templeton, NBC, New York ("Every time we say goodbye", "Accentuate the positive", with Melton, Templeton, "Close as pages in a book", with Melton).
17 Feb.	Recital, Symphony Hall, Boston, Massachusetts.
23 Feb. 5 Mar.	*Der Rosenkavalier*: (Octavian), Lotte Lehmann (Marschallin); Emanuel List (Baron Ochs); Nadine Conner (Sophie); Walter Olitzki; Alessio de Paolis (Valzacchi); Martha Lipton (Annina); Kurt Baum (Singer); Georg Szell (Cond). (MO); Mar.5 Irene Jessner (Marschallin).
25 Feb.	Radio, *Texaco star theater*, James Melton, NBC, New York ("Yesterday", "Ai nostri monti", with Melton).
8 March	Recital, Evansville, Indiana.
11 March	Concert, Victor Alessandro, Cond., Oklahoma Symphony Orch., Oklahoma City, Oklahoma ("Mon coeur", "Habañera", "Seguidilla").
13 March	Recital, College Station, Texas.
15 Mach	*Texaco star theater* w. James Melton, Alec Goodman, Al Goodman ("Tristesse eternelle", Schubert's "Ave Maria", "O Canada", "Battle Hymn of the Republic" w. Melton, Chorus, "National Anthem" w. Melton, Chorus) CBS.
17 March	Concert, Max Reiter, Cond, San Antonio Symphony, San Antonio, Texas ("Connais-tu le pays", "Mon coeur", "Habañera", "Seguidilla").
Recitals	20 March New Orleans, Louisiana; 23 Jacsonville, Florida; 26 Fort Pierce, Florida; 29, Augusta, Georgia.
30 March	Radio, *Mail call*, Bing Crosby, Andrews Sisters, Peggy Ryan, Garry Moore ("Habañera", dedicated to the boys overseas).
Recitals	2 April Columbus, Georgia; 5 Dayton, Ohio; 7 Columbus, Ohio; 9 Sidney, Ohio; 11 Beaver Falls, Pennsylvania.
14 April	*Mignon*, same as 17 Jan. (MO-Boston, Massachusetts) (started 12:30 p.m. to be completed by 4 p.m. the hour set aside for national mourning of Franklin D. Roosevelt).
15 April	Radio, *Texaco star theater*, James Melton, NBC, New York (Chopin's, "Eternal Sorrow", Schubert's, "Ave Maria", "O Canada", "Battle hymn of the Republic", with Melton and Chorus).
Recitals	24 April Los Angeles, California; 26 Redlands, California; 30 War Memorial Opera

	House, San Francisco, California ("Where'er you walk" replaced "Lascia"); May 2 Eugene, Oregon.
4 May	Concert, "United Nations Conference", Eugene Goosens, Cond, San Francisco Symphony, Civic Auditorium, San Francisco, California ("Connais-tu le pays", "Voi che sapete", "None but the lonely heart", "I love thee", "The song is you"; encores: "Look, Edwin", "Songs my mother taught me", "Ave Maria"); (also) Private recital given by RS for Anthony Eden and Delegates.
6 May	Recital, San José, California.
16 May	Radio, Frank Sinatra Show, Hollywood, California. (*Carmen Jones*: "Dat's love" "Habañera", "Stand up and fight" "Toreador Song" with Sinatra; also a comedy routine).
18 May	7th War Loan Drive, including Bing Crosby, Barry Fitzgerald, Andrews Sisters, Abbott & Costello, Paulette Goddard, Don Wilson, Eddie Anderson, Carl Hoff and his band, Hollywood Bowl, California.
26 May	Recital, Eugene, Oregon.
31 May	Radio, *Kraft music hall*, Frank Morgan, Hollywood, Calif. ("They didn't believe me", Schubert's, "Ave Maria").
20 June	Radio, Walgreen Birthday Show by transcription from Hollywood w. Bing Crosby, the Andrews Sisters, Paulette Goddard, Abbott and Costello. ("Habañera", "I hear music")
Radio	2 July RS Show, Paramount Studio: "Dream lover", *The love parade*, title song, *Out of this world*, "Irish lullaby", "Habañera" (*Carmen*), *Going my way*, Bing Crosby, Robert Emmet Dolan, Guest Conductor; 9 Universal Studio: Title song, *Can't help singing*, "I'll walk alone", *Follow the boys*, "More and more", *Can't help singing*, "Falling in love with love", *Boys from Syracuse*, "Begin the Beguine", *Hers to hold*, Charles Previn, Guest Conductor; 16 Warner Brothers Studio: Music from *Rhapsody in blue*, "S'wonderful", "Man I love", "Love walked in", "Somebody loves me", Leo Forbstein, Guest Conductor; 23 Columbia Studio: Title song, *One night of love*, Title song, *A song to remember*, "Long ago and far away", *Cover girl*, "Stars in my eyes", *The King steps out*, H. Soploff, Guest Conductor; 30 United Artists Studio: "Together", *Since you went away*, "Moon of Manicura", *Hurricane*, Title song, *I'll be seeing you*, "My heart at thy sweet voice", *Samson et Dalila* (by request), Lou Forbes, Guest Conductor; 6 Aug. Sam Goldwyn Studio: "Now I know", *Up in arms*, "Moonlight madonna", *Stella Dallas*, "Blue skies", "My hero" (by request), Carmen Dragon, Guest Conductor; 13: Walt Disney Studio: Brazil, *Saludas amigos*, "Some day my Prince will come", *Snow White*, "You belong to my heart", *The three caballeros*, "When you wish upon a star", *Pinocchio*, Charles Wolcott, Guest Conductor; 20 Paramount Studio: "Lover", *Love me tonight*, Title song, *Love letters*, "My silent love", "Only a rose", "Someday", *The vagabond King*, Victor Young, Guest Conductor; 27 R. K. O. Studio: "The music stops", *Higher and higher*, "Smoke gets in your eyes", *Roberta*, "Alice blue gown", *Irene*, "Night and day", *The gay divorcee*, Constantine Bakaleinikoff, Guest Conductor; 3 Sept. Universal Studio: "A room of my own", "Can't help lovin' dat man o' mine", *Showboat*, "In love with love", Shady lady, "Seguidilla", *Carmen* (by request), Edgar Fairchaild, Guest Conductor. All of the RS programs originated from Hollywood, California on Mondays.
19 Aug	*Command performance*: "Victory Program". A special radio show celebrating the end of the War. Joseph Cotton, Hollywood, California. (Pre-empted *Crime doctor*)

The format of the show is of particular interest and was very similar to the *Victory Caravan*: Meredith Wilson led the Armed Forces Radio Service (AFRS) Orchestra; Ken Carpenter was the announcer for radio station; Bing Crosby served as Master of Ceremonies; Risë Stevens, "Ave M Dinah Shore, "I'll walk alone"; Bette Davis and Jimmy Durante, Comedy routine around a lav his motel; Jimmy Durante and José Iturbi, Comedy routine to do with piano playing; Lionel Pitch for good music; José Iturbi, Chopin, "Polonaise" in A flat; Marlene Dietrich, Tribute Pyle; Burgess Meredith, Poem by Ernie Pyle; Ginny Simms. "You'll be so nice to come b; Sinatra and Bing Crosby, Comedy routine plus "You are my sunshine" sung by both, "Clin knee Bingy boy" sung by Sinatra, "Your the top" sung by both; Frank Sinatra, "The ho' Walk on appearances by Rita Hayworth, Ida Lupino, Ginger Rogers, Ruth Hussy, Cla?

Wilson, Bill Mauldin, George Montgomery, John Conte, Jinx Faulkenberg, Diana Lewis, Ronald Coleman; Janet Blair, "What is this thing called love"; William Powell, Introduction for Bing Crosby; Bing Crosby, "San Fernando Vally"; Harry von Zell and Lucille Ball, Comedy routine around "familiar sounds from home"; King Sisters, "Shoo-Shoo Baby"; Cary Grant, Introduction for Robert Montgomery; Robert Montgomery, Franklyn Delano Roosevelt on Victory; Loretta Young, Prayer; Lena Horne, "The man I love"; Johnny Mercer, "GI jive"; Edward G. Robinson and Orson Wells, Readings from General McArthur, Admiral Nimitz, General Eisenhower; Bing Crosby, Tribute to Bob Hope; Lena Romai, "Chiyo, Chiyo, Chiyo"; Danny Kaye and Bing Crosby, Comedy routine; Danny Kaye, from film *Up in arms* take off on Hollywood musicals; Marilyn Maxwell, "I got rhythm"; Carmen Miranda, "Tico, Tico"; Claudette Colbert and Ed Gardner as Archie of *Duffy's tavern*, Comedy routine; Greer Garson, Four Christmases at war; Bing Crosby, "White Christmas"; Orson Wells, Prayer by a serviceman; "National Anthem".

1945-1946

Recital Program, same as 1943-1944 except, Handel *Semele*, "Where'er you walk", replaced "Lascia". Robert Payson Hill, Accompanist.

25 Sept. 11 Oct., 10 Nov.	*Carmen*: (Carmen); Raoul Jobin (Don José); Eleanor Steber (Micaela); Mack Harrell (Escamillo); Walter Olitzki (Zuniga); George Cehanovsky (Morales, Dancaïro); Thelma Votipka (Frasquita); Claramae Turner (Mercedes); Alessio de Paolis (Remendado); Gaetano Merola (Cond). (SF); Nov. 10 Nadine Conner (Micaela). (SF-Los Angeles, California)
2, 6, 18 Oct.	*Der Rosenkavalier*: (Octavian); Lotte Lehmann (Marschallin); Lorenzo Alvary (Baron Ochs); Eleanor Steber (Sophie); Walter Olitzki (Faninal); Alessio de Paolis (Valzacchi); Herta Glaz (Annina); Bruno Landi (Singer); Georges Sebastian (Cond). (SF); Oct. 18 Nadine Conner (Sophie).
Radio	21 Oct. *Standard symphony hour*, San Francisco, California (abridged *Carmen* w. Charles Kullman, Eleanor Steber and Mack Harrell, Gaetano Merola and the San Francisco Opera Orchestra ("Habañera", Final duet); 25 *Sealtest show*, Jack Haley, Los Angeles, California ("Seguidilla", *Rigoletto,* comedy quartet).
29 Oct.	Concert, Bond Rally, Denver Symphony, Denver, Colorado.
4 Nov.	Radio, *Electric hour*, Nelson Eddy, Los Angeles, California ("Chanson Bohème", "My hero", with Eddy, "I'll follow my secret heart").
22 Nov.	Radio, *The pause that refreshes: the Coca-Cola hour* André Kostelanetz, Cond, CBS, New York ("My hero", "Mon coeur", Schubert's, "Ave Maria").
30 Nov. 12 Dec. 5 April, 17 May	*Der Rosenkavalier*: (Octavian); Irene Jessner (Marschallin); Emanuel List (Baron Ochs); Eleanor Steber (Sophie); Frederick Lechner (Faninal); Alessio de Paolis (Valzacchi); Herta Glaz (Annina); Kurt Baum (Singer); Georg Szell (Cond). (MO); Dec. 12 Thomas Hayward Singer); Apr. 5 Nadine Conner (Sophie); Walter Olitzki (Faninal); Thomas Hayward (Singer). (MO-Boston, Massachusetts); May 17 Hugh Thompson (Faninal); Martha Lipman (Annina); Thomas Hayward (Singer); Max Rudolf (Cond). (MO-Dallas, Texas)
4 Dec.	War Activities Commemorative Dinner, Lt. Charles Brendler, Cond., U.S. Navy Orchestra, Hotel Willard, Washington, D.C. (RS listed on program, unspecified contribution).
16 Dec.	Radio, *International harvester*, Raymond Massey, Howard Barlow, Cond. ("O little town of Bethlehem", "Silent night", Christmas medley).
1 Dec., ̇an., 16 Mar. ̇il, 8 May	*La Gioconda*: (Laura); Zinka Milanov (Gioconda); Richard Tucker (Enzo); Leonard Warren (Barnaba); Ezio Pinza (Alvise); Margaret Harshaw (La Cieca); Emil Cooper (Cond). (MO); Mar, 16 Giacomo Vaghi (Alvise). (MO-Texaco Broadcast)
̇c. ̇an. ̇ril, ̇y	*Carmen*: (Carmen); Raoul Jobin (Don José); Licia Albanese (Micaela); Alexander Sved (Escamillo); Louis d'Angelo (Zuniga); John Baker (Morales); Thelma Votipka (Frasquita); Lucielle Browning (Mercedes); Alessio de Paolis (Remendado); George Cehanovsky (Dancaïro); Wilfred Pelletier (Cond). (MO); Jan 7 Jacques Gérard (Don José); Robert Merrill (Escamillo); Lorenzo Alvary (Zuniga); Anthony Marlowe (Remndado); Jan 18 Jacques Gérard (Don José); Robert Merrill (Escamillo); Florence Quartararo (Micaela);

| | Frances Greer (Frasquita); Martha Lipton (Mercedes); Richard Manning (Remendado); Arthur Kent (Dancaïro). (MO-student performance); Apr. 10 Martial Singher (Escamillo). (MO-Boston, Massachusetts); April 22 Eleanor Steber (Micaela); Lorenzo Alvary (Zuniga). (MO-Cleveland, Ohio); May 14 Hugh Thompson (Escamillo); Lorenzo Alvary (Zuniga). (MO-St. Louis, Missouri); May 20 Dorothy Kirsten (Micaela); Frank Valentino (Escamillo); Lorenzo Alvary (Zuniga). (MO-Memphis, Tennessee) |

20 Jan. Radio, *The Ford program*, Detroit, Michigan ("Sequidilla", "None but the lonely heart", "Roving in the dew", "Oh dear! What can the matter be", "A Scottish fantasy", "O sing a new song").

Recitals 23 Jan. Kalamazoo, Michigan; 25 Rockford, Illinois; 28 Dayton, Ohio; 31 Roanoke, Virginia; 3 Feb. Norfolk, Virginia; 5 Charlotte, North Carolina; 7 Greenville, South Carolina.

10, 13 Feb. Concert, Dr. Hans Kindler, Cond., National Symphony, Constitution Hall, Washington, D.C. ("Connais-tu le pays", "Mon coeur"; encore: "None but the lonely heart", "Habañera", "Seguidilla" encores: "Chanson Bohème", "Irish lullabye").

12 Feb. Recital, Louisville, Kentucky.

14 Feb. Recital, Paducah, Kentucky.

19, 24 Feb. *Carmen*: (Carmen); Frederick Jagel (Don José); Frances Yeend (Micaela); Walter Cassel (Escamilllo); Walter Olitzki (Zuniga); Wilfred Engleman (Morales, Dancaïro); Jean Parelli (Frasquita); Helen Olheim (Mercedes); Costante Sorvino (Remendado); Max Reiter (Cond); Symphony Society of San Antonio, Texas

26 Feb. Concert, Max Reiter, Cond., Waco Symphony, Waco, Texas. ("Connais-tu le pays", "Mon coeur", Bach's, "With one foot in the grave I stand", "Habañera", "Seguidilla").

Recitals 28 Feb. Dallas, Texas; March 3 Little Rock, Arkansas; 5 Fort Smith, Arkansas; 9 Lansing, Michigan; 11 Grand Rapids, Michigan; 13 Temple Sholom, Chicago, Illinois.

Recitals 19 March Utica, New York; 21 Battle Creek, Michigan. 24 March Gala, *La Gioconda*, Act 3, same as 21 Dec. except Stella Roman (Gioconda); Giacomo Vaghi (Alvise). 30 March same as 28 Dec. except Mary Henderson (Micaela); Robert Merrill (Escamillo); Frances Greer (Frasquita).

18 April Radio, *Chrysler show*, New York w. Andre Kostelanetz (*Carmen* aria, Schubert's "Ave Maria", "Irish lullabye", "Will you remember") WABC, 9 p.m.

25 April Recital, Bridgeport, Connecticut.

Radio 30 April Radio, Paula Stone, New York; 2 May *Hobby lobby*, New York ("All the things you are").

11 May (Personal appearance Lyon & Healy Book Store) followed by matinee *Der Rosenkavalier*, same as 30 Nov. except Hugh Thompson (Faninal); Martha Lipman (Annina); Thomas Hayward (Singer). (MO-Chicago, Illinois)

Recitals 23 May Palo Alto, California; 26 Los Angeles, California; 28 San Diego, California.

29 May Radio, Frank Sinatra show, Hollywood, California ("The song is you", "Strange music", with Sinatra).

Recitals 30 May Redlands, California; 3 June Tacoma, Washington.

11,17 July *Samson et Dalila*: (Dalila); Raoul Jobin (Samson); Louis d'Angelo (Abimélech); Angelo Pilotto (High Priest); Virgilio Lazzari (Old Hebrew); Fausto Cleva (Cond), (CZO)

14. 25 July *Carmen*: (Carmen); Raoul Jobin (Don José); Marita Farell (Micaela); Martial Singher (Escamillo); Louis d'Angelo(Zuniga); Wilfred Engelman (Morales, Dancaïro); Mildred Ippolito (Frasquita); Thelma Altman (Mercedes); Francesco Curci (Remendado); Georges Sébastion (Cond). (CZO); July 25 Jacques Gérard (Don José); Christina Carroll (Micaela).

23 July Concert, "Music Under the Stars", Jerzy Bojanowski, Cond., Milwaukee, Wisconsin ("Mon coeur", "Habañera"; encore: "Seguidilla", "None but the lonely heart", "Songs my mother taught me", "Irish lullabye", "My hero"; encores: "Trees", Schubert's, "Ave Maria").

Radio 30 July *Chesterfield supper club*, Martin Block, NBC, New York ("Stars in my eyes", "Irish lullabye", "The song is you"); Aug. 1 *Chesterfield supper club* ("Falling in love with love", "The man I love", "Smoke gets in your eyes"; program ended at 7:15 p.m. but RS sang, "Trees", and the "Seguidila", for the studio audience); 4 Aug. *Let's go to the opera*, Eugene Conley, New York ("Che farò", "Seguidilla", *Mignon*, Act 3 duet, with Conley. All selections performed in English); 8 Alma Kitchel show, WJZ, New York.

Chronology

(During this period RS filmed her scene in *Carnegie Hall*)
Carnegie Hall, (Herself); Marsha Hunt (Nora Ryan); William Prince (Tony Salerno, Jr.); Frank McHugh (John Donovan); Hans Yaray (Tony Salerno, Sr.); Olin Downes (Himself); Alfonso d'Artega (Tchaikovsky); Walter Damrosch (Himself); Martha O'Driscoll (Ruth Haines); Guest Artists in order of appearance: Bruno Walter, Lily Pons, Gregor Piatigorsky, Risë Stevens, Artur Rodzinski, Artur Rubenstein, Jan Peerce, Ezio Pinza, Vaughn Monroe, Jascha Heitetz, Fritz Reiner, Leopold Stokowski, Harry James. Boris Morros, William LeBaron (Producers). Edgar G. Ulmer (Director). Charles Previn, Cond. for RS ("Seguidilla", "Mon coeur"). Released, May, 1947.

1946-1947
Recital Program, see 1943-1944 except, Handel *Semele*, "Where'er you walk", replaced "Lascia". Robert Payson Hill, Accompanist.

Recitals	8 Oct. Almeda, California; 18 El Paso, Texas; 20 Peoria, Illinois; Denver, Colorado; 23 Emporia, Kansas; 25, 26 Kansas City, Missouri; 28 Cedar Rapids, Idaho; 2 Nov. Johnstown, Pennsylvania.
10 Oct.	Radio, Jack Haley program, Los Angeles, Ca ("Gypsy song", comedy routine w. Jack Haley and John Dunn, parody w. music from *Rigoletto).*
13 Nov., 17, 24, 28 Apr., 5, 8, 13, 19 May	*Le nozze di Figaro*: (Cherubino); Ezio Pinza (Figaro); Frances Greer (Susanna); John Brownlee (Count); Eleanor Steber (Countess); Salvatore Baccaloni (Don Bartolo); Herta Glaz (Marcellina); Alessio de Paolis (Don Basilio); Leslie Chabay (Don Curzio); Mimi Benzell (Barbarina); Lorenzo Alvary (Antonio); Fritz Busch (Cond). (MO); Apr, 17 Florence Quartararo (Countess); John Garris (Don Curzio); Marita Farell (Barbarina). (MO-Minneapolis, Minnesota); Apr. 24 Florence Quartararo (Countess); John Garris (Don Curzio); Marita Farell (Barbarina). (MO-Chicago, Illinois); Apr. 28 Bidú Sayão (Susanna); Florence Quartararo (Countess); Claramae Turner (Marcellina); Marita Farell (Barbarina); John Garris (Don Curzio). (MO-Atlanta, Georgia); May 5 Bidú Sayão Susanna); John Garris (Don Curzio); Marita Farell (Barbarina). (MO-San Antonio, Texas); May 8 Bidú Sayão (Susanna); Marita Farell (Barbarina); John Garris Don Curzio). (MO-New Orleans, Louisana); May 13 Bidú Sayão (Susanna); John Garris (Don Curzio), Marita Farell (Barbarina). (MO-Memphis, Tennessee); May 19 Bidú Sayão (Susanna); Marita Farell (Barbarina). (MO-Rochester, New York)
15 Nov.	Radio, Preview of the Milk Fund for Babies *Carmen* benefit, Robert Merrill, Ramon Vinay, Mrs William Randolph Hurst.
21 Nov., 7, 20 Dec., 21 Apr., 3, 16 May	*Boris Godunov*: (Marina); Ezio Pinza (Boris); Richard Tucker (Grigory); Nicola Moscona (Pimen); Frank Valentino (Rangoni); Alessio de Paolis (Shouisky); Salvatore Baccaloni (Varlaam); Anthony Marlowe (Simpleton); Emil Cooper (Cond). (MO); Dec.20 Virgilio Lazzari (Pimen); Apr. 21 John Garris (Shouisky); Virgilio Lazzari (Pimen). (MO-Chicago, Illinois); May 16 John Garris (Shouisky); Mario Berini (Grigory). (MO-St. Louis, Missouri)
22 Nov.	Radio, *Serenade to America*, NBC, New York.
24 Nov., 2 Dec, 2 Jan. 6 Jan., 22 Feb. 20 Mar.	*Carmen*: (Carmen); Ramon Vinay (Don José); Renée Mazella (Micaela); Robert Merrill (Escamillo); Lorenzo Alvary (Zuniga); John Baker (Morales); Thelma Votipka (Frasquita); Martha Lipton (Mercedes); Alessio dePaolis (Remendado); George Cehanovsky (Dancaïro); Louis Fourestier (Cond). (MO); Dec. 2 Nadine Conner (Micaela); Martial Singher (Escamillo); Jan.2 Raoul Jobin (Don José); Florence Quartararo (Micaela); Philip Kinsman (Zuniga); Hugh Thompson (Morales); Lucielle Browning (Mercedes); Leslie Chabay (Remendado); Jan. 6 Mario Berini (Grigory); Feb 22 Nadine Conner (Micaela); William Hargrave (Zuniga); Lucielle Browning (Mercedes); Leslie Chabay (Remendado); Max Rudolf (Cond). (MO-Texaco Broadcast); Mar. 20 Raoul Jobin (Don José); Nadine Conner (Micaela); Martial Singher (Escamillo). (MO-Boston, Massachusetts).
28 Nov.	Radio, *Treasure hour of song*, Frank Valentino, Alfredo Antonini, Cond. New York ("My hero", "Gypsy song", "Only make believe", with Valentino).
1 Dec.	Recital, Lewiston, Maine.
8 Dec.	Radio, *The family hour*, CBS, New York, 5:00 p.m., Sponsored by Prudential Life

	Insurance Co., w. Jimmy Carroll, Al Goodman, Ted Malone, Frank Gallup, ("Habañera", "Seguidilla", "Chanson Bohème", "With a song in my heart", "You are love").
9 Dec.	Radio, Victor Borge show, New York. ("Moon love").
14, 30 Dec.	*Der Rosenkavalier*, (Octavian); Irene Jessner (Marschallin); Emanuel List (Baron Ochs);
8 Feb.,	Eleanor Steber (Sophie); Frederick Lechner (Faninal); Alessio de Paolis (Valzacchi);
18 Mar.	Herta Glaz (Annina); Kurt Baum (Singer); Fritz Busch (Cond). (MO-Texaco Broadcast); Feb. 8 Desző Ernster (Baron Ochs); Walter Olitzki (Faninal); John Garris (Valzacchi); Martha Lipton (Annina); Thomas Hayward (Singer); Mar. 18 Desző Ernster (Baron Ochs); Nadine Conner (Sophie); Hugh Thompson (Faninal); Herta Glaz (Annina); John Garris (Valzacchi); Thomas Hayward (Singer). (MO-Baltimore, Maryland)
16 Dec.	Radio, *The family hour* ("Ave Maria", sung to "Intermezzo" from *Cavalleria rusticana*, "Night and day", "Someday"). Guest: Jean Sablon (Singer)
22 Dec.	Radio, *The family hour* (Schubert's, "Ave Maria", "White Christmas").
27 Dec.,	*Hänsel und Gretel*: (Hansel); Nadine Conner (Gretel); John Brownlee (Peter); Claramae
11, 31 Jan.,	Turner (Gertrud); Thelma Votipka (Witch); Fritz Stiedry (Cond). Performed in English.
22 Mar., 11 Apr.	Followed by *Faust*, "Walpurgis night". (MO-student performance) Performed in English; Jan.11 Preceeded by world premiere of *The Warrior*. (MO-Texaco Broadcast); Jan 31 preceeded by *The Warrior*; Mar. 22 Followed by *Faust*, "Walpurgis night". (MO-Boston, Massachusetts); Apr. 11 Followed by *Faust*, "Walpurgis night". (MO-Cleveland, Ohio)
29 Dec.	Radio, *The family hour* ("My heart at thy sweet voice", "The song is you", "Auld lang syne"). Guest: Albert Spalding (violinist)
5 Jan.	Radio, *The family hour* ("One night of love", "Through the years", *Finian's rainbow*, medley). Guests: Andrews Sisters (Singers)
12 Jan.	Radio, *The family hour* ("Because", "Stars in my eyes", "I love but thee", Norwegian medley) Guests: Les Paul Trio (Singers); *Carmen*, same as Nov. 24 except Mario Berini (Don José); Florence Quartararo (Micaela); Lucielle Browning (Mercedes); Max Rudolf (Cond).
19 Jan.	Radio, *The family hour* ("Ciriciribin", "A dream Team", *Sweethearts* medley incl. "Land of romance and Waltz"). Guest: Jack Smith (Singer)
Recitals	21 Jan. Purdue University; 23 Macon, Ohio; 25 Lafayette, Indiana.
26 Jan.	Radio, *The family hour* ("Dream lover", "Full moon and empty arms", Templeton "Coffee song" adaptation with Jimmy Carroll, Al Goodman). Guest: Alec Templeton (Pianist)
28 Jan.	Recital, Detroit, Michigan (Encore: "Ave Maria" in memory of Grace Moore).
2 Feb.	Radio, *The family hour* ("My hero", "Adieu, forêts", "They say that falling is love is wonderful"). Guest: Ethel Merman (Singer)
4 Feb.	*Mignon*, Hartford, Connecticut.
9 Feb.	Radio, *The family hour* ("Masquerade", "Homing", *Street scene* medley incl. "What good would the moon be"). Guest: Diana Lynn (Pianist)
12, 24 Feb.	*La Gioconda*: (Laura); Zinka Milanov (Gioconda); Richard Tucker (Enzo); Leonard Warren (Barnaba); Giacomo Vaghi (Alvise); Margaret Harshaw (La Cieca); Emil Cooper (Cond). (MO); Feb 24 Lucielle Browning (La Cieca).
Radio	13 Feb. *Treasury hour of song*, Frank Valentino, Alfredo Antonini, Cond. ("I'm falling in love with someone", "Mon coeur", "One alone", with Valentino); 16 *The family hour*, *Sari* waltzes, "In the silent night", *Helen goes to Troy* medley, "Barcarolle", with Jimmy Carroll). Guest: Robert Maxwell (Harpist)
23 Feb.	Radio, *The family hour* ("Strange music", "When you're away", Templeton "Open the Door Richard", adaptation with Jimmy Carroll, Al Goodman). Guest: Alec Templeton
March	Concert, Howard Mitchell, Cond., National Symphony Orchestra, Washington, D.C. ("Agnus Dei", "Che farò", "In the silence of the night", "Adieu, forêts").
1 March	Radio, Intermission, *Rigoletto*, "Opera News on the Air" with Boris Goldovsky (discussion of the opera).
Radio	2 March *The family hour* ("I'll follow my secret heart", "At dawning", "Will you remember") Guest: Olga San Juan (Entertainer); 9 *The family hour* ("Poincianna", "I'm

	falling in love with someone", *Vagabond King* medley). Guest: Doris Stockton (Marimbist)
11 March	Vladimir Bakalanikoff, Cond, Pittsburg Symphony, Pittsburg, Pennsylvania. ("Printemps qui commence", "Mon coeur", "Habañera", "Seguidilla", "Chanson Bohème").
13 March	Recital, Allentown, Pennsylvania; 13 eve. National Symphony Orchestra, Constitution Hall, Washington, D.C. ("Agnus Dei", "Che farò", "In the silence of the night", "Adieu, forêts"; encores: "I'm falling in love with someone", "My hero").
16 March	Radio, *The family hour* ("When Irish eyes are smiling", "Irish lullabye", "Thine alone"). Guest: Jack Berch (Singer)
19 March	Recital, R. Payton Hill, piano acc., Prudential Business Conference Dinner, Hotel Commodore, New York. (Selections from *Robin Hood, New moon* and *Sweethearts.*).
Radio	23 March *The family hour* ("Oh what a beautiful morning", "Trees", "How are things in Gloccamora") Guests: Vera Appleton and Michael Field (Duo-Pianists); 30 *The family hour* ("April in Paris", "Where'er you walk", Templeton *Faust* parody, with Jimmy Carroll, Al Goodman, Chorus) Guest: Alec Templeton (Pianist); 6 April *The family hour* ("Easter parade", *Hänsel und Gretel* Prayer (English), "Agnus Dei", *Easter parade* medley) Guest: Lauritz Melchior (*Parsifal*, "Nur eine waffe Taugt"); 10 *Treasury hour of song*, Thomas Hayward, Alfredo Antonini, Cond. ("Allah's holiday", "Habañera", "Lover come back to me", with Hayward).
13 April	Radio, *The family hour* ("Smilin' thru", "Seguidilla", *Brigadoon*, medley).
20 April	Radio, *The family hour* (Springtide, One more waltz with Jimmy Carroll, Alec Templeton, piano, Templeton operatic adaptation of, "Miragua, Nicaragua", with Carroll, Al Goodman, Frank Gallup, Ted Malone). Guest: Alec Templeton (Pianist).
27 April	Radio, *The family hour* ("One kiss", "My heart at thy sweet voice", "Ah sweet mystery of life", with Jimmy Carroll).
30 April	Recital, Baton Rouge, Louisiana.
11 May	Radio, *The family hour* (Brahms, "Lullaby", "Adieu, forêts", "Always", with Jimmy Carroll, "Bless this house").
18 May	Radio, *The family hour* ("'Neath a southern moon", *Tannhäuser*, "Evening star", "Strange music"). Guest: Alec Templeton (Pianist)
Radio	25 May *The family hour* ("A kiss in the dark", "Chanson Bohème", 'America', with Jimmy Carroll); 1 June *The family hour* ("One night of love", "Moon love", "I'll see you again", with Jimmy Carroll); 31 July, *Sealtest show*, Eve Arden ("Chanson Bohème", Comedy routine with Arden as waitresses in a cafe singing the menu to the music of the "Toreador song", duet from *Il Trovatore* presumably, "Ai nostri monti", sung mainly by RS).

(In addition to the recitals listed above, RS also appeared in Chattanooga, Tennessee, Lake Charles, Louisiana and Veterans Administration Hospitals)

1947-1948

Recital Program: Handel, *Semele*, "Where'er you walk"; Malotte, "The Lord's prayer"; Schumann, "Widmung"; Wolf, "Das verlassene Mägdlein" and "Mausfallensprüchlein"; R. Strauss, "Traum durch die Dämmerung" and "Wie sollten wir geheim sie halten"; Donizetti, *La Favorita*, "O mio Fernando"; Hageman, "Charity"; Britten, arr., "The ash grove"; Bantoc, "A feast of lanterns"; Rachmaninoff, "To the children"; Bizet, *Carmen*, "Habañera", "Seguidilla", "Chanson Bohème". Brooks Smith, Accompanist.

Radio	5 Sept. Maggie McNallis; 7 *The family hour* ("Ouvre ton coeur", "Our love", "Lullaby", "Temptation"); 14 *The family hour* (Waltzes from *Sari*, "Play Gypsies"); 15 *Betty Crocker show.*
19 Sept.	Recital, Adelphi College, Long Island, New York. (the program sung at Adelphi contained variations on the one which was arranged for the Community Concert tours. Opening the recital were, "Thanks be to Thee", "Evening prayer" and "The Lord's prayer"; the group in English had an additional song, "Look, Edwin!").
Radio	21 Sept. *The family hour* ("Command", "As years go by", "Since first I met thee"); 27 Luncheon at Sardi's; 28 *The family hour* ("I wonder as I wander", "In the still of the night").
Recitals	30 Sept. Scranton, Pennsylvania; 3 Oct. Atlantic City, New Jersey.
5 Oct.	Radio, *The family hour* ("Liebestraum", "Yours is my heart alone", "Breeze and I").
8 Oct.	Recital, Endicott, New York.

374

12 Oct.	Radio, *The family hour* ("Love's old sweet song", "Still as the night", "Balalaika serenade", "While there's a song to sing").
Recitals	14 Oct. Spartanburg, South Carolina; 16 Oct. Washington, D.C.
19 Oct.	Radio, *The family hour* ("Donkey serenade", "Engagement waltz", "Pilgrim's song", "Daybreak").
Recitals	21 Oct. Gladsden, Alabama; 23 Oct. Beaumont, Texas.
26 Oct.	Radio, *The family hour* ("Intermezzo", "Moon love", *Allegro* medley).
28 Oct.	Recital, New Haven, Connecticut.
Radio	1 Nov. *Twenty questions*; 2 *The family hour* ("All my love", "Il est doux", "I love you"); 4 *Tea-time ballroom*: Bob Clayton Show, Boston, Massachusetts. WHDH, 5-6 p.m. (Preceeding this program RS held a press conference at 10 a.m. in the Ritz Carlton Hotel, between then and 3 p.m. she visited Horticultural Hall where a chrysanthemum was named in her honor, she then spoke at the New England Conservatory of Music, next was a stint on the switchboard of Community Fund Headquarters followed by a speech at a Rally at the Parkman Bandstand on Boston Common on behalf of the Community Fund; 3:30 p.m., RS signed records and albums at Paines Department Store until it was time to report to the radio station).
Recitals	5 Nov. Symphony Hall, Boston, Massachusetts (encores included, "Mon coeur", in first half and, "Look, Edwin", "I'm falling in love with someone", "Irish lullabye", "Songs my mother taught me", Schubert's, "Ave Maria" at conclusion); 7 Milwaukee, Wisconsin.
9 Nov.	Radio, *The family hour* ("Lamp is low", "Full moon and empty arms", "Hawaian medley").
Recitals	11 Nov. Zanesville, Ohio; Nov. 13 Lorain, Ohio.
16 Nov.	Radio, *The family hour* ("Masquerade", "You and the night and the music", "Habañera", "Seguidilla", "Chanson Bohème").
18 Nov. 6 Dec., 19 Jan., 7 Feb., 1, 13, 27 Apr., 15 May	*Carmen*: (Carmen); Ramon Vinay (Don José); Claudia Pinza (Micaela); Martial Singher (Escamillo); Philip Kinsman (Zuniga); Clifford Harvuot (Morales); Thelma Votipka (Frasquita); Martha Lipton (Mercedes); Alessio de Paolis (Remendado); George Cehanovsky (Dancaïro); Louis Fourestier (Cond). (MO); Dec. 6 Kurt Baum (Don José); Robert Merrill (Escamillo); John Baker (Morales); Leslie Chaby (Remendado); Jan. 19 Kurt Baum (Don José); Nadine Conner (Micaela); Robert Merrill (Escamillo); Lorenzo Alvary (Zuniga); Lucielle Browning (Mercedes); Feb. 7 Nadine Conner (Micaela); Lucielle Browning (Mercedes); Wilfred Pelletier (Cond). (MO-Texaco Broadcast); Apr. 1 Kurt Baum (Don José); Nadine Conner (Micaela); Wilfred Pelletier (Cond). (MO-Atlanta, Georgia); Apr. 13 Nadine Conner (Micaela); John Baker (Morales); Wilfred Pelletier (Cond). (MO-Los Angeles, California); Apr. 27 Lorenzo Alvary (Zuniga); John Baker (Morales); Lucielle Browning (Mercedes); Wilfred Pelletier (Cond). (MO-Denver, Colorado); May 15 Eleanor Steber (Micaela); Robert Merrill (Escamillo); Thelma Altman (Mercedes); Wilfred Pelletier (Cond). (MO-Cleveland, Ohio)
Radio	23 Nov. *The family hour* ("Jealousy", "Touch of your hand", Brahms, "Lullaby", "Thanks be to thee").
30 Nov. 4, 15 Dec., 16, 29 Apr., 3, 6, 17 May	Radio, *The family hour* ("None but the lonely", "L'amour toujour l'amour", "Night and day"). *Der Rosenkavalier*: (Octavian); Irene Jessner (Marschallin); Emanuel list (Baron Ochs); Apr. 16 Nadine Conner (Sophie); Hugh Thompson (Faninal); Alessio de Paolis (Valzacchi); Fritz Busch (Cond). (MO-Los Angeles, California); Apr. 29 Nadine Conner (Sophie); Hugh Thompson (Faninal); Martha Lipton (Annina). (MO-St.Louis, Missouri); May 3 Nadine Conner (Sophie); Hugh Thompson (Faninal); Martha Lipton (Annina). (MO-Bloomington, Indiana; May 6 Nadine Conner (Sophie); Hugh Thompson (Faninal); Martha Lipton (Annina). (MO-Minneapolis, Minnesota); May 17 Nadine Conner (Sophie); Hugh Thompson (Faninal); Martha Lipton (Annina); Fritz Busch (Cond). (MO-Rochester, N.Y)
15 Mar.	Eleanor Steber (Sophie); Frederick Lechner (Faninal); John Garris (Valzacchi); Herta Glaz (Annina); Kurt Baum (Singer); Max Rudolf (Cond). (MO); Dec. 15 Erna Schlüter (Marschallin); Mar. 15 Deszö Ernster (Baron Ochs); Hugh Thompson (Faninal); John Garris (Valzacchi); Martha Lipton (Annina); Fritz Busch (Cond). (MO-Boston, Massachusetts).
7 Dec.	Radio, *The family hour* ("My heart at thy sweet voice", "When day is done", "Speak

	low").
Recitals	9 Dec. Bluefield, West Virginia; 11 Wincester, Virginia
14 Dec.	Radio, *The family hour* ("Zigeuner", "Eventide", "All the things you are").
18 Dec.,	*La Gioconda*: (Laura); Danitza Ilitsch (Gioconda); Richard Tucker (Enzo); Leonard; Jan. 26
26 Jan., 3 Feb.	Frank Valentino (Barnaba); Nicola Moscona (Alvise); Feb 3 Frank Valentino (Barnaba); Nicola Moscona (Alvise). (MO-Philadelphia, Pennsylvania)
17 Jan.	Warren (Barnaba); Giacomo Vaghi (Alvise); Margaret Harshaw (La Cieca); Emil Cooper (Cond). (MO); Jan. 17 Frank Valentino (Barnaba).
21 Dec.	Radio, *The family hour* (Schubert's, "Ave Maria", *Hänsel und Gretel*, "Prayer" (English), "White Christmas").
26 Dec.	*Hänsel und Gretel*: (Hänsel); Nadine Conner (Gretel); Claramae Turner (Gertrude); John Brownlee (Peter); Thelma Votipka (Witch); Max Rudolf (Cond). Performed in English Followed by *A mid-summer night's dream*). (MO)
27 Dec.	Appeared on the intermission feature, "Opera News on the Air", with Boris Goldovsky and John Brownlee during the Metropolitan Opera broadcast of *Il Trovatore*.
Radio	Dec. 29 *The family hour* ("Poinciana", "Thru' the years", "Over the rainbow"); Jan. 4 *The family hour* ("Best things in life are free", "Here is my heart", "Adieu, forêts", "Night was made for love"); 11 *The family hour* ("Amour, amour", "Wild Irish rose", "Only a rose").
18 Jan.	Radio, *The family hour* ("How deep is the ocean", "Because", "So near so far", "Almost like being in love").
25 Jan.	Radio, *The family hour* ("Orchids in the moonlight", "Deep river", "Sympathy", "My hero").
30 Jan.	Franklin Delano Roosevelt Birthday Memorial Concert, Ezio Pinza, Larry Adler, Paul Draper, Yehudi Menuhin, Dorothy McGuire, Hugh Ross and the Schola Cantorum, Brooks Smith, acc., Waldorf-Astoria Hotel, New York ("Widmung", "Habañera", "Seguidilla", "Chanson Bohême").
1 Feb.	Radio, *The family hour* ("Midnight in Paris", "Ouvre ton coeur", "Sweethearts", "My life I love thee").
8 Feb.	Radio, *The family hour* ("What'll I do", "Homing", "I got you under my skin").
11 Feb.	Recital, Lexington, Kentucky.
15 Feb.	Radio, *The family hour* ("Will you remember", "I love you truly", "Our love").
21 Feb.	Recital, Washington Dinner, Southern Hotel, Baltimore, Maryland.
Radio	22 Feb. *The family hour* ("Golden Earings", "Strange music", "Oh promise me", "Black magic"); 29 *The family hour* ("Spanish song", "Deep in my heart", "Ave Maria", sung to "Intermezzo" from *Cavalleria rusticana*, "Someday").
5 March	Recital, Martial Singher, Horace Mann School, New York("Lieder", "Habañera", "Seguidilla", three duets with Singher, "Strange music", "One alone", "My Hero").
7 March	Radio, *The family hour* ("Song is you", "Temptation", "Banjo song", "Blue Danube waltz").
9 March	Concert, Benefit for Italian War Orphans, Licia Albanese, Stella Roman, Kurt Baum, Robert Merrill, Salvatore Baccaloni, Washington, D.C. ("O mio Fernando", "Habañera", "Seguidilla").
10 March	Prudential Business Conference, Newark, New Jersey ("Homing", "Through the years", "Strange music").
14 March	Radio, *The family hour* ("Smoke gets in your eyes", "Irish Lullaby", with Jack Berch, "Seguidilla", Irish medley)..
Radio	21 March *The family hour* ("Stars in my eyes", "Smilin' through", "Without a song", "The palms"); 28 *The family hour* ("Agnus Dei", "Easter parade", "Holy city", *Cavalleria rusticana*, "Regina celli", with Chorus).
30 March	Recital, Fort Benning, Georgia.
April 4	Radio, *The family hour* ("April showers", "April in Paris", "Songs my mother taught me", Schubert's "Serenade", "Springtime").
7 April	Concert, Baltimore, Maryland.
11 April	Radio, *The family hour* (Drigo's "Serenade", "Now is the hour", "Chanson Bohême", "Falling in love with love").

25 April	Radio, *The family hour* ("Come boys", "Because", "O mio Fernando", "Just we two", with Leonard Stokes).
2 May	Radio, *The family hour* ("'Neath a southern moon", "Oh what a beautiful morning", "Going home", "Begin the beguine").
9 May	Radio, *The family hour* ("Mighty like a rose", "Granada", "Will you remember", "Haunted house").
16 May	Radio, *The family hour* ("Yesterday", "Because", *Der Rosenkavalier* Waltzes adapted for voice, "Love of life").
19 May	Recital, College Park, Maryland.
Radio	23 May *The family hour* ("Lover", "Old refrain", "Vissi d'arte", *Say it with music* medley); 30 May *The family hour* ("I wonder as I wander", "You are my song of love", "Song of songs", "Habañera").
Concerts	11 June Dr. Delbert Johnson, Cond., Krug Park, St. Joseph, Missouri ("Habañera", "Strange music", "I'm falling in love", "My hero"); 18 Dimitri Mitropoulos, Cond., Robin Hood Dell Orchestra, Philadelphia, Penn. ("Strange music", "Seguidilla"); 21, 22 June Atlantic City, New Jersey.
27, 29 June	*Der Rosenkavalier.* (Octavian); Irene Jessner (Marschallin); Emanuel List (Baron Ochs); Mary Henderson (Sophie); Osie Hawkins (Faninal); Karl Laufkötter (Valzacchi); Thelma Altman (Annina); William Horne (Singer); Max Rudolf (Cond). (CZO)
28 June	Atlantic City, First Long Playing record shown, Goddard Lieberson, Howard Scott (Columbia Technical Department).
2 July	*Carmen*: (Carmen); Charles Kullman (Don José); Frances Yeend (Micaela); Walter Cassel (Escamillo); Carlo Tomanelli (Zuniga); Wilfred Engelman (Morales, Dancaïro); Francesco Curci (Remendado); Thelma Votipka (Frasquita); Thelma Altman (Mercedes); Fausto Cleva (Cond). One hour broadcast over WLW and WLWA. (CZO)
6 July	Concert, Music Under the Stars, Jerzy Bojanowski, Cond., Milwaukee, Wisconsin ("Che farò", "Adieu, forêts", "El amor Brujo", "Homing", "One night of love", "Strange music").
9 July	Recital, Omaha, Nebraska.
16 July	Concert, Buffalo, N.Y.

(In addition to the recitals listed above, RS also appeared through Community Concerts in Winchester, Virginia)

1948-1949

Recital Program: Handel, *Semele*, "Where'er you walk"; Massenet, *Herodiade*, "Il est doux, il est bon"; Boatner, arr., "Oh, what a beautiful city"; Burleigh, arr., "Were you there"; Johnson, arr., "My good Lord done been here"; Schumann, "Widmung"; R. Strauss, "Traum durch die Dämmerung"; Brahms, "Meine liebe ist grün"; Wolf, "Das verlassene Mägdlein" and "Mausfallensprüchlein"; Rachmaninoff, "To the children"; Brooks Smith, "An ocean idyl"; Britten, arr., "The ash grove"; St. Leger, "April"; Bizet, *Carmen*, "Habañera", "Seguidilla", "Chanson Bohème". Brooks Smith, Accompanist.

3 Oct.	Radio, *Carnegie Hall*, ABC.
Recitals	4 Oct. West Chester, Pennsylvania; 6 Clemson, S. Carolina; 8 Richmond, Virginia; 12 Appleton, Wisconsin; 14 Duluth, Minnesota.
18 Oct.	Radio, *Railroad hour*, "The cat and the fiddle", Gordon MacRae, host, Fortunio Bonanova, Adolf Menjou, Norman Luboff Choir ("She didn't say 'yes'", "Try to forget", "One moment alone", with MacRae, "Night was made for love", "Poor Pierrot", Finale).
20 Oct.	Radio. Hammond, Indiana; 22 South Bend, Indiana; 26 Academy of Music, Brooklyn, New York; 30 Tulsa, Oklahoma; 1 Norman, Oklahoma.
8 Nov.	Radio, *Voice of Firestone*, Howard Barlow, Cond ("It's a lovely day tomorrow", "Estrellita", "I dream of you", "My heart at thy sweet voice").
Recitals	16 Nov. Gastonis, N. Carolina; 19 Tallahasee, Florida; 22 Alexandria, Virginia.
Concerts	27 Nov. Max Reiter, Cond., San Antonio Symphony, San Antonio, Texas ("El amor Brujo", "Adieu, forêts", "Widmung", "Daemmerung", "Meine liebe ist grun"; encores: "Ouvre to coeur", "Strange music"); Nov. 30, Dec. 2 Victor Alessandro, Cond., Oklahoma Symphony, Oklahoma City, Oklahoma ("Il est doux" for "El amor Brujo", otherwise same as 27 Nov).

4, 8, 23 Dec.,   *Mignon*: (Mignon); James Melton (Wilhelm Meister); Marilyn Cotlow (Philine); Nicola
17 Jan.,   Moscona (Lothario); John Garris (Laërte); Jean Madeira (Frédéric); Wilfred Pelletier
26 Mar.,   (Cond). (MO-Texaco Broadcast); Dec 8 Jerome Hines (Lothario); Dec. 23 Giuseppe di
19, 23 Apr.,   Stefano (Wilhelm Meister); Patrice Munsel (Philine); Nicola Moscona (Lothario); Alessio
4, 10, 13 May de Paolis (Laërte); Jean Madeira (Frédéric); Jan. 4 Patrice Munsel (Philine); Jerome Hines
  (Lothario). (MO-Philadelphia); Jan 17 Jerome Hines (Lothario).; Mar.26 Giuseppe di
  Stefano (Wilhelm Meister); Mimi Benzell (Philine); Jerome Hines (Lothario). (MO-
  Boston, Massachusetts); Apr. 5 Giuseppe di Stefano (Wilhelm Meister); Patrice Munsel
  (Philine); Jerome Hines (Lothario). (MO-Cleveland, Ohio); Apr. 19 Giuseppe di Stefano
  Wilhelm Meister); Patrice Munsel (Philine); Jerome Hines (Lothario). (MO-Atlanta,
  Georgia); Apr. 23 Giuseppe di Stefano (Wilhelm Meister); Patrice Munsel (Philine);
  Jerome Hines (Lothario); Leslie Chabay (Laërte). (MO-Dallas, Texas); May 4 Jerome
  Hines (Lothario); Leslie Chabay (Laërte). (MO-Los Angeles, California; May 10
  Giuseppe di Stefano (Wilhelm Meister); Jerome Hines (Lothario); Alessio de Paolis
  (Laërte). (MO-Denver, Colorado); May 13 Jerome Hines (Lothario); Alessio de Paolis
  (Laërte). (MO-Minneapolis, Minnesota)
9 Dec.   Radio, USA theater
14 Dec.,   *Carmen*: (Carmen); Ramon Vinay (Don José); Licia Albanese (Micaela); Frank Guarrera
1, 20 Jan.,   (Escamillo); Lorenzo Alvary (Zuniga); John Baker (Morales); Thelma Votipka
2, 18 Feb.,   (Frasquita); Lucielle Browning (Mercedes); Alessio dePaolis (Remendado); George
5, 30 Mar.,   Cehanovsky (Dancaïro); Wilfred Pelletier (Cond). (MO); Jan 1 Paula Lenchner
29 Apr.,   (Micaela); Anne Bollinger (Frasquita); Jan 20 Kurt Baum (Don José); Nadine Conner
7, 17, 20 May (Micaela); Clifford Harvuot (Morales); Feb. 2 Charles Kullman (Don José); Eleanor
  Steber (Micaela); Robert Merrill (Escamillo); Clifford Harvuot (Morales); Anne Bollinger
  (Frasquita); Feb. 18 Kurt Baum (Don José); Florence Quartararo (Micaela); Robert
  Merrill (Escamillo); Philip Kinsman (Zuniga); Anne Bollinger (Frasquita); Martha Lipton
  (Mercedes); Mar 5 Kurt Baum (Don José); Nadine Conner (Micaela); Clifford Harvuot
  (Morales); Martha Lipton (Mercedes). (MO-Texaco Broadcast); Mar. 30 Anne Bollinger
  (Micaela); Robert Merrill (Escamillo); Philip Kinsman (Zuniga); Martha Lipton
  (Mercedes). (MO-Boston, Massachusetts); Apr. 29 Florence Quartararo (Micaela);
  Clifford Harvuot (Morales). (MO-Los Angeles, California); May 7 Kurt Baum (Don
  José). (MO-Los Angeles, California); May 17 Anne Bollinger (Micaela); Clifford Harvuot
  (Morales); Jean Madeira (Mercedes). MO-Bloomington, Indiana); May 20 Florence
  Quartararo (Micaela); Clifford Harvuot (Morales); Martha Lipton Mercedes). (MO-St.
  Louis, Missouri)
9 Jan.   Concert, Victor Alessandro, Oklahoma City, Oklahoma.
Recitals   11 Jan. Sheffield, Alabama; 13 Jan. Hattiesburg, Mississippi.
16 Jan.   Radio, Carnegie Hall, ABC.
Recitals   25 Jan. Syracuse, New York; 28 Lowell, Massachusetts.
4 Feb.   Concert, Haddonfield, New Jersey.
7 Feb.   Radio, *Voice of Firestone* ("When you're in love", "Don't ever leave me", Bach-Gounod,
  "Ave Maria", "Seguidilla", "Chanson Bohème").
19 Feb.   Radio, Intermission, *Aida*, fund raiser with Kirstin Thorborg, Louis d'Angelo, John
  Brownlee, Regina Resnik, Nicola Moscona. (MO-Texaco Broadcast)
Concerts   21 Feb.Greenville, N. Carolina; 23 Charleston, South Carolina.
Recitals   1 March Urbana, Illinois; 3 Oxford, Ohio.
Recitals   7 March Sioux City, Iowa; 10 Minneapolis, Minnesota.
13 March   Concert, Max Leon, Cond., Philadelphia Pops, Academy of Music, Philadelphia,
  Pennsylvania ("Mon coeur", "Habañera", "Homing", "Strange music", "My hero";
  encore: "Seguidilla").
14, 22 March *Le nozze di Figaro*, (Cherubino); John Brownlee (Figaro); Bidú Sayão (Susanna); Frank
  Valentino (Count); Polyna Stoska (Countess); Salvatore Baccaloni (Don Bartolo);
  Herta Glaz (Marcellina); Alessio de Paolis (Don Basilio); Leslie Chabay (Don Curzio);
  Mimi Benzell (Barbarina); Fritz Busch (Cond). (MO); Mar. 22 Italo Tajo (Figaro);

	Eleanor Steber (Countess); Anne Bollinger (Barbarina); Fritz Reiner (Cond). (MO-Baltimore, Maryland)
19 March	Appeared on, "Opera News on the air", intermission feature of the Metropolitan Opera broadcast of *Rigoletto* with Boris Goldovsky and Clifton Fadiman.
20 March	TV, Maxwell House Coffee Presents, "Lambs gambol", NBC, 8-8:30 p.m. w. William Gaxton, Bert Wheeler, Guy Kibbee ("Habañera").
8 April	Concert, Baltimore, Maryland.
17 April	Radio, *Carnegie Hall*, ABC ("Agnus Dei", Bach-Gounod, "Ave Maria", "The Lord's prayer", "Onward Christian soldiers").
30, May	*Der Rosenkavalier:* (Octavian); Hilde Konetzni (Marschallin); Emanuel List (Baron
3, 6 June	Ochs); Julia Moore (Sophie); Marko Rothmueller (Faninal); Hans Georg Hartig (Valzacchi); Dagmar Hermann (Annina); Rafaël Romagnoni (Singer); Louis Fourestier, (Cond). (PO)

(In addition to the recitals listed above RS also appeared through Community Concerts in Hammond, Indiana).

1949-1950

Recital	Program, same as 1948-1949
7, 9 Sept.	*Der Rosenkavalier:* (Octavian); Marie Reining (Marschallin); Emanuel List (Baron Ochs); Lisa della Casa (Sophie); Karl Kamann (Faninal); Hans Georg Hartig (Valzacchi); Dagmar Hermann (Annina); Raphaël Romagnoni (Singer); Louis Fourestier, (Cond). (PO)
25 Sept.	Radio, *Harvest of stars*, James Melton ("Habañera", *Chocolate soldier* excerpts).
27 Sept	Recital, Sherbrooke, Quebec.
4 Oct.	Radio, *Carnegie Hall*, ABC ("Seguidilla", "None but the lonely heart", "I'll follow my secret heart", "Vissi d'arte").
Recitals	6 Oct. Pittsfield, Massachusetts; Richmond, Virginia.
10 Oct.	Radio, *Voice of Firestone* ("The night was made for love", "Until", "I dream of you", "Ouvre ton coeur").
Recitals	11 Oct. Amherst, Massachusetts; 13 Milwaukee, Wisconsin; 15, 16 Madison, Wisconsin; 18 Fargo, North Dakota; 20 Oct. Grand Forks, North Dakota; 24 Salisbury, North Carolina; 26 Paterson, New Jersey; 29 Kenoska, Wisconsin; 31 Danville, Illinois; 3 Nov. Wilmette, Illinois; 5 Witchita, Kansas; 8 Kansas City, Missouri.
6 Nov.	Radio, *Omnibus of music*. Presented by U. S. Army recruiting. RS spoke about music favorites w. illustrations ("Seguidilla" Columbia recording, "Because", "Say it with music"). Thank you!!!
21 Nov.,	*Der Rosenkavalier:* (Octavian); Eleanor Steber (Marschallin); Emanuel List (Baron Ochs);
3, 14 Dec.,	Erna Berger (Sophie); Hugh Thompson (Faninal); Peter Klein (Valzacchi); Martha Lipton
1 Apr.	(Annina); Giuseppe di Stefano (Singer); Fritz Reiner (Cond). (MO-Opening Night Telecast); Dec. 14 Herta Glaz (Annina); Apr. 1 Nadine Conner (Sophie); Alessio de Paolis (Valzacchi); Kurt Baum (Singer). (MO-Boston, Massachusetts)
26, 30 Nov.,	*Samson et Dalila:* (Dalila); Ramon Vinay (Samson); Robert Merrill (High Priest); Ossie
8, 27 Jan.,	Hawkins (Abimélech); Deszö Ernster (Old Hebrew); Emil Cooper (Cond). MO-Texaco
10, 18,	Broadcast) The third intermission featured a broadcast back stage visit of Edward
22, 30 Apr.	Johnson by RS, Merrill and Vinay; Jan. 8 Brian Sullivan (Samson); Lorenzo Alvary (Abimélech); Jerome Hines (Old Hebrew); Jan. 27 Kurt Baum (Samson); Nicola Moscona (Old Hebrew); Apr. 10 Jerome Hines (Old Hebrew). (MO-Cleveland, Ohio), Apr. 22 Kurt Baum (Samson). (MO-St.Louis, Missouri)
28 Nov.	Radio, *Voice of Firestone* ("Strange music", "How deep is the ocean", "Homing", "O mio Fernando").
8, 19 Dec.,	*Carmen:* (Carmen); Charles Kullman (Don José); Nadine Conner (Micaela); Martial
4 Feb., 15 Apr.,	Singher (Escamillo); De Paolis Alvary (Zuniga); Clifford Harvuot (Morales); Thelma
3, 7, 9 May	Votipka (Frasquita); Martha Lipton (Mercedes); Alessio de Paolis (Remendado); George Cehanovsky (Dancaïro); Jonel Perlea (Cond). (MO); Feb. 4 Kurt Baum (Don José); Frank Guarrera (Escamillo); Philip Kinsman (Zuniga); Lucielle Browning (Mercedes). (MO-Texaco Broadcast); Apr. 15 Frank Guarrera (Escamillo); John Baker (Morales); Inge Manski (Frasquita); Lucielle Browning (Mercedes). (MO-Cleveland, Ohio) May 3

Ramon Vinay (Don José); Robert Merrill (Escamillo); Philip Kinsman (Zuniga); Anne Bollinger (Frasquita); Jean Madeira (Mercedes). MO-Oklahoma City, Oklahoma); May 7 Ramon Vinay (Don José); Robert Merrill (Escamillo); Anne Bollinger (Frasquita); Jean Madeira (Mercedes). (MO-Minneapolis, Minnesota); May 9 Ramon Vinay (Don José); Robert Merrill (Escamillo); Anne Bollinger (Frasquita); Jean Madeira (Mercedes). (MO-Chicago, Illinois)

12 Dec.	Recital, Ann Arbor, Michigan.
18 Dec.	TV, *This is show business*, Clifton Fadiman, Abe Burrows, George S. Kaufman, Gloria Swanson.
23 Dec.	Recital, Quebec, Canada.
10 Jan.	Radio, *Carnegie Hall*, ABC ("Ouvre ton coeur", "I'll see you again", "Widmung", "Il est doux").
Recitals	11 Jan. Reading, Pennsylvania; 16 Pueblo, Colorado, Jan Popper, acc; 18 Salt Lake City, Utah, Jan Popper, acc; 23 San Francisco, California, War Memorial Opera House, Jan Popper, acc. (Wolf, "Kennst du das Land", in place of the three spirituals).
30 Jan.	Radio, TV, *Voice of Firestone*, NBC ("They say falling in love is wonderful", "A dream", "One night of love", "Seguidilla").
16, 25 Feb.	*Khovanshchina*: (Marfa); Lawrence Tibbett (Ivan); Brian Sullivan (Andrey); Jerome Hines (Dosifey); Charles Kullman (Golitsyn); Robert Weede (Shaklovity); Anne Bollinger (Emma); Polyna Stoska (Susanna); Emil Cooper (Cond). (MO-Premiere)
21 Feb.	Radio, *Carnegie Hall*, Dr. Frank Black, Cond., ABC ("Vilia", "Songs my mother taught me", "Habañera", "Vissi d'arte").
Recitals	27 Feb. Denver, Colorado; 4 March Hollywood, California; 7 Palm Springs, California; 11 Fort Worth, Texas; 21 New Castle, Pennsylvania; 23 Youngstown, Ohio; 26 Fitchburg, Massachusetts; 28 Sumter, South Carolina.
4 April	Concert, Raymond A. Schoewe, Cond., Huntington Symphony, Huntington, West Virginia ("Mon coeur", "Habañera", "Agnus Dei", "Songs my mother taught me", "Stars in my eyes").
11 April	Recital, Buffalo, New York.
25, 26 April	Recital, Columbia, Missouri.
4 June	Damon Runyon Cancer Fund Benefit, Vivian Blaine, Jack Benny, Rochester, Phil Harris, Frank Sinatra, Fred Allen, Milton Berle, Danny Kaye, Carnegie Hall, New York ("Habañera", "One night of love"; encore: "I'm falling in love with someone").
26 June	Concert, William Steinberg, Cond., Robin Hood Dell Orchestra, Philadelphia, Pennsylvania ("Habañera", "Seguidilla", "Chanson Bohème", "Adieu, forêts", "Moncoeur"; encores: "I'm falling in love with someone", "Stars in my eyes", "One night of love").
2 July	Radio, United States Steel Summer Concerts, Milton Katims, Cond., NBC Symphony ("I wonder as I wander", "Lover", "Deep river", "Younger than springtime").
25 July	Concert, "Music under the stars", Jerzy Bojanowski, Cond., Milwaukee, Wisconsin ("Il est doux", "Ouvre ton coeur", "At dawning", "Because", "Through the years", "The song of songs").
7 August	Radio, TV, *Voice of Firestone* ("People will say we're in love", "Voi che sapete", "It might as well be spring", "A kiss in the dark").
19 August	Recital, Chicago, Illinois.

(In addition to the above RS also presented a recital through Community Concerts in Wauwatosa, Wisconsin)

1950-1951

Recital Program: Handel, *Semele*, "Where'er you walk"; Bizet, "Agnus Dei"; Schumann, "Widmung"; R. Strauss, "Traum durch die Dämmerung"; Brahms, "Meine Liebe ist grün"; Wolf, "Das verlassene Mägdlein" and "Mausfallensprüchlein"; Puccini, *Tosca*, "Vissi d'arte"; Brooks Smith, "An ocean idyl"; Britten, arr., "The ash grove"; St. Leger, "April"; Dougherty, "Declaration of Independence"; Bizet, *Carmen*, "Habañera", "Seguidilla", "Chanson Bohème"). Brooks Smith, Accompanist.

17 Sept.	TV, *This is show business*, RS appeared on the panel w. regulars Clifton Fadiman, Abe Burrows and George S. Kaufman. Guests included Billy Daniels, Sheilah Bond and Jan Murray.

24 Sept.	TV, *Colgate comedy hour*, w. Fred Allen, Monty Wooley and Sono Osato, WNBC, 8 p.m.
27 Sept.	TV, *What's my line*, Hal Block, Arlene Francis, Dorothy Kilgallen, Louis Untermeyer and John Daly.
2 Oct.	Radio, TV, Voice of Firestone ("La vie en rose", "My heart at thy sweet voice", "Two hearts in 3/4 time").
4 Oct.	*Carmen*: (Carmen); Raoul Jobin (Don José); Nadja Wilkowska (Micaela); Frank Guarrera (Escamillo); Wilfred Pelletier, Cond., Philadelphia La Scala Opera Company, Detroit, Michigan.
Recitals	6 Oct. Jackson, Michigan; 9 Pittsburgh, Kansas; 11 Topeka, Kansas; 13 Albuquerque. New Mexico; 16 Lubbock, Texas; 18 Kilgore, Texas.
20 Oct.	Radio, Views of the news (interview).
21 Oct.	Concert, Henry Sopkin, Cond., Atlanta Symphony, Atlanta, Georgia ("Il est doux", "Mon coeur", "Air de Lia", Dedication, "Widmung"; encores: "Habañera", "Seguidilla", "I'm falling in love with someone").
Recitals	24 Oct. Knoxville, Tennessee; 26 Chapel Hill, N. Carolina ("Oh, what a beautiful city", "Were you there", "My good Lord done been here", in place of "Vissi d'arte").
29,30 Oct.	Concert, Modeste Alloo, Cond., Miami Symphony, Miami, Florida ("Habañera", "Seguidilla", "Card song"; encores: "Chanson Bohème", "Ouvre ton coeur", "I'm falling in love with someone").
Recitals	2 Nov. Gainsville, Florida; 9 Norristown, Pennsylvania; 14 Waverly, Iowa.
17 Nov.	Concert, Hermann Herz, Cond., Duluth Symphony, Duluth, Minnesota ("Agnus Dei", "Adieu, forêts", "Ouvre ton coeur", "Widmung", "O mio Fernando"; encores: "One night of love", "Seguidilla").
20 Nov.	Recital, Freemont, Nebraska.
27 Nov.	Concert, Simon Asen, Cond., Mt. Vernon Symphony, Mt. Vernon, New York ("Il est doux", "Mon coeur", "Habañera", "Seguidilla", "Chanson Bohème"; encores: "Strange music", "My hero").
Recitals	29 Nov. University, Mississippi; 1 Dec. Memphis, Tennessee.
16 Dec.	TV, Jack Carter Show ("Habañera", "La vie en rose").
20, 27,31 Dec., 13, 20 Jan.	*Fledermaus*: (Prince Orlofsky); Ljuba Welitsch (Rosalinde); Set Svanholm (Eisenstein); Patrice Munsel (Adele); Richard Tucker (Alfred); John Brownlee (Dr.Falke); Hugh Thompson (Frank); Jack Guilford (Frosch); Eugene Ormandy (Cond). (MO); Dec. 31 Charles Kullman (Eisenstein); Jan. 13 Eugene Conley (Alfred); Tibor Kozma (Cond). Jan 20 Marguerite Piazza (Rosalinde); Charles Kullman (Eisenstein). (MO-Texaco Broadcast)
28 Dec.	Fetes des Artistes Ball for Hospitalized Veterans, Eleanor Steber, Gladys Swarthout ("Minnie the Moocher").
5, 11 Jan.	*Der Rosenkavalier*: (Octavian); Helen Traubel (Marschallin); Fritz Krenn (Baron Ochs); Erna Berger (Sophie); John Brownlee (Faninal); Alessio de Paolis (Valzacchi); Herta Glaz (Annina); Kurt Baum (Singer); Fritz Reiner (Cond). (MO)
8 Jan.	Radio, TV, *Voice of Firestone.*
15 Jan.	*Fledermaus*, same as 20 Dec. except Charles Kullman (Eisenstein); Brian Sullivan (Alfred); Tibor Kozma (Cond).
Recitals	29, 30 Jan. Great Falls, Montana; 1 Feb. Moscow, Idaho; 4 Aberdeen, Washington; 6 Victoria, British Columbia; 8 Vancouver, British Columbia; 10 Portland, Oregon; 13 Minneapolis, Minnesota; 15 Milwaukee, Wisconsin; 17 Chicago, Illinois; 28 Trenton, New Jersey.
5 March	Radio *Voice of Firestone* ("Che farò"; "The night was made for love", "Love's rondelay").
11 March	Radio, Sid Fields at 2:30 p.m. (Interview); Ed Sullivan's, *Toast of the town*, ("Stars in my eyes", "Ouvre ton coeur")
Recitals	12 March Bangor, Maine; 14 Hamilton, Ontario w. Kurt Adler, acc.
19 March	Radio, *Bell telephone hour*, Donal Voorhees, Cond., Clifford Curzon, Claudio Arrau ("Chanson Bohème").
Recitals	28 March Columbia, South Carolina; 30 Macon, Georgia.

2 April	Radio, TV, *Voice of Firestone* ("Widmung", "It might as well be spring", "They say that falling in love is wonderful", "Chanson Bohème").
3 April	Recital, Bangor, Maine.
19, 21 April	*Carmen*: (Carmen); David Poleri (Don José); Audrey Schuh (Micaela); Randolph Symonette (Escamillo); Norman Treigle (Zuniga); Henri Feux (Morales, Dancaïro); Viletta Russell (Frasquita); Marietta Muhs (Mercedes); Charles (Anthony); Caruso (Remendado); Walter Herbert, Cond. New Orleans, Louisiana.
29 April	TV, *Showtime USA*.
2 May	Thirty-ninth Annual Dinner, Chamber of Commerce, Washington, D.C., Brooke Smith, acc.
4 May	Recital, Cleveland, Ohio.
5 May	Concert, Eugene Ormandy, Philadelphia Orchestra, Ann Arbor, Michigan ("Che farò", "Voi che sapete", "Il est doux", "Air de Lia", "Habañera", "Seguidilla"; encores: "Chanson Bohème", "Ouvre ton coeur").
Recitals	7, 8 May Omaha, Nebraska, 10, Lawrence, Kansas
14 May	Radio, TV, *Voice of Firestone* ("Songs my mother taught me", "Amour, viens aider", "Lover come back to me"),
24 May	Radio, Metropolitan Opera Jamboree, Jimmy Durante, Giuseppe Valdango, Lucine Amara, Brian Sullivan, Anne Bollinger. ABC. (re Metropolitan Opera Fund).
23 July	Radio, TV, *Voice of Firestone* ("People will say we're in love", "Seguidilla", "The sweeetest story ever told", "I'm falling in love with someone").
5 August	Radio, *U.S. Steel Summer Concerts*, Vladimir Bakalein, NBC Symphony ("Songs my mother taught me", "One night of love", "Adieu, forêts").

1951-1952

Recital Program: Handel, *The Messiah*, "He shall feed His flock"; Halsey Stevens, arr., "Early one morning"; Gluck, *Orfeo ed Euridice*, "Che farò senza Euridice"; Massenet, *Herodiade*, "Il est doux, il est bon"; Schubert, "Gretchen am Spinnrade" and "Wohin"; R. Strauss, "Heimkehr"; Brahms, "O liebliche Wangen"; Wolf, "Elfenlied"; Dougherty, "Loveliest of trees"; Hughes, arr., "A Ballynure ballad"; Bacon, arr., "The lonesome grove"; Bernstein. "The Indian"; Bizet, *Carmen*, "Habañera", "Seguidilla", "Chanson Bohème". Brooks Smith, Accompanist. Alternate program substituted "Oh, what a beautiful city"; "Were you there" and "My good Lord done been here", for the Halsey Stevens and the Gluck arias.

5 Sept.	Recital, American Chemical Society, Waldorf Astoria Hotel, New York, w. Brooks Smith, acc. ("Mon coeur", "Seguidilla", "Stars in my eyes", "I'm falling in love with someone").
1 Oct.	Radio, TV, *Voice of Firestone* ("Falling in love with love", *Carmen*, "Card scene", "L'amour toujours l'amour").
3 Oct.	Recital, Toledo, Ohio.
5 Oct.	Radio, *News show* with Dorothy Fuldheim, Cleveland, Ohio, 6.30 p.m. (discussion of *Carmen* album); Recital, 8:30 p.m.
Recitals	8 Oct. Savannah, Georgia; 10 Montgomery, Alabama; 13 Birmingham, Alabama; 16 College Station, Texas; 22 Jackson, Mississippi.
26 Oct.	Concert, Eugene Ormandy, Philadelpha Orchestra, Worcester, Massachusetts ("Che farò", "Voi che sapete", "Il est doux", "Air de Lia", "Amour viens aidé", "Seguidilla"; encore: "Mon coeur", "Habañera").
4 Nov.	Recital, Orchestra Hall, Chicago, Illinois.
11 Nov.	Concert, Henry John Brown, Cond., Tri-City Symphony, Davenport, Iowa ("Habañera", "Seguidilla", "Card scene", "Chanson Bohème").
Recitals	13 Nov. Chicago, Illinois; 17 Winnipeg, Canada; 19 Regina, Canada; 22 Saskatoon, Canada; 24, 26 Edmonton, Canada; 28 Calgary, Canada; 3 Dec. Seattle, Washington; 6 San Bernardino, California.
Carmen rehearsals:	31 Dec. Act 1, RS, Tucker, Hawkins, Harvuot, 2:30 p.m., MO-Guild Room; 2 Jan. Acts 2, 3 Reiner, RS, Vinay, Roggero, Amara, Guarrera, Cehanovsky, de Paolis, 11:30 a.m. MO-Guild Room; 3 RS French coaching w. Singher, 12:00 p.m., MO-Ladies Parlor, Guthrie, RS, Guthrie, Tucker (MO-Radio Room), 2:30 p.m.
7 Jan.	Radio, TV, *Voice of Firestone* ("The world is waiting for the sunrise", "Voi che sapete",

"You and the night and the music", "Two hearts in 3/4 time").

Carmen rehearsals: 9 Jan. RS, Tucker, Guarrera, Reiner, 11:30 a.m. MO-Guild Room, RS, Tucker, Guthrie, Pardoll, (Martin) Rich, 3:15 p.m. MO-Radio Room; 11 Act 1, RS, Tucker, Lenchner, Harvuot, Chorus, piano acc. MO-Stage 11:00-2:30 p.m.; 12 Guthrie, Rich, RS, Amara, Roggero, 4:00 p.m., MO-Roof Stage; 14 Act 2, RS, Tucker, Hawkins, Guarrera, Chorus, (Luncheon meeting at Rostoff's with the Press, RS and Guthrie, guests of honor), RS, Tucker, de Paolis, Cehanovsky, Amara, Roggero; 15 Act 4 w. piano, RS, Amara Roggero 10.p.m., MO-Stage; Tucker, Stevens, Guthrie, 1;30 p.m., (MO-Radio Room); 16 Act 3 RS, Tucker, Amara, Roggero, Franke, Cehanovsky, de Paolis, Conner, Guthrie, Adler, piano acc., 12:00 p.m. MO-Stage, RS, Tucker, Guarrera, Guthrie, 3:30 p.m. MO-Roof Stage; 17 Act 1, RS, Conner, Harvuot, Guthrie, Chorus, Baer, piano acc., 11:45 a.m., MO-Stage, RS, Hawkins, Guthrie, 4:30 p.m. MO-Roof Stage; 18 Act 4, Guthrie, Reiner, RS, Tucker, Guarrera, Amara, Roggero w. piano MO-Stage, 3:00 p.m. Guthrie, RS, De Paolis, Cehanovsky, Amara, Roggero, Tucker, Conner, Hawkins MO-Roof Stage; 19 11:15 Guthrie, Vinay, RS, Guarrera MO-Roof Stage; 21 10:30 a.m. Act 1 complete with Chorus, lights and partially costumed, piano acc. MO-Stage; 22 10:00 a.m. Act 2, 12:45 Guthrie w. RS, Amara, Roggero, dePaolis, Cehanowsky MO-Opera Club, 8:00 p.m. Guthrie with RS, Tucker MO-Roof Stage; 23 10:00 a.m. Acts 3, 4; 24 10:00 a.m. Acts 1, 2 with orchestra MO-Stage; 25 10:00 a.m. Act 3, 11:15 a.m. with orchestra MO-Stage; 26 6:00 p.m. Guthrie, Stevens MO-Roof Stage; 28 11:15 a.m. Acts 1, 2 Final Dress; 29 11:30 a.m. Acts 3,4 Final Dress.

On 12 January, RS was heard on an intermission feature, "Opera news on the air", with Boris Goldovsky during the Metropolitan Opera broadcast of *Cosi fan tutte.*

31 Jan., 7 12 16, 19 Feb., 1, 5, 17, 25, 28 Mar., 5, 17, 23, 29, Apr., 2, 7, 11, 15, 17, 21, 23, 28, 31 May	*Carmen*: (Carmen); Richard Tucker (Don José); Nadine Conner (Micaela); Frank Guarrera (Escamillo); Ossie Hawkins (Zuniga); Clifford Harvuot (Morales); Lucine Amara (Frasquita); Margaret Roggero (Mercedes); Alessio dePaolis (Remendado); George Cehanovsky (Dancaïro); Janet Collins, Loren Hightower (Dancers); Fritz Reiner (Cond). (MO-New Production); Feb. 12 Paolo Silveri (Escamillo). (MO-Philadelphia, Pennsylvania); Feb. 16 Paolo Silveri (Escamillo). (MO-Texaco Broadcast); Feb.19 Mario del Monaco (Don José); Paolo Silveri (Escamillo); Norman Sctt (Zuniga); Kurt Adler (Cond). Mar. 1 Ramon Vinay (Don José); Hilde Gueden (Micaela); Kurt Adler (Cond); Mar. 5 Ramon Vinay (Don José); Hilde Gueden (Micaela); Paula Lenchner (Frasquita); Kurt Adler (Cond); Mar. 17 Mario del Monaco (Don José); Paolo Silveri (Escamillo); Kurt Adler (Cond); Mar. 25 Mario del Monaco (Don José); Hilde Gueden (Micaela); Norman Scott (Zuniga); Paula Lenchner (Frasquita). (MO-Baltimore, Maryland); Mar. 28 Mario del Monaco (Don José); Hilde Gueden (Micaela); Paula Lenchner (Frasquita); Kurt Adler (Cond); Apr. 5 Mario del Monaco (Don José); Victoria de los Angeles (Micaela); Robert Merrill (Escamillo); Norman Scott (Zuniga); Paula Lenchner (Frasquita); Herta Glaz (Mercedes); Apr. 17 Robert Merrill (Escamillo). (MO-Cleveland, Ohio); Apr. 23 Hilde Gueden (Micaela); Herta Glaz (Frasquita). (MO-Boston, Massachusetts); Apr. 29 Hilde Gueden (Micaela); Robert Merrill (Escamillo); Herta Glaz (Mercedes). (MO-Washington, D.C.); May 2 Hilde Gueden (Micaela); Robert Merrill (Escamillo); Herta Glaz (Mercedes); Tilda Morse (Dancer). (MO-Atlanta, Georgia); May 7 Mario del Monaco (Don José); Herta Glaz Mercedes); Tilda Morse (Dancer). (MO-Memphis, Tennessee); May 11 Kurt Baum (Don José); Herta Glaz (Mercedes). (MO-Dallas, Texas); May 15 Kurt Baum (Don José); Herta Glaz (Mercedes); Tilda Morse (Dancer); Kurt Adler (Cond). (MO-Des Moines, Iowa); May 17 Ramon Vinay (Don José); Robert Merrill (Escamillo); Herta Glaz (Mercedes). (MO-Minneapolis, Minnesota); May 21 Ramon Vinay (Don José); Herta Glaz (Mercedes). (MO-Lafayette, Indiana); May 23 Ramon Vinay (Don José); Paula Lenchner (Frasquita); Herta Glaz (Mercedes). (MO-St. Louis, Missouri); May 28 Ramon Vinay (Don José); Robert Merrill (Escamillo); Herta Glaz (Mercedes). (MO-Toronto, Canada); May 31 Norman Scott (Zuniga); Herta Glaz (Mercedes). (MO-Montreal, Canada)
21 Feb.	Recital, Reading, Pennsylvania.
3 March	Radio, TV, *Voice of Firestone* ("I dream of you", "Il est doux", Brahms, "Lullaby", "Novillero").

| 7 March | Benefit for the National Music League, David Garvey, piano (Group of Lieder). |

7 March   Benefit for the National Music League, David Garvey, piano (Group of Lieder).

11 March   TV, *Texaco star theatre*, Milton Berle, Phil Reagan ("Ouvre ton coeur", "Irish Lullabye", "When Irish eyes are smiling", with Berle and Reagan).

13 March   Recital, Shamokin, Pennsylvania. Earlier in the day, she appeared on an intermission, "Opera news on the air", feature with Boris Goldovsky and Dr. Frank Columbo during the Metropolitan Opera broadcast of *La Bohème*.

Recitals   21 March Rochester, New York; 23 Youngstown, Ohio.

14 April   Radio, TV, *Voice of Firestone* ("Look for the silver lining", "Sweet and low", "O mio Fernando", "Siboney").

15 April   Annual Men's Club Award Dinner, Reform Congregation Keneseth Israel, David Sarnoff, awardee, RS guest artist, Philadelphia, Pennsylvania.

25 April   Recital, Hanover, New Hampshire.

23 June   Radio, TV, *Voice of Firestone* ("Lover", "Printemps qui commence", "To the children", "I give my heart").

3 July   Concert, André Kostelanetz, Cond., Robin Hood Dell, Philadelphia, Pennsylvania ("Voi che sapete", "Mon coeur", "Seguidilla", "Kiss me again", "All the things you are", "One night of love").

5 July   Concert, André Kostelanetz, Cond., Lewisohn Stadium, New York ("Voi che sapete", "Mon coeur", "Seguidilla", "Kiss me again", "All the things you are", "One night of love").

20 July   TV, Ed Sullivan's, *Toast of the town* ("Chanson Bohème", "One night of love").

18 Aug.   Radio, TV, *Voice of Firestone* ("Huguette Waltz", "In the still of the night", "Alice blue gown", "Chanson Bohème").

20 Aug.   Concert, Harry John Brown, Cond., Evansville, Indiana ("Habañera", "Seguidilla", "Chanson Bohème", "One night of love", "Stars in my eyes", "I'm falling in love with someone").

22 Aug.   Chicagoland Music Festival Luncheon, Guest of Honor, Chicago, Illinois.

23 Aug.   Concert, Chicagoland Music Festival, Soldiers Field, Guest of Honor, vocal competition, Chicago, Illinois.

1952-1953

Recital Program, same as alternate program for 1951-1952.

27 Sept.   TV, *All star review*, Martha Raye, Rocky Graziano, Caesar Romero.

Recitals   1 Oct. San Diego, California; 3, Ventura, California; 6   San José; 8 University of Arizona. (all accompanied by Norman Johnson).

13 Oct.   Radio, TV, *Voice of Firestone* ("People will say we're in love", "Habanara", "Widmung", "Vienna, city of my dreams").

Recitals   15 Oct. Detroit, Michigan (acc. by Norman Johnson); 17 Ann Arbor, Michigan; 20 Lansing, Michigan; 23 Denver, Colorado; 25 Santa Fé, New Mexico; 27 Colorado Springs, Colorado; 29 Casper, Wyoming. 2, 3 Nov. Concert, James P. Robertson, Cond, Wichita Symphony, Wichita, Kansas ("Che farò", "Voi che sapete", "Il est doux", "Habañera", "Seguidilla", "Chanson Bohème").

Recitals   5 Nov. Dodge City, Kansas; 7 Kansas City, Missouri.

10 Nov.   Concert, H. Arthur Brown, Tulsa Philharmonic Orchestra, Tulsa, Oklahoma ("Che farò", "Voi che sapete", "Il est doux", Ravel, "Alborado del Gracioso", "Air de Lia", "Habañera", "Seguidilla").

19, 29 Nov.,   *Carmen*: (Carmen); Mario del Monaco (Don José); Nadine Conner (Micaela); Frank
11, 15, 30, Dec., Guarrera (Escamillo); Osie Hawkins (Zuniga); Clifford Harvuot (Morales); Lucine Amara
11, 15, 22 Apr., (Frasquita); Margaret Roggero (Mercedes); Alessio de Paolis (Remendado); George
4, 11, 26 May   Cehanovsky (Dancaïro); Janet Collins, Loren Hightower (Dancers); Fritz Reiner (Cond). (MO); Dec. 11 Richard Tucker (Don José); Robert Merrill (Escamillo). (MO-Televised via closed circuit); Dec. 15 Kurt Baum, Act 1/Brian Sullivan (Don José); Lucine Amara (Micaela); Norman Scott (Zuniga); Paula Lenchner (Frasquita); Kurt Adler (Cond); Dec 30 Victoria de los Angeles (Micaela), Norman Scott (Zuniga); Kurt Adler (Cond); Apr. 11 Ramon Vinay (Don José); George London (Escamillo); Paula Lenchner (Frasquita); Apr. 15 Hilde Gueden (Micaela); Robert Merrill (Escamillo). (MO-Cleveland, Ohio); Apr. 22

	Norman Scott (Zuniga). (MO-Boston, Massachusetts); May 4 Richard Tucker (Don José); Hilde Gueden (Mocaela); George London (Escamillo); Tilda Morse (Dancer). (MO-Birmingham, Alabama); May 11 Hilde Gueden (Micaela); Robert Merrill (Escamillo); Tilde Morse (Dancer). (MO-Houston, Texas); May 26 Ramon Vinay (Don José). (MO-Toronto, Canada)
1 Dec.	Radio, Community Concerts Twenty-fifth Anniversary, Frederick Shang, jr., Arthur Judson, Hosts, with Richard Crooks, Nadine Conner, Charles Kullman, James Melton, Igor Gorin, Cesare Siepi, Dimitri Mitropoulos, ("Sextet", *Lucia*, RS, Conner, Kullman, Melton, Gorin, Siepi, Mitropoulos, piano; Quartet by Gerald Devlin, RS, Conner, Melton, Gorin, Sascha Gorodnitzki, piano) Other guests, Arthur Whittemore and Jack Lowe, Alec Templeton. (Municipal Broadcasting Co.)
6 Dec.	Radio, *Great moments from opera*, Milk Fund Broadcast with Leonard Warren, Giacinto Prandelli (Brahms, "Lullaby") (NBC); *Carmen*, same as Nov. 19 except Kurt Baum (Don José); Lucine Amara (Micaela); Paula Lenchner (Frasquita); Kurt Adler (Cond).
21 Dec.	TV, *Colgate comedy hour*, Ray Bolger ("Chanson Bohème", "Dearie, do you remember?" with Bolger, followed by dance routine).
5 Jan.	Radio, TV, *Voice of Firestone* ("At dawning", "Vissi d'arte", "Trees", "Love has wings).
Recitals	8 Jan. Atlanta, Georgia; 10 Orlando, Florida.
22, 26 Jan.,	*Der Rosenkavalier*: (Octavian); Astrid Varnay (Marschallin); Endre Koreh (Baron Ochs);
28 Feb.,	Nadine Conner (Sophie); Erich Kunz (Faninal); Alessio de Paolis (Valzacchi); Martha
12 Mar.,	Lipton (Annina); Kurt Baum (Singer); Fritz Reiner (Cond); Jan 26 Lorenzo Alvary
18 Apr, 9,	(Baron Ochs); Roberta Peters (Sophie); Feb. 28 John Brownlee (Faninal); Herta Glaz
15 May	(Annina); Thomas Hayward (Singer). (MO-Texaco Broadcast); Mar. 12 Hilde Gueden (Sophie); John Brownlee (Faninal); Herta Glaz (Annina); Giulio Gari (Singer); Apr. 18 Lorenzo Alvary (Baron Ochs); Hilde Gueden (Sophie); John Brownlee (Faninal).; May 9 Lorenzo Alvary (Baron Ochs); Hilde Gueden (Sophie); John Brownlee (Faninal); Max Rudolf (Cond). (MO-Dallas, Texas; May 15 Lorenzo Alvary (Baron Ochs); Hilde Gueden (Sophie); John Brownlee (Faninal); Giulio Gari (Singer); Max Rudolf (Cond). (MO-Minneapolis, Minnesota)
31 Jan.	Radio, *Music through the night* (spoken tribute on first anniversary of show) (NBC)
Recitals	2 Feb. Rock Hill, South Carolina; 5 Goshen, Indiana; 9 Vermillion, South Dakota; 12 East Lansing, Michigan.
15, 17 Feb.	Concert, Josef Krips (Cond), Buffalo Philharmonic Orchestra, Buffalo, New York ("Non so piu", "Voi che sapete", "Che farò"; encore: "Card song").
19 Feb.	Recital, Syracuse, New York.
3, 14, 30 Mar.,	*Samson et Dalila*: (Dalila); Ramon Vinay (Samson); Sigurd Björling (High Priest); Norman
29 Apr., 1, 6	Scott(Abimélech); Lubin Vichey (Old Hebrew); Fausto Cleva (Cond). (MO); Apr. 29 Kurt
23 May	Baum (Samson); Deszö Ernster (Old Hebrew). (MO-Washington,D.C.); May 1 Kurt Baum (Samson); Deszö Ernster (Old Hebrew). (MO-Atlanta-Georgia); May 6 Deszö Ernster (Old Hebrew). (MO-Memphis, Tennessee); May 23 Nicola Moscona (Old Hebrew). (MO-Montreal, Canada)
9 March	Recital, Atlantic City, New Jersey.
Recitals	16 March Bloomington, Indiana; 19 Kingsville, Texas.
21 March	Concert, Victor Alessandro, San Antonio Symphony, San Antonio, Texas ("Che farò", "Voi che sapete", "Il est doux", "Habañera", "Seguidilla", "Chanson Bohème").
23 March	Recital, Lafayette, Louisiana.
29 March	TV, Ed Sullivan's, *Toast of the town* (two Rodgers and Hammerstein songs).
5 April	Easter recital, General Motors sponsorship, Flint, Michigan ("Habañera", "Seguidilla", "Chanson Bohème", "One night of love", "I'm falling in love with someone", "Because"; encore: Handel, "Largo").
13 April	Radio, TV, *Voice of Firestone* ("Songs my mother taught me", "My heart at thy sweet voice", "Onward Christian soldiers", "Say not love is a dream").
3 June	TV, *Scott music hall*, Robert Russell Bennett, Host, Oscar Hammerstein 2nd, Danny Daniels, William Warfield, Leontyne Price. NBC, 8:30-9 p.m. ("The song is you").

15 June	Radio, TV, *Voice of Firestone* ("Lover come back to me", "Voi che sapete", "Novillero").
Concerts	17 June *Music under the stars*, American Fund for Israel, Milton Katims Cond., NBC Symphony Orchestra, Brian Sullivan, Ossy Renardy, Sam Levenson, Ebbets Field, Brooklyn, New York ("Habañera", "Seguidilla", "Chanson Bohème", "One night of love", "I'm falling in love with someone"); 3 July Daniel Saidenberg, Cond., Connecticut Pops, Bridgeport, Connecticut ("Habañera", "Seguidilla", "Chamson Bohème", "Kiss me again", "Strange music", "One night of love"); 21 Thor Johnson, Cond., *Music Under the Stars*, Symphony Orchestra, Milwaukee, Wisconsin ("Habañera", "Seguidilla", "Kiss me again", "Strange music", "One night of love").
25 July	TV, Larry Storch Show ("Chanson Bohème", comedy routine with Storch, "Man I love").

1953-1954

Recital Program, same as 1952-1953. James Shomate, Accompanist.

5 Oct.	Radio, TV, *Voice of Firestone* ("Bluebirds", "Voi lo sapete", "Brazil").
Recitals	7 Oct. Oak Park, Illinois; 9 Saginaw, Michigan; 13 Oberlin, Ohio; 15 Quincy, Massachusetts; 18 Constitution Hall, Washington, D.C.; 20 Blacksburg, Virginia; 26 Chattanooga, Tennessee.
Concerts	29 Oct. Arthur Bennett Lipkin, Cond., Birmingham Symphony, Birmingham, Alabama ("Che farò", "Voi che sapete", "Widmung", "Amour, viens aider", "Printemps qui commence", "Mon coeur") Muni Auditorium, Broadcast over WAFM; 1 Nov. Miami Beach Auditorium and 2. Dade County Auditorium, John Bitter, Cond., University of Miami Symphony Orchestra, Miami, Florida ("Che farò", "Air de Lia", "O mio Fernando", "Mon coeur").
8 Nov.	TV, *Toast of the town*, Ed Sullivan's "Salute to the Met", Richard Tucker, Roberta Peters, Robert Merrill, Cesare Siepi, Paul Franke, Metropolitan Opera Orchestra (members), Max Rudolf, Cond. The program took place in the Metropolitan Opera House (*Carmen*, Act 4, abbreviated final scene, with Tucker; *Rigoletto*, Ouartet, with Peters, Tucker, Merrill). Sam Levenson and Victor Borge provided the comedy.
Recitals	9 Nov. Salisbury, North Carolina; 12 Tuscaloosa, Alabama; 14 Decatur, Alabama; 18 New Orleans, Louisiana; 20 Lake Charles, Louisiana; 2 Asheville, North Carolina.
30 Nov.	Radio, TV, *Voice of Firestone*, Anniversary Show with Thomas L. Thomas, Eleanor Steber, Jerome Hines, Robert Rounseville, Brian Sullivan (*Rigoletto*, Quartet, Sullivan, Steber, Thomas; "Chanson Bohème"; *Lucia*, Sextet with Hines, Rounseville, Steber, Sullivan, Thomas). Detroit, Michigan.
3 Dec.	Recital, Baltimore, Maryland.
4 Dec.	Guest Speaker, Music Research Foundation 1954 Fund Raising Drive Dinner, Waldorf-Astoria Hotel, New York.
12, 18, 30 Dec., 10, 18 Jan., 3, 10 Apr.	*Carmen*: (Carmen); Richard Tucker (Don José); Lucine Amara (Micaela); Frank Guarrera (Escamillo); Osie Hawkins (Zuniga); Clifford Harvuot (Morales); Heidi Krall (Frasquita); Margaret Roggero (Mercedes); Alessio dePaolis (Remendado); George Cehanovsky (Dancaïro); Pierre Monteux (Cond). (MO); Dec. 18 Nadine Conner (Micaela); Dec 30 Tibor Kozma (Cond); Jan 10 Kurt Baum (Don José); George London (Escamillo); Tibor Kozma (Cond); Jan 18 George London (Escamillo); Tibor Kozma (Cond); Apr. 3 Victoria de los Angeles; Tibor Kozma (Cond). (MO-Broadcast); Apr. 10 Kurt Baum (Don José); Victoria de los Angeles (Micaela); Robert Merrill (Escamillo); Algerd Brazis (Morales); Tibor Kozma (Cond).
15 Jan.	Recital, Greensboro, South Carolina.
Recitals	25 Jan. Danville, Virginia; 27 Anderson, S. Carolina; 29 Columbia, S. Carolina; 1 Feb. Nashville, Tennessee; 3 Baton Rouge, Louisiana; 8 Lubbock, Texas; 17 Monroe, Louisiana.
20 Feb.	Radio, *American Heart Association*, a musical toast from "Your Heart Fund to your heart", w. Robert Merrill, Deems Taylor. 27 Feb. Flys to Milan, Italy, to start La Scala rehearsals)
24, 27, 30 Mar., 1 Apr.	*La Figlia del Diavolo*: (Erodiade); Gian Giacomo Guelfi (Erode); Angelo Mercuriali (L'Eunuco); Eugenio Fernandi (Giovanni); Giuliana Barabaschi (Salome); Angela Ravani (Berlicche); Nino Sanzogno (Cond). Paired with: Menotti's, *Amelia al ballo* and

	Peragallo's *La gita in campagna* (LS); Mar 30 paired with *Amelia al ballo* and Ravel's *Bolero* (Ballet); Apr. 1 paired with *Amelia al ballo* and De Falla's *El amor brujo* (Ballet).
2 April	Flys to New York for *Carmen* broadcast
Recitals	5 April Springfield, Massachusetts; 7 Amherst, Massachusetts.
1954-1955	
Recitals	12 April Vineland, New Jersey; 20 Bloomington, Illinois; 22 El Dorado, Arkansas; 26 Junction City, Kansas; 29 Kearney, Nebraska; 2 May Manhattan, Kansas; 4 Lincoln, Nebraska.
10 May	Radio, TV, *Voice of Firestone* ("Beautiful dreamer", "Neath a southern moon", "Vissi d'arte", "Two hearts in 3/4 time").
20 June	TV, Ed Sullivan's, *Toast of the town* ("Come rain or come shine", acc. by the composer, Harold Arlen; "Stars in my eyes").
28 June	Radio, TV, *Voice of Firestone* ("Sing to me guitar", "One night of love", "Mon coeur", "Love's roundelay").
6 July	Concert, Frank Brieff, Cond., New Haven Symphony, New Haven, Connecticut ("Che farò", "Voi che sapete", "Mon coeur", "Strange music", "One night of love", "Stars in my eyes"; encores: "Habañera", "Seguidilla", "Chanson Bohème").
8 July	Pennsylvania Night, Madison Square Garden, New York, David Stephens, CBS Symphony, Jimmy Nelson, June Taylor Dancers (selections not specified, appeared in Part 2 and finale).
12 July	Radio, TV, *Voice of Firestone* ("Songs my mother taught me", "You are the song in my heart", "Bluebirds").
13 July	Recital, Kent, Ohio.
28 Aug.	Recital, Anthony Drake's Boys Harbor Camp Benefit, ("Divinites du Styx", "Were you there", "The Ballynure ballad", "The Indian", "Habañera", "Seguidilla", "Chanson Bohème"; encores: "Look, Edwin", "Songs my mother taught me").

1954-1955
Recital Program: Handel, *Semele*, "Where'er you walk"; Mozart, *Le nozze di Figaro*, "Voi che sapete"; Grieg, "With a water lily", "Morning dew", "The first meeting", "A dream"; Erich Wolf, "Alle Dinge haben Sprache"; Wolf, "Begegnung"; Brahms, "Dein blaues Auge"; R. Strauss, "Nichts"; Saint-Saëns, *Samson et Dalila*, "Mon coeur s'ouvre à ta voix"; Cowles, "The fragerence of a song"; Naginski, "The pasture"; Duke, "Wild swans"; Boardman, "Monastery evening", "Arcady"; Bizet, *Carmen*, "Habañera", "Seguidilla", "Chanson Bohème"). James Shomate, (Accompanist).

11 Oct.	Radio, TV, *Voice of Firestone* ("Smoke gets in your eyes", "Habañera", "Ave Maria", "Siboney").
Recitals	13 Oct. Cedarhurst, New York; 18 Newport News, Virginia; 21 Atlanta, Georgia; 25 San Antonio, Texas; 27 San Angelo, Texas; Nov. 3 Oklahoma City, Oklahoma; 6 Clovis, New Mexico; 8 Borger, Texas; 10 Denver, Colorado; 15 Morgantown, West Virginia; 23 Staten Island, New York; 29 New Britain, Connecticut; 1 Dec. Lawrence, Massachusetts.
6 Dec.	Radio, TV, Voice of Firestone ("Some day my Prince will come", "I give my heart", "Connais-tu le pays", "Say not love is a dream").
9 Dec.	Music Research Foundation, North Shore Chapter, Benefit dinner dance, with Claudia Pinza, Burl Ives, Manhassat, New York.
29 Dec., 3 Jan., 5, 12 Feb., 7, 11 Apr., 22 May	*Carmen:* (Carmen); Kurt Baum (Don José); Lucine Amara (Micaela); Frank Guarrera (Escamillo); Norman Scott (Zuniga); Calvin Marsh (Morales); Heidi Krall (Frasquita); Margaret Roggero (Mercedes); Alessio de Paolis (Remendado); George Cehanovsky (Dancaïro); Max Rudolf (Cond). (MO); Feb. 5 Mario del Monaco (Don José). (MO-Texaco Broadcast); Feb. 12 Hilde Gueden (Micaela); Robert Merrill (Escamillo); Osie Hawkins (Zuniga); Tibor Kozma (Cond); Apr. 7 Mario del Monaco (Don José); Nadine Conner (Micaela); Osie Hawkins (Zuniga); Herta Glaz (Frasquita); Apr. 11 Robert Merrill (Escamilllo); Clifford Harvuot (Morales). (MO-Cleveland,Ohio); May 22 Richard Tucker (Don José); Clifford Harvuot (Morales). (MO-Chicago, Illinois)
Recitals	11 Jan. Chapel Hill, N. Carolina; 13 Hickory, N. Carolina; 15 Daytona Beach, Florida.
2 Feb.	Fritz Kreisler Eightieth Birthday Celebration, Eleanor Steber, Hilde Gueden, Gladys

	Swarthout, serenade to Kreisler, St. Regis Hotel, New York.
7 Feb.	Radio, TV, *Voice of Firestone* ("Look for the silver lining", "Amour viens aider", "Under the starlight", "Dancing in the dark").
24, 28 Feb.,	*Orfeo ed Euridice*: (Orfeo); Hilde Gueden (Euridice); Roberta Peters (Amore); Laurel
11, 30 Mar.	Hurley (Spirit); Alicia Markova, Zachary Solov (Dancers); Pierre Monteux (Cond). (MO);
9 Apr.	Mar. 11 Laurel Hurley (Amore); Shakeh Vartenissian (Spirit); Apr. 9 Laurel Hurley (Amore); Shakeh Vartenissian (Spirit). (MO-Broadcast)
3 March	Recital, Portland, Maine.
15 March	Juilliard Benefit, Josef Lhevinne Scholarship, Rosina Lhevinne, Juilliard String Quartet, James Shomate, acc., Juilliard School of Music, New York ("Alle dinge haben sprache", "Begegnung", "Dein blaues auge", "Nichts", "Voi che sapete", "Mon coeur", "Habañera").
Recitals	20 March Detroit, Michigan; 22 Ft. Wayne, Indiana; 24 Carbondale, Illinois.
27 March	Concert, Leo Kucinski, Cond., Sioux City Symphony, Sioux City, Iowa ("Che farò", "Voi che sapete", "Il est doux", "Habañera", "Seguidilla", "Chanson Bohème").
1 April	Recital, Indianapolis, Indiana.
10 April	One TV and two radio appearances, Cleveland, Ohio.
Recitals	16 April Burlingame, California; 18 Palo Alto, California; 19 War Memorial Opera House, San Francisco,California (program differed from standard format for this season in so far as, *Alceste*, "Gods of eternal night", trans. by John Gutman, was added and *Carmen* excerpts dropped); 22 Berkeley, California; 25 Salem, Oregon; 27 Longview, Washington; 29 Pasco, Washington; 2 May Helena, Montana; 4, 5 Billings, Montana.
8 May	Concert, Eugene Ormandy, Cond., Philadelphia Orchesra, Ann Arbor, Michigan ("Gods of eternal night", "Adieu, forêts", "Mon coeur", "Habañera", "Seguidilla").
16 May	Radio, TV, *Voice of Firestone* ("I'll see you again", *Carmen*, "Card scene", "Songs my mother taught me", "Two hearts in 3/4 time").
19 May	Recital, Jefferson City, Missouri.
4 June	TV, *Chocolate soldier*: Nadina; Eddie Albert (Bumerli); Akim Tomeroff (Major Ludek); David Atkinson (Major Alexius Spiridoff); George Ebeling (General Masakroff); Will Scholz (General Kirkovitch); Earl Wrightson; Joan Chambers, Bambi Lynn, Rod Alexander; Charles Sanford, Cond. Jeffrey Hayden (Director). 9-10:30 p.m., NBC.
June	American Fund for Israel, Dinner in honor of Spyros P. Skouros, Robert Merrill, Pierre Monteux, Diana Adams, André Eglevsky, Symphony of the Air ("Mon coeur", "Chanson Bohème").
(15 June Sailed to Europe)	
2, 7 July	*Le nozze di Figaro*: (Cherubino); Sesto Bruscantini (Figaro); Elena Rizzieri (Susanna); Sena Jurinac (Countess); Franco Calabrese (Count); Ian Wallace (Don Bartalo); Monica Sinclair (Marcellina); Hugue Cuenod (Don Basilio); Daniel McCoshan (Don Curzio); Jeannette Sinclair (Barbarina); Vittorio Gui (Cond). (GFO)
27 Aug.	*Orfeo ed Euridice*: (Orfeo); Anna Tassopoulou (Euridice); Vilma Georgiou (Amore); Philoctepes Economidis (Cond). The State Symphony. Dino Yannopoulos, Director, Anthony Tudor, Choreographer. First Athens Festival. There were two additional performances.

(In addition to the recitals listed above, RS also appeared through Community Concerts in Houston, Texas)

1955-1956
Recital Program, same as 1954-1955.
(22 Sept. left Italy for New York)

Recitals	5 Oct. Bala-Cynwyd, Pennsylvania; 7 Spartanburg, North Carolina.
11 Oct.	Concert, David Van Vector, Cond., Knoxville Symphony, Knoxville, Tennessee ("Che farò", "Voi che sapete", "Connais-tu le pays", "Habañera", "Seguidilla", "Chanson Bohème").
16 Oct.	Music Research Foundation, Fall cocktail party in Mrs. John P. Ohe's home with Burl Ives, Sands Point, New York.
17 Oct.	Concert, Dr. Erno Daniel, Cond., Wichita Falls Symphony ("Habañera", "Seguidilla", "Chanson Bohème").

24 Oct.	Radio, TV, *Voice of Firestone* ("Speak to me of love", "The night was made for love", "Voi che sapete", "Vienna, city of my dreams").
28 Oct.	Concert, Worcester Music Festival, Eugene Ormandy, Philadelphia, Pennsylvania, Worcester, Massachusetts ("Gods of eternal night", "Adieu, forêts", Wolf, "Kennst du das land", "Widmung"; encore: "Chanson Bohème").
2 Nov.	Metropolitan Opera Guild's Twentieth Anniversary Party.
4 Nov.	Recital, Brooklyn College, Brooklyn, New York.
6 Nov.	TV, Ed Sullivan's *Toast of the town*, Phil Silvers, Liberace ("Falling in love with love", "Cement mixer", with Liberace, "Dancing in the dark").

14, 23 Nov., *Les contes d'Hoffman*: (Giulietta); Richard Tucker (Hoffmann); Roberta Peters; May 2
2 May Thomas Schippers. (MO-Atlanta, Georgia)
3, 20 Dec. (Olympia); Lucine Amara (Antonia); Martial Singher (Lindorf, Coppélius, Dappertutto, Dr. Miracle); Mildred Miller (Nicklausse) Alessio de Paolis (Andrès, Cochenille, Pittichinaccio, Frantz); Paul Franke (Spalanzani); Clifford Harvuot (Schlemil); Norman Scott (Crespel); Sandra Warfield (Mother's voice); Pierre Monteux (Cond). (MO-Opening Night)

19, 25, 30 Nov., *Carmen*: (Carmen); Richard Tucker (Don José); Lucine Amara (Micaela); Frank Guarrera
21 Jan., 5, (Escamillo); Norman Scott (Zuniga); Calvin Marsh (Morales); Heidi Krall (Frasquita);
19 Apr., Margaret Roggero (Mercedes); Paul Franke (Remendado); George Cehanovsky
27, 30 May (Dancairo); Max Rudolf (Cond). (MO); Nav. 25 Kurt Baum (Don José); Osie Hawkins (Zuniga); Alessio de Paolis (Remendado); Nov. 30 Giuseppe di Stefano (Don José); Jan. 21 Giuseppe di Stefano (Don José); Robert Merrill (Escamillo). (MO-Texaco Broadcast); Apr. 5 Nadine Conner (Micaela); Robert Merrill (Escamillo); Tibor Kozma (Cond); Apr 19 Nadine Conner (Micaela); Osie Hawkins (Zuniga); Alessio de Paolis (Remendado). (MO-Boston, Massachusetts); May 27 Nadine Conner (Micaela); Frank Valentino (Escamillo); Alessio de Paolis (Remendado). (MO-Chicago, Illinois); May 30 Frank Valentino (Escamillo); Alessio de Paolis (Remendado). (MO-Toronto, Canada)

20 Nov.	Concert, Henry Sopkin, Cond., Atlanta Symphony, Atlanta, Georgia ("Lieder eines fahrenden Gesellen", "Songs of a Wayfarer", "Connais-tu le pays", "Adieu, forêts", "Mon coeur").
28 Nov.	Recital, Southampton, New York.
5 Dec.	Radio, TV, *Voice of Firestone* ("Allah's holiday", "L'amour tojours l'amour", "Adieu, forêts", "Kiss in the dark").
Recitals	7 Dec. Wilkes-Barre, Pennsylvania; 9 Springfield, Pennsylvania.
29 Dec., 9 Jan.	*Samson et Dalila*: (Dalila); Ramon Vinay (Samson); Martial Singher (High Priest); Norman Scott (Abimélich); Nicola Moscona (Old Hebrew); Pierre Monteux (Cond). (MO)
7 Jan.	Recital, Wilkes-Barre, Pennsylvania.
Recitals	11 Jan. Rocky Mountain, North Carolina; 13 Clearwater, Florida; 16 Wilmington, North Carolina; 18 Manhassett, New York.
30 Jan.	TV (color), *Festival of music*, Marian Anderson, Jussi Björling, Zinka Milanov, Mildred Miller, Jan Peerce, Roberta Peters, Gregor Piatigorsky, Arthur Rubenstein, Isaac Stern, Renata Tebaldi, Blanche Thebom, Leonard Warren, Charles Laughton, Host. Max Rudolf, Music Director. NBC (*Carmen*, "Card scene").

6, 18 Feb., *Der Rosenkavalier*: (Octavian); Lisa della Casa (Marschallin); Otto Edelmann (Baron
9, 22, 31 Mar., Ochs); Hilde Gueden (Sophie); Ralph Herbert (Faninal); Alessio de Paolis (Valzacchi);
11, 28 Apr. Martha Lipton (Annina); Thomas Hayward (Singer); Rudolf Kempe (Cond). (MO-Revised Production); Feb. 18 (MO-Texaco Broadcast); Evening: Radio and TV Correspondents Association Dinner, Steve Allen, M.C., Bambi Lynn, Rod Alexander, Dennis Day, Clifford Guest, West Point Glee Club, V.P. Richard Nixon representing President Dwight D. Eisenhower, Washington, D.C. (Unspecified selection); Mar 9 John Brownlee (Faninal); Kurt Baum (Singer), Mar. 22 John Brownlee (Faninal); Kurt Baum (Singer); Mar 31 John Brownlee (Faninal); Herta Glaz (Annina); Apr. 11 Eleanor Steber 9 Marschallin); Nadine Conner (Sophie); John Brownlee (Faninal); Herta Glaz (Annina); Albert da Costa (Singer); Max Rudolf (Cond).; Apr. 28 Eleanor Steber (Marschallin);

	Nadine Conner (Sophie); John Brownlee (Faninal); Albert da Costa (Singer); Max Rudolf (Cond). (MO-Cleveland, Ohio)
13 Feb.	Radio, TV, *Voice of Firestone* ("Dearly beloved", "Falling in love with someone", *Les Contes d' Hoffmann*, "Barcarolle", "You are the song in my heart").
Recitals	21 Feb. Springfield, Illinois; 24 Kansas City, Kansas; 27 Houston, Texas.
19 March	Radio, TV, *Voice of Firestone*, Springtime, U.S.A.
17 April	TV, Martha Raye Show, James Shomate, acc.
21 April	Schubert Club Annual Concert, Schubert Male Singing Group, Grand Rapids, Michigan; ("Habañera", "Seguidilla", "Chanson Bohème", Frank Goodwin, Cond.; with the Glee Club, Brahms, "Lullaby", "Strange music").
8 May	Recital, Hollywood, Florida.
14 May	Radio, TV, *Voice of Firstone* ("'Neath the southern moon", "Dear hearts and gentle people", "Moon love", "Love's rondelay").
15 May	Friars Club Testimonial Dinner in honor of Ed Sullivan, Waldorf-Astoria Hotel, New York.
4 June	Rotary Interaction Night, Philadelphia, Pennsylvania (unspecified selection).
10 July	Red Rocks Music Festival, Saul Caston, Cond., Denver Symphony, Denver, Colorado.
15 July	*Carmen*, (Carmen); Charles Kullman (Don José); Helen George (Micaela); Cesare Bardelli (Escamillo); William Wilderman (Zuniga); Edgar Keenon (Morales); Rita Haaser (Frasquita); Ruth Thorsen (Mercedes); Virginio Assandri (Remendado); Wilfred Engelman (Dancaïro); Fausto Cleva (Cond). (CZO)
6 Aug.	Radio, TV, *Voice of Firestone* ("Lover", "I'll take romance", "Connais-tu le pays", "I could have danced all night").
14 Aug.	Candlelight Concert, Brevard Music Center, James Christian Pfohl, Gala Festival Orchestra ("Che farò", "Voi che sapete", "Mon coeur", "Habáñera", "Seguidilla", "Chanson Bohème").
28 Aug.	New Haven Pop Concert Series, Harry Berman, New Haven Symphony Orchestra ("Habáñera", "Seguidilla", "Chanson Bohème", "Moon love", "The man I love", "I could have danced all night")

1956-1957
Recital Program, same as 1954-1955.

30 Sept.	Luncheon in honor of David Sarnoff's fifty years in radio and television, Jan Peerce, Tony Cabot Orchestra, Waldorf-Astoria Hotel, New York (unspecified selections).
1 Oct.	Radio, TV, *voice of Firestone* ("Greensleeves", "I give my heart", "Adieu, forêts", *Merry Widow*, Waltz).
9 Oct.	Recital, Greensboro, Pennsylvania.
11 Oct.	Concert, John Anello, Cond., Milwaukee Pops Orchestra, Milwaukee, Wisconsin ("Mon coeur", "Seguidilla", "Lover", "Moon love", "I could have danced all night").
14 Oct.	TV, Ed Sullivan's, *Toast of the town* ("I could have danced all night" and unspecified aria). Other guests were Vivian Blaine and Johnny Carson.
Recitals	18 Oct. Stockton, California; 20 Angwin, California; 22 Yakima, Washington; 24 Wenatchee, Washington; 26 Idaho Falls, Idaho.
31 Oct.	Concert, Maurice Abravanel, Utah Symphony, Salt Lake City, Utah ("Che farò", "Where'er you walk", "Voi che sapete", "Lieder eines fahrenden gesellen" "Songs of the Wayfarer", "Seguidilla", "Chanson Bohème").
Recitals	1 Nov .Ogden, Utah; 17 Charlotte, North Carolina; 20 Atlanta, Georgia; 26 Ft. Lauderdale, Florida; 1 Dec. Joplin, Missouri; 4 Fayetteville, Arkansas; 7 Denton, Texas.
10 Dec.	TV, *Producer's showcase*: RS, *Carmen*, "Card scene", Other guests included Marian Anderson, Victoria de los Angeles, Boris Christoff, Renata Tebaldi, Jussi Björling, Zinka Milanov, Leonard Warren, Roberta Peters, Blanche Thebom. (NBC).
16 Dec.	TV, Ed Sullivan's, *Toast of the town* ("I wonder as I wander", "O holy night", "Strange music").
27 Dec., 2,	*Carmen*: (Carmen); Richard Tucker (Don José); Lucine Amara (Micaela); George London
12, 19, 25 Jan.,	(Escamillo); Norman Scott (Zuniga); Clifford Harvuot (Morales); Heidi Krall (Frasquita);
11 Feb., 9 Mar.,	Margaret Roggero (Mercedes); Alessio de Paolis (Remendado); George Cehanovsky
18, 25 Apr.,	(Dancaïro); Dimitri Mitroupolis (Cond). (MO); Jan 2 Robert Merrill (Escamillo); Paul
26, 30 May	Franke (Remendado); Jan 12 Mario del Monaco (Don José); Frank Guarrera (Escamillo);

Paul Franke (Remendado). (RS 100th Met Carmen) (MO-Texaco Broadcast); Jan. 19 Mario del Monaco (Don José); Hilda Gueden (Micaela); Frank Guarrera (Escamillo); Osie Hawkins (Zuniga); Jan 25 Mario Del Monaco (Don José); Nadine Conner (Micaela); Frank Guarrera (Escamillo); Osie Hawkins (Zuniga); Rosalind Elias (Mercedes); Calvin Marsh (Dancaïro); Feb. 11 Nadine Conner (Micaela); Ettore Bastianini (Escamillo); Calvin Marsh (Morales); Paul Franke (Remendado); Mar. 9 Giulio Gari (Don José); Emelia Cundari (Micaela); Clifford Harvuot (Morales); Kurt Adler (Cond); Apr. 18 Kurt Baum (Don José); Heidi Krall (Micaela); Frank Guarrera (Escamillo); Gloria Lind (Frasquita); Paul Franke (Remendado); Martin Rich (Cond); Apr, 25 Frank Guarrera (Escamillo); Calvin Marsh (Morales); Paul Franke (Remendado); Martin Rich (Cond). (MO-Cleveland, Ohio); May 26 Kurt Baum (Don José); Paul Franke (Remendado). (MO-Chicago-Illinois); May 30 Raoul Jobin (Don José); Emelia Cundari (Micaela); Frank Valentino (Escamillo); Calvin Marsh (Morales); Paul Franke (Remendado). (MO-Toronto, Canada)

9 Jan.	Recital, Columbiana, Ohio.
14 Jan.	Association of Master Knights of the Sovereign Militry Order of Malta in the U.S., dinner, Waldorf-Astoria Hotel, New York (Unspecified selections).
Recitals	31 Jan. St. Louis, Missouri; Feb. 2 Chicago, Illinois; 6 Peoria, Illinois.
14 Feb.	Recital, Quebec, Canada.
2 March	Metropolitan Life, James Shomate, acc., Waldorf-Astoria Hotel, New York (unspecified selections).
4 March	Radio, TV, *Voice of Firestone* ("A dream", "You and the night and the music", "Vissi d'arte", "One night of love").
12 March	Recital, York, Pennsylvania.
14 March	Haarlem Philharmonic Society, Stanley Babin, Piano, James Shomate, acc., Waldorf-Astoria Hotel, New York ("Alle dinge haben sprache", "Begegnung", "Dein blaues auge", "Nichts", "Habañera", "Seguidilla", "Chanson Bohème").
Recitals	24 March Baltimore, Maryland; 27 Ypsilanti, Michigan; 28 Sewickley, Pennsylvania; 30 Pittsburgh, Pennsylvania; 3 April Minneapolis, Minnesota; 6 Elkhart, Indiana; 9 Dayton, Ohio; 11 Winston-Salem, North Carolina; 15 Auburn, Alabama.
22 April	Recital, Columbus, Ohio.
30 April	Recital, Englewood, New Jersey.
5 May	Concert, Eugene Ormandy, Cond., Philadelphia Orchestra, Ann Arbor, Michigan ("Lieder eines fahrenden gesellen" "Songs of a Wayfarer", "Connais-tu le pays", "Air de Lia", "Amour, viens aider"; encore: "Chanson Bohème").
19 May	Ed Sullivan's, *Toast of the town* with Clyde Beatty and his lions, the Glen Miller Band, Tommy Sands and Julie Wilson (*The Bells are ringing*, "Drop that name", with Wilson).
3 June	Radio, TV, *Voice of Firestone* ("Getting to know you", "Songs my mother taught me", "Yours is my heart alone", "Connais-tu le pays", "It's a grand night for singing").
7 June	Committee to Help Concert Fund for Israel, Dimitri Mitropoulos, N.Y. Philharmonic (members), Jennie Tourel, Robert Merrill, Daniel Barenboim, Waldorf Astoria Hotel, New York (unspecified selections).
14 July	Recital, "Music by the Lake series", Chicago, Illinois.
22 July	*Carmen*, (Carmen); Richard Tucker (Don José); Laurel Hurley (Micaela, Frasquita); Robert McFerrin (Escamillo); LouisSgarro (Zuniga); Helen Vanni (Mercedes); Charles Anthony (Remendado); Calvin Marsh (Dancaïro); Margaret Hillis Chorus; Max Rudolf (Cond) Lewisohn Stadium, New York.(abridged version with main arias, duets, interludes)
3 Aug.	Newport Festival, Vic Damone, Geoffre Holder, Stan Freeman, Peggy Hitchcock, Joseph Welch, Newport, Rhode Island.

1957-1958
Recital Program, same as 1954-1955.

23 Sept.	TV, *Voice of Firestone* ("Always", Irving Berlin medley, "Seguidilla", "Dancing in the dark").
Recitals	3 Oct. Ann Arbor, Michigan; 8 Carlisle, Pennsylvania 10 Tampa, Florida.
Concerts	14 Oct. Orlando Barera, Cond., El Paso Symphony, El Paso, Texas ("Che farò", "Voi

	che sapete", "Habañera", "Seguidilla", "Chanson Bohème"); 19 Victor Alessandro,Cond., San Antonio Symphony, San Antonio, Texas ("Lieder eines fahrenden gesellen" "Songs of the Wayfarer", "Connais-tu le pays", "Adieu, forêts", "Mon coeur").
Recitals	22 Oct. Rome, Georgia; 25 Bowling Green, Kentucky; 27 Park Ridge, Illinois; 29 Worcester, Massachusetts.
4 Nov.	TV, *Voice of Firestone* ("Dear hearts and gentle people", Memory lane medley, *Les Contes d'Hoffmann* "Barcarolle", "Grand night for singing").
Recitals	6 Nov. Toledo, Ohio; 8 Mount Holyoke College, New York.
22, 26 Nov.	*Der Rosenkavalier*: (Octavian); Lisa della Casa (Marschallin); Otto Edelman (Baron
9 Dec., 26 Feb.,	Ochs); Hilde Gueden (Sophie); Ralph Herbert (Faninal); Alessio de Paolis (Valzacchi);
22 Mar.,	Martha Lipton (Annina); Kurt Baum (Singer); Karl Böhm (Cond). (MO); Dec. 9 Roberta
16, 28 Apr.,	Peters (Sophie); Feb 26 Eleanor Steber (Marschallin); Laurel Hurley (Sophie); Nicolai
2, 17, 20 May	Gedda (Singer); Max Rudolf (Cond); Mar 22 Eleanor Steber (Marschallin); Laurel Hurley (Sophie); Max Rudolf (Cond). (MO-Texaco Broadcast; Apr. 16 Eleanor Steber (Marschallin); Laurel Hurley (Sophie); Max Rudolf (Cond). (MO-Boston, Massachusetts); Apr. 28 Eleanor Steber (Marschallin); Laurel Hurley (Sophie); Albert da Costa (Singer); Max Rudolf (Cond). (MO-Washington, D.C.); May 2 Eleanor Steber (Marschallin); Roberta Peters (Sophie); Albert da Costa (Singer); Max Rudolf (Cond). (MO-Atlanta, Georgia); May 17 Eleanor Steber (Marschallin); Roberta Peters (Sophie); Albert da Costa (Singer); Max Rudolf (Cond). (MO-Minneapolis, Minnesota); May 20 Eleanor Steber (Marschallin); Roberta Peters (Sophie); Nicolai Gedda (Singer); Max Rudolf (Cond). (MO-Bloomington, Indiana)
4, 29 Dec.,	*Carmen*: (Carmen); Richard Tucker (Don José); Emelia Cundari (Micaela); Frank
14 Jan.	Guarrra (Escamillo); Norman Scott (Zuniga); Calvin Marsh (Morales); Heidi Krall (Frasquita); Margaret Roggero (Mercedes); Paul Frank (Remendado); George Cehanovsky (Dancaïro); Thomas Schippers (Cond). (MO); Dec. 29 Carlo Bergonzi (Don José); Lucine Amara (Micaela); Robert Merrill (Escamillo); Clifford Harvuot (Morales); Jan. 14 Lucine Amara (Micaela); Gloria Lind (Frasquita).
8 Dec.	Israel Bond Chanukah Festival, Madison Square Garden, New York.
10 Dec.	Constance Hope's farewell party for the Begum Aga Kahn, Guests: Leonard Bernstein, Samuel Barber, André Kostelanetz, Alicia Markova, RS).
16, 26 Dec.,	*Orfeo ed Euridice*: (Orfeo); Hilde Gueden (Euridice); Emelia Cundari (Amore); Mildred
10, 18, 25 Jan.	Allen, Helen Vanni (Spirits); Alicia Markova, Michael Maule (Dancers); Max Rudolf (Cond). (MO); Jan. 10 Lucine Amara (Euridice).; Jan. 18 Lucine Amara (Micaela). (MO-Texaco Broadcast); Jan. 25 Mildred Allen (Amore).
22 Dec.	TV, Ed Sullivan's, *Toast of the Town* ("I wonder as I wander", with Maryknoll Group, "Let it snow", "Merry little Christmas").
Recitals	20 Jan. Waynesboro, Virginia; 22 Charleston, West Virginia.
Recitals	28 Jan. Chester, Pennsylvania; 31 Dothan, Alabama; 2 Feb. Dallas, Texas; 4 Paris, Texas; 7 Abilene, Texas; 9 Midland, Texas; 12 Modesto, California; 15 Los Angeles, California; 18 Pasadena, California; 20 Escondido, California.
3 March	TV, *Voice of Firestone* ("A kiss in the dark", "I'll take romance", "Che farò", "The song is you").
13, 31 Mar.,	*Samson et Dalila*, (Dalila); Mario del Monaco (Samson); Martial Singher (High Priest);
12, 23 Apr.,	Norman Scott (Abimélech); Giorgio Tozzi (Old Hebrew); Fausto Cleva (Cond.) (MO);
5, 15, 24 May	Mar. 31 William Wilderman (Old Hebrew); May 5 Clifford Harvuot (High Priest); William Wilderman (Old Hebrew). (MO-Birmingham, Alabama); 9 (Dallas, Texas); May 15 William Wilderman (Old Hebrew). (MO-St. Louis, Missouri); May 24 William Wilderman (Old Hebrew). (MO-Chicago, Illinois); 29 (Toronto, Canada).
Recitals	16 March College Point, Pennsylvania; 18 Lebanon, Pennsylvania.
26 March	Recital, St. Catherine, Ontario, Canada.
27 April	TV, *Hansel and Gretel*, (Mother); Rudy Vallee (Father); Red Buttons (Hansel); Barbara Cook (Gretel); Hans Conreid (Witch); Stubby Kaye (Town Crier); Paul Hartman (Good Night Watchman); Will Able (Eenie); Paula Laurence (Meenie); Shai K Ophir (Miney);

	Sondra Lee (Moe); Glen Osser (Cond). Paul Bogart (Producer/Director). Music by Alec Wilder and William Engvick. NBC. ("Children in our hearts", Finale)
12 May	Recital, New Kensington, Pennsylvania.
20 June	I.B.M. Dedication, James Melton, James Shomate, Endicott, New York.
1,2 Aug.	*Carnival of music*, Gordon MacRae, Newport, Rhode Island.
8 Aug.	Concert, Evan Whallon, Cond., Connecticut Pops, Fairfield, Connecticut ("Voi che sapete", "Mon coeur", "Ouvre ton coeur", "Stars in my eyes", "Getting to know you", "I could have danced all night").

(In addition to the recitals listed above RS also appeared through Community Concerts in Charlotte, North Carolina)

1958-1959

Recital Program: Vaughan Williams, "Orpheus with his lute"; Hatton, "Bid me to live"; Bantock, "Silent strings"; Schumann, "Widmung"; R. Strauss, "Ruhe, meine Seele,"; Wolf, "Mausfallensprüchlein"; R. Strauss, "Heimkehr"; Brahms, "O liebliche Wangen"; de Falla, "Séguidille" and "Séguidilla murciana"; Bizet, *Carmen*, "Seguidilla"; Quilter, "Love's philosophy"; Bernstein, "Rabbit at top speed"; Barber, "Sure on this shining night"; Levitski, "Do you remember"; Hughes, arr., "A Ballynure ballad"; Saint-Saëns, *Samson et Dalila*, "Mon coeur s'ouvre à ta voix"; Bizet, *Carmen*, "Chanson Bohème").

8 Sept.	TV, *Voice of Firestone*
Recitals	8 Oct. Genesco, New York; 11 Wappingers Falls, New York.
16 Oct.	TV, *Little women*, (Margaret March); Florence Henderson (Meg); Jeannie Carson (Jo); Margaret O'Brien (Beth); Zina Bethune (Amy); Joel Grey (Theodore Lawrence); Bill Hayes (John Brooks); Roland Winters (Mr. Lawrence); Hal Hastings (Cond). Albert Selden (Producer). William Corrigan (Director). Music and lyrics by Richard Adler. CBS.
Recitals	18 Oct. Milford, Connecticut; 21 Uniontown, Pennsylvania; 23 Hazleton, Pennsylvania; 25 New Castle, Pennsylvania; 28 Shreveport, Louisiana; 30 Norman, Oklahoma; 7 Nov. Louisville, Kentucky; 10 Indianapolis, Indiana.
21, 29 Nov. 10 Dec., 28 Mar., 15, 21 Apr., 17, 21 May	*Carmen*: (Carmen); Richard Tucker (Don José); Hilde Gueden (Micaela); Mario Zanasi (Escamillo); Louis Sgarro (Zuniga); Calvin Marsh (Morales); Heidi Krall (Frasquita); Margaret Roggero (Mercedes); Alessio de Paolis (Remendado); George Cehanovsky (Dancaïro); Jean Morel (Cond). (MO); Dec. 10 Dimiter Uzunov (Don José); Heidi Krall (Micaela); Frank Guarrera (Escamilla); Madelaine Chambers (Frasquita); Paul Franke (Remendado); Mar 28 Laurel Hurley (Micaela); Mario Sereni (Escamillo); Lorenzo Alvary (Zuniga); Clifford Harvuot (Morales); Gloria Lind (Frasquita); Helen Vanni (Mercedes); Paul Franke (Remendado); Apr 15, 21 Carlo Bergonzi (Don José); Heidi Krall (Micaela); Frank Guarrera (Escamillo); Clifford Harvuot (Morales); Gloria Lind (Frasquita); Helen Vanni (Mercedes); Paul Franke (Remendado); May 17 Heidi Krall (Micaela); Gloria Lind (Frasquita); Helen Vanni (Mercedes). (MO-Minneapolis, Minnesota); May 21 Heidi Krall (Micaela); Mario Sereni (Escamillo); Mildred Allen (Frasquita); Helen Vanni (Mercedes). (MO-Detroit, Michigan)
25 Nov.	TV, Arthur Godfrey Show
15 Dec.	Chanukah Festival for Israel, Ed Sullivan, M.C., Madison Square Garden, New York, w. Arthur Fiedler, New York Philharmonic (members), Jan Peerce, Sir Cedric Hardwick, Earl Lang, Bruce Marks ("Habañera", "Chanson Bohème", "Mon coeur", "I could have danced all night").
21 Dec.	TV, Ed Sullivan's, *Toast of the town* ("Silent night", "Hark the herald angels sing", "It came upon a midnight clear", "O come all ye faithful").
20 Jan.	TV, *Voice of Firestone*, Brian Sullivan, Oscar Shumsky, Wilfred Pelletier, Cond., White House, Washington, D.C. ("My hero", "Falling in love with love", with Brian Sullivan, "Mon coeur", "Ah sweet mystery of life", with Sullivan).
Recitals	5 Feb. Ft. Myers, Florida; 7 Miami Beach, Florida.
10 Feb.	TV, *Telephone hour*, "American song festival" (Scene from Victor Herbert's, *Natoma*).
16 Feb.	TV, *Voice of Firestone*, Walter Hendl, Chicago Symphony, Chicago, Illinois ("Voi che sapete", "Air de Lia", "Mon coeur").
22 Feb.	TV, David Susskind, *Open end* (Interview).
Recitals	7 March Odessa, Texas; 9 Carlsbad, New Mexico; 12 Winona, Minnesota; 16 East

	Liverpool, Ohio; 18 Trenton, Michigan.
26 March	Lighthouse Music School of the N.Y. Association for the Blind w. Milton Cross (tribute to organization).
6 Apr.	TV, *Voice of Firestone*, Heidi Krall, Richard Tucker, Jerome Hines, Detroit, Michigan ("Seguidilla", "Connais-tu le pays").
10 May	Concert, Jan Peerce, Giuseppe Bamboschek, Cond., Philadelphia Academy of Music, Philadelphia, Pennsylvania ("Habañera", "Seguidilla", "Chanson Bohème", "Wanting you" and "Thine alone", with Peerce).
14 May	Lincoln Center Ground Breaking Ceremony. In attendance, President Dwight D. Eisenhower, Anthony Bliss, John D. Rockefeller, Mayor Robert F. Wagner, Lauder Greenway, Rudolf Bing, Reginald Allen, William Schuman, Robert Moses; Leonard Bernstein, New York Philharmonic, Juilliard Chorus, Leonard Warren. 11 a.m., Sixty-fourth Street and Broadway, New York ("Habañera").
25 May	TV, *Voice of Firestone*, Brian Sullivan, Heidi Krall, Jerome Hines, Akron, Ohio ("Il est doux", *Student Prince*, "Serenade", with Krall, Sullivan, Hines).
28 May	Dinner in honor of King Baudouin of Belgium, Francis Cardinal Spellman, Herbert Hoover, Maurice Scott Orchestra, Waldorf-Astoria Hotel, New York (unspecified selections).
3-18 August	Moscow, USSR, 19-25 August, Leningrad, Ed Sullivan Show)

1959-1960
Recital Program, same as 1958-1959.

27 Sept.	TV, Ed Sullivan's, *Toast of the town*. Highlights from Russian trip ("Getting to know you", sung in Russian as those on stage wave U.S. flags).
17 Oct.	Concert, Victor Alessandro, San Antonio Symphony, San Antonio, Texas (Wolf, "Kennst du das land"; "Il est doux", "Air de Lia", "Chanson Bohème").
19 Oct.	TV, Jack Paar Show ("Getting to know you").
22 Oct.	Eighth Alfred E. Smith Memorial Dinner. Speakers: Mayor Robert Wagner, Governor Nelson Rockefeller, Senator John F. Kennedy, Francis Cardenal Spellman. Guest Soloist: RS, acc. by James Shomate. Waldorf-Astoria Hotel, New York.
3 Nov.	Cerebral Palsey Humanitarian Award Dinner. Soloists: RS, Robert Merrill, Nat King Cole, Tony Cabot Orchestra. Waldorf-Astoria Hotel, New York.
12, 23 Nov., 6 Dec., 6 Feb.	*Carmen*: (Carmen); Dimiter Uzunov (Don José); Heidi Krall (Micaela); Mario Sereni (Escamillo); Norman Scott (Zuniga); Clifford Harvuot (Morales); Teresa Stratas (Frasquita); Margaret Roggero (Micaela); Paul Franke (Remendado); George Cehanovsky (Dancaïro); Jean Morel, (Cond). (MO); Nov. 23 William Olvis (Don José); Maria Louisa Nache (Micaela); Robert Merrill (Escamillo); Helen Vanni (Mercedes); Alessio de Paolis (Remendado); Dec. 6 William Olvis (Don José); Heidi Krall (Micaela); Robert Merrill (Escamillo); Alessio de Paolis (Remendado); Feb 6 Richard Tucker (Don José); Lucine Amara (Micaela); Frank Guarrera (Escamillo). (MO-Texaco Broadcast)
Recitals	30 Nov. Jackson, Tennessee; 2 Dec. East St. Louis, Illinois.
9, 10 Dec.	Concert, Henry Mozer, Cond., Wheeling, West Virginia (Selections from *Orfeo, Nozze, Carmen, Herodiade*).
Recitals	13 Dec. Trenton, New Jersey; 15 Albany, New York.
24 Dec.	TV, Jack Paar Show (with Nicolas Surovy).
29 Dec.	Eleventh Annual Tiara Ball. RS Mystery Guest "Juliette Marglen". Prize awarded to person who guessed her true identity. Benefit Spence-Chapin Adoption Service, Waldorf-Astoria Hotel, New York.
4 Jan.	TV, Steve Allen Plymouth Show ("In the still of the night") Other guests were Keenan Wynn and Roger Williams).
7 Jan.	Recital, Peekskill, New York.
10 Jan.	Goodspeed Opera House Foundation, "Intimate Musicale". Licia Albanese, Barry Morell, Cornell MacNeil, Sally Leff, acc., Greenwich, Connecticut ("Che farò", "Voi che sapete", "Sure on this shining night", "Rabbit at top speed", "My hero", with MacNeil).
Recitals	17 Jan. Boston, Massachusetts (Program ended with the "Lord's Prayer" dedicated to

| | Richard Cardinal Cushing, assisted by the Regis College Glee Club and St. Teresa Chorale, Symphony Hall); 20 El Dorado, Kansas; 22 Lufkin, Texas; 26 Grand Junction, Colorado; 28 Missoula, Montana; 1 Feb. Jackson, Michigan. |

Recitals 9 Feb. Lewisburg, Pennsylvania; 12 Detroit, Michigan.

16 Feb. Concert, Robert Hull, Cond., Fort Worth Symphony, Fort Worth, Texas ("Che farò", "Voi che sapete", "Mon coeur", "Habañera", "Seguidilla", "Chanson Bohème").

22, 24 Feb. *Carmen*, (Carmen); Brian Sullivan (Don José); Dorothy Warenskjold (Micaela); Walter Cassel (Escamillo); Emerson Buckley (Cond). Miami, Florida; Feb. 24 Irene Patti (Micaela).

8 March Concert, Arthur Bennett Lipkin, Cond., Birmingham Symphony, Birmingham, Alabama ("Che farò", "Voi che sapete", "Mon coeur", Ravel, "Seguidilla marciana", "Jota", "Polo").

17 March *Der Rosenkavalier*: (Octavian); Leonie Rysanek (Marschallin); Oskar Czerwenka (Baron Ochs); Hilde Gueden (Sophie); Marko Rothmüller (Faninal); Charles Kullman (Valzacchi); Martha Lipton (Annina); Da Costa (Singer); Erich Leinsdorf (Cond). (MO)

18 March *Golden Jubilee Gala*, Boy Scouts of America, Don Ameche, M.C., Henry Belafonte, Hotel Astor, New York.

Recitals 21 March Williamsport, Pennsylvania; 23 Sharon, Pennsylvania; 25 McKeesport, Pennsylvania.

31 Mar, 2 Apr. *Samson et Dalila*: (Dalila); Ramon Vinay (Samson); Joseph Mordino (High Priest); Arthur Cosenza (Abimélech); Ara Berberian (Old Hebrew); Renato Cellini (Cond). New Orleans Opera.

Recitals 5 Apr. Albany, Georgia; 7 Milledgeville, Georgia; 9 Marietta, Ohio; 24 Dover, Delaware; 30 Montreal, Canada; 3 May Muncie, Indiana; 6 University Glee Club, James Shomate, acc., Academy of Music, Philadelphia, Pennsylvania ("Ruhe meine seele", "Mausfallensprüchlein", "Heimkehn", "O lieblachewangen", Ravel, "Seguidilla", Bizet. "Seguidilla", "Mon coeur", "I'm falling in love with someone" and "You'll never walk alone" with Glee Club.)

15 May Concert, Calvin Rogers, Cond., Akron Symphony, Akron, Ohio ("Che farò", "Voi che sapete", "Mon coeur", "Habañera", "Seguidilla", "Chanson Bohème").

26 June TV, Ed Sullivan's, *Toast of the town* ("Climb every mountain", "So in love").

2 July Concert, Arthur Fiedler (Cond), Chicago Symphony, Ravinia, Illinois ("Che farò", "Voi che sapete", "Air de Lia", "Habañera", "Seguidilla", "Chanson Bohème").

26 July Concert, Zubin Mehta , Cond. ("Che farò", "Voi che sapete", "Mon coeur", "Adieu, forêts", "Air de Lia", "Chanson Bohème") Lewisohn Stadium, New York.

(In addition to TV shows listed above, RS appeared on *Masquerade party* disguised as a conductor who was a combination of Fritz Reiner, Leonard Bernstein and Arturo Toscanini; Alma Dettinger, WQXR, New York, interview re *Subway to the Met*).

1960-1961

Recital Program, same as 1958-1959.

18 Sept. TV, Ed Sullivan's, *Toast of the town* ("Getting to know you", sung in Russian).

10, 11 Oct. Concerts, Joseph Levine, Cond., Omaha Symphony, Omaha, Nebraska ("Che farò", "Voi che sapete", "Mon coeur", "Habañera", "Seguidilla", "Chanson Bohème").

14 Oct. Recital, Ottumwa, Iowa.

Concerts 17 Oct. John Hoover, Cond., Mobile Symphony, Mobile, Alabama ("Habañera", "Seguidilla", "Chanson Bohème", "Che farò", "Voi che sapete"); 24 Jacques Singer, Cond., Corpus Christi Symphony, Corpus Christi, Texas ("Che farò", "Voi che sapete", "Air de Lia", "Habañera", "Seguidilla", "Chanson Bohème"); 2 Nov. Paul Katz, Cond., Dayton Philharmonic, Dayton, Ohio ("Che farò", "Voi che sapete", "Mon coeur", "Habañera", "Seguidilla", "Chanson Bohème").

Recitals 4 Nov. Greenville, South Carolina; 7 U.S. Naval Academy, Annapolis, Maryland; 9 Utica, New York.

19 Nov. Concert, Alfredo Antonini, Cond., Tampa, Florida ("Che farò", "Voi che sapete", "Mon coeur", "Habañera", "Seguidilla", "Chanson Bohème").

12 Dec. Recital, Hartford, Connecticut.

19 Dec., 2 Jan. *Chanukah Festival for Israel*, Mike Wallace, M.C., David Bar-Illan, Nathan Milstein, Jan Peerce, Maurice Levine, Cond., New York Philharmonic (members), Madison Square Garden, New York ("Il est doux", "In the still of the night", "Anu, Banu Artza", "Agada",

Israeli folk songs, arr. by Arthur Harris).
23 Dec. TV, *Telephone hour*, Special Christmas Program.
1 Jan. TV, *Grand illusion*, Michael Manuel, Thomas Schippers, George London (round table discussion on opera).
8 Jan. Recital, University of Florida.
11 Jan. Concert, Evan Whallon, Cond., Columbus Symphony, Columbus, Ohio ("Lieder eines fahrenden gesellen" "Songs of the Wayfarer", "Habañera", "Seguidilla", "Chanson Bohème").
Recitals 20 Jan. Salt Lake City, Utah; 25 Seattle,Washington.
28 Jan. Concert, Johnny Green, Cond., Los Angeles Philharmonic, Los Angeles, California ("Habañera", "Seguidilla", "Chanson Bohème", "One night of love", "Getting to know you", "I could have danced all night").
Recitals 2 Feb. Honolulu, Hawaii (encores: "Look, Edwin", "Habañera", "Were you there"); 6 Pomona, California; 28 Pittsburgh, Pennsylvania (encore: incl. "Were you there"); 9 Ponca City, Oklahoma; 11 Arlington, Texas; 14 Harlingen, Texas; 2, 3 March Tallahas see, Florida; 6 Harrisonburg, Virginia; 8 Hopkinsville, Kentucky; 10 Portsmouth, Ohio; 14 University of Massachusetts; 20 Warsaw, Indiana; 3 Pine Bluff, Arkansas; 25 Kansas City, Missouri; Evanston, Illinois.
12 April *Carmen*: (Carmen); William Olvis (Don José); Lucine Amara (Micaela); Robert Merrill (Escamillo); Norman Scott (Zuniga); Clifford Harvuot (Morales); Gloria Lind (Frasquita); Margaret Roggero (Mercedes); Paul Franke (Remendado); George Cehanovsky (Dancaïro); Jean Morel Cond). (MO)
Recitals 15 April Manchester, New Hampshire; 18 Toronto, Ontario; 23 Chicago, Illinois; 27 Kohler, Wisconsin; 30 Cleveland, Ohio; 3 May Grand Rapids, Michigan.
14 May Recital, Jamaica, New York, Jewish Center (Two concluding arias were replaced by, "Anu, Banu Artza" and "Agada").
17 May Detroit Friends of Yeshiva University, David Diamond and Orchestra, Detroit, Michigan.
28 June American Medical Education Foundation Benefit, Norman Masonson, Cond., Brian Sullivan, Doctors'Orchestral Society, Carnegie Hall, New York ("Che farò", "Voi che sapete", "Mon coeur", "Habañera", "Seguidilla", "Chanson Bohème").
(In addition to the recitals listed above RS also appeared through Community Concerts in the following cities: Sumter, South Carolina; Pampa, Texas)
1961-1962
Recital Program, same as 1958-1959.
30 Sept. Queens College Inaugural Concert, w. James Shomate. Queens, New York.
Recitals 10 Oct. Florence, South Carolina; 14 Sumter, South Carolina.
7 Nov. Denver Symphony, Saul Coston, Cond., Denver, Colorado ("Air de Lia", "Mon coeur", "Habañera", "Seguidilla", "Chanson Bohème").
Recitals 22 Nov. Cleveland Heights, Ohio; 1 Dec. Ohio University; 15 Philadelphia, Pennsylvania ("Love's philosophy", "Sure on this shining night", "Widmung", "Ruhe meine seele", de Falla, "Seguidilla", "Habañera", "Mon coeur"; encore: "My hero", with Pennsylvania Glee Club).
17 Dec. Man of the Year Award, Chicago, Illinois. (guest)
5 March Charlotte Symphony, Henry Janiec, Cond., Charlotte, North Carolina ("Che farò", "Voi che sapete", "Mon coeur", "Habañera", "Seguidilla", "Chanson Bohème").
Recitals 10 March Hollywood, California; 14 Portland, Oregon.
19 May Detroit Symphony, Gregory Miller, Cond., Detroit, Michigan .
29 June General Federation of Women's Clubs, Sheraton Park Hotel, Washington, D.C., Ryan Edwards, acc. ("Love's Philosophy", "Sure on this shining night", "Habañera", "Seguidilla", "Mon coeur", "Falling in love with someone").
5 Aug. TV, Ed Sullivan's, *Toast of the town* ("Getting to know you", sung in Russian and English).
(In addition to the recitals through Community Concerts in the following cities: Belvedere, Illinois; Altus, Oklahoma; Fredericton, N.B., Canada; St. John, N.B., Canada; State Isles, Quebec, Canada; Sault St. Marie, Ontario, Canada; Rochester, Minnesota; Sioux Falls, South Dakota; Clarksdale, Missouri;

Gastonia, North Carolina; Key West, Florida; Ocala, Florida; Sarasota, Florida; Portsmouth, Virginia; Seaford, Delaware; Riverhead, New York; Kingston, New York; Greensburg, Pennsylvania.

1962-1963

Recital Program, same as 1958-1959, except "Habañera" substituted for "Chanson Bohème").

Concerts	19 Sept. *Symphony of the Air*, Arthur Fiedler, Cond., Robert Merrill, Carnegie Hall, New York ("Habañera", "Seguidilla", "Mon coeur", "Will you remember", with Merrill); 10 Oct. Florence, South Carolina; 20 Detroit Symphony, Paul Paray, Cond.,103rd Worcester Festival, Worcester, Pennsylvania ("Mon coeur", "Lieder eines fahrenden gesellen" "Songs of a Wayfarer"; 23 Jacksonville Symphony, John Canarina, Cond., Jacksonville, Florida ("Che puro ciel", "Che farò", "Habañera", "Seguidilla", "Chanson Bohème"; encore: "One night of love"); 26, Milwaukee Symphony, Henry John Brown, Cond., Milwaukee, Wisconsin ("Habañera", "Seguidilla", "Mon coeur", "One night of love", "Stars in my eyes", "I could have danced all night"); 27 same as 26 except program for young adults ("Habañera", "Seguidilla", "Mon coeur").
30 Sept.	TV, *Voice of Firestone*, Arthur Fiedler, Cond., Cesare Siepi, Mischa Elman, Sally Ann Howes (Opening theme, "Mon coeur", "I love you" and "Shall we dance", with Siepi, Howes).
18 Nov.	Recital, Sheraton Park Hotel, Wahington, D.C.
5 Dec.	TV, *Voice of Firestone*, Howard Barlow, Cond., Brian Sullivan, Columbus Boy's Choir (Opening theme, "Silent night", "O Christmas tree", with Sullivan, "Here we come a-wassailing", "Deck the halls", with Chorus and Sullivan, "What Child is this", "O little town of Bethlehem", with Sullivan, "We wish you a Merry Christmas", with entire cast, "Joy to the world", "Adeste fideles" and Closing theme, with entire cast). Shown 23 Dec.
8 Dec.	Appeared on the intermission feature, "Opera News on the Air", during the Metropolitan Opera broadcast of *Cavalleria rusticana* and *Pagliacci*. Other guests included Robert Merrill, Teresa Stratas, Charles Anthony, Ezio Flagello, Norman Mittelmann, George Shirley and Howard Hook, Jr.
Concerts	7 Jan. Waco Symphony, Danial Sternberg, Cond., Waco, Texas ("Lieder eines fahrenden gesellen" "Songs of a Wayfarer", "Habañera", "Seguidilla"); 12 Feb. Tucson Symphony, Frederic Balzas, Cond., Tucson, Arizona ("Che farò", "Mon coeur", "Lieder eines Fahrenden gesellen", "Songs of a Wayfarer").
28 March	Recital, University of Virginia.
14 April	TV, *Voice of Firestone*, Arthur Fiedler, Cond., Theodore Uppman, Maria Tallchief, Oleg Tupine (Opening theme, "Hello young lovers", "Habañera", Gounod, "Ave Maria", Closing theme, with entire cast).
18 April	Recital, Bristol, Virginia
12 May	TV, *Voice of Firestone*, Henry John Brown, Cond., Colman Blumfeld, Alfred Drake (Opening theme, with Drake, "A kiss in the dark", "Whispering", with Drake, "Lover come back to me", "Can't help lovin'that man", "S'wonderful" and Closing theme, with entire cast).
31 May	Rotterdam Hilton Flower Show, Gerard von Krevelen and his Orchestra (selections unspecified).
16 Aug.	Concert, Henri Rene, Cond., C. W. Post College, New York.

(In addition to the recitals listed above RS also appeared through Community Concerts in the following cities:New Jersey; Anderson, South Carolina; Waycross, Georgia; Lake Wales, Florida; Goldsboro, North Carolina; Paducah, Kentucky; Mason City, Iowa; Hutchinson, Kansas; Bay City, Michigan; Iron Mountain, Michigan; Traverse City, Michigan, Petoskey, Michigan; Minot, North Dakota; Glendale, California; Oneonta, New York).

RS appeared in the documentary film, *A legend is born*, which related the development of Lincoln Center.

1963-1964

Recital Program, same as 1958-1959 except "Habañera" for "Chanson Bohème".

7 Sept.	*Harvest Moon Ball*, Madison Square Garden, New York.
Recitals	15 Oct. Nashville, Tennessee (encores: "Nichts", "Because", "Were you there"); 4 Nov. Elizabeth, New Jersey (encore: "Nichts"); 8 Naperville, Illinois; 9 Jan. Northeast Mission,

State Teachers College; 4 Feb. China Lake, California; 15 March Chicago, Illinois w. Bjornson Male Chorus.

(In addition to the recitals listed above RS also appeared through Community Concerts in the following cities: Hinsdale, Illinois; Farmingham, Massachusetts; Greenville, Missouri). and heard in: *Journey back to Oz*, (Glinda, "You have only you"); Milton Berle (Cowardly Lion); Herschel Bernardi (Woodenhead the Horse); Paul Ford (Uncle Harry); Margaret Hamilton (Aunt Em); Jack E. Leonard (Signpost); Paul Lynde (Pumpkinhead); Ethel Merman (Mombi); Liza Minelli (Dorothy); Mickey Rooney (Scarecrow); Danny Thomas (Tinman); Mel Blanc; Larry Storch. Music and Lyrics: Sammy Cahn and James van Huesen. Director: Hal Sutherland. Performers provided the voices for this animated film in color made in 1964 and released in 1974.

1964-1965

Recital Program, same as 1958-1959 except "Habañera" for "Chanson Bohème".

Recitals	5, 6 Oct. Kalamazoo, Michigan; 8 Garden City, Kansas; 10 Chicago, Illinois; 27 Freeport, Texas.
12 Dec.	Radio, Intermission, *Rigoletto*, Marcia Davenport, Michael Manuel (discussion re National Company). (MO)
23 March	Radio, Luncheon with Mimi Benzell, Drake Hotel, New York. 12-2 NBC (Interviewed re Albert Einstein Award).
30 April	Recital, Congressional Club Luncheon, Washington, D.C.
6 July	*King and I*, (Anna); Darren McGavin, (The King); Lee Venora (Tuptim); Patricia Neway (Lady Thiang); Frank Poretta, (Lun Tha); Michael Kermoyan (Kralhome); James Harvey (Louis Leonowens); Franz Allers, Cond. Edward Greenberg, Stage Director; Irene Sharaff, Costumes; Paul G. McGuire, Sets; Jerome Robbins, Choreography (reproduced by Yuriko).
17 July	Concert, "Music under the stars", Alfredo Antonini, Cond., Milwaukee, Wisconsin ("Che farò", "Habañera", "Mon coeur"; encore: "Getting to know you")

(In addition to the recitals listed above RS also appeared through Community Concerts in Augusta, Georgia). Although the chronology ends with RS' retirement from performing, two memorable television events that occurred later were:

22 April, 1972 TV, Host for Rudolf Bing Gala. One hour of the more than six hour program was telecast.

2 Dec., 1990 (TV delayed) Kennedy Center award to RS, Katherine Hepburn, Julie Styne, Gene Wilder; Dizzy Gillespie.

NATIONAL COMPANY

1965-1966

Susannah: Robert La Marchina, Cond., José Quintero, Director; David Hayes, Set Designer; Jane Greenwood, Costume Designer; Rhoda Levine, Choreographer.

Madama Butterfly: Samuel Krachmalnick, Cond.; Yoshio Aoyama, Director; Ming Cho Lee, Designer. Sung in Italian or English.

La Cenerentola: Samuel Krachmalnick, Conductor; Gunther Rennert, Director; Beni Montresor, Designer; Rhoda Levine, Choreographer; Ruth and Thomas Martin Translation.

Carmen: Robert La Marchina, Cond.; Louis Ducreux, Director; Bernard Daydé, Designer; Luis Olivares, Choreography. Sung in French or in English Translation by John Gutman.

1966-1967

Le Nozze di Figaro: Robert La Marchina, Cond.; Kirk Browning, Director; Ming Cho Lee, Set Designer; Jane Greenwood, Costume Designer; Rhoda Levine, Choreographer; Ruth and Thomas Martin, Translation.

La Traviata: Samuel Krachmalnick, Cond.; Yoshio Aoyama, Director; Rolf Gérard, Designer; Rhoda Levine, Choreographer. Sung in Italian or English.

La Bohème: Samuel Krachmalnick, Cond.; José Quintero, Director; David Hayes, Set Designer; Jane Greenwood, Costume Designer; Rhoda Levine, Choreographer. Sung in Italian or English.

The Rape of Lucretia: Robert La Marchina, Cond.; Gunther Rennert, Director; Alfred Sierke, Designer

DISCOGRAPHY

* = unreleased

RCA Victor
1935
DC24   *Gems from Romberg Operettas*
             Blossom time: "My springtime thou art" w. chorus (12951-A)
             My Maryland: "Mother" (12954-A)
Risë Stevens uncredited
also appearing uncredited:
             Helen Marshall, Helen Olheim, Morton Bowe, Thomas L. Thomas, Milton
             Watson Nathaniel Shilkret, Conductor, Salon Symphony Orchestra (also on
             Camden LP239)
Columbia Masterworks
1941
21 Feb.   *CO-29794   Dvorak, "My song resounds"
             *CO-29795   Dvorak, "I love thee"
             *CO-29796   Leoni, "A little China figure" Weaver, "Moon-marketing"
             *CO-29797   Folk Song, "Roving in the dew" Diack, "Little Jack Horner
13 March   *CO-30001   Brahms: "Sonntag"; "Meine liebe ist grun"
             *CO-30002   Brahms: "Der tod"; "Das ist die kuhle nacht"
             CO-30003   Schumann: "Widmung"; "Du meine seele"
             CO-30004   H. Wolf: "In dem schatten meiner lachen"
                          "Mansfallen-spruchlein" (17297-D Feb.,1942)
7 April   *XCO-30265   Thomas, "Connais-tu le pays", *Mignon*
             *XCO-30266   Bizet, "Habañera", *Carmen*
17 Sept.   XCO-30514   Bizet, "Habañera", *Carmen*
             XCO-30515   Thomas, "Connais-tu le pays", *Mignon*
                          Orchestra conducted by Frieder Weissmann (first recordings
                          issued, 71192-D Sept., 1941;
21 Sept.   HCO-516   Mozart, "Non so più", *Le Nozze di Figaro*
             HCO-517   Mozart, "Voi che sapete",   "
             XHCO-518   Gluck, "Che puro ciel", *Orfeo ed Euridice*
             XHCO-519   Gluck, "Che farò senza Euridice",
                          Orchestra conducted by Erich Leinsdorf (1*, 2* 17298-D March*,
                          1942, 3, 4 71365-D May, 1942; 1, 2, 4 Odyssey Y 31738, March,
                          1969; no. 4 Odyssey 32 16 0304)*included in Lebendige
                          Vergangenheit CD 89556
5 Oct.   HCO-534   O. Straus, "Forgive", with Nelson Eddy (4283-M)
             HCO-535   O. Straus, *Chocolate soldier*, with Nelson Eddy (4283-M)
             HCO-536   O. Straus, "Ti-ra-la-la" (4282-M)
             HCO-537   O. Straus, "Sympathy", with Nelson Eddy (4281-M)

6 Oct.	HCO-541	O. Straus, "My hero", with Nelson Eddy (4281-M)
	HCO-542	O. Straus, "My lady sleeps", Nelson Eddy The chocolate soldier Orchestra conducted by Robert Armbruster (M-482 Jan. 1942; ML 4060; ML 54060; CSP P-13707; no. 5, Nelson Eddy's Greatest Hits, CS 9481)
		The student Prince and the chocolate soldier (ML4060; ML54060)
		The chocolate soldier and Naughty Marietta (CSP-P13707)
		Naughty Marietta features Nadine Conner and Nelson Eddy.
		Hear them again, Reader's Digest, 1968 "My hero" (RD3-49)

1942

21 June	XCO-32980	Gluck, "Divinites du Styx", *Alceste*
	XCO-32981	Meyerbeer, "Ah! mon fils", *Le Prophête*
	XCO-32982	Donizetti, "O mio Fernando", *La Favorita*
	XCO-32983	Tchaikovsky, "Adieu forêts", *Jeanne d'Arc*
		Orchestra conducted by Erich Leinsdorf; (1, 2 71486-D Nov., 1943, 3, 4 71440-D Feb. 1943; Odyssey Y 31738, 1972)
30 June	*CO-32992	Brahms, "Der tod das ist"
	*CO-32993	Grieg, "I love thee"
	*CO-32994	Delibes, "Sweet Suzanne"
	*XCO-32995	Kingsford, "Command"; Leoni, "A little China figure"
	*CO-32996	Weinberger, "Olympia", "Conversation"
	"CO-32997	Weaver, "Moon-marketing"; Bridge, "Love went a' riding"
	*CO-32998	Brahms, "Der schmied"
	*CO-33026	Dvorak, "Songs my mother taught me"
	*CO-33027	Purcell, "I attempt from love's sickness"
	*CO-33028	Rachmaninoff, "In the silence of the night"

1944

A night at Carnegie Hall
Sound track for *Carnegie Hall* film
"Mon coeur s'ouvre à ta voix", *Samson et Dalila*; "Seguidilla", *Carmen* (ML 2113, Set MM-676)

NB: During this period numerous unaccounted for radio transcription discs were made for the Armed Forces radio service, War and Navy Departments. Among them are an undated 15 minute program in which RS sang: "Moonlight madonna", "All of my life", "You belong to my heart" and "Together". Radio program #711. This recording was for broadcast use only. Transcription discs were also made for each war bond purchased through Records for our Fighting Men project, one song per bond. Songs included, "The sweetest story ever told", "Love has wings" (V disc #413).

1945

8 Feb.	XCO-34258	Kern, "Look for the silver lining", *Sally* (7422-M)
	XCO-34259	Kern, "They didn't believe me", *The Girl from Utah* (7421-M)
	XCO-34260	Kern, "All the things you are", *Very Warm for May* (7423-M)
		Songs of Jerome Kern with Sylvan Schulman, Conductor (M568, ML54270, Feb., 1950)

15 Feb.	XCO-34229	Schubert, "Ave Maria" (7425-M)
	XCO-34230	Shannon, "Too-ra-loo-ra-loo-ra" (Irish lullaby) (7425-M, June, 1945; no. 2 in Collectors'Choice A34228 CD)
	XCO-34280	Kern, "Don't ever leave me", *Sweet Adeline* (7424-M)
	XCO-34281	Kern, "The touch of your hand", Roberta *Songs of Jerome Kern* with Sylvan Schulman, Conductor (M568; ML54270, Feb., 1950; no.1 in Odyssey Y31738; no.2 in MET 254)
6 Feb.	XCO-34315	Kern, "Can't help lovin' dat man", *Show Boat* (7421-M)
	XCO-34316	Kern, "Smoke gets in your eyes", *Roberta* (7422-M)
	XCO-34317	Kern, "The song is you", *Music in the Air* (7422-M) *Songs of Jerome Kern* with Sylvan Schulman,Conductor M568; ML54270, Feb., 1950; nos.2, 5, 6, 7 in Collectors' Choice A34228 CD)
25 June	HCO-1437	Romberg, "Lover come back to me", *New Moon* (4331-M0)
	HCO-1438	Kern, "Dearly beloved", *You were Never Lovelier* (4331-M)
	HCO-1439	Fields, "I love you", *Mexican Hayride* (remade 27 June)
	HCO-1440	Gershwin, "Love walked in", *Rhapsody in Blue* *Love songs* with Sylvan Schulman (M595; ML4179, Feb.,1946; no. 2 on MET-205))
27 June	HCO-1439	Porter, "I love you" (remake, 4333-M)
	HCO-1447	Gershwin, "The man I love", *Lady, be Good* (4332-M)
	HCO-1448	Rodgers, "Lover", *Love Me Tonight*
	HCO-1449	Herbert, "I'm falling in love with someone", *Naughty Marietta* (4333-M)
	HCO-1450	Rodgers, "Falling in love with love", *The Boys from Syracuse* (4333-M) *Love songs* with Sylvan Schulman (M595;ML4179, Feb.,1946 nos. 4,6,7,9 in Collectors' Choice A34228 CD)
31 Dec.	XCO-35566	Bizet, "Chanson bohème" (71740-D)
	XCO-35567	Bizet, "Air des cartes" (71742-D)
1946		
14 Jan.	XCO-35627	Bizet, "Habañera" (71739-D)
	XCO-35628	Bizet, Final scene, with Raoul Jobin (71743-D)
	XCO-35629	Bizet, Final scene (concluded) (included in Raoul Jobin Preiser 89517)
15 Jan.	XCO-35630	Bizet, "Seguidilla", with Raoul Jobin (71740-D) Also included "Prelude", Act 1, "Votre toast" (Weede),"La fleur que tu m'avais jetée", (Jobin), "Je dis que rien ne m'épouvante" (Conner). Metropolitan Opera Orchestra and Chorus conducted by George Sebastian with RS (Carmen), Jobin (Don José), Nadine Conner (Micaela), Robert Weede (Escamillo) (above selections recorded as part of *Carmen* highlights album M-607, 71739-43-D March, 1946; A-607 May 1954; ML4013 May, 1950; Odyssey Y32102 April, 1973; Odyssey YT 32102

cassette.no. 6 on M-676, 71974-D April, 1947 and MM-676, 71978-D, April, 1947; "Seguidilla" and duet on MET- 100 and MET 254;Final scene on MET-607; "Habañera", Sony Classical 64594: Sony Classical 89370, Sony Classical 66707).

3 April	XCO-36046	Porter, "Ev'ry thing I love", *Let's Face It*
	XCO-36047	Porter, "What is this thing called love", *Wake Up and Dream*
	XCO-36048	Porter, "I've got you under my skin", *Born to Dance* with Sylvan Schulman, Conductor (MM630, Oct., 1946)
16 April	XCO-36116	Porter, "In the still of the night", *Rosalie*
	XCO-36117	Porter, "Night and day", *Gay Divorce*
	XCO-36118	Porter, "Begin the Beguine", *Jubilee* Album of Cole Porter songs with Sylvan Schulman, Conductor (MM630, Oct., 1946; nos.1, 2, 3, 5, 6)
29 April	CO-36221	del Riego, "Homing"
	CO-36222	Nevin, "The rosary"
	CO-36223	Tate, "Somewhere a voice is calling"
	CO-36224	Cadman, "At dawning" with Sylvan Schulman, Conductor (issued as *Sincerely yours*, MM654; ML4179, Feb., 1947)
1 May	CO-36231	Rasbach, "Trees"
	CO-36232	Stults, "Sweetest story ever told"
	CO-36233	Bartlett, "A dream"
	CO-36234	Molloy, "Love's old sweet song" with Sylvan Schulman, Conductor (issued as *Sincerely yours*, MM654; ML4179, Feb., 1947) (no. 2, no. 4, no. 6, no. 8 comprise 45rpm A-1539; no. 1 on Odyssey Y31738) *Risë Stevens: songs* "At dawning", "The Rosary", "Love's old sweet song", "The sweetest story ever told", with Sylvan Schulman (Columbia A-1539). Originally in *Sincerely yours.*

1947

7 Feb.	XCO-37361	Saint-Saëns, *Samson et Dalila,* "Mon coeur s'ouvre à ta voix" Metropolitan Opera Orchestra conducted by Fausto Cleva (M-676, 71974-D April, 1947; MM-676, 71978-D April, 1947; ML-2113 May, 1950).
	XCO-37363	Ponchielli, *La Gioconda,* "Bella così, madonna", with Ezio Pinza
	XCO-37364	Thomas, *Mignon,* "Légères hirondelles", with Ezio Pinza. Metropolitan Opera Orchestra conducted by Fausto Cleva (72371-D Dec., 1947; Odyssey Y31148; Philips SBF 290; No. 2 MET 114-A)
14 Feb.	XCO-37332	Herbert, "A kiss in the dark", *Orange Blossoms*
	XCO-37333	Herbert, "Kiss me again", *Madamoiselle Modeste*
	XCO-37381	Herbert, "When you're away", *The Only Girl* with Sylvan Schulman, Conductor and Male Chorus (M682, June, 1947; ML2013)

28 Feb.		Herbert, "Ah, sweet mystery of life", *Naughty Marietta* with Sylvan Schulman, Conductor.
5, 6 June	XCO37849- XCO-3787	Humperdinck, *Hansel and Gretel* Metropolitan Opera Orchestra and Chorus with Max Rudolf,Conductor, RS (Hansel), Nadine Conner (Gretel), Thelma Votipka (Witch & Sandman), John Brownlee (Peter),Claramae Turner (Gertrude), Lillian Raymondi (Dewman) (MOP-26, Sept., 1947; Ml4078/9; Oct., 1948; Odyssey Y2-32547/8, Nov., 1973)
30 July	CO-39068	"Moon love", Tchaikovsky, Symphony no. 5
	CO-39069	"Full moon and empty arms", Rachmaninoff, piano concerto no. 2
	CO-39070	"Tonight we love", Tchaikovsky, piano concerto no. 1
	CO-39071	"As years go by", Brahms, Hungarian dance no. 4 with Morris Stoloff, Conductor (MM826; ML2039, May, 1949)
8 Aug.	CO-39072	"Strange music", Grieg, "Nocturne" and "Wedding day at Troldhaugen" from Wright, Forrest, *Song of Norway*
	CO-39073	"Our love",Tchaikovsky, *Romeo and Juliette*
	CO-39074	"The lamp is low", Ravel, "Pavane" (remade 0 Aug.) with Morris Stoloff, Conductor (MM826; ML2039, May, 1949)
11 Aug.	CO-39078	Romberg, "Golden days"
	CO-39079	Romberg, "Just we two"
	CO-39080	Romberg, "Serenade" *The student Prince* with Nelson Eddy, Chorus, Rombert Armbruster, Conductor (MM724; ML4060, Jan., 1948; ML54060; CSP-13707)
18 Aug.	CO-39089	Romberg, "Come boys"
	CO-39090	Romberg, "Deep in my heart" no. 2 with Nelson Eddy, Chorus,Rombert Armbruster, Conductor (MM724; ML4060, Jan., 1948; ML54060; CSP-13707) CO-39091, "Drinking song", Eddy solo *The student Prince and The chocolate soldier,* (ML4060; ML54060)
20 Aug.	CO-39092	Rubinstein,"Since first I met thee"
	CO-39074	"The lamp is low", Ravel, "Pavane" (remake) with Morris Stoloff, Conductor (MM826; ML2039, May, 1949)
	CO-39094	Youmans, "Through the years"
	CO-39095	"Bless this house" with Morris Stoloff, Conductor (4501-M, Nov., 1947; no. 2 in Collectors' Choice A34228 CD)
22 Dec.	CO-39710	Berlin, "They say it's wonderful", *Annie Get Your Gun*
	C0-39711	Berlin, "Always"
	CO-39712	Berlin, "How deep is the ocean", *Mammy*
	CO-39713	Berlin, "Remember" with Dudley King, Conductor (MM784, Oct., 1948; nos. 2, 3, 4 in Collectors' Choice A34228 CD)
	CO-39714	Gade, "Jalousie",with Dudley King, Conductor (remade 31 Dec., 4528-M, July, 1948)

29 Dec.	CO-39830	d'Hardelot, "Because"
	CO-39831	de Koven, "Oh promise me" (4515-M)
	CO-39832	Romberg, "Wanting you", *Desert Song*
	CO-39833	Romberg, "Will you remember", *Maytime* with Dudley King, Conductor (ML4270, MX332, Feb., 1950; ML54270)
31 Dec.	CO-39863	Brown, Freed, "Temptation",with Dudley King, Conductor (4528-M, July, 1948)
	CO-39864	Berlin, "Easter parade", *As Thousands Cheer*
	CO-39865	Berlin, "Say it with music", *Music Box Review* with Dudley King, Conductor (MM784, Oct., 1948; Collectors' Choice A34228 CD)
	C0-39866	Romberg, "One alone", *The Desert Song*
	CO-39867	Romberg, "One kiss", *New Moon* with Dudley King, Conductor (ML4270, MX332, Feb., 1950; ML54270)
	CO-39714	Gade, "Jalousie", with Dudley King, Conductor (remake, 4528-M, July, 1948)

1949

16 Feb.	*XCO-41003	Wolf, "Das verlassene Magdlein" (remade 14 April)
	*XCO-41004	Wolf, "Ich hab in penna einen liebsten"
	*XCO-41005	Brahms, "Meine liebe ist grun"
	*XCO-41006	Brahms, "Von ewiger liebe" (remade 14 April)
	*XCO-41007	R. Strauss, "Zuneigung" (remade 14 April)
	*XCO-41008	R. Strauss, "Traum durch die dammerung"
14 April	*XCO-41151	Wolf, "Mignon"
	*XCO-41152	Wolf, "Mignon"
	*XCO-41153	Wolf, "Verborgenheit"
	*XCO-41154	Brahms, "Weigenlied", "Sonntag"
	*XCO-41155	Brahms, "Der tod das ist die kuhle nacht"
	*XCO-41003, *XCO-41006, *XCO-41007 (remade)	
1 May	CO-41273	Lehar, "In Marsovia"
	CO-41274	Lehar, "Ladies' choice",with Dennis Morgan
	CO-41275	Lehar, "Vilia"
	CO-41276	Lehar, "The cavalier", with Dennis Morgan
	CO-41278	Lehar, "My marriage will be one arranged" with Dennis Morgan
	CO-41280	Lehar, "I love you so", with Dennis Morgan *Merry widow* with Dennis Morgan, Max Rudolf, Conductor (MM849, Sept., 1949; ML2064, Sept., 1949)
	CO-41277	"Maxims",
	CO-41279	"Women", Dennis Morgan solos 1962-1963 23/1, 22/5

Weil *Lady in the dark* with RS (Liza Elliott); Adolph Green (Beekman and Ringmaster); John Reardon (Randy Curtis); Stephanie Augustine (Sutton); Kenneth Bridges (Charley Johnson); Roger White(Kendal Nesbitt); Lehman

Engel (Cond) Oh, fabulous one"; "Huxley"; "One life to live"; "Girl of the moment"; Wedding dream, "Liza,Liza"; "Mapleton High chorale"; "This is new"; "The Princess of pure delight"; "Circus dream"; "The best years of his life"; "Tchaikovsky", "The saga of Jenny"; Childhood dream, "My ship") (OL-5990; OS-2390; "My ship", Odyssey Y31738; "Saga of Jenny", MET 252; SONY CD MHK 62869

CD album includes Danny Kaye in, "One life to live"; "The Princess of pure delight"; "It's never to late to Mendelssohn"; "Tchaikovsky and other Russians"; "Jenny"; "My ship". Maurice Abravanel, Cond. Recorded 28/2/41).

Anthologies

Odyssey   Legendary performances: Risë Stevens Album consists of reissues of Columbia recordings: "Habañera" (17 September, 1941); "Che farò senza Euridice (21 September, 1941); "Connais-tu le pays"(18 September, 1941); "Voi che sapete", (21 September, 1941); "Non so più" (21 September, 1941); "Ah! mon fils" (21 June, 1942); "Divinités du Styx" (21 June, 1942); "Adieu, forêts" (21 June, 1942); "O mio Fernando (21 June, 1942); "Homing" 29 April, 1946); "Ah, sweet mystery of life" (28 February, 1947); "Look for the silver lining" (7 February, 1945); "My ship" (2 August, 1963). *The fabulous forties at the Met*: "Che farò" (21 September, 1941).

SONY Classical

The pop side Compilation of previously released recordings for Columbia"Can't help lovin' dat man" (26 February, 1945); "Lover" (27 June, 1945); "Love walked in" (25 June, 1945); "What is this thing called love" (3 April, 1946); "Easter parade" (31 December, 1947); "Through the years" (20 August, 1947); "Ev'rything I love (3 April, 1946); "Always" (22/12/47); "they didn't believe me" (8 February, 1945); "I love you" (27 June, 1945); "The man I love" (27 June, 1945); "The song is you" (26 February, 1945); "Night and day" (16 April, 1946); "How deep is the ocean" (22 December, 1947);"Love's old sweet song" (1 May, 1946); "The touch of your hand" (15 February, 1945); "Say it with music" (31 December, 1947);"Falling in love with love" (27 June, 1945). "Smoke gets in your eyes" (26 February, 1945); "I've got you under my skin" (3 April, 1946); "Remember" (22 December, 1947); "Begin the Beguine (16 April, 1945); "Too-ra-loo-ra-loo ral (15 February, 1945)Collectors' Choice (Sony Music Special Products) A34228. RCA Victor

1949-1950

19 May	EO-RB-4640	Herbert, "Moonbeams", *The Red Mill*
	EO-RB-4641	Herbert, "I'm falling in love", *Naughty Marietta*
	EO-RB-4642	Herbert, "Toyland", *Babes in Toyland*
	EO-RB-1463	Herbert, "Neath the Southern moon", *Naughty Marietta*
26 May	EO-RB-4707	Herbert, "The rose of Algeria", title song

	EO-RB-4708	Herbert, "Because you're you", *The Red Mill*
	EO-RB-4709	Herbert, "Gypsy love song", *The Fortune Teller*
	EO-RB-4710	Herbert, "I can't do the sum", *Babes in Toyland Songs of Victor Herbert*, Frank Black, Conductor (LM-79; also issued as 45rpm 1, 49-1245-B; n. 2, 49-1247-B; no. 3, 49-1244-A; no. 4, 49-1246-A; no. 5, 49-1247-A; no.6, 49-1245-A; no. 7, 49-1246-B; no. 8, 49-1244-B)
2 June	EO-RC-1033	Frank, "Panis Angelicus" *
	EO-RC-1034	Bizet, "Agnus Dei"
	EO-RC-1035	Adams, "The holy city"
9 June	EO-RC-1036	Monk, "Abide with me"
	EO-RC-1037	Mason, "Nearer my God to Thee"
	EO-RC-1038	Steffe, "Battle hymn of the Republic" *Religious songs*, Frank Black, Conductor (LMX-38; also issued as 45rpm no. 1 49-1300-A; no.2, 49-1298-A; no. 3, 49-1299-B; no. 4, 49-1300-B; no. 5, 49-1299-A; no. 6, 49-1298-B; no.1 *Met stars sing sacred music*, Met 231 CD) Recorded in the Manhattan Center, New York

1950-1951

12 Sept.	EO-RC-1752	Gershwin, "Bess, you is my woman" (also issued on Preiser 89592)
13 Sept.	EO-RC-1750	Gershwin, "Summertime"
	EO-RC-1751	Gershwin, "My man's gone now"
	EO-RC-1755	Gershwin, "Gone, gone, gone" *Porgy and Bess*, with Robert Merrill, Robert Russell Bennett, Conductor, Robert Shaw Chorale (LM-1124; also issued as 45rpm, WDM-1946, 49-3160-49-3163)
	EO-RC-1757	"A woman is a sometime thing"; EO-RC-1753, "I got plenty o'nuttin"; EO-RC-1754, "It ain't necessarily so"; EO-RC-1756, "Where is my Bess", Robert Merrill, solos. Recorded in the Manhattan Center, New York.
18 Sept.	EO-RC-1780	J.Strauss, "Come along to the ball" "To part is such sweet sorrow"
	EO-RC-1782	J.Strauss, Entr'acte and chorus: "What a joy to be here" "From time to time I entertain" (RS solo) "My friends your kind attention"
	EO-RC-1788	J.Strauss, "Last night I had adventures" "Oh Eisenstein"
19 Sept.	EO-RC-1784	J.Strauss, Finale, Act 2 "Champagne's delicious"
	EO-RC-1785	Strauss, "Brother dear, Sister dear" "Enough, my friends, enough"
25 Sept		(RS not included in this session) *Die Fledermaus*, Prince Orlofsky; Patrice Munsel (Adele); Regina Resnik (Rosalinde);Paula Lenchner (Ida);Jan Peerce (Alfred); James Melton (Eisenstein);Robert Merrill (Falke); Hugh Thompson(Frank);Johnny Silver (Blind); Fritz Reiner,Conductor; The Robert

Shaw Chorale. Ruth and Thomas Martin translation. (LM 1114; also issued as 45rpm no 1 & 2, 49-3083-A; no. 3, 49-3080-B; no. 4 & 5, 49-3084-B; no. 6, 49-3082-B; LRM 7026)

Also included Overture,"Turtle dove who flew aloft"; "When these lawyers don't deliver"; "Drink, my darling drink"; "Good Sir, what can you think of me"; "Frank, you set my doubts at rest"; "Ever since I was a baby". Recorded in the Manhattan Center, New York.

12 Nov.	EO-RB-6100	Berlin, "It's a lovely day today", *Call Me Madam*
	EO-RB-6101	Berlin, "You're just in love", *Call Me Madam* with Robert Merrill; Ted Dale, Conductor (10-3108-B, A; 45rpm 49-3108)
	*EO-RB-6103	Stolz, "Don't ask me why"
	*EO-RB-6102	O. Straus, "My hero" with Robert Merrill; Ted Dale, Conductor
1 Dec.	EO-RB-6228	Anon. "All thro' the night"
	EO-RB-6231	Penn, "Smilin' through"
	EO-RB-6232	Nevin, "Mighty lak a rose"
	EO-RB-6233	Weatherly, Adaptation, "Danny boy"
3 Dec.	EO-RB-6229	Anon,"Flow gently, sweet Afton"
	EO-RB-6230	Shannon,"Too-ra-loo-ra-loo-ral"
	EO-RB-6234	Brahms,"Cradle song" ("Wiegenlied")
	EO-RB-6235	Dvorak, "Songs my mother taught me" *Songs my mother taught me*, Milton Katims, Conductor (LM-59; also made as 45rpm, no. 1, 49-3169-B; no. 2, 49-31718-A; no. 3, 49-3171-B; no. 4, no. 5, 49-3169-A; no. 6, 49-3170-A; no.7, 49-3170-B; no. 8, 49-3168-B; no. 9, 49-3168-A; nos. 2, 4 ERA-88-A; nos. 1, 7 ERA-88-B; nos. 1, 8 issued as late 78rpm Vr 10-3297; issued as 45 rpm album, "Irish Folk Songs", includes no. 1, 2, 4, 7) Recorded in the Manhattan Center, New York.
22 Jan.	E1-RB-137	Youmans, "More than you know", *Great Day*
	E1-RB-139	Ayer, "If you were the only girl"
	E1-RB-140	Porter, "I get a kick out of you", *Anything Goes*
	E1-RB-135	Schwartz, "If there is someone lovelier than you", *Revenge with Music*
25 Jan.	E1-RB-136	Porter, "Just one of those things", *Jubilee*
	E1-RB-138	McHugh, "I'm in the mood for love", *Every Night at Eight*
	E1-RB-141	Schwartz, "You and the night and the music", *Revenge with Music*
	E1-RB-142	Rodgers, "If I loved you", *Carousel A cavalcade of musical comedy*, with Robert Merrill, Chorus, Ted Dale, Conductor (LOX-329; also issued as 45rpm, no. 1, 49-3332-A; 49-3331-A; no. 3, 49-3334-A; no. 4, 49-3333-A; no. 5, 49-3332-B; no. 6, 49-333-B; no. 7, 49-3334-B; no. 8, 49-3331-B) Recorded in the Manhattan Center, New York
21 March	E1-RC-3175	Gluck, "Che puro ciel"

	E1-RC-3176	Gluck, "Che farò senza Euridice"
	E1-RC-3177	Mozart, "Non so più"
	E1-RC-3178	Mozart, "Voi che sapete"
5 April	E1-RC-3195	R. Strauss, "Mir ist die ehre"
	E1-RC-3196	R. Strauss, "Ist zeit und ewigkeit"
	E1-RC-3197	R. Strauss, "Ist ein traum" (part 1)
	E1-RC-3198	R. Strauss, "Ist ein traum" (part 2) *Scenes from opera, Der*

Rosenkavalier, Orfeo ed Euridice, Carmen with Erna Berger; Fritz Reiner, Conductor (LM9010; also issued as 45rpm, no. 1, 49-3847-B; no. 2, 49-3846-B; no. 3, 49-3849-B; no. 4 49-3848-B; no. 5, 49-3846-A; no. 6, 49-3847-A; no. 7, 49-3848-A; no. 8, 49-3849-A; nos. 7, 8 ERA-138-A; nos. 2, 3, 4 ERA-138-B; nos. 1, 3, 4, 5 MET-114; no. 4 MET-515). Album also includes the final scene from *Carmen* extracted from complete set. Recorded in the Manhattan Center, New York 28, 29, 31 May Bizet,*Carmen* also 12, 14, 15, 16, 19, 21, 22 June and 6 July with RS; Jan Peerce (Don José); Robert Merrill (Escamillo); Licia Albanese (Micaela); Paula Lenchner (Frasquita); Margaret Roggero (Mercedes);George Cehanovsky (Dancaïro); Alessio de Paolis(Remendado); Osie Hawkins (Zuniga); Hugh Thompson (Moralès); Fritz Reiner, Conductor, RCA Orchestra,Robert Shaw Chorale, Lycée Français Children's Chorus.

E1-RC-3719 through E1-RC-3750

(LM 6102; 45rpm 49-3452 through 49-3467; Highlights LM 1749; Victrola AVM3-0670; CD 7981-2-RG) "Habañera", "La fleur que tu m'avais jetée" included in *60 years of music America loves best,*vol. 2. LM-6008, 45 rpm 49-3729 A, B; Final scene included in *Scenes from opera*, LM-9010; *The Metropolitan Centennial Collection of Great Opera,*scenes from Carmen, Time Life Recods STL-OP03;Final scene MET-114; Quintet, MET-50) *The best of Carmen*, Highlights PLATCO 1224 (2004); "Habañera" RCA Victor 68823. Recorded in the Manhattan Center, New York

1951-1952

20 Dec.   E1-RC-7010 Massenet, "Elegie"

E1-RC-7011 Offenbach, "Barcarolle", *Les Contes d'Hoffmann* with Mischa Elman, Violin; Brooks Smith,Piano, included in *Great combinations* LM-1703; contents: "Ombra mai fu", "In the silence of the night", Robert Merrill, Yehudi Menuhin, C. Hollister; "Angel's serenade", "O dry those tears", Jan Peerce, Mischa Elman, W.Rosé; "None but the lonely heart", "Calm as the night", Ezio Pinza, Nathan Milstein, G. King;"My old Kentucky home", Marian Anderson, Gregor Piatigorsky, Franz

Rupp); also issued as 45rpm 49-3809-B, A) Recorded in the Manhattan Center, New York

1952-1953

5 June   E3-RC-2381   Firestone, "In my garden"

E3-RC-2382   Firestone, "If I could tell you"

E3-RC-2383   Firestone, "You are the song in my heart"

E3-RC-2384   Firestone, "Bluebirds" *Songs of Idabelle Firestone*, Howard Barlow, Conductor (no. 1 ERA-149; no. 2 ERA-149-B) Recorded in the Manhattan Center, New York

1954-1955

4-9, 11-12/7   Mozart *Le nozze di Figaro* with RS (Cherubino); Sesto Bruscantini (Figaro); Graziella Sciutti (Susanna); Hugues Cuenod Don Basilio); Monica Sinclair (Marcellina); Franco Calabrese (Count Almaviva); Sena Jurinac (Countess Almaviva); Ian Wallace (Dr. Bartolo); Gwyn Griffiths (Antonio); Jeanette Sinclair (Barbarina); Daniel McCoshan (Don Curzio); Vittorio Gui (Cond.); Glyndebourne Festval Orchestra and Chorus. (LM 6401; Highlights LM 2053; HMV ALPS 1312; ASDS 274; ALP 1313-15; ASD 275-6-7; CD 72435738452-0) Recorded in Studio No. 1, Abbey Road, London, England.

7, 9, 10,   Saint-Saëns, *Samson et Dalila*, highlights with RS, Jan Peerce
14 Sept.   (Samson); Robert Merrill (High Priest); Leopold Stokowski, Conductor, Members of the NBC Orchestra, The Robert Shaw Chorale. (LM-1848) Includes "Arrètez, ô mes frères!, "Printemps qui commence", "Amour! viens aider ma faiblesse!", "Se pourrait-il? "C'est toi", "Mon coeur s'ouvre à ta voix", "Vois ma misère", Bacchanale, "Gloire à Dagon" [Recording data are missing from RCA Victor files] (LM-1848; "Mon coeur" included in MET-114; "Amour! viens aider" included in MET-405) Recorded in the Manhattan Center, New York

1955-1956

13 March   Kern, *Showboat*, highlights G2-RB-1679 "Can't help loving dat man" G2-RB-1689 "Bill" G2-RB-1691 "Dance the night away" with RS (Julie); Patrice Munsel (Magnolia); Robert Merrill (Gaylord Ravenal, Joe); Janet Pavek; Kaherine Graves, Kevin Scott; Lehman Engel, Conductor (LM 2008). Also includes the Overture,Opening Chorus, "Where is the mate for me","Make believe", "Ol'man river","Love on the wicked stage", "Till good luck comes my way", "I might fall back on you", "You are love", Opening of Act 2, "Why do I love you?", "After the ball" (Harris interpolation), Finale. Recorded

in Webster Hall, 125 East 11th Street, New York. n. d. *Gypsy Love Song:* "Gypsy love song", "I'm falling in love with someone", "Because you're you" *The Red Mill*, "Moonbeams". RCA Victor Orchestra and Chorus, Frank Black. RCA 45 EP ERA-246

1956-1957

15-26/6   Gluck, *Orfeo ed Euridice* RS (Orfeo); Lisa della Casa (Euridice) Roberta Peters (Amor); Pierre Monteux (Cond.); Rome Opera House Orchestra and Chorus. (LM-6136; Victrola VICS-1435; RB-16058-60; CD RER 09026-6353-2) Highlights LM/LSC-2253; Met 230 Met Legends: Roberta Peters, "Amore assistera"). Recorded in the Rome Opera House.

1957-1958

28/3, 3/4   O. Straus *The Chocolate Soldier* with RS (Nadine); Robert Merrill (Bumerli); Sadie McCollum (Aurelia); Jo Sullivan (Mascha); Peter Palmer (Alexius); Michael Kermoyan (Popoff);Eugene Morgan (Masakoff); Lehman Engel and his Orchestra. (LOP/LSO-6005; Abridged LOP/LSO-1506; Abridged FPS-175). Recorded in Webster Hall.

15/4   Saint-Saëns *Samson et Dalila* with RS (Dalila); Mario del Monaco (Samson); Clifford Harvuot (High Priest); Ezio Flagello (Abimelech); Fausto Cleva(Cond.), Metropolitan Opera Orchestra and Chorus. includes: "Arretèz, o mes frères"; "Amour! viens aider ma faiblesse"; "En ces lieux"; "Mon coeur s'ouvre à ta voix"; "Vois ma misère"; "Gloire à Dagon vainqueur!". (Abridged LM/LSC 2309; 731083 France Stereo) Recorded in Symphony Hall,Boston.

1962-1963

J. Strauss *Die Fledermaus* with RS (Orlofsky); Anna Moffo (Rosalinde); Jeannette Scovotti (Adele); Richard Lewis (Eisenstein); George London (Falke); Sergio Franchi (Alfred); John Hauxwell (Frank); Oscar Danon (Cond). Vienna State Opera Orchestra and Chorus (Highlights LM-2728) Recorded in Vienna. BMG Reissue: CD 09026-6 S468-2

17-25/6   J. Strauss *Die Fledermaus* with RS (Orlofsky); Adele Leigh (Rosalinde); Anneliese Rothenberger (Adele); Eberhard Wächter (Eisenstein); George London (Falke); Sándor Kónya (Alfred); Erich Kunz (Frank); Erich Majkut Blind); Oscar Danon, Cond.; Vienna State Opera Orchestra and Chorus. (LM/LSC-7029; FTC-7004). Recorded in the Sofiensaal, Vienna, Austria.

1963-1964

12/7   Rodgers and Hammerstein *The King and I* with RS (Anna Leonowens); Darren McGavin (The King); Patricia Neway

(Mrs. Tiang); Lee Venora (Tuptim); Frank Poretta (Lun Tha); James Harvey (Louis Leonowens); Franz Allers (Cond). (LOC/LSO-1092). Recorded in the St. George Hotel, Brooklyn, New York). Overture; "Whistle a happy tune"; "My lord and master"; "Hello, young lovers!"; March of the Siamese children; "A puzzlement"; "Getting to know you"; "We kiss in a shadow"; "Shall I tell you what I think of you?"; "Something wonderful";"I have dreamed"; "The small house of Uncle Thomas"; "Shall we dance"; "Something wonderful (reprise).

Non-Columbia and RCA Victor releases:

A 1940's Radio Hour, Vol. 3 *Carmen* with RS, Charles Kullman Standard Hour broadcast, 22 October, 1944

Final scene: "Tu ne m'aimes donc plus?". IRCC-CD809

Die Walküre: live performance from Buenos Aires, Teatro Colòn, 1938 (see chronology for cast listing) 1938. (Eklipse EKR63)

Le nozze di Figaro, live performance from San Francisco (see chronology for cast listing) October 1940. (EJS 301); (Guild 2238/40).

Der Rosenkavalier, Act 3 with RS (Octavian); Lotte Lehmann (Marschallin); Nadine Conner (Sophie); Lorenzo Alvary (Baron Ochs); Walter Olitzki (Faninal); Herta Glaz (Annina); Alessio de Paolis (Valzacchi); George Sebastian, Cond., San Francisco Opera Orchestra and Chorus, 18 October, 1945 (Eklipse EKR CD25). Includes interview with Lehmann on her eighty-fifth birthday; Act 3. (Guild 228789).

Samson et Dalila with RS (Dalila); Ramón Vinay (Samson); Joseph Mordino (High Priest); Arthur Cosenza (Abimélech); Ara Berberian (Old Hebrew); Tony Lopez (Messenger); Thomas Carter, Joseph Knight (Philistines);Renato Cellini, Cond., New Orleans Opera Orchestra and Chorus.Live performance of April 2, 1960. (VAIA 1055-2)

Die Walküre with RS (Fricka); Marjorie Lawrence (Brünnhilde); Irene Jessner (Sieglinde); René Maison (Siegmund); Herbert Janssen (Wotan); Emanuel List (Hunding); Eric Kleiber, Cond., Teatro Colon Orchestra and Chorus. Live performance August 23, 1940. (Gebhardt JGCD 0028-3)

Little Women: soundtrack of television presentation, October, 1958. Kapp records (no album number)

Journey back to Oz: music and lyrics by Sammy Cahn and James van Huesen. Recording issued in conjunction with the television showing of the animated film on the SFM Holiday Network, 1974 (filmed 1964). Voices supplied by RS ("You have only you" and Finale). Other participants are Herschel Bernardi, Jack E. Leonard, Paul Lynde, Ethel Merman, Liza Minelli, Mickey Rooney and Danny Thomas. Walter Scharf, Cond., with Oz Symphony Orchestra. (no album number)

Metropolitan Opera Recordings

Great artists at the Met "Che puro ciel", "Che farò senza Euridice"; "Non

do più", "Voi che sapete" with Fritz Reiner, Cond. recorded 21 March, 1951
"Mir ist die ehre", with Erna Berger, Fritz Reiner, Cond. recorded 5 April, 1951
(all entries originally appeared in RCA Victor LM-9010)
"Connais-tu le pays", with Frieder Weissmnn, Cond. recorded 18, September,
1941 (originally appeared on Columbia 71192-D)
"Légères hirondelles", with Ezio Pinza, Fausto Cleva, Cond. recorded 7
February, 1947. (originally appeared as Columbia 72371-D).
"Mon coeur s'ouvre à ta voix", with Jan Peerce, Leopold Stokowski, Cond.
recorded 7 September, 1954. (originally appeared on RCA Victor LM-1848)
"Habañera", "Seguidilla", "Chanson Bohème", Final scene, with Jan Peerce,
Fritz Reiner, Cond. recorded May-June, 1951. (originally appeared on RCA
Victor LM-6102 (MET-114)
*Great artists at the Met This is CD new edition of the earlier disc issued in
this series. New selections added, "Printemps qui commence", "Amour!
viens aider", with Stokowski in place of "Légères hirondelles". (CD 04229)*
Met stars sing sacred music: RS "Panis Angelicus" (MET-231 CD)
One hundred years at the Met Volume 1: *The Johnson years,* "Seguidilla" and
duet, with Raoul Jobin, George Sebastian, Metropolitan Opera Orchestra
(MET 404, originally in set Columbia M-607)
Volume 2: *The Bing years,* vol. 1. "Amour! viens aider", with Leopold
Stokowski (MET 505, originally on RCA Victor LM-1848)
One hundred singers, one hundred years: Der Rosenkavalier, "Ist ein
traum", with Erna Berger and Fritz Reiner (RCA Red Seal CRM8-5177)
Originally recorded, 5 April 1951 (E1-RC3197/8).
Met centennial collection: 1939-1950 *Mignon,* excerpt Act 3: RS (Mignon);
Richard Crooks (Wilhelm Meister); Josephine Antoine (Philine); Willfred
Pelletier, Cond., Metropolitan Opera Orchestra and Chorus. 17 December,
1938. (MET 100)
Great operas at the Met: *Carmen:* "Habañera", "Seguidilla", with Jan Peerce,
"Chanson Bohème", Fritz Reiner, Cond. (originally on RCA Victor LM-6102);
Final scene, with Raoul Jobin (originally on Columbia M 607).
Le nozze di Figaro: "Non so più", with Erich Leinsdorf, Conductor (originally
on Columbia 17298-D) (MET 505)
Der Rosenkavalier: Presentation of the rose, with Erna Berger, Fritz Reiner,
Metropolitan Opera Orchestra. (originally on RCA Victor LM 9010)
Fifty years of Guild performances at the Met: Quintet, Act 2, with RS, Paula
Lenchner, Margaret Roggero, Alessio de Paolis, Georg Cehanovsky, Fritz
Reiner, Cond. (originally on LM 6102) (MET-50)
La Gioconda: "Bella così, madonna", with Ezio Pinza, Fausto Cleva,
Metropolitan Opera Orchestra. (originally on Columbia 72371-D). MET-524)
Old Met Christmas: "Friendly beasts". (MET-206; MET-206 C; MET-206 CD)
Met stars on Broadway: "My ship" (originally on Columbia OL/S-5990). (MET-204)
Met stars in Hollywood: "Dearly beloved" (originally on Columbia 4331-M). (MET-205)

Met stars on Broadway and Hollywood: "My ship", "Dearly beloved", I've got you under my skin" (originally on Columbia MM-630)(MET-204CD)

Met stars sing operetta: "Chacun a son gout", Act 2 finale, *Die Fledermaus*, performed in the Ruth and Thomas Martin translation, conducted by Fritz Reiner. Originally on RCA Victor LM114; "Because you're you", Matrix no. RCA eorb4707, recorded 5/26/50. (MET-244CD)

Growing up with Broadway: "Getting to know you", originally on RCA Victor LOC/LOS 1092. (MET 241CD)

An old Met treasury: "Seguidilla" originally on Columbia XCO-35530 (MET254CD)

Met Stars Sing the Great American Songbook: "The touch of your hand", "The Song is you", "Saga of Jenny" (originally issued no. 1 Columbia M568; no. 2 Columbia M568; no. 3 Columbia OL 5990 monaural, OS 2390 stereo)

Der Rosenkavalier with RS (Octavian); Lotte Lehmann (Marschallin); Emanuel List (Baron Ochs); Marita Farell (Sophie); Friedrich Schorr (Faninal);Nicholas Massue (Singer); Artur Bodanzky, Cond. Metropolitan Opera Orchestra and Chorus. Historic Broadcast, 7 January, 1939 (MET-5)

La Gioconda with RS (Laura); Zinka Milanov (Gioconda); Margaret Harshaw (La Cieca); Richard Tucker (Enzo); Leonard Warren (Barnaba); Giacomo Vaghi (Alvise); Ossie Hawkins (Zuàne); Lodovico Oliviero (Isèpo);William Hargrave (Monk); John Baker (Steersman); Emile Cooper, Cond. Metropolitan Opera Orchestra and Chorus. Historic Broadcast, 16 March, 1946. (MET-17/CD)

Les contes d'Hoffmann with RS (Giulietta); Roberta Peters (Olympia); Lucine Amara (Antonia); Mildred Miller (Nicklausse); Richard Tucker (Hoffmann);Martial Singher (Lindorf, Coppélius, Dappertutto, Miracle);Alessio de Paolis (Andrès, Cochenille, Pitichinaccio, Frantz);Lawrence Davidson (Luther); James McCracken (Nathanael);Paul Franke (Spalanzani); Norman Scott (Crespel); Clifford Haruot (Schlemil); Sandra Warfield (Mother's Voice); Pierre Monteux, Cond. Metropolitan Opera Orchestra and Chorus. Historic Broadcast, 3 December, 1955. (MET-14)

Miscellaneous Anthologies

Goodspeed Opera House Foundation, Inc. Intimate Musicale As presented on January 10, 1960 with RS, Licia Albanese, Barry Morell, Cornell MacNeil and Sally Leff at the piano.

Part 1: Barry Morell, "E lucevan le stelle", *Tosca*; Licia Albanese, "Vissi d'Arte", *Tosca*; Cornell MacNeil, "Di Provenza",*La Traviata,* "Si può", Pagliacci; RS, "Che farò", "Voi che sapete"; Barry Morell, "Che gelida manina", *La Bohème*; Licia Albanese, "Mi chiamano Mimi", *La Bohème*; "O soave fanciulla", *La Bohème.*

Part 2: Cornell MacNeil, "The gambler's lament"; "The rovin' gambler"; RS, "Sure on this shining night" (Barber); "Rabbit at top speed" (Bernstein);Barry Morell, "O Paradis", *L'Africaine*; "The pipes of Gorden's men"; Licia Albanese, "Roma mia"; "The star"; RS and Cornell MacNeil, "My hero", *The Chocolate Soldier.*(MUS-103) Private recording sold to benefit the

Foundation.

Favorite Christmas Carols, Vol. 1 Voice of Firestone with RS and Brian Sullivan Firestone Orchestra and Chorus

Medley ("Joy to the world"; "Away in a manger"; "We three Kings of Orient are; "Hark! the herald angels sing"); "What child is this"; "O come all ye faithful"; Medley ("A Virgin unspotted"; "God rest ye merry gentlemen"; "Deck the halls"); "O little town Bethlehem";"O holy night"; "It came upon a midnight clear"; "The friendly beasts"; Medley ("Here we come a-wassailing"; "Good King Wenceslas"; "O Christmas tree"); "The first Noel"; "Silent night";Medley ("Jingle bells"; "Up on the house-top"; "Jolly old Saint Nicholas"; "We wish you a merry Christmas"). FTP Records (MLP/SLP 7005)

Your Favorite Christmas Carols, Vol. 2 Voice of Firestone with RS, Brian Sullivan and The Columbus Boy Choir Firestone Orchestra and Chorus

Opening ("O holy night"; "O come all ye faithful"); "O come , o come Emanuel"; Medley ("Hark the herald angels sing"; "The first Noel"); Medley ("We three Kings of Orient are"; "God rest ye merry gentlemen"); "O angels we have heard on high"; "Carol of the bells"; "Hallelujah"; "Deck the halls"; Medley ("Away in a manger"; "It came upon a midnight clear"); "Joy to the world"; Medley ("Away in a manger"; "It came upon a midnight clear"); "Joy to the world"; Medley ("Silent night"; "O little town of Bethlehem"; "Jingle bells"); "The twelve days of Christmas". FTP Records (MLP/SLP 7006)

Great voices on radio: * (Sandy Hook 41)

Opera goes Hollywood: "One night of love", *One Night of Love* (1943) from unidentified radio broadcast (Star-Tone ST-211)

Opera goes Broadway: "They say it's wonderful" (1946) from unidentified radio broadcast (Star-Tone ST 223)

A lyric Christmas: "Friendly beasts", originally on Voice of Firestone Christmas album, vol. 1. (Lyric LCD 217)

Risë Stevens: Historic Recordings

"Che farò" (1941 Columbia 71365-D); "Divinites du Styx" (1942 Columbia 71486-D); "Non so più" (1941 Columbia 17298-D); "Voi che sapete" (1941 Columbia 17298-D); "O mio Fernando" (1942 Columbia 17440-D);"Ah! mon fils" (1942 Columbia 71486-D); "Connais-tu le pays" (1941 Columbia 71192-D); "Adieux forêts" (1942 Columbia 71440-D); "Habañera" (1946 Columbia 71739-D, XCO 35627); "Seguidilla" with Raoul Jobin (1946 Columbia 71740-D, XCO-35-630); "Chanson bohème" (1945 71740-D, XCO35566); "Card scene" (1945 Columbia 71742-D, XCO 35567); "C'est toi" with Jobin (1946 Columbia 71743-D, XCO35628/9); "Mir ist die Ehre" with Erna Berger (1951 RCA Victor LM9010, EL-RC-3195/6); "Ist ein Traum" (1951 RCA Victor LM9010 EL-RC-3197/8) Lebendige Vergangenheit 89556

Four Famous Mezzo-Sopranos of the Past "Non so più" (1941 Columbia 17298-D); "Voi che sapete" (1941 Columbia 71440-D); "O mio Fernando" (1942 Columbia 71440-D); "Ah! mon fils (1942 Columbia 71486-D); "Adieux forêts"

(1942 Columbia 71440-D). Jennie Tourel, Gladys Swarthout and Blanche Thebom are also featured. Historic Recordings 89958.

VIDEOTAPES

Carnegie Hall film (Bel Canto BCS0791)

Risë Stevens in Opera and song: Volume 1 (VAI 69106)

Telecasts from *The voice of Firestone*, Howard Barlow, Conductor.

1 Oct., 1951: "Falling in love with love"; Card song, *Carmen*; "L'amour toujours l'amour".

2 April, 1951: "Widmung"; "It mght as well be spring"; "They say its wonderful"; "Chanson Bohème", *Carmen.*

11 Oct.,1954: "Smoke gets in your eyes"; "Argonaise", *Carmen* (Orchestra); "Habañera", *Carmen*; "Ave Maria (Schubert); "Siboney".

Risë Stevens in Opera and song: Volume 2 (VAI 69123)

Telecasts from *The voice of Firestone*

23 July, 1951: "People will say we're in love"; "The sweetest story ever told"; "I'm falling in love with someone".

23 June, 1952: "Printemps qui commence", *Samson et Dalila*; "To the children";

7 Feb., 1955: "If I could tell you"; Bacchanale (Orchestra) and "Amour! viens aider ma faiblesse", *Samson et Dalila*; "Under the starlight";

16 Feb., 1959: "Voi che sapete", *Le nozze di Figaro*; "Air de Lia",*L'enfant prodigue.*

23 Sep., 1957: "Always"; "Seguidilla", *Carmen*; "Dancing in the dark"; "In my garden".

30 Sept., 1962: "Mon coeur s'ouvre à ta voix", *Samson et Dalila.* Wilfred Pelletier, Conductor (2 Feb., 1955) Walter Hendl, Conductor (16 Feb., 1959) Howard Barlow, Conductor (remainder)

Great Stars of Opera: Vol. 1 (VAI 69715) 10 Feb., 1959: "Beware of a hawk, my baby", "Lonely am I", *Natoma;* Donald Voorhees, Conductor, The Bell Telephone Hour Orchestra.

San Francisco Opera Gems, Vol. 1: *Le Nozze di Figaro*, Act 2, 12 Oct., 1940: with RS, Ezio Pinza, Elisabeth Rethberg, John Brownlee, Bidú Sayão, Gerhard Pechner, Alessio de Paolis; Erich Leinsdorf, Conductor, San Francisco Opera Orchestra. (Guild 2238/40)

San Francisco Opera Gems, Vol. 2: *Carmen, excerpts,* 21 Oct., 1945: with RS, Charles Kullman, Eleanor Steber; Georges Sebastian, Conductor, San Francisco Opera Orchestra and Chorus.

18 Oct., 1945: *Der Rosenkavalier,* Act 3 with RS, Lotte Lehmann, Nadine Conner, Mack Harrell, John Garris, Walter Olitzki, Herta Glaz, Lorenzo Alvary, John Garris; Georges Sebastian, Conductor,

San Francisco Opera Orchestra. (Guild 228789)

Robert Merrill Lebendige Vergangenheit: "Bess, you is my woman now", *Porgy and Bess;* Robert Russell Bennett, Conductor. (Preiser 89592)

Raoul Jobin Lebendige Vergangenheit: "C'est toi? C'est moi"; Georges Sebastian, Conductor. (Preiser 89517)

Bizet Greatest Hits: "Habañera", *Carmen;* Georges Sebastian, Conductor, Metropolitan Opera Orchestra and Chorus. (Sony Classical 64594)

Escape Through Opera: "Habañera", *Carmen;* Georges Sebastian, Conductor, Metropolitan Opera Orchestra and Chorus. (Sony Classical 89370)

Opera Greatest Hits: "Habañera", *Carmen;* Georges Sebastian, Conductor, Metropolitan Opera Orchestra and Chorus. (Sony Classical 66707)

The Only Opera CD You'll Ever Need: "Habañera", Fritz Reiner, Conductor, RCA Victor Symphony Orchestra. (RCA Victor 68823)

28 February, 1953: *Der Rosenkavalier,* Act 1, 3 excerpts: RS, Astrid Varnay, Nadine Conner. Fritz Reiner, Conductor. (Guild 2285/6)